Praise for
Nine Quarters of Jerusalem

"[Teller] writes with affection and compassion for Jerusalem's wide variety of peoples but a sharp-eyed lack of deference for a city whose past and present he explores with insight, sensitivity, and wry humor...a refreshing portrait of the 'Holy City' that is vibrant and engaging."
—Jonathan Dimbleby, author of *Operation Barbarossa:*
The History of a Cataclysm

"This book is so good. It peels away the layers of deception to debunk the myth that the Old City is composed of four distinct quarters—a notion that continues to plague Jerusalem and underpins the assumption that the present-day conflict comes down to age-old hatred between religions. Teller celebrates the complexity of the city."
—Raja Shehadeh, author of *Palestinian Walks:*
Forays into a Vanishing Landscape

"This must-read book lays bare the role of arrogant British colonialists and missionaries in shaping Jerusalem's Old City according to their vision. It challenges the misleading maps that serve the Israeli narrative and encourages visitors to see beyond the facade."
—Diana Darke, author of *Stealing from the Saracens:*
How Islamic Architecture Shaped Europe

"There has been no book like this written in the last twenty years. Matthew Teller has resurrected this city."
—George Hintlian, author of *History of*
the Armenians in the Holy Land

"A lyrical and electric book, rich and intensely evocative (with a twist of cumin), as the author shares his lifelong obsession for one of the most over-documented and misunderstood cities on earth. This is not another biography but an altogether more important book, about the human tapestries that could, possibly, weave together a new Jerusalem."
—Louisa Waugh, author of *Meet Me in Gaza:*
Uncommon Stories of Life Inside the Strip

"A marvel. Teller deftly braids the historical, the political, and the experiential to offer a multifaceted gem, brilliant and finely cut. Frequently philosophical, his work resonates beyond the physical boundaries of a city and its most apparent features—occupation and organized religion. This book is at once universal in scope and intimate, and it is as enjoyable as it is poignant."

—Massoud Hayoun, author of *When We Were Arabs: A Jewish Family's Forgotten History*

"For any other city, a book that tells the stories of its residents might be unremarkable—but for Jerusalem, so often weighed down by ancient history and the politics of occupation, Teller has produced a book that is borderline radical in its focus on the people who live there."

—Zora O'Neill, author of *All Strangers Are Kin: Adventures in Arabic and the Arab World*

"A terrific book that holds to scholarly levels of research, critique, and questioning, but is also packed full of fresh, original insights."

—Dr. Sarah Irving, editor-in-chief, *Contemporary Levant*

"Teller presents a more complete picture of Jerusalem than any overview could provide…an essential addition to your travel reading, whether you've been to Jerusalem or not."

—Pam Mandel, author of *The Same River Twice: A Memoir of Dirtbag Backpackers, Bomb Shelters, and Bad Travel*

"A love letter to the people of the Old City…Teller's book [is] a rare treasure." —*Jerusalem Post*

"Teller excels in piecing together the old and the new, religion and politics, money and family, combining academic research with powerful human stories. In his colorful style, he brings the city and its occupants to life, taking readers on a breathtaking journey…a remarkable book."

—*Arab News*

"An original and engaging take on the city…packed with fascinating material." —*Tel Aviv Review of Books*

"This telling of history spotlights the characters, communities, and institutions that have given the Old City a heartbeat underneath all the grandeur and mythology…Teller's stories are informed by dogged detective work."

—*Middle East Eye*

"Teller is a travel writer by background, and it shows in his descriptions of Jerusalem…seemingly little things are what make this book stand out."

—*Asian Review of Books*

NINE QUARTERS OF JERUSALEM

*A New Biography
of the Old City*

MATTHEW TELLER

Other Press
New York

Production editor: Yvonne E. Cárdenas
Text designer: Henry Iles
This book was set in Minion Pro.

1 3 5 7 9 10 8 6 4 2

Library of Congress Cataloging-in-Publication Data
Names: Teller, Matthew, author.
Title: Nine quarters of Jerusalem : a new biography of the Old City /
Matthew Teller.
Description: New York : Other Press, [2022] | "First published in Great Britain
in 2022 by Profile Books." | Includes bibliographical references and index.
Identifiers: LCCN 2022018852 (print) | LCCN 2022018853 (ebook) |
ISBN 9781635423341 (hardcover) | ISBN 9781635423358 (ebook)
Subjects: LCSH: Religious communities—Jerusalem. | Ethnology—Jerusalem. |
Jerusalem—Description and travel.
Classification: LCC DS109.15 .T45 2022 (print) | LCC DS109.15 (ebook) |
DDC 956.94/42—dc23/eng/20220505
LC record available at https://lccn.loc.gov/2022018852
LC ebook record available at https://lccn.loc.gov/2022018853

To Q and to Doc, who, long ago, believed in me

For my family

Contents

A note on "Jerusalem" and transliteration

Throughout this book, and unless I'm specifically talking about the city as a whole, by "Jerusalem" I mean what has been called for the last hundred years or so the Old City – that is, the area enclosed by sixteenth-century walls that comprised all of Jerusalem until the city began to expand in the middle of the nineteenth century. That said, for ease of understanding I also sometimes use the unsatisfactory formulations of "East Jerusalem" and "West Jerusalem," as well as the outdated but still current term "Middle East."

There is no single, consistent way to render Arabic or Hebrew words in English. Academics use several different systems, which don't always tally with methods used by journalists and the media, none of which may satisfy general readers and speakers trying to communicate a message across a language boundary. I have opted for simplicity and readability, eliminating diacritical marks and apostrophes, and have preferred familiar usages wherever possible.

Meet people in such a way that, if you die,
they will weep for you.
ALI IBN ABI TALIB, c.599–661

What is the city but the people?
SHAKESPEARE, *Coriolanus*, 1608

The street is a library. People are books.
SULAIMAN ADDONIA, Twitter, 2020

City of Icebergs

AN INTRODUCTION TO JERUSALEM

WE ALL HAVE OUR JERUSALEM. Our place of heavenly perfection, our city of joy. The culmination of our hopes and embodiment of our dreams. A true home, where we will live in communion with humanity and the higher powers in the comfort of certainty and the certainty of comfort.

Just please don't get your Jerusalem mixed up with the real one. Because the real one's in a bit of a state right now.

"I don't see Jerusalem as holy at all. What even is holy? You feel the Old City is the most pressured city in the whole world. Behind that wall you see so many aggressive, tense people. It's supposed to be this holy city, city of love and sharing, but honestly, I don't see it." That's what a Jerusalemite friend, Amoun Sleem, told me, when I asked her what it meant to live in a holy city. But then she added: "I'm connected with the Old City beyond politics and what people feel. I can't change that. I love it." And she wrote as much in her memoir: "Nothing is more beautiful than my home, Jerusalem. My morning walk in the Old City has a beautiful magic."

You find this a lot in Jerusalem, this push and pull, hot and cold. It's a prerogative of ownership, of belonging – to criticize, disparage, even to hate, but at the same time to love. I've had a friend tell me he knows the Jerusalem stories he grew up with are fiction, but still he would die to defend the stones that bred them. That's only a part of what makes this city so hard to understand. Inevitably, too, there's a gap between how a person might live their city each day, and how they might communicate that experience to peers and insiders, let alone to outsiders like me.

Here is John Tleel, Jerusalemite author, who died in 2018:

> Only by living inside the Old City, enclosed by its walls, can you really come to know Jerusalem. Along its narrow streets you begin to feel its force. You are changed by its shrines and holy places, you are baptised by the city of stone. But it is not easy to be a Jerusalemite. A thorny path runs alongside its joys. The great are small inside the Old City.
>
> You don't know how to treat Jerusalem. Most people treat Jerusalem as a city. It is not a city. It's not London, it's not New York, it's not Paris. This is a person, Jerusalem is a living person. It breathes, it talks, it fights. It is not a city. Every minute in Jerusalem is a special minute. It is something that gives you a new life. You become a new person, every minute.

Ten thousand metaphors have grasped at Jerusalem. Layers of an onion is a popular image, not least since it evokes the layers of history diggable beneath every street. Mustafa Abu Sway, professor of Islamic studies, told me the benefit of living here was "like having the right plug. It lets you plug directly into the energy source." And I'm fond of what another friend, the writer Yuval Ben-Ami, said. He called Jerusalem "the city of the frozen moment." That encapsulates nicely the idea that everything you see is just a snapshot. Each tiny cross of the hundreds carved into the stone walls of the Church of the Holy Sepulchre speaks of the life of a single pilgrim, in the moment of their arrival at their destination. And if, as long suspected, the tiny crosses date from the Crusader era (recent research suggests they may be earlier), then they also speak of the moment of conquest, frozen in stone by the sword hand of a pilgrim-knight.

Another example. The dome of the Dome of the Rock wasn't always gold. From 1022 to 1959 – some 937 years – it was dark gray lead. Then it was renovated with sheets of anodized aluminium that looked golden, before in 1993 being re-covered in copper panels plated with a two-micron layer of actual gold. Over the last few decades, a blip in time, our image-saturated era has elevated the golden dome to be the emblem of Jerusalem. The golden dome, so often pictured against a sky of penetrating blue, *means* Jerusalem.* It asserts the reality of Islamic Jerusalem. It even stands, gloriously, for Islam itself. It's inconceivable, now, that it was ever gray, or could ever return to gray. The golden dome is another frozen moment, a function of the building's late twentieth-/early twenty-first-century role at the nexus of religion and geopolitics.

So the frozen moment idea is good. But it doesn't go far enough. There's something still more challenging playing below the surface. The core truth of Jerusalem today, it seems to me, is a jagged dislocation between appearance and reality. Whatever you see here is not what's really going on.

All my life cumin has meant my first trip to Jerusalem. I can't make an informed comparison – I was only a child, then – but I'd guess the city I saw in 1980 was very different from the city today. What I have in my mind's eye from then is a scatter of impressions: flagstones worn smooth underfoot, gaudy colors and textures hung high over my head in narrow alleyways, my father doing something he wouldn't dream of doing today: changing money at a Palestinian-owned booth inside Damascus Gate. And the smells. So many smells. Sweet things. Burnt things. Rotting things. Laundry soap. Hot bread. New leather. Smells I knew nothing about.

It was years later, at a time when spices had become a more normal thing for a suburban London family to buy and use, that I was able to put a name to the earthy scent I'd filed in my head for years as "Jerusalem." So *that's* what it was. Cumin. Then as now, cumin's

---

* This is literally true in Palestinian Sign Language, in which Jerusalem is signed by the fingers of the right hand forming a dome shape over the back of the left hand. (By contrast, in Jewish Israeli society and elsewhere, Jerusalem is signed by kissing the fingertips of the right hand and then turning the palm outwards, as if pressing the fingertips to the Western Wall.)

crimson-brown sniff of old warmth would plant me mentally in the middle of Jerusalem's walled Old City, amid a crush of elbows on the crossroads of glittering, dizzying roofed pathways where the Souk al-Bazaar, or David Street market, turns left to Souk al-Lahameen, the Butchers' Market, as multiple smaller markets crash in from both sides and the main alleyway doglegs downward to form Tariq Bab al-Silsila, the Road of the Gate of the Chain, on its way towards holy places. Everything was there, at that intersection: gold, fabrics, money, fresh bread, fresh fruit, fresh meat, leather, fenugreek, perfumes, heat, sweat, color, new faces, new languages, new people, new ways of being. I watched but I didn't understand. I didn't know how much I didn't know. That was cumin.

For years I put cumin in everything. I was really putting Jerusalem in everything.

Jerusalem shouldn't exist. I mean, there shouldn't be a city there at all. That's hard for us, who are not city-builders, to grasp, but in the era when Jerusalem began, if you were going to build somewhere to live, you wouldn't choose that spot. Its water sources are too remote, down in steep valleys or far distant. Its hilltop ridges – which aren't the highest around – are threateningly overlooked. Major trade routes pass nowhere near. Everything's wrong. Yet, here it is. "Knowledge does not dispel mystery," wrote Nan Shepherd.

When the pharaohs cursed "Rusalimum," in texts written in the decades either side of 1900 BCE, maybe they were cursing Jerusalem. We don't know. But Jerusalem – perhaps named for Shalim, the god of the setting sun – was certainly a place by the time its ruler, Abdi-Heba, wrote to the Pharaoh Akhenaten, in the 1330s BCE. Later, around 1000 BCE, in a foundational tradition of Judaism, something special about Jerusalem prompted David, perhaps a ruler of Judah, a region to the south, to seize it and its fortress of Zion, then controlled by the Jebusites.

It seems the Jebusites – a nation or just a family; we don't know – and all of Canaan, as the country was then known, may already have venerated Jerusalem as the center of the world. Spiritual energy could have been why they wanted to live here, despite the logistical shortcomings. Either way, when David's son Solomon built a temple on one of Jerusalem's stony summits, he probably incorporated pre-existing forms of Jebusite (that is, Canaanite) worship into his new, Israelite devotions. A rock at the peak of that summit, enclosed within the Temple buildings, became revered in Judaism – named after Judah – as the Foundation Stone, the interface between earth and heaven, source of creation and center of the world, beneath which raged the waters of the Flood. It was where God had collected the dust that formed Adam. It was where Abraham had bound his son, believed in Judaism to be Isaac, for sacrifice.

The Temple was destroyed in 586 BCE, rebuilt and destroyed again in 70 CE. By then, the first Christians knew of Jewish traditions focused on the Rock, but for them, the foundational drama of faith in Jerusalem played out five hundred meters to the west, at a rocky knoll known as Golgotha (and, later, as Calvary). A kilometer to the east on the Mount of Olives, pilgrims venerated a rock bearing the footprint of Jesus from his ascent to heaven. Jerusalem remained the center of the world in Christianity but the Temple's demolition twice over obviously demonstrated God's displeasure with the Jews. Christ's teachings signalled a transference of understanding, and a new beginning for humanity.

The first Muslims also knew of Jewish traditions, and Christian ones. Jerusalem was, to them, already a site of cosmic importance.* It was where the prophets Abraham, David, Solomon and Jesus had lived and prayed. It was linked with Mecca by the Night Journey of the Prophet Muhammad. "There is not an inch in Jerusalem where a prophet has not prayed or an angel has not stood," said Ibn Abbas, cousin of Muhammad. The Foundation Stone took on new significance: now it bore the footprint of Muhammad from his ascent to heaven, when he received God's instruction to pray five times a day.

---

* Jerusalem is not mentioned by name in either the Quran or the five books of the Torah – see the notes to this chapter for more on this – yet it is central to both and many other texts in both Islam and Judaism (as well, of course, as Christianity). The city has always been pivotal to religious observance and spiritual yearnings throughout all three traditions.

Below it gaped the Abyss of Chaos, source of the Rivers of Paradise. In Islam the Rock stood as the focus of the Quranic site Al-Aqsa, a mosque that some believed had been built by the first human, Adam, and renovated by Solomon. Over and around the Rock, Jerusalem's new Muslim rulers designed an architectural evocation of the city's crucial role as the location of the Day of Judgment – a building that was octagonal, like the Throne of God, with a golden dome beaming the message of Islam to the world. The esplanade around this new Dome of the Rock was where the souls of the dead would gather to hear the archangel Israfil blow the trumpet announcing the end of the world. Islam, in its turn, signalled a transference of understanding, and a new beginning for humanity.

As in the previous traditions, there was a physical Jerusalem and a moral, spiritual one; an old, corrupted message and a new, clear one. So it didn't matter that the city had no river, no strategic value and no natural sources of commercial wealth. It had God.

I travelled once through Jordan with a friend from Vancouver who is blind. It was a revelation. He conceived of new places in an entirely fresh way. How do you convey the diversity of wildflowers on a rural hillside to a blind person? He tasted different kinds of local honey – one rich, one light, one floral-scented, one bland – and understood. How do you convey the longevity of occupation at an ancient archaeological site to a blind person? He walked on a spoil heap, hearing the centuries of discarded pottery crunch, fingering fine ware and coarse, and understood. How do you describe a city to a blind person? Helsinki had flummoxed him at first, he told me, because the streets were silent and odorless: he was forced indoors to understand. Amman in the open air, with its topographical echoes of traffic and music and languages, its smells of dust and cooking, its market thrum, its street food, rich with olive oil, he understood.

That journey left me convinced that the world we create through our eyes is only one world, and there are others. Is my impression of the rural hillside any more valid because I can see

it? If we listen to a poem declaimed in an open-air theater, but my eyes work, does that mean my understanding of Roman society or architecture is better than my friend's? Does seeing a market make the place more real?

Eyes, truthfully, aren't much help in Jerusalem. Whatever you're looking at – this street, that building, these people, those weapons – you can't know the truth of it from what you see. When racists want to attack strangers here, they (sometimes) ask them who they are first. Skin color and physical features give nothing away. Distinctive clothing aside – a *hijab*, say, or a *kippah*,* or traditional garb such as kaftans or knickerbockers – you can't tell by looking who is Israeli and who is Palestinian, who is Arab or Kurdish or Armenian, who is Muslim or Jewish or something else. What you see no more embodies truth than our face embodies our inner reality.

Sighted people cannot recreate the insights of blindness, but they can learn to take visual evidence with a pinch of salt – and I know no better place for that than Jerusalem, city of icebergs. What you see here is only ever the 10 percent above the surface, and if you attempt to navigate on the evidence of your eyes alone, you may find yourself holed beneath the waterline and sinking fast.

In 1965, when an international border ran through the middle of Jerusalem – or, rather, when Jerusalem consisted of two cities in different countries – a king arrived to open a hotel. A photo of the event survives, showing Hussein of Jordan, only twenty-nine years old, striding through the lobby of the swish new St. George Hotel, his smile as tight as his suit, buttoned and narrow-lapelled.

"There was a time, you know, when anything happened, it happened here." Bookseller and literary impresario Mahmoud Muna leans over his till, casting shadow onto a monograph by a Palestinian artist. "Umm Kalthoum, Fairouz, Abdel Wahab – they all came

---

* *Hijab*: headscarf worn by some Muslim women. *Kippah*: skullcap worn by some Jewish men.

first to Jerusalem," Mahmoud says, naming the three megastars of twentieth-century Arab music. "This city has lost its charm."

He talks about the Nakba (Arabic: catastrophe), the dispossession and loss that accompanied war and the declaration of the State of Israel in 1948, when Palestinian society was destroyed. In another war in 1967 – or, more accurately, another part of the same war – Israel defeated Jordan to become military occupier of Jerusalem's east. That area includes the Old City, enclosed by its sixteenth-century walls, site of the most significant Christian, Muslim and Jewish holy places. Israel defined new boundaries for East Jerusalem and later annexed it to the Israeli state, shunting the locus of urban energy westwards, marginalizing Palestinian character and expanding Jewish presence and influence, in particular within the Old City. It still calls East Jerusalem's 370,000 or so Palestinians merely residents, and strips them of even that status if they do not continuously furnish proof that their "center of life" is in the city.

As West Jerusalem was constrained by the Jordanian border before 1967, so East Jerusalem has become constrained since by a ring of Israeli settlements, illegal under international law, that encircles the city, along with what's euphemistically called Israel's Separation Barrier, an eight-meter-high wall of concrete through the suburbs. The wall physically and psychologically slices Palestinian Jerusalem away from its rural hinterland and isolates Jerusalemites from wider Palestinian society and economy. Not a single international hotel has opened in East Jerusalem in the decades since King Hussein did his walkabout. Visitors almost without exception approach Jerusalem via Israel. Of the city's 12,000 hotel rooms, nearly 11,000 are in the west. That ratio of 90:10 is mirrored in the marketing profiles of the Israeli and Palestinian tourism ministries, and in the relative visibility of government and nongovernment messaging in media and social media. A single narrative of Jerusalem dominates, locally and globally.

Underpinning this is Britain's invasion of Palestine in 1917, which brought to an end more than twelve hundred years of Muslim rule in Jerusalem, a period broken only by the eighty-eight-year aberration of a Crusader kingdom in the twelfth century. British colonial rule furthered the ambitions of Palestine's Jewish communities over all others. Jerusalem wasn't always a zero-sum game, but Britain made it so, in our time. For Arabs and Muslims around the world – as, once, for Jews – Jerusalem has become distant, a symbol of longing, more potent in imagination than reality. Most cannot even visit. Those who lack Israeli citizenship must apply first for visas to enter Israel; if a visa is granted, the holder then faces interrogation by border officials, who often deny entry. Even Palestinians living in the West Bank and Gaza cannot enter Jerusalem without Israeli permission, rarely given.

"There's a weird energy in the Old City," Bashar Murad, a musician who lives in East Jerusalem outside the walls, told me. "It's a beautiful place, but if you go down there you see Israeli soldiers everywhere, standing around with their guns, and if you go to visit Al-Aqsa you're questioned by them at the door, treated as if you're a criminal. It makes you not want to go at all."

Then there are the provocateurs. Extremist elements on the Zionist religious right – in Israel and elsewhere, both Jewish and evangelical Christian – espouse the idea of razing the Dome of the Rock and replacing it with a Third Temple, as a prelude to, or in conjunction with, the return of the Messiah. For more than fifty years, rogue rabbis have been emboldened to act out the fantasy, leading illicit prayer services, building coalitions of the zealous and displaying models in the Old City itself of what such a temple might look like.

"The 1967 war transformed Jerusalem from a vessel of humanity's most noble aspirations of sanctity into a playground for pyromaniacs," tweeted one Israeli human rights lawyer, gloomily.

If the area inside Jerusalem's walls were a free-standing city, it would be one of the twenty most harshly surveilled in the world, roughly on a par with Dubai or China's Uyghur capital, Urumqi. Israeli police in a remote control center monitor a network of four hundred CCTV cameras, watching every street and alleyway in the

Old City 24/7. In some areas cameras are mounted every twenty meters. They place the Palestinian people who live and work there – as well as every tourist and visitor – under fearsome levels of scrutiny. Israeli intelligence uses satellite technology to follow the movement of individual smartphones through the streets, while drones monitor activity from the air. In 2019 NBC News reported that face-recognition software was being used to track individuals in East Jerusalem; the Israeli police denied it.

Current estimates put the population of the Old City around 35,000 or slightly more, over 90 percent of whom are Palestinian. Around two-thirds are under the age of thirty. Israel's occupation exacerbates poverty, poor mental health, alcohol and drug abuse and other social ills, not least overcrowding. In some Old City neighborhoods, more people are packed in per *dunam** than in the densest districts of Karachi, Hong Kong or Nairobi. Yet even though ideologically driven Jewish Israeli settler organizations harry Old City residents with offers of millions of dollars (often via deceptively sympathetic middlemen) for any property, large or small, by which to expand their presence, most people are determined to stay put.

The Baedeker guidebook of 1876 wrote: "It is only by patiently penetrating beneath the modern crust of rubbish and rottenness which shrouds the sacred places from view that the traveller will at length realize to himself a picture of the Jerusalem of antiquity." Fifty years later, T.E. Lawrence could do little better. "Jerusalem was a squalid town … [The] united forces of the past and the future were so strong that the city almost failed to have a present. Its people, with rare exceptions, were characterless as hotel servants, living on the crowd of visitors passing through."

A century after Lawrence, there are still those who value stones over people. You see it often in Jerusalem, when tourists (let alone the authorities) treat Jerusalemites as not just tangential to their goals, but an impediment to them, worthy only of contempt and dismissal. "The shine in their eyes has gone," writer George Hintlian

---

* An Ottoman-originated measure of land area, equal to 1,000 square meters.

told me one afternoon, of his fellow Jerusalemites. "You can tell what the mood is like because people's shoulders are down."

Here's a story about walls, and the spaces they enclose.

When the Jewish Temple existed, it was designed as a sequence of concentric courtyards. After Herod's rebuilding, the outermost was named the Court of the Gentiles, accessible to all. Next came the Court of the Women, restricted to Jews only. From there, only Jewish men could access the Court of the Israelites. The inner Court of the Priests held the temple building itself, within which a vestibule led to a holy chamber. At the back of this chamber, the core of the whole complex was the ornately decorated Holy of Holies, a space holding the Ark of the Covenant, a chest out of which God spoke to Moses and which contained the stone tablets of the Ten Commandments. Only one man, the High Priest, could enter the Holy of Holies, and then only on one day a year, Yom Kippur, the Day of Atonement. But the Ark had disappeared, perhaps during the destruction of Solomon's Temple in 586 BCE. By Herod's day, the Holy of Holies had been empty for more than five hundred years. There was nothing there.

Hold that image.

To reach the Church of the Holy Sepulchre, two gated entrances from public streets open to the parvis, the enclosed courtyard before the church door. From here, worshippers enter the church itself, and pass through the building to a central rotunda known as the Anastasis ("Resurrection"). Here, beneath a great dome, stands the decorated Edicule, a small building-within-a-building at the core of the whole complex. Within the Edicule, a vestibule chapel leads through to the holiest of spaces, which contains the tomb of Jesus. Since the Son of God triumphed over death by rising on the third day, the tomb is empty.

The Haram al-Sharif, or Al-Aqsa mosque compound, has ten gates currently in use, which open from surrounding streets to an enclosed esplanade atop the levelled summit of the mountain. Once within this enclosure, worshippers ascend to a second raised platform, demarcated by free standing arcades. Atop this platform rises the glitteringly decorated Dome of the Rock. Entering through the doors of this building brings you first to an outer ambulatory, then an inner ambulatory that encircles the exposed Rock itself, the Foundation Stone, the interface between earth and heaven, and the point from which Prophet Muhammad ascended to an audience with God. Steps from the inner ambulatory access the holiest space of all, a cave beneath the Rock known as the Well of Souls, where the spirits of the dead await Judgment Day. Apart from a niche indicating the direction of prayer, the cave is empty.

These three spaces – the Holy of Holies, the Tomb of Christ and, to a lesser extent, the Well of Souls – are fundamental to belief and practice in Judaism, Christianity and Islam. Jerusalem is a city of walls, and gates, and stones, accreted in concentric layers. Their encirclement, as Hisham Matar wrote about Siena, "does not repel so much as intensify" the Jerusalem-ness within. We pass the walls, we walk through the gates, we touch the stones. We navigate our path from the outer courtyards of our everyday world to the inner courtyards of what is most holy, most Jerusalem. Once we have done enough to gain access, once every barrier has dissolved and every gate has fallen open, we arrive, emotional, awestruck, in a room that has nothing in it. Penetrating to the very heart of the mystery brings us to ourselves, in empty space.

Such an encounter with the invisible and the intangible – the ineffable, if you like – is why this city exists. Whatever you see here is not what's really going on.

PLAN OF JERUSALEM

BY

F. CATHERWOOD

ARCHITECT. JULY 1835

1 PLACE WHERE CHRIST WAS SCO
2 SCALA SANCTA BY WHICH CHRIST EN
PILATES HOVSE
3 PILATES HOVSE AND NOW RESIDE
OF TVRKISH GOVERNOR SPOT
WHENCE THE PANORAMA WAS T
4 CHAPEL OF THE CROWNING WITH T
5 ARCH OF THE ECCE HOMO
6 PLACE WHERE CHRIST SAID S
MATER
7 SPOT WHERE SIMON ASSISTED
CARRY THE CROSS
8 DWELLING OF LAZARVS
9 DWELLING OF THE RICH MAN
10 COLVMN ERECTED BY THE EMP
HELENA
11 HOSPITAL OF THE EMPRESS H
12 CHVRCH OF THE HOLY SEPVLC
13 PALACE OF THE KNIGHTS OF ST J
14 ST PETERS PRISON
15 IRON GATE WHICH OPENED ITS
TO ST PETER
16 SPOT WHERE CHRIST APPEAR
THE WOMEN AFTER HIS RESVRRE
17 SPOT WHERE JESVS TAVGHT
APOSTLES THE LORDS PRAYE
18 SPOT WHERE JESVS WEPT O
JERVSALEM
19 SPOT WHERE THE DICIPLES S
20 SPOT WHERE JVDAS KISSED
REDEEMER
21 SPOT WHERE JESVS SWEATED
22 PLACE WHERE ST STEPHEN WAS S
23 SPOT WHERE JVDAS HANGED H
24 SPOT WHERE THE PROPHET IS
WAS SAWN ASVNDER
25 COENACVLVM WHERE CHRIST
TVTED THE LAST SVPPER
26 CATHOLIC BVRIAL GROVND
27 ARMENIAN BVRIAL GROVND

SCALE OF FEET.

1

The Subdivisions Are Unimportant

HOW JERUSALEM WAS QUARTERED

LET'S TALK ABOUT MAPS. Maps of Jerusalem show the Old City divided into four quarters: top left Christian Quarter, top right Muslim Quarter, bottom left Armenian Quarter, and bottom center Jewish Quarter. Such neat divisions.

Nearly all modern maps do this. Many are even color-coded, with solid blocks of shading for each quarter, and precise borders marking frontiers from one quarter to the next. This makes somewhere like, say, Jaffa Gate a bit complicated. It straddles one of those borders. So which quarter does it fall in – the Christian Quarter to the north, or the Armenian Quarter to the south? (What a mad question! As if Armenians weren't Christians!)

The idea of these four Jerusalem quarters is not old. It dates from the nineteenth century. That's not in doubt. But in all my reading, for this book, and before, I've never seen any explanation of who came up with the idea, whether in media, literature or even academia. But it's vital to examine where that idea came from and why it has persisted, because four quarters underpins the common assumption that the present-day conflict in Jerusalem comes down to age-old hatred between religions – and that is a falsehood worth debunking. But nobody does. The emergence of four quarters is always described as if it just happened spontaneously, during the time when Europeans started exploring Jerusalem in greater numbers and mapping the place. One day Jerusalem was whole, the next it had four quarters.

Ridiculous. And yet everyone accepts it as true: "the Old City is divided into four." Every description. Every article. Every map. Every guidebook. Scholarly papers by learned academics analyze Ottoman census data in meticulous detail, tracing Jerusalem's patterns of settlement from the Crusades onwards and keenly questioning causes, influences and motivations – but then they just accept the abrupt nineteenth-century transition to four quarters without comment. A fact of life. Unquestioned. Uninvestigated.

If you're lucky, you might find someone saying something like "maps made by nineteenth-century explorers divided the city into four for the first time" – but as far as I can tell, nobody has ever looked into the whos, whens and whys of that.

So I did. And I think I've found the person responsible. And when they did it. And, at least roughly, why.

"The lanes of Jerusalem are striped like a tiger. You pass perpetually from strips of sunlight into bands of shadow," a visitor wrote, compellingly, eighty years ago. The busiest of those lanes is Souk Khan al-Zeit. *Souk* means market, a *khan* is a caravanserai, and *zeit* is oil, specifically olive oil. For hundreds of years, into the twentieth century, this crowded street was lined with workshops where olives would be pressed and the oil either stored and sold or processed for products such as olive-oil soap. I'm no shopping influencer, but honestly, if you've never scrubbed up with an aromatic bar of handmade olive-oil soap before, well, there's a whole new world of bathroom bliss waiting for you. It's wonderful. Soap-making with olive oil survives in Nablus, which is famous for it, and was also a mainstay of the souk in Aleppo, before the Syrian war, but in Jerusalem, as far as I know, it has completely vanished.

Now *there's* a business opportunity.

Khan al-Zeit, a stone-paved alley only a couple of meters wide despite its importance and the quantity of its foot traffic, stretches due south–north, climbing from Damascus Gate into the heart of the Old City, flanked by shops, shouts and fluster the whole way along. You could buy children's shoes, orange juice or gold earrings. An antique religious icon or a sandwich, a SIM card, saffron or a kitchen sink. Pilgrims dawdle, shoppers browse, cats scavenge, the occasional nun or becloaked priest swishes by in a waft of incense, professionals speed-walk, barrow boys hiss, click and yell for passage and the only vehicles that can get through are filthy diesel-powered mini-tractors that pull trailers up and down the stepped alleyways for dropping off deliveries or collecting rubbish. It's the most intense, bewildering and absorbing shopping street in the world.

And nobody knows which "quarter" it's supposed to be in. Most maps say it's in the Muslim Quarter, but then again it has chapels, it includes part of the Via Dolorosa – the centuries-old Christian pilgrimage route – and it leads directly to the Church of the Holy Sepulchre. Some maps treat it as a dividing line, with the east side of the street counting as the Muslim Quarter, and the west side as the Christian Quarter. Does that make the apricot I dropped one day in the middle of the road a Muslim apricot, or a Christian one?

You could say it doesn't matter which quarter Khan al-Zeit is in. It just is. Well, exactly. None of the quarters matter. The whole city just is. But some maps get pushy. Because the Muslim Quarter would otherwise take up so much space – spreading from the northeast corner to cover more than half the Old City – they choose to squash a shrunken "Muslim Quarter" label up near Herod's Gate. This creates a vacuum in the central portion of the city around Khan al-Zeit, an undefined zone awaiting an eager claimant.* This

---

* It hasn't always been undefined. Jerusalem's Old Yishuv Court Museum displays a Hebrew-language map, published for Zionist pioneers early in the twentieth century, that gives the Old City five quarters – the usual four, plus this area in the middle which it labels *rova meorav*, "Mixed Quarter." In reality, most of the city had a mixed population at this time: the label was created to stake a claim for future expansion of the Jewish Quarter. That claim persists. One Hebrew-language map from 1984 tried to realize the same ambition by printing its "Jewish Quarter" label in the same place, north of Bab al-Silsila Street.

conveniently suits a set of political aspirations in Israel that espouse displacement of Jerusalem's long-settled Palestinian populations.

Other maps, similarly tempted, might spread their Jewish Quarter label westwards, laying claim to extra slices of territory nudging up against the walls of the Armenian compound. And if you look in an Israeli tourist office you'll find Jerusalem maps that turn the Old City around, putting west at the bottom, since that's the direction from which most Israel-based visitors approach. In this configuration, Jaffa Gate becomes the main focus, rendered unrealistically large in an elevated 3D-like perspective. The Christian Quarter, with the Holy Sepulchre church, is at ten o'clock, and the Jewish Quarter, with its tourist hub, the Western Wall, at two o'clock. Between them, in a subtly manufactured central vacuum, lies the souk and the majority of the city. The Armenian Quarter appears an afterthought, and the Muslim Quarter is isolated at the far margin of the page, flattened by the perspective and largely detail-less.

Thus do maps shape our perceptions, deliberately concealing truth while perhaps unintentionally revealing motivation.

More problems arise. The "four quarters" configuration leaves out the Haram al-Sharif, but the Haram is almost always shown as a neatly walled-off rectangle, visually separated from the rest of the Old City. It is generally labelled using a different typographic convention from the quarters. Is the Haram inside the Muslim Quarter, or not? Considering its status within Islam, it would make sense, but every map of Jerusalem shows it surrounded by clear, straight boundary lines that divide it from the streets around. The Haram's status as a holy place, open and undeveloped, might suggest it is not residential in the same way as the rest of the Old City, though in truth people have for centuries lived within it, and still do. And then there's its status in Judaism as the site of the now-destroyed Jewish Temples, which for some militates against including it in a Muslim quarter at all.

So the Haram stands alone on the map, rarely, if ever, covered by a "Muslim Quarter" cartographic label. We visitors might therefore imagine it is some sort of special fifth quarter. It's not, of course. The Haram is a Muslim space, intimately linked with the lives of the people who live within and around its perimeter – as well as countless more distant others – in ways that belie the hard, fast lines on a map. As the writer Ahdaf Soueif put it, "The north and west walls of al-Aqsa are not walls at all; they are a porous urban border that houses people, schools, libraries and archives."

This quartering plagues Jerusalem. If you're approaching the city for the first time, you might reasonably assume that the four quarters (or are there five?), and their attribution to specific religious communities, are, somehow, holy. A holy city, divided, holily, into holy quarters. From that mistake, it's a short step to the next – thinking that only Christians live (or, perhaps, *could* live) in the Christian Quarter. After all, the West retains a residual memory of its ghettoes, strictly demarcated and often walled areas of cities into which, historically, Jews were forced. The word clings on in our own time, tainted by the Holocaust and by Black trauma in the United States and the continued suffering of underserved communities of color in Western cities. Are Jerusalem's color-coded "quarters," you might legitimately ask, in fact ghettoes?

From that double mistake, it would then be easy to absorb the unspoken message that you, an innocent visitor, might be more welcome in one quarter than another. Seeing all these zones of religiousness on the map, you might conclude that you should just stick tight with your own people, whoever they happen to be, for your own safety and so as not to unwittingly offend anyone else.

Such conclusions suit a narrative based on division and exclusion. In reality, Christians live in the Muslim Quarter, and Muslims live in the Jewish Quarter. (And Jews live across the Old City, too, but their presence in the Christian, Muslim and Armenian quarters currently is an anomaly, stemming not from organic community growth but from Israel's state-sanctioned policies of property seizure and settlement, in contravention of international law, following Jordan's expulsion of the Old City's Jewish population in 1948.)

Yet on the maps we all use today, Jerusalem's Old City looks like a jigsaw of no-go zones. It appears to be the kind of place you might approach gingerly in order to do what you want to do, or see what you want to see, and then leave.

There's a reason for that.

But first, food. And an excursion across a border to an earlier map of Jerusalem, in Jordan.

You can eat very well in Madaba, a cheerful, medium-sized market town set among fields of wheat on the hilltops east of the Dead Sea. It's not a rich place and not especially pretty, but every so often it lets you glimpse a fragment of deep time – a dry stone wall, a narrow balcony on the curve of a street that could be a nineteenth-century photograph, something about how the main-road traffic – a mix of Mercs, delivery vans and farmers' pickups carrying fearful sheep – still passes slap bang through the center of town rather than being bypassed through suburbs. Aside from bakeries and pastry-houses and aromatic hole-in-the-wall falafel joints, lanes behind Madaba's old fruit and veg market hide a handful of restaurants in Ottoman stone courtyards where suave waiters serve puffy hot flatbreads sprinkled with nigella seeds, tangy sheep's cheeses, cubes of lemony grilled chicken and bright, floral Jordanian Chardonnays.

Wealthy Ammanis enjoy Madaba. It's also a comfortable, uncomplicated place for foreigners to visit, and if you go looking, it yields evidence of still deeper time. The hills are strewn with dolmens. Behind a line of shops selling rugs and olive-wood crucifixes is a long stretch of Roman road. Mount Nebo, from atop which Moses saw the land God had promised to the descendants of Abraham, as recounted in the Book of Deuteronomy, is a few miles away. And surviving as a mosaic on the floor of Madaba's main Greek Orthodox church, built 130 years ago over the ruins of a much bigger predecessor, is the world's oldest map of Jerusalem.

I saw it first in 1997. The way I remember it, I stood for hours at the rope strung across the jagged border on that dusty church floor where modern ceramic tiles between the pews give way to Byzantine tesserae. I lost myself, staring down at Jerusalem, an evocative, pixellated ovoid filled with 1,400-year-old detail. The mosaic depicts the city in oblique perspective, as if from a high vantage point: you see the outside of the encircling west wall and the inside of the east wall. Buildings inside cluster in a 3D rendering. You can walk the streets in your mind, it is that clear. You see the main gates, in the same locations they are today, and trace the lines of the market lanes, the same as today. You smell the animal filth on the map's minuscule alleys in front of the map's open doorways.

The Madaba map was created to glorify the works of God, but also to help direct Christian pilgrims to holy sites. Conveying, like maps before and since, factual information mixed with partial values and assumptions, it is mostly cartographically accurate, even today. Jerusalem, united, quarterless, is just one part. It extends from modern Lebanon in the north to the Nile Delta in the south, and from the Mediterranean coast in the west to open desert further east. The artist included every major town and city – Jerusalem, Bethlehem, Nablus, Jericho, Gaza and others. Boats cross the Dead Sea laden with wheat, perhaps, and salt. Holy places, from the Garden of Gethsemane to the Sanctuary of Lot, carry precise labels in Greek. Roaming the Jordan Valley are gazelles and lions.

When the map was created, probably in the 550s, Madaba was a place of some importance. Christian life was thriving and the town was a regional center of art: dozens of intricate mosaics from the period survive all over the modern town, and in nearby villages. When Persian armies came through sixty years later, followed shortly afterwards by Arab Muslim ones, Madaba surrendered without a fight, and so retained its Christian identity and population: churches were still being built and mosaics laid for another hundred years or more. A mosaic discovered nearby mentions a bishop of Madaba as late as 785. Were Christians at that time still gathering here – right here, where I'm standing – to consult this mosaic map on the floor of the church, as old to them as Wollstonecraft's *A Vindication of the Rights of Woman* is to us now? Did they use it to visit nearby Jerusalem, by then an Islamic city?

Madaba's tide turned, and for centuries through what we call the Middle Ages it lay abandoned under rubble. Memory of its mosaics, and its wondrous map, faded. It was only in the 1880s, as Madaba was being repopulated, that the map came to light – a unique work, embodying the insight of those living on Jerusalem's doorstep.

In the thousand-plus years between the Madaba map's creation and its rediscovery, almost every map of Jerusalem was created by outsiders. Some were drawn, many were painted, almost all were figurative or purely imaginary. Maps became symbolic representations of ideal locations or landscapes – an especially powerful idea when it came to Jerusalem, holiest of yearned-for holy cities.

In many maps produced in medieval Europe, Jerusalem is depicted as circular, a literal expression of the idea of the city as *omphalos*, a Greek word meaning navel (that is, of the world), drawn from God's words in the Book of Ezekiel: "This is Jerusalem: I have set it in the midst of the nations and countries that are round about her." As in Islamic-world cartography at this time, the idea of a map wasn't so much to function as a practical aid, since travellers would rely on oral and written accounts and journey together under the supervision of knowledgeable guides. Often, maps were drawn *after* travel, to serve as a rendering of how an individual – or a community – conceived of a place. To observers, particularly to European Christians, what Jerusalem looked like, or where it was, mattered far less than what it represented – a place of perfection and the location of the *axis mundi*, the point of connection between heaven and earth. A map became a visual expression of religious belief.

Then, in 1798, Napoleon invaded first Egypt, then Palestine. He brought with him a large contingent of scientists, artists and scholars. Their investigations and publications sparked a surge of European interest in Arab and Turkish culture. Painters painted. Explorers explored. Domingo Badía, a Barcelona-born spy for Napoleon who disguised himself as a Muslim and went by the name Ali Bey, gained entry to the Haram al-Sharif in 1807 and, seven years later, published the first measured drawings of the mosque compound.

The first nonfigurative map of Jerusalem, based on measurements taken in the field, appeared soon afterwards in 1818, the work of Franz Wilhelm Sieber, a young botanist from Prague. Oriented with east at the top, it shows the main streets and some major buildings in what we would recognize today as more or less the right locations. Most of the area inside the walls is shaded as being populated, or at least built-up, though a few patches of gardens and orchards stand out in the southwestern corner by the Armenian compound, the northeastern corner inside Herod's Gate, and in the south by the Dung Gate. Its most noticeable difference from a modern map is the lack of physical or conceptual divisions within the city. The long western edge of the Haram – usually shown nowadays by a thick line signifying a rigid separateness from the streets beyond it – is only lightly marked. The one neighborhood defined by religion is the *Judenstadt*, meaning "Jewish Quarter," here comprising an area south of Bab al-Silsila Street and immediately east of the Cardo (both of which are unidentified). There is no "Muslim Quarter" or any other quarter marked.

I would have liked to have spent time in Sieber's Jerusalem.

The next major cartographic advance was a map by the English explorer-architect Frederick Catherwood. Later to become famous for his pioneering drawings of Mayan ruins in Central America, Catherwood visited Jerusalem in late 1833 with two companions as part of a years long journey around the eastern Mediterranean. It was a business trip: Jerusalem's monuments and holy places were little understood in Europe and, having gained technical drawing and engineering experience in Athens and Egypt, Catherwood wanted to draw them for publication.

On arrival in Jerusalem Catherwood made a point of gaining the confidence of the governor, a vital step if he was to be able to fulfill his mission. Even so, he would not have been welcome on the

Haram, from which Ottoman law barred non-Muslims. Undeterred, Catherwood wasn't the first, and would not be the last, non-Muslim to try to use subterfuge to get access to Muslim-only holy places. According to his own account, quoted in a guide to Jerusalem by English artist W.H. Bartlett published eleven years later, it was 13 November 1833 when Catherwood screwed up his courage and walked onto the Haram disguised as an Egyptian officer, accompanied by an Egyptian servant he names only as Suleyman. The two entered the Dome of the Rock, where Catherwood sat down and began to sketch, "not without some nervousness."

At first he was ignored, he says, but then some of the worshippers "began to think all could not be right. They gathered at a distance in groups, suspiciously eyeing me ... They approached, broke into sudden clamor [and] uttered loud curses."

Suleyman brandished a whip to defend his master. With an eye for his admiring audience back home, Catherwood spices up the encounter. "Escape was hopeless," he writes. "I was completely surrounded by a mob of two hundred people." Is our hero to be torn limb from limb? Catherwood, who by this stage has apparently neither spoken to his objectors nor defended himself, tells us he was only seconds from certain death when the governor appeared. "As we had often smoked together, and were well acquainted," murmurs Catherwood, "he saluted me politely."

A word from this debonair life-saver – described patronizingly as "a latitudinarian as to Mahometanism" (that is, a liberal Muslim) – was enough to placate and then disperse the crowds, whereupon Catherwood sat back down and continued drawing. With violent murder at the hands of a dauntingly large and "fanatic" mob averted by a whisker, we can only marvel at how Catherwood's *camera lucida* – a delicate technical sketching aid with mirrors – remained undamaged throughout.

Catherwood stayed on in Jerusalem for another six weeks, and the drawings that resulted include what is thought to be the first-ever architectural survey of the Dome of the Rock. But, back at home, London publishers showed little interest, and Catherwood eventually gave away most of his still-unpublished Jerusalem drawings to other artists, who used them as the basis for their own works. It was a Catherwood original that inspired a 360-degree panoramic painting of the Jerusalem skyline, done by his friend and fellow artist-entrepreneur Robert Burford and displayed in 1837 in the IMAX cinema of its day, a purpose-built multilevel viewing rotunda located off Leicester Square in London.

Catherwood's map of Jerusalem, published in July 1835, was a substantial improvement on Sieber's. It isn't quite right – he gets a bit mixed up in the alleys either side of Al-Wad Street – but the detail is absorbing, particularly on and around the Haram, where twenty-six points of interest are marked and keyed. As on Sieber's map, tantalizing fragments of city life begin to emerge, from the soap factories identified along Khan al-Zeit to the previously unlabelled open space in the city's northeast corner, which is now evocatively marked "Gardens of olive, fig and prickly pear." The Wailing Wall – or any indication of a Jewish holy place there or anywhere else in the city – is lacking, even though the Wall's importance at the time, and access to it, is attested by travellers' accounts. Was it not considered significant enough to mark?

As before, the only neighborhood Catherwood identified with its residents was the "Jews Quarter," located in roughly the same area as on Sieber's map. There is no other mention of quarters: the Armenian convent, for instance, is shown as a building, marked in the same way as the Latin and Greek convents. The same size and weight of typography used for "Jews Quarter" is also used to identify other, geographically defined neighborhoods, all anachronistically given Latin names, including "Calvary" (consisting, curiously, of the whole area from Jaffa Gate virtually to Damascus Gate), "Acra" (along today's Bab al-Wad Street), "Bezetha" (outside Herod's Gate) and "Moria" (the Haram). Catherwood also marks mosques and churches all across the city, including twenty-seven points of interest relating to Christianity that are not restricted to his nominally Christian "Calvary" area.

It was only two years later, in 1837, that the first map of Jerusalem showing the presence of religiously defined quarters appeared. Viennese lithographer Hermann Engel essentially translated Catherwood's work into German, reproducing the earlier ground plan line for line but introducing new elements, such as variations in typography to differentiate geographical features, such as hills, from ethnoreligiously defined districts. Thick, bold lettering gave new prominence to "Acra," "Moria" and "Bezetha," as well as "Berg Sion" (Mount Zion) and other areas. By contrast, Engel's *Juden Quartier*, shifted slightly eastwards, is marked in a lighter typeface that he also uses for entirely new labels: a Latin Quarter, in the northwest corner; a Greek Quarter, north of Bab al-Silsila Street; a Turkish Quarter, inside Herod's Gate; and an Armenian Quarter, to the north and east of the Armenian convent. This is the first time any of these names appear on a map.

On what did Engel base this innovation? Did he go to Jerusalem himself, or was he just printing a map from another source? I wish I knew. Almost nothing has been written about his work.

It's worth pausing here to look more closely at the words that keep cropping up. What do we have in English to designate parts of a city? There are informal terms – district, neighborhood, zone, area – and also formal or legal usages, whose meanings vary according to jurisdiction: borough, parish, ward, and so on. They are all pretty neutral. But then there's "quarter" – a problematic word.

Quarter, of course, need not imply exactly one-fourth, though that meaning has a solid foundation in Latin. Roman urban design often involved the division of a settlement – or, specifically, a military camp – into four by the creation of a straight north–south road (the *cardo*) intersecting with a straight east–west road (the *decumanus*). Each quarter was then given over to a particular rank, or perhaps a discrete unit. Such military echoes survive in modern English, which has "married quarters," "headquarters," "quartermaster," and to "give no quarter" meaning to deny shelter to an enemy. This usage slid into civilian life three or four centuries ago – every grand house had its servants' quarters – though its undertone remained.

Despite the semantic shift, "quarter" in the sense of a city district seems to survive in a gray area in English: a conceptual link to fourths is not overt yet somehow lingers in the background of the word. This is particularly the case for Jerusalem, where outsiders unaccountably expect the term to reflect a precise division into four. Yet other cities get by fine with fewer. New Orleans has only one – the French – as does Copenhagen – the Latin, named for Latin-speaking scholars congregating around a university. Paris has a Latin Quarter, and a few others. Many European cities also have, or had, one – a Jewish Quarter, often named as such (*La Juiverie, Jodenbuurt, Judería, Judiaria*), sometimes not (Prague's was in Josefov; Krakow's in Kazimierz). Birmingham has Chinese and Irish quarters, and a Jewellery Quarter, named for its artisans. There's an Indian Quarter in Durban. Moscow once had a German Quarter.

That hints at the nuances of power carried by the word in English, nuances of military origin, class hierarchies and cultural, nationalistic or ethnoreligious separation. Quarters, it seems, are for minorities. But they are rarely defined by their own residents, to whom they're just home. Outsiders tend to assume that right, whether they be the municipal authorities, a local demographic majority, colonial overseers and/or some social grouping that is excluded from whatever characteristic links the residents of the quarter.

None of this is hard and fast. It's well understood that from the very beginning of urban settlement, people sharing similar back-grounds, trades or outlooks have tended to want to stick together. Then, as now, people who self-identify together, and live side by side, may also choose to name and demarcate their shared living space, particularly if they face social or political oppression from wider society. The urge to seek security in community can gener-ate self-defined quarters. Nevertheless, when English uses "quarter," more often than not it means a place where Other People live.

Arabic has a completely different conceptual framework. Grasping its basics can help when trying to understand how Jerusalem fits together. A handful of words are relevant here, in the Jerusalem context. The most important is *hara* (which can also be transliterated in colloquial constructions as *haret*; plural *harat*). A *hara* can be both a street and a small neighborhood, often at the same time: the one lends its name to the other. As well as its neutral meaning – a thoroughfare – the word also carries what's been called a socio-geographical meaning, defining "an area inhabited by people bound by faith, origin or occupation."

In 1495, Jerusalemite historian Mujir al-Din identified eighteen *harat* in his city. (Another count has identified even more, as many as thirty-nine quarters in Jerusalem during the thirteenth and fourteenth centuries.) Some were defined by landmarks: *Haret Bab Hutta* comprised, as it still does, the network of alleys in the northeast corner of the city running off the street that emerges from Bab Hutta (Gate of Forgiveness), the middle gate in the north wall of the Haram. Others were named for a local trade, such as *Haret al-Jawaldeh* ("Tanners"), a street inside New Gate. Still others were defined by the origin of their population, such as *Haret al-Yahud* ("Jews"). All had emerged organically.

By the nineteenth century, some of Mujir al-Din's *harat* had changed or disappeared, but many persisted, and others emerged. Beside *Haret Bab Hutta*, for instance, was *Haret as-Sa'diyya*, named after the Bani Sa'd tribe, who had long ago settled in the lanes between Herod's Gate and Damascus Gate. There was *Haret Haddadin*, named for a tribal grouping of Christian Arabs; *Haret al-Mawarneh*, named for Maronite Christians; *Haret an-Nasara* (Christians in general); *Haret al-Qattanin* (the Cotton Merchants, named after a long-established covered market); *Haret Khan al-Zeit* (the [Olive] Oil Caravanserai, named after a market street); *Haret al-Magharba* ([Muslim] North Africans); *Haret al-Wad*, spreading around the central section of the main artery Al-Wad Street; and several more.

On top of this self-defined patchwork, the Ottoman authorities attempted to impose their own administrative divisions, in the form of census districts. These large areas drew from the traditional *harat*, and in some cases more or less overlaid them, though they often subsumed – and thus erased – the smaller ones. Two notable examples were the *harat* traditionally named after the Armenians and the Jews, which roughly bordered each other in the south of Jerusalem. It seems the Ottoman authorities balked at actually naming either community in their official paperwork. So we find Ottoman censuses first renaming *Haret al-Yahud* (Jews) as *Maslakh*, meaning slaughterhouse, referring to the abattoir that stood in the area – but then, by the nineteenth century, subsuming both *Haret al-Yahud* and *Haret al-Arman* (Armenians) into a broader district under the title *Haret al-Sharaf*, another traditional neighborhood name referencing the nearby tomb of fourteenth-century dignitary Sharaf al-Din Musa.

Nonetheless, populations across the city remained mixed, despite prevailing patterns of settlement linked to religious affiliation. From the fourth century onwards, Christians of all denominations had gravitated to the area around the Church of the Holy Sepulchre in the west of the city (Armenians were an exception, since their monastery had been established in its current location further to the south early in the fourth century). After the arrival of Islam in the seventh century, Muslims often settled in the north and east of the city, close to the gates giving access to the Haram. Jews tended to settle close to the Wailing Wall in the south.

But these patterns were neither fixed nor exclusive. In the eleventh century, there was a Jewish quarter in the city's northeast, inside what is now Herod's Gate. Many churches still thrive today in areas traditionally framed as Muslim, such as St. Anne's, which for the last 150 years has been a Roman Catholic church and seminary located immediately opposite the northern gates of the Al-Aqsa compound. The Muslim quarter of *Haret al-Magharba* lay directly beside the Jewish holy place of the Wailing Wall, until it was almost completely destroyed by Israel in 1967. By the turn of the twentieth century, more than a third of Jerusalem's Muslims lived *outside* what is now called the Muslim Quarter, and both Christians and Jews lived *inside* it. There were non-Armenian Christians in the Armenian Quarter, Jews in the Christian Quarter, and Muslims in almost every part of the city.

(Beware: it's tempting to infer from this that Jerusalem was some kind of paradise of coexistence, with everybody getting on famously until twentieth-century intolerance broke the spell. As strongly as we should resist that fantasy, we should also allow room for the image of Jerusalemites living the daily reality of sharing limited space with others. Ethno-religious identification does not, in and of itself, foment conflict. Political manipulation does that.)

Another Arabic word that's useful here is *hawsh*, meaning "courtyard." In Jerusalem, as in towns and villages across the region (and far beyond), people often shared intimate living space, different families frequently occupying rooms off a communal *hawsh*. Several of these courtyards might comprise a *hara*. Jerusalem also has words such as *ziqaq* (alley), *aqaba* (a steep, often stepped, alleyway) and different terms for street, road or way (*tariq, sharia, khatt*) and market (*suq*) – but *hara* has been the principal term defining the city's urban settlement for more than five hundred years, and it carries none of the baggage burdening the English word "quarter."

In bigger cities, several *harat* could comprise a *hayy*, meaning district. Several of these, forming a large area in a metropolis, could be termed *roba*, literally quarter.* But such definitions are slippery. What's clear from listening to people, and as one Jerusalemite, the writer Khalil Assali, confirmed to me: "Palestinians never use *roba*. Some people say *hayy*, but that's new. Everybody still uses *hara*."

By contrast, in Hebrew the universal term is *rova*, meaning both one-fourth and a city quarter. When talking about the Jewish Quarter, Jewish Israelis will often refer to it simply as *ha-rova*, "The Quarter." The omitted adjective implies exceptionalism and a sense of possessiveness as well as, perhaps, helping to avoid attention being drawn to the existence of other quarters with other adjectives.

The bottom line is that Jerusalem had – and still has – a multitude of neighborhoods. All throughout its long, long history, it was never divided into four, neat, religious quarters.

Until the British arrived.

To tell this part of the story we need to return to the 1830s – for Jerusalem, a time of political upheaval. In 1831 the reform-minded governor of Egypt, Muhammad Ali Pasha (*pasha* is an honorific), and his son Ibrahim Pasha, had rebelled against their Ottoman overlords. They invaded the Ottoman-controlled eastern Mediterranean,

---

* Size is relevant: the vast desert of sand that spreads across the entire southern third of the Arabian Peninsula is known as *Al-Roba Al-Khali*, the Empty Quarter.

conquering Syria (which included modern Lebanon and Palestine) and marching on to Constantinople itself before declaring an intent to proclaim independence. To make matters worse – or, some said, better – in 1839 the Ottoman sultan suddenly died, and was succeeded by his sixteen-year-old son. Then the commander-in-chief of the navy defected to Muhammad Ali and took the fleet with him.

The Ottoman Empire was apparently about to collapse. The European powers scrambled to reimpose order, seize influence and, in Britain's case, keep routes open to colonial possessions further east in India. They also identified a power vacuum in Palestine. An 1834 popular uprising there against Muhammad Ali's new policies of conscription and taxation had failed, but it left lasting impact as a challenge to political authority. Amid the turmoil, Britain in particular sensed an opportunity to influence hearts and minds. The first British Consulate opened in Jerusalem in 1839.

The following July Britain, Austria, Prussia and Russia intervened on the side of the Ottoman sultan, first with a diplomatic initiative, then with military force. Britain, in essence, bombed Palestine (and Lebanon) into submission, then handed it back to Constantinople. By November it was all over. Muhammad Ali withdrew.

But British forces remained.

Along with the Royal Navy, a select band of Royal Engineers had been sent to the eastern Mediterranean to support the campaign and survey terrain. British interests having prevailed, their commanding officer, Colonel Ralph Alderson, directed his men to make detailed plans of fortified positions up and down the coast. A few weeks later two of them – lieutenants Edward Aldrich and Julian Symonds – arrived in Jerusalem. They stayed throughout March 1841, surveying, sketching and drawing, and eventually producing an intricate, but contentious, map.

Aldrich and Symonds's work superseded Catherwood's of six years before, forming the basis of cartography in the city for decades afterwards. But it found controversy in its own time through its depiction of the walls of the Haram. Like Catherwood, the two Christians would not have been welcome to enter the Haram, but unlike Catherwood they didn't push the issue and instead surveyed the compound from outside, recycling Catherwood's work for the interior. This led to a slight discrepancy in one corner, around the Gate of the Chain, corrected on later maps.

What wasn't corrected, though – and what, in retrospect, should have raised much more controversy than it did (it seems to have passed completely unremarked for the last 170-odd years) – was the map's labelling. Because here, newly arcing across the familiar quadrilateral of Jerusalem, are four double labels in bold capitals. At top left *Haret En-Nassara* and, beneath it, *Christian Quarter*; at bottom left *Haret El-Arman* and *Armenian Quarter*; at bottom center *Haret El-Yehud* and *Jews' Quarter*; and at top right – the big innovation, covering perhaps half the city – *Haret El-Muslimin* and *Mohammedan Quarter*.

No map had shown this before. Every map has shown it since.

The idea, in 1841, of a Mohammedan (that is, Muslim) quarter of Jerusalem is bizarre. It's like a Catholic quarter of Rome. A Hindu quarter of Delhi. Nobody living there would conceive of the city in such a way. At that time, and for centuries before and decades after, Jerusalem was, if the term means anything at all, a Muslim city. Many people identified in other ways, but large numbers of Jerusalemites were Muslim and they lived all over the city.

A Muslim quarter could only have been dreamt up by outsiders, searching for a handle on a place they barely understood, intent on asserting their own legitimacy among a hostile population, seeing what they wanted to see.

Its only purpose could be to draw attention to what it excludes.

But it may not have been Aldrich and Symonds.

Below the frame of their map, printed in italic script, a single line notes that "The Writing" had been added by "the Revd. G. Williams" and "the Revd. Robert Willis."

The machinations of 1840 had not all been about geopolitics. British Christian missionaries had long had their eye on the unevangelized peoples of the Ottoman Empire – and, specifically, the so-called Holy Land. Since the Crusades* there had been an unrequited urge to restore Christian rule over Jerusalem. Shades of opinion within Christian theology – then as now – saw the conversion of the Jews as a vital step towards the second coming of Christ. In Britain a group of concerned Anglicans had in 1809 founded the London Society for Promoting Christianity Among the Jews (known for short, misleadingly, as the London Jews' Society). Among its other works, the society had sent two missionaries to Jerusalem in 1836, but whereas Roman Catholics enjoyed official French protection, and the Greek Orthodox church was protected by Russia, Jerusalem's tiny number of Protestants struggled alone, with no recognition locally and no international support.

Their savior appeared from an unexpected quarter. In 1841 the King of Prussia, Friedrich Wilhelm IV, keen to boost evangelical Protestantism by capitalizing on Britain's existing missionary activity in Jerusalem, proposed a joint Anglican-German bishopric. After some misgivings, the English church adopted the idea. The first Protestant bishop of Jerusalem, Michael Alexander – appropriately enough, once a rabbi who had converted to embrace the aims of the London Jews' Society – was ordained that December and arrived to a downpour in Jerusalem on Friday, 21 January 1842. Chosen to accompany him as chaplain was George Williams.

Alexander's story, and the tale of the short-lived bishopric, is for another time and place. Our focus is that young chaplain, twenty-seven years old when he arrived in Jerusalem. He stayed for fourteen months before departing to St. Petersburg, Dublin and other postings. Some sources suggest he arrived before Alexander, in 1841. If so, did he meet Aldrich and Symonds? We don't know. But Williams became their champion, defending them when the Haram

---

* Before the nineteenth century, the Crusader period was the only other era in Jerusalem's long history in which rulers created ethnoreligious districts within the city. Having killed all the Jews and killed or driven out all the Muslims, the European occupiers repopulated the north and east of Jerusalem with Christian Arabs from the countryside, inventing a Syrian Quarter. They created the office of Latin Patriarch and established a Patriarch's Quarter around the Holy Sepulchre church, and partitioned smaller, semiautonomous zones for their various knightly orders, including a Templars' Quarter and Hospitallers' Quarter.

inaccuracy came up and then publishing their work. The survey the two Royal Engineers did was not intended for commercial release (Aldrich had originally been sent to Syria under "secret service"), and it was several years before their military plan of Jerusalem came to public attention, published first in 1845 by their senior officer Alderson in plain form, without most of the detail and labelling, and then in full in 1849, in the second edition of Williams's book *The Holy City*.

Did Aldrich and/or Symonds invent the idea of four quarters in Jerusalem? It's possible, but they were military surveyors, not scholars. It seems more likely they spent their very short stay producing a usable street-plan for their superior officers, without necessarily getting wrapped up in details of names and places. The 1845 publication, shorn of street names, quarter labels and other detail, suggests that.

It's the 1849 publication that we need to focus on.

The other figure named on the map, Reverend Robert Willis, was the son and grandson of doctors to George III and a Cambridge professor of mechanical engineering who dabbled in architectural history. He never went to Jerusalem. Regardless, he wrote a long essay on the Holy Sepulchre church and published it in Williams's book. Even his own obituary of 1875 called his work "old-fashioned."

So we come back to Williams as the provider of captions and labels for the 1849 map. Here he is, in *The Holy City*, introducing the main gates into Jerusalem – the western "named of Jaffa," the northern "of Damascus," the southern "of Sion" and the eastern, "called by the natives 'The Gate of St. Mary.'" He adds: "They have all of them other designations, but with these we need not ... concern ourselves." Ah.

Then Williams takes it upon himself to "assign names" to Jerusalem's main streets, since "the inhabitants have, for the most part, dispensed with ... this convenient practice." This is false, as we've already seen: the inhabitants had names for every corner.

Re-examining the map, which, cartographically, is reasonably accurate, it becomes apparent that most of the labelling is way off. On the plus side, Williams transliterates Arabic terms such as *haret* as well as some place names (*Bab en Nebi Daud* for the Gate of Prophet Dawoud/Zion Gate; *Tarik el Alam* for Via Dolorosa; and others) so he obviously had some local assistance – though there are mistakes too (e.g. *Miryam* for *Maryam*). But bizarrely, for the most part Williams ignores contemporary Arabic and instead gives the main streets English names last used by the Crusaders. He has "Street of the Temple" for Bab al-Silsila (Street of the Chain); "Street of the Arch of Judas" for Haret al-Yahud (Street of the Jews or, today, Jewish Quarter Road); "Street of Saint Stephen" for Souk Khan al-Zeit ([Olive] Oil Caravanserai Market). These are names that are centuries out of date, as if a modern map of London labelled Marble Arch "Tyburn," or a plan of the New York subway had "New Amsterdam" at the top. Who had Williams been talking to?

Compounding his anachronisms, and perhaps with an urge to reproduce Roman urban design in this new context, Williams writes how two main streets, north–south and east–west, "divide Jerusalem into four quarters." Then the crucial line: "The subdivisions of the streets and quarters are numerous, but unimportant."

Historians will, I hope, be able to delve more deeply into Williams's work, but for me, this is evidence enough. For almost two hundred years, virtually the entire world has accepted the ill-informed, dismissive judgmentalism of a jejune Old Etonian missionary as representing enduring fact about the social makeup of Jerusalem. It's shameful.

Williams – who, at a guess from his work, did not understand Arabic – had no clue what he was looking at. Or, he saw what he wanted to see. Harking back to a Christian-ruled era and carving up the city mattered desperately to him and his mission. The newly arrived Protestant evangelicals could not convert Muslims, since Ottoman law punished converts with execution. They despised Catholicism and the rituals of the Eastern Orthodox churches but could gain little traction in drawing converts (also, provoking those communities' protecting powers, France and Russia, could have had unforeseen diplomatic consequences). For this reason, and their own millenarian eschatology, all their political, financial and spiritual resources went into converting Jews.

With Britain's increased standing in Palestine after 1840, and the growth of interest in biblical archaeology that was to become an obsession a few decades later, it was vital for the Protestant missionaries to establish boundaries in Jerusalem. They needed to know exactly who lived where, in order to be able to know where to target their evangelising efforts, and where to avoid. As British newcomers did elsewhere, in India and other colonies, they imported their home-grown conceptions of social division to Jerusalem.*

"We never use 'Muslim Quarter' in Arabic," Mustafa Abu Sway, professor of Islamic Studies at Al Quds University, told me. "I am more than sixty years old, and I have never used that term except in an academic setting and media interviews. Among ourselves, we don't say it. 'Where are you going?' 'I'm going to Al-Wad Street,' 'I'm going to Al-Aqsa,' 'I'm going to the market,' 'I'm going to the Redeemer church' – not 'I'm going to this quarter or that quarter.' The notion of 'Muslim Quarter' is absent from our daily language."

Here is Laura C. Robson, a historian of colonialism in the Middle East: "[The] evangelical Protestant worldview did a great deal to determine the nature of the encounter between the British and the local Arab populations … in nineteenth-century Palestine. It determined the British focus on local Christian and Jewish populations, rather than the much larger Arab Muslim community. Furthermore … it assisted the emergence of an understanding of Palestine as a place whose significance lay primarily in its Christian and Jewish heritage – an idea that would be used from the

---

* Williams spread his ideas around. Ernst Gustav Schultz, who came to Jerusalem in 1842 as Prussian vice-consul, writes in his 1845 book *Jerusalem: eine Vorlesung* ("A Lecture"): "It is with sincere gratitude I must mention that, on my arrival in Jerusalem, Mr. Williams … willingly alerted me to the important information that he [and] another young Anglican clergyman, Mr. Rolands, had discovered about the topography of [Jerusalem]." Later come the lines: "Let us now divide the city into quarters," and, after mentioning Jews and Christians, "All the rest of the city is the Mohammedan Quarter." Included was a map, drawn by Heinrich Kiepert, that labelled the four quarters, mirroring Williams's treatment in *The Holy City*.

mid-nineteenth century onwards to legitimize a British political claim to the so-called Holy Land."

Thus was a Muslim Quarter created.

The four quarters took hold in outsiders' imaginations. They appeared, reinforced in large, bold capital letters, in Titus Tobler's map of 1849, the 1858 Van de Velde map, the hugely influential map known as the Ordnance Survey of Jerusalem done by Charles Wilson in 1864–65, and then in Charles Warren's Jerusalem volume in the magisterial *Survey of Western Palestine*, published in 1884.

From then until today, pretty much every map of Jerusalem's Old City published in any language in the non-Islamic world (and often within it) divides the place into four quarters. All because the Reverend George ridiculous Williams said so.

In truth, of course, it's not just because of George. If his framing, and the fostering of sectarian division it codified, hadn't suited the British and other European governments, such cartographic fantasy would never have persisted. The fact that it has, to the extent that it's now all over the internet and available for free at every tourist office, speaks volumes about the colonial ambitions of successive waves of Jerusalem's rulers, down to our own time.

"Religious, ethnic and racial difference underpinned European conceptions of state and society, and ethnographic maps became a tool of empire- and nation-building," writes historian Michelle Campos. "The unease that European observers repeatedly expressed at the messy taxonomies of other heterogeneous Ottoman and Levantine cities such as Istanbul, Salonica, Izmir, Beirut and Jaffa ... contributed to a lasting desire to place Jerusalem's residents in neatly sealed quarters."

Jerusalemites lived – and live – in another Jerusalem. To take just one source, Jerusalemite musician Wasif Jawhariyyeh (1897–1972) wrote vividly about the shared experience of religious celebrations and the fluidity of intercommunal relations in the city before the British Mandate. Historian Salim Tamari, who edited

Jawhariyyeh's diaries for publication, notes the absence of ethno-religious demarcation lines at that time, theorizing – rightly – that they were a British creation. Jawhariyyeh's lived experience and Tamari's analysis of it offer a compelling repudiation of the colonial worldview presented by George Williams and his heirs.*

Yet opinions differ, naturally. Jerusalem's Armenians are a very small ethnoreligious minority elevated by colonial intervention to unusually high status by the allocation of an entire "quarter" of the city (actually one-sixth of the area inside the walls). Many Armenians remain proud of, and grateful for, the prominence their quarter brings them and for the benefit Hebrew and English linguistic ambiguity bestows: the Armenian "Quarter" (neighborhood) has come to mean the Armenian "quarter" (one-fourth part). They appear to be one among four, rather than one among a dozen or more.

Nevertheless, there's a reason why Jerusalem's Old City looks on the map like a jigsaw of no-go zones. The Palestinians of the Old City are a thorn in Israel's side. Israel devotes enormous political, economic, legal and bureaucratic resources to making their lives difficult. Exerting visible control is part of that, and embedding the idea of deep-seated sectarian enmities, pitting one group against another in order to maintain power over all, has always been a useful tool of control. George Williams's idea of four sharply delineated quarters has survived so long because it supports the poisonous old narrative of divide and rule.

Wherever you see it, know that it is false.

---

* Despite being from a family that was both middle class and Christian, Jawhariyyeh's education and his profession granted him a degree of valuable social capital, which may have allowed him to overlook ethno-religious or class divisions. For less privileged groups in the nineteenth and early twentieth centuries – Jews, say – the idea of four quarters may have loomed larger.

2

A Product of British Imagination

STORIES OF JERUSALEM'S WALLS

"WHAT DO YOU THINK OF JERUSALEM?" a Jerusalemite friend asked me one afternoon. "How does it look to you?"

How to reply? You could say it looks beautiful or tense, or ugly or calm, or inspiring, or smelly, or hopeless, and it would all be true. You could say I'm sorry life has been made so hard for you, or you could say when I stood on the roof last night and watched the sun go down, lighting up the domes and the steeples against a low sky streaked with grime, and I thought of the sea and how I miss those who are gone, your heavenly city seemed to me such a miserably human and ignoble place, peaceless and powerless, condemned to carry the albatross of its eternal significance. You could say thank god the rain has come (it was autumn) or I wonder why it's so hot these days. You could say it seemed busy yesterday in the souk but not busy enough, or you could say where have all the people gone, or you could say it looks like things are getting worse. All of it would be true.

But then I knew what to say.

I said – It looks different to me all the time. It just depends which gate you walk in through.

I didn't know my friend well enough to precisely judge the look that passed over his face, but I haven't forgotten it, even now. Then he smiled, in his cheerful, disarming way, and nodded. "That's good," he said. "Nobody's said that before."

They haven't? I thought. They must have done.

So I thought I'd write about the gates. But to write about Jerusalem's gates, you have to start with the walls that flank those gates. And the best way to do *that* is to consider a small village in the English countryside.

Everywhere you look in Chipping Campden, there are ghosts. They hang about in St. James's, the high-towered "wool church" at the top of the village, built thanks to the deep pockets of fifteenth-century textile merchants who were making a killing from the shaggy-fleeced local Cotswold sheep. Nearby, an elaborate honeystone Jacobean gateway looks out onto spectral fields, since the mansion it once shielded was burnt to the ground during the Civil War. Opposite is a row of gabled almshouses, haunted as a medieval woodcut. Then, try following the undulating, weather-beaten roofs that jag against each other all along the gentrified High Street down to the old silk mill, repurposed as a gallery. There, among the showrooms of painters and ceramicists, up some stairs, hides a dim silversmith's workshop under a low ceiling, its artisans perched by mullioned windows studiously bending metal for brooches while the starch-collared dead flit about in the shadows, rattling chains at you.

The silversmith's is the last survivor from the Guild of Handicraft, a workers' enterprise relocated to this corner of rural Gloucestershire in 1902 from London's East End by architect, designer and social reformer Charles Ashbee. Ashbee was one of the leading lights of Arts and Crafts, a deeply romantic, nostalgic movement in British decorative art that formed as a reaction against industrialization, just before modernism arrived to sweep the board clean. To an Arts and Crafts sensibility, chilly old Chipping Campden embodied perfection – a preindustrial landscape of pristine beauty and simplicity where working people could enjoy the benefits of fresh air and social dignity, free from the ugliness of urban life. Ashbee, and many other Arts and Crafts luminaries, adored the place. Their vision was both utopian and patronizing.

The Guild collapsed after five years, but Ashbee stayed on in Campden (locals drop the "Chipping"), becoming a father for the first time in 1911, aged forty-eight, despite having told his wife before their wedding thirteen years earlier that he was attracted to men, at a time when homosexuality was illegal. Three more children followed in rapid succession, then he departed hurriedly in 1917 to take a government teaching job in Cairo. There he wrote *Where the Great City Stands*, a manifesto arguing for an appreciation of art and beauty to influence postwar civic planning.

Cairo, at that time, was Britain's regional military headquarters. Among the officers and civil servants Ashbee met there was Ronald Storrs, then Oriental Secretary. Storrs liked *Where the Great City Stands* and remembered a talk he'd heard Ashbee give at his old school, Charterhouse, twenty years before. Consequently, when General Allenby appointed Storrs as Britain's Military Governor of Jerusalem in December 1917, Storrs straightaway invited Ashbee to Palestine to direct the new administration's planning policy for the city. Thus was the empire forged.

What resulted was a dose of English Arts and Craftsiness from which Jerusalem may, still, never recover.

Jerusalem's walls are old but, for Jerusalem, not that old. They are the work of the Ottoman sultan Suleiman, tediously dubbed "the Magnificent" in English but more interestingly known in Arabic as "the Lawgiver" – though from inscriptions he left, Suleiman would refer to himself ever-so-modestly as "the Second," bonding his legacy to that of his Old Testament namesake, the Jerusalemite prophet and wise old Temple-builder King Solomon.

Suleiman's accession in 1520, at the age of twenty-five, energized his empire. Besides military campaigning in Europe and Persia, and maritime expansion from Aden and the Somali coast to Gujarat, the first years of his reign saw a flurry of building work in Jerusalem. The Dome of the Rock was repaired, public fountains went up as part of an overhaul of the city's water supply, the Citadel was reinforced – and then, in 1535, Suleiman ordered that the city walls be rebuilt. It was to be Jerusalem's largest building project for hundreds of years, perhaps the largest in the entire period between construction of the Dome of the Rock and the modern era.

Author Evliya Çelebi, writing a century later, put it down to supernatural intervention. "The Prophet appeared to [Suleiman] and told him: 'You should spend [your wealth] on embellishing Mecca and Medina and fortifying Jerusalem's citadel, in order to repulse the unbelievers when they try to seize Jerusalem during the reigns of those who come after you.' ... Suleiman at once rose from his sleep and sent one thousand purses to Medina and another thousand to Jerusalem ... [His governor] gathered all the master builders, architects and sculptors of Cairo, Damascus and Aleppo and sent them to Jerusalem to rebuild it."

Walls had defended Jerusalem since its foundation, though their size and extent, straddling the various valleys and hills, had altered many times to match the city's changes. By the sixteenth century Jerusalem had been wall-less for three hundred years, after the previous set had been dismantled in 1219–27 to frustrate any Crusader reoccupation. There had been piecemeal restoration of parts of the Haram wall since then, but otherwise, by Suleiman's time, Jerusalem was encircled mostly by a line of rubble.

Logically, the new walls followed that line. Work began in 1537 under project manager Muhammad al-Naqqash, assisted by his Syrian sidekick Darwish al-Halabi, master builder from Aleppo, and Muslih ad-Din ibn Abdullah from Turkey, who handled the finances. (Despite the talk of purses, no record has yet been found of budget or expenditure.) Their masons proceeded by uncovering the former walls' foundations, making good, then laying new courses on top. The northern wall was first, then teams worked simultaneously to extend walls on the east to the Haram, and on the west as far as the Citadel. It was while they were exposing the foundations of the old southern wall, probably in the early summer of 1539, that workers including Hussein ibn Nammar, a Jerusalemite mason, and clerk Yacoub al-Yaziji discovered treasure – a ceramic pipe filled with old coins that had been buried in the rubble. The two faithful employees dug out the trove and delivered it to the sultan's representatives. Were they rewarded? The archives are silent.

By 1541 the walls were complete – just over four kilometers in length, averaging twelve meters high and more than two meters thick, and pierced by seven gates: two each to the north, east and south, and one to the west. One of the seven – Bab ar-Rahma, the Gate of Mercy, also known as the Golden Gate – was immediately sealed shut. Much later, in the nineteenth century, a new gate was created in the north. (There's also a new gate in the south, but it is small and insignificant.) All the gates are discussed individually in alternate chapters throughout this book.

Suleiman never made it to Jerusalem himself, but for the next three hundred years his walls marked a hard border around the city. The five functioning city gates were locked shut overnight and on Fridays in the middle of the day, to thwart a surprise attack during the noon congregational prayer. Outside lay only cemeteries, orchards, temporary encampments and – by the early nineteenth century – a handful of buildings put up by wealthy families as rural retreats. Permanent settlement outside the walls began in the middle of that century and accelerated rapidly, but despite deepening sectarian divides the commercial, cultural and spiritual focus of city life remained the area within the walls, which were themselves incorporated into the urban conversation. Shops, offices, cafés and hotels clustered outside the most important city gates, as new streets developed from parades of buildings put up against the external line of the walls. Community ties preserved the continuity between older districts within the walls and the newer ones developing outside.

Late nineteenth- and early twentieth-century photographs show souvenir shops and photo studios clustered outside New Gate, and rows of commercial premises outside Damascus Gate and Zion Gate. The area outside Jaffa Gate was a node of business: around eighty shops stormed up the slope towards New Gate, owned by the Greek

Orthodox Church and rented to Jews, Muslims and Christians alike – a bakery, a stationer, a furniture outlet, a blacksmith, an ironmonger, newspaper sellers, coffee stands. Jerusalemite historian George Hintlian has compiled memories of this area, including of Abou Petro, a short, round restaurateur with a fine mustache, who served simple, cheap meals of meat and rice in a large garden here with space to seat a hundred. For hummus you would go to Afghani, for fancy dining the Syria-Palestine restaurant, for sophisticated chitchat the Muallakah, an upper-floor café with a wooden balcony. Abou El Haj restaurant made excellent kebabs. Maaref hosted famous singers. Café Bristol was known for gambling and dancing girls. Here too, says Hintlian, was "the European market, where it was possible to find alcohol, quality cheeses, biscuits and other delicatessen items." In the next street over, still just outside Jaffa Gate, were greengrocers – both retail and wholesale – pharmacies, tailors, printers, confectioners and mechanics. There were shoe shops, perfumeries and boutiques, as well as the deluxe three-story Fast Hotel. Immediately beside Jaffa Gate stood a pet shop with a parrot that had been trained to greet customers by squawking "Can I help you?" (Unfortunately, local boys managed to retrain the bird to screech obscenities instead, leading the shop owner, Mr. Totah, to "terminate the services of his assistant," as Hintlian puts it gloomily.)

By the time the British had finished with Jerusalem, all of this was gone.

Charles Ashbee arrived in Jerusalem in July 1918, and immediately wrote: "I've never felt so pagan and repelled in my life ... this medievalism [...] is something of a shock." He spent a little over four years in the "picturesque but filthy" town, also bringing his wife and daughters over from England.

His position as Civic Advisor was uniquely privileged. Thanks to his personal friendship with his sympathetic boss, the colonial governor Storrs, Ashbee had the legal authority to enact, in effect, whatever regulations he wanted. At that time, Storrs and the British administration also enjoyed sufficient prestige among Jerusalemite elites to be able to smooth over any local opposition to their planning decisions. Ashbee's whim was law. And Jerusalem was about to get that whim right between the eyes.

Ashbee adored Jerusalem's walls. They were ancient. They were romantic. They had battlements. They embodied the kind of past he expected to find and wanted to preserve. One of his first acts was to order all the shops and cafés and other buildings clustered against them cleared away, the better to be able to view them from afar. Then he created an exclusion zone around them, beautifying it with green lawns – lawns! – and forbidding any encroachment by builders or developers. Next, he created a scenic walkway along the top of them, to allow their splendor – and the splendor of the ancient stones they enclosed, not to mention the lives lived among those stones – to be admired from a suitably elevated perspective.

This was a triple blow under which Jerusalem still staggers. At a stroke, Ashbee and Storrs transformed the city's enclosed core from a living urban space at the heart of its communities to a sliced and diced "Old City" – it was around this time that the phrase entered use – showcased for the admiration of onlookers. Later occupiers, notably Israel, adopted this approach and extended it into commodification. Today, accessing Ashbee's Ramparts Walk requires payment to an Israeli public company and the walls have become a powerful visual device for Israel's national tourism marketing: floodlights illuminate them as a backdrop to sound-and-light shows offering visitors an Israeli reading of Jerusalem's history.

Ashbee's lawns survive, too, a buffer zone of colonial green that isolates the walls – and thus the Old City as a whole – both physically and psychologically from life elsewhere in the city. They demonstrate an imposed exceptionalism. British rule was set on creating, then entrenching, a division between the walled "Old City" – the idealized Jerusalem of imagination – and the altogether less desirable "New City" outside the walls, just as British influence in the nineteenth century had highlighted, then attempted to exacerbate, sectarian divisions within the walls. Today, Israeli policy adapts the same idea, using new walls – this time of concrete – alongside tools such as economic and demographic manipulation to further divide Jerusalem and cut the city off from its Palestinian hinterland, objectifying it again in the service of the state. Israel has extended Ashbee's lawns and, with the bestowal of National Park status in 1974, rendered them inviolable.

The Pro-Jerusalem Society, founded by Ashbee and Storrs soon after their arrival, was the vehicle for British restoration and preservation. It wasn't all bad. The Society funded renovations in the souk, established workers' guilds for weavers and other trades, supported apprenticeships, offered micro-grants for repairs – though all of this came with Arts-and-Crafts strings attached: renovations had to be like-for-like, using only traditional materials and methods. Modernization was prohibited.

One early stipulation – stemming from that devotion to local materials – was that all new buildings must be clad in "Jerusalem stone," a few varieties of distinctive pale-colored limestone that have been quarried in nearby mountains for millennia. This British-conceived municipal law, still in force today, has given the whole of Jerusalem a remarkable visual unity, even as it has crushed innovation and eclecticism. It has fetishized the visual regularity of blocks of limestone to such an extent that those blocks have come to symbolize not just Jerusalem but, in a strange sense, a particular idea of holiness itself. A building clad in Jerusalem stone is not just any building. It has Jerusalem status. It demands Jerusalem reverence. New must appear old. Inanimate stone has absorbed the pomposity of the colonial officials who were so set on promoting its use. The only way Jerusalem may be imagined, they said – and their heirs still say – is in textured* rectangles of creamy-yellow limestone. (And, in a happy side effect, since stone is expensive, only the wealthy may build.) A look that King Herod achieved two thousand years ago is the same look the entire city and every person living in it remain bound to by law, yesterday, today and forever. It's hateful.

Architectural analysts Wendy Pullan and Lefkos Kyriacou are more measured. "The Society set a collision course between an idealized

---

* The standard Jerusalem style is *tubza*, a stone block left with – or given – a rough, bumpy face.

vision for Jerusalem and the urban structures that supported the day-to-day lives and incomes of the city's inhabitants," they note.

Ashbee liked to see himself in the vanguard of a battle against urban ugliness and the dehumanization of modern society, as an ennobler of work and a dignifier of public space. Yet he seemed unable to empathize. "An industrialized Palestine ... is a questionable benefit and, I think, a futile hope," he wrote. "[M]ay it not be better to leave as it is that peasant society, which still has so much dignity and beauty?"

Even for 1920, his aesthetic and social vision was at least fifty years out of date. But he wasn't alone. Storrs, who came from a devoutly Anglican background, shared many of the same outlooks: he ordered all the bars in Jerusalem that served alcohol to be closed, on grounds of public morality. Then there was William MacLean, a British planner who had worked in Khartoum and Alexandria, and who, like Ashbee, was brought in by Storrs in 1918. After two months in Jerusalem, MacLean submitted his master plan. In essence, it said preserve everything old and ban everything new. Much of it was implemented. Another colleague was Patrick Geddes, a town planner who had worked across British India and who wrote a report for Storrs in 1919 called *Jerusalem Actual and Possible*. (He was later commissioned to design a layout for nascent Tel Aviv, still discernible in that city's streets today.) Geddes characterized Jerusalem, catastrophically, as a "Sacred Park" with "many modern disfigurements," and decreed that "squalid buildings ... will naturally be removed." The groupthink is shocking.

Early in his tenure, Ashbee sketched a city plan – fortunately not taken up – for a greater Jerusalem, showing what he called the "Holy City" preserved in aspic behind its walls at the center of a web of neatly intersecting streets radiating out from an encircling green belt. Historian Simon Goldhill has juxtaposed this with Ashbee's 1917 sketch plan for Letchworth, a garden city in Hertfordshire, north of London, that was conceived and built in the years either side of the First World War. The two images are cousins. From Chipping Campden to Letchworth to Jerusalem: in Ashbee's mind, it seems, all of humanity yearned to live in a nice, neat little country town in southern England. "Ashbee brought the Cotswolds to Jerusalem," Goldhill says, approvingly.

Perhaps I'm being unfair. After all, Storrs was in charge. And the buck ultimately stopped with Storrs's superiors. Then again, listen to social historian Yair Wallach: "Jerusalem today, as it is perceived by many within and outside the region, is largely a product of British imagination. The stone-built city, eternally holy and ever divided between its quarrelling sects, was the brainchild of Ronald Storrs, Herbert Samuel [British High Commissioner for Palestine 1920–25] and a generation of British administrators, who named its streets after prophets and kings [and] covered its new buildings with a stone mask ... The effect of that colonial makeover was overwhelming. The inhabitants of the city lost control over its meaning, probably irrecoverably. [Jerusalem] is crushed by its historicist aesthetics and what it symbolizes."

The core tragedy is that such ideas remain current. An Israeli government director of planning wrote less than thirty years ago: "Since the British planning perspectives of Jerusalem were laid down, no other dominant town planning elements were formed in the city." So today, when you look at Jerusalem's walls, or walk its ramparts, or approach its gates, hold in your mind that what you are seeing is essentially an Arts-and-Crafts vision of an idealized medieval walled city. Our twenty-first-century experience of Jerusalem is rooted in, and framed by, a regressive nineteenth-century British rural sensibility.

Ashbee would have approved.

3

Living in Eternity

A STORY OF PLACEMENT
AND DISPLACEMENT

NOT MUCH IS COMMON TO PUBLIC SPACES across the Old City. Design is different, street furniture is different ... But one thing that's the same whichever neighborhood you're in is the trilingual street nameplates fixed on every corner. They always comprise three rows of square white tiles, showing the street's name in Hebrew on the top, then Arabic, then English underneath, the text hand-painted in black and the whole sign finished by a thin border of green olive leaves. They're very clear and rather elegant, even if the translation (or transliteration) between languages is sometimes a bit clunky.

Some residents use the nameplates to make their own statements. In Jewish Israeli neighborhoods you may see the Arabic text scratched out or obscured with stickers. Elsewhere, some have the Hebrew text obliterated – and, occasionally, the English too. Erasure of language is an unmistakable message.

Most signs have a single border around all three languages. But across the Old City you'll notice that some signs have a complete border around the Arabic and English text, but a separate part-border around the Hebrew text above. Why the difference? And why tiles at all? As you might have guessed, there's a story to tell.

Tavit Ohannessian had come back to Kutahya to save lives. It had been a terrible time there since he'd left. This ancient town southeast of Istanbul, for centuries the center of Armenian ceramics production, had been torn asunder. Starting in 1915, Armenians across Anatolia had suffered arbitrary arrests, expulsions, forced marches and massacres at the hands of Turkish officials and military. As many as one and a half million people died in what became known as the Armenian genocide. But following his own arrest and deportation, Ohannessian had had the good fortune to escape first to Aleppo, then by a stroke of exceptional luck to Jerusalem.

Years earlier, in 1911, before the violence, Ohannessian's ceramics atelier in Kutahya had hosted a visit from the British diplomat Mark Sykes. Sykes was rebuilding his country pile in Yorkshire, Sledmere House, after a fire, and commissioned Ohannessian to create a set of decorative wall tiles. That project, fulfilled by 1914, turned out to be – literally – a life-saver for Ohannessian, as word of Sykes's dazzling "Turkish Room" spread among British diplomats and officials. After the British occupied Jerusalem in 1917, the governor they installed, Ronald Storrs, decided to have the tilework decorating the Dome of the Rock replaced – but artisans to do such skilled work could not be found locally. When Sykes by chance met Ohannessian again in Aleppo, among thousands of destitute Armenian refugees, he offered him the Dome of the Rock commission and an introduction to his old friend Storrs. Ohannessian jumped at the chance. He arrived in Jerusalem with his family in December 1918.

Storrs, Ashbee and other British officials from the Pro-Jerusalem Society took Ohannessian under their wing, offering moral, technical and financial support. But it was clear that Ohannessian couldn't tackle such a mammoth commission alone. He needed specialists to help him, and there was only one place to find them.

Ohannessian travelled back to Kutahya.

With atrocities continuing all around, Ohannessian offered his hometown's surviving artisans and their families the chance to return with him to Jerusalem. Notable among the eight who accepted were potter Neshan Balian, and Megerditch Karakashian, whom the American author Sato Moughalian describes as "a refined master of black brush drawing and painting of traditional designs" in her biography of her grandfather Tavit Ohannessian, *Feast of Ashes*.

Moughalian tells the enthralling story of Ohannessian's career and journeyings superbly well. Back in Jerusalem in the autumn of 1919, Ohannessian – who anglicized his first name to David, to ease his new working relationships – and his freshly assembled team for the Dome of the Rock renovations soon ran into technical then budgetary problems. Public opposition followed, from the prominent Turkish architect Ahmet Kemalettin, and in 1922 the British abruptly cancelled the project.* Return to Kutahya was out of the question, so Ohannessian made the best of a bad situation. His studio on Jerusalem's Via Dolorosa turned to private commissions and the burgeoning tourist trade, manufacturing tile designs as well as bowls, plates, mugs, candlesticks and ashtrays by the score, decorated with traditional floral motifs, peacocks, gazelles or songbirds. That same year, keen to exploit a rising market, Balian and Karakashian split away to form their own ceramics studio. Thanks in part to British patronage, Kutahya's distinctive blue and white designs began to take on emblematic status for Jerusalem.

Over the 1920s and beyond, these three pioneering Armenian craftsmen working out of two studios, with their families and employees, successfully introduced to Palestine the previously unknown art of decorative tile-making. Public buildings still display their work today. Examples around Jerusalem include wall-sized tile panels flanking the entrance lobby of the American Colony Hotel, and a beautiful tiled fountain alcove at the Rockefeller Museum, both by Ohannessian; and the façade of the Armenian church of St. James and a Garden of Eden panel in the Legacy Hotel, both by Balian and Karakashian. There are more, particularly by Ohannessian, in West Jerusalem and worldwide from Cairo to California.

But Ohannessian himself, already once a refugee, was forced to flee his new home, Jerusalem, during the fighting of 1948. He went first to Cairo, and then Beirut, where he died in 1953, his family dispersed.

---

* The Dome of the Rock's tiles didn't get replaced until the 1960s, in a project sponsored by Jordan's King Hussein and fulfilled by Turkish artisans.

Ohannessian's studio in Jerusalem did not survive his departure. However, the Balian family still operates on Nablus Road just north of the walls, the building's original stonework adorned with their own tiles. Marie Balian, daughter-in-law of Neshan, became a world-renowned ceramic artist, staging a solo show at the Smithsonian Institution in Washington, DC, her work collected by London's V&A Museum. She died in 2017, and her son, Neshan Jr., continues at the head of the business today.

That's two families. What about the third?

"Jerusalem gave us shelter. This art survived because we found shelter here." Hagop Karakashian reaches over to a shelf and picks up a tile with a beautiful curlicued floral design. "This represents us nicely, the vine. Whoever eats from this fruit lives in eternity. Jerusalem is like the vine tree and we were the ones eating from it. Our art flourished and became part of Jerusalem. We have been able to express our artistic identity here, even though we've gone through a hundred difficult years – the genocide, war in 1948, war in 1967, a couple of intifadas … It wasn't easy to keep going."

Hagop, fifty-something grandson of Megerditch, tall, gently smiling, speaks quietly in his company workshop, which fills a space off his showroom on a back street between the Greek Orthodox Patriarchate and the Franciscan monastery. If you didn't know it was here, you'd be unlikely to find it. Thanks to the Karakashians' stellar reputation, though, plenty of customers know it's here.

Hagop talks about his father, Stepan, born in 1929, who grew up in the pottery building on Nablus Road where the Balians and the Karakashians lived and worked together. "The market was not that big back then. Balian and my father were able to serve the demand," he says. But in 1963 Megerditch died, and Stepan made the decision with his brother Berge, Hagop's uncle, to set up on their own. Their first studio was on Via Dolorosa and almost immediately they bagged a juicy new commission from the Jordanian government, then in control of the Old City.

This is a story that's been told through official records, but never from the family's perspective. It started with a visit from Santiago and Ursula Lopez, a husband-and-wife team – Santiago Spanish (or perhaps Gibraltarian; sources differ) and Ursula British – who had been appointed by Jordan's King Hussein to manage his royal stud. In the process of designing new stables at Hummar, outside Amman, they visited Jerusalem and asked Stepan to incorporate a design using an Arabian horse and the royal crown onto a set of tiles for a fountain. Hagop shows me one of the tiles, perhaps a memento of his father's. It has been signed in the corner: "U. Lopez, 1967."

One commission led to another. In 1965, with the stables complete, the Lopezes visited Jerusalem again. Through personal connections at the Amman office of UNESCO, they proposed that the Jordanian government commission Stepan to make street-name tiles for the whole of the Old City. Tourism was a key plank of Jordan's strategy for Jerusalem, but tourists were wandering the city with no idea where they were. Hagop emphasizes that the idea came from the Lopezes. "It was a personal initiative [on their part]," he says. "The [Jordanian] government agreed with them."

As we've seen, street names in Jerusalem have always been fluid, changing from generation to generation and often disputed. In an echo of George Williams a hundred years earlier, Jerusalem's last British mayor, Richard Graves, in office during 1947–48, grumbled: "One of the minor defects of the city of Jerusalem … is the absence of street names." His mild words may have concealed an angrier sentiment: the British had tried for more than a decade to either impose street names or have various local committees agree on names, largely without success.* The process of naming streets, then displaying the chosen name, is a form of administrative control. Britain had signally failed. Jordan wanted to succeed.

---

* A few streets outside and inside Jerusalem's walls still display original British-era trilingual name-plates in blue. These are notable for showing English at the top, above Arabic and Hebrew. Israel has since affixed nameplates in a similar design to Dung Gate and New Gate, but with the order of languages reversed. When the Jordanians commissioned Stepan Karakashian to make nameplates, they put Arabic at the top. Under the Israeli occupation, Hebrew is at the top again.

Regardless of his client's motivations, Stepan was not about to look such a gift horse in the mouth, and took the job. It soon ballooned almost out of control. He took fifteen years to finish.

There's a much longer story to tell here about how each street was named, who decided on the (sometimes ropey) translations and transliterations between languages, who signed off on the (unusual) calligraphic style, and so on. That would necessitate digging around in the municipality archives to uncover processes and personalities. Hagop pointedly jokes with me, "Someone needs to write a book about it" – but until that happens, here's the short version.

In 1965 Stepan began the process of producing hand-painted street-name tiles in Arabic and English, framed with that distinctive olive-green border. The work proceeded in batches as the municipality underwent the process of surveying the city, defining the start- and end-point of each street and deciding on spellings and transliterations for names which, in some cases, may only ever have been spoken before. Hagop shows me the process his father followed. "The English he would have done himself," Hagop says. "But the Arabic needs a calligrapher. My father would have found someone, ordered [text] from him on a piece of paper, then copied it."

Once he had the text, Stepan used a pin to prick tiny holes in a sheet of tracing paper placed over the designed words, following the outline of each letter. Hagop copies the process as he is talking to me. Stepan would then spread the tracing paper over a blank tile and rub charcoal across it. Hagop does the same. What results is the outline of the text picked out on the tile in charcoal pinpricks. These serve as guidelines. Stepan would then have used his brushes to paint each letter onto the tile by hand, using black underglaze paint imported – like his kilns – from the English company Blythe.

The tiles themselves, Hagop says, were made by Berge, according to the same basic formula used forty-five years earlier in the original Dome of the Rock project – reddish clay mixed with kaolin and quartz for strength, hand-pressed and dipped in white slip, a thin slurry that

provides a surface for the text. They were up to fifteen millimeters thick, two or three times thicker than the decorative tiles used today.

Hagop hands me a black-and-white photo from 1966, showing the Jordanian mayor of Jerusalem, Ruhi al-Khatib, in a *qalbaq** at the center of a semicircle of dour officials and ministers standing bundled in winter coats at the corner of Al-Wad Street and Via Dolorosa, marking the installation of the new bilingual street signs, visible on the wall above them. He puts a finger on his father, who's been pushed to the back of the group on one side, as if tangential to the project; Stepan is craning his neck to be seen.

Soon after the photo was taken, in June 1967 Israel invaded and occupied. Days later, Al-Khatib was ousted. With the project

---

* From Turkish *kalpak*: a tall hat of black goatskin or sheepskin common in Turkey and the Caucasus. The notes to this chapter give detail on some of the people shown in Hagop's photograph, reproduced above.

barely begun, and two previous administrations having failed to resolve the street-names issue, Israel extended Stepan's commission. From then until around 1979 Stepan labored to complete his task. For all the existing bilingual nameplates, he had to add an extra row of tiles above to show Hebrew, hence the mismatched borders that persist to this day. For streets not yet covered, he had to produce new trilingual nameplates, with all three languages within one border.

Much of Stepan's work survives intact, fifty years on, or more. His nameplates look fresh and crisp, and it's hard to believe they are all hand-painted originals. Only a few streets have new or replacement nameplates; they copy Stepan's style but are less pleasing to the eye.

While Stepan was fulfilling the street-names commission, he was also stabilizing and expanding his business with private commissions and tourist sales. The evolution of Armenian ceramic art in Jerusalem is another subject that deserves a book of its own.

"Slowly they [Karakashian and Balian] started taking designs from local sources – church mosaics, the Madaba map, the birds mosaic, the Tree of Life mosaic.* So the art changed, and it became specifically Jerusalem. It's nothing to do with Armenia or Turkey anymore," says Hagop.

Their work inevitably bred imitators. During the 1960s and 1970s a number of factories in Hebron began to copy the Armenian-Jerusalem style, turning out mass-produced ceramics cheaply for the souvenir market, to the extent that Jerusalem's souks today are full of Armenian-originated designs, even if very little of it is actually Armenian-made. Then in the 1980s a few Jerusalemite Armenian families began using their own kilns to

---

* The "birds mosaic" is a sixth-century floor discovered in 1894 outside Damascus Gate, showing vine leaves, grapes and many kinds of birds, inscribed: "For the memory and redemption of all the Armenians whose names God knows." The "Tree of Life" is an eighth-century mosaic floor at the early Islamic site of Khirbet al-Mafjar (Hisham's Palace) near Jericho, showing a tree flanked by wild animals.

produce handmade, hand-painted pottery of their own, alongside Balian and Karakashian. They still thrive today, with studios near New Gate and around the Armenian convent, most prominently Garo and Sonia Sandrouni, George and Dorin Sandrouni, and Harry Sandrouni – the men all brothers – Hagop Antreassian and Vic Lepejian.

It seems to me there's room in the market for artistic variety, but Hagop Karakashian's smile has become a little forced. "It makes me feel a bit competitive to be honest. It's not easy to accept. There are differences." He selects a tile to show me. "This is one of my father's designs. Look at the accuracy. When I look at it I examine every element, every leaf, I see every curve, how it's painted. When I look at the other families' works I don't see anything binding the design together. There's something missing. Maybe it's the process, the way we mix our colors, the way I was taught by my father to be very exact."

He puts the tile down, and, beaming again, directs my attention to a part-finished bowl on the workshop table in front of us. I see familial pride in his expression, but there's something else too, and I wonder if I'm imagining some hint shadowing his words of the trauma and displacement that is this quiet man's inheritance.

"My daughter Patil. This is her work. She's seventeen and she does this freehand. It's not traditional, it has a different touch. The Armenians brought the arts to Jerusalem, in ceramics, photography, as goldsmiths. We are part of this city's mosaic. I'm fifty-two years old now. A few years ago I didn't feel what I feel today, this artistic connection to my daughter. I need to teach her, pass this art on to her. It's emotional for me. Getting older makes you more emotional" – at this he smiles ruefully – "but I believe as Armenians we enrich this city with our art. It seems very important to me to pass it on, otherwise it will be lost."

4

In Movement Is Blessing

STORIES OF BAB AL-AMOUD/
DAMASCUS GATE

"HISTORY IS VALUABLE. I love carrying the past on my shoulders. I love it, and I want to do it. It's not about the money – less money is better for you anyway, I tell my sons. It's about the meaning of this shop. One son studied psychology at university, another studied politics. He could have gone into public life, but he turned it down because he wanted to follow in the family business. Our family have a good influence here in Jerusalem. People know Izhiman."

The names of Jerusalem's many gates are a poem. There's been a Water Gate, a Horse Gate, a Fish Gate, a Spring Gate, a Valley Gate, a Song Gate, a Garden Gate and a Beautiful Gate. Today there's a Lions Gate, a Flowers Gate, a Golden Gate. If we include the gates into the Haram, we could add a Gate of Forgiveness, a Gate of Darkness, a Gate of Tranquillity, a Gate of Paradise. And that's not even all of them. Some of the vanished gates we can locate; most are now just words, unattached to places.

As often in Jerusalem, names are like clouds, beautiful but elusive. How a gate is known in English doesn't necessarily correspond with its Arabic name – or, rather, names, since most places have more than one name in Arabic, one or two more in English, and quite often others in Hebrew, too.

It's the same with the city itself. Jerusalem has essentially the same name in English as in Hebrew (*Yerushalayim*), drawn from the ancient past via Greek, but a set of other names in Arabic with other derivations. The most common is *Al-Quds*, literally "The Holy One," derived from the linguistic root Q-D-S, connoting holiness and purity. It's spoken in Jerusalem dialect with the *q* as a glottal stop, so *'Uds.** You may also hear the more literary names *Bayt al-Maqdis* or *Bayt al-Muqaddas*, "The Sanctified House," derived from Hebrew.

This is the first in a series of stories from each of Jerusalem's gates, starting in the north and, for no special reason, going clockwise.

There's a saying in Arabic that could have been invented for the Damascus Gate: *fil-haraka baraka.*

Haraka is movement. *Baraka* is blessing or benefit – spiritual and, sometimes, material. Both are emphasized on the first syllable. *Fee* just means "in," here elided with the definite article *al* (some people say *al-haraka baraka* without *fee*). The phrase comes out literally as "In movement is blessing," or, more idiomatically, something like "It's good to keep moving." People say it literally, implying exercise is healthy, but also figuratively, to mean "Work hard, get results" or "Time waits for no one."

But I've also heard *fil-haraka baraka* said in awe, to hint at the euphoria of wandering loose in the midst of an absorbing street or market, full of movement and people and color and life, watching goods being bought and sold, money being made, wreathed in a dozen smells, hearing the shouts of a dozen sellers, revelling in the

---

* Since 1967 Israeli officialdom has tried to suppress the term *Al-Quds*. Roadsigns, for instance, if they show *Al-Quds* at all, will generally have it in small script and parentheses, after Israel's "official" Arabic name for the city *Urshalim*, which features in Christian liturgy (and which was used by some Palestinian writers before 1948). No Arab says *Urshalim*.

hubbub of humanity all around. If you're loving your day, excited to be alive in the big city, high on all the streetlife, you might reflect on the joy to be found in a crowd. *Fil-haraka baraka.*

Damascus Gate is never dull. This is the main transit point between the Old City and Palestinian Jerusalem beyond the walls. The streets nearby are a terminus for public transport from all points of the city and wider West Bank, bringing people and taking them away. The gate is a bottleneck, through which everybody passes, in both directions. It is life, and community, and commerce, and – too often – drama, and tension, and confrontation, and it never sleeps. There is movement 24/7. Make your own way. *Fil-haraka baraka.*

The gate's names in Hebrew and English are simple pointers: the ancient and modern road leading northwards from Jerusalem begins from here. The Hebrew name *Shaar Shekhem* (*shaar* is gate) refers either to the ancient Canaanite city of Shekhem, first capital of Israel's kingdom 2,900 years ago, or to its post-Roman successor Nablus (*Shekhem* in Hebrew). Until Ramallah grew bigger than village-sized in the late nineteenth century, Nablus was the first major city on the road north of Jerusalem. And if you kept going past Nablus you could – before modern borders – reach the bright lights of Damascus. Hence the name in English. *Fil-haraka baraka.*

By contrast, the Arabic name *Bab al-Amoud* draws on a lost memory. It means Gate of the Column. There's been no column here for more than a thousand years, but before that, the gate's Roman predecessor had rising just inside it a column, depicted on the sixth-century Madaba map. That gate was built by the emperor Hadrian, originally as a triumphal arch (only later were the city walls extended to bond with it), so perhaps the column supported a statue of Hadrian himself. Or maybe it was Victory; another name for the gate is *Bab an-Nasr*, the Gate of Victory – but that's from later, referring to Salah ad-Din's recapture of Jerusalem from the Crusaders. They, the Crusaders, called this St. Stephen's Gate after the first martyr of Christianity, whose bones reputedly lay nearby. Such mobile webs of association are this city's undergirding.

Damascus Gate has menace, too. In 1981 Israeli authorities rebuilt the gate's external approach, turning it into a Roman-style theater. Their design adapts a British plan from 1948 – thankfully never implemented – for a pair of curving processional ramps enclosing a circular piazza. Today, people use the semicircle of steps to sit and chat, or eat, or smoke, shifting round as the shadows move, but in 2018 Israel built three watchtowers here, staffed day and night by Israeli armed police. Constant hostile surveillance has lessened the appeal of hanging out on the steps, though the symbolic power of the place remains. In 2021, when police sought a high-profile location at which to restrict Palestinian freedom of assembly during the Muslim holy month of Ramadan, they chose Damascus Gate, and placed barriers across the steps to bar access. That led, predictably, to a reassertion of ownership of public space by Palestinian people, who gathered nightly on the steps to demonstrate their resistance. Within days the restrictions were lifted.

From inside the gate, past the bags guy on the left, the clothes guy on the right, the pharmacy on the left, the café on the right, the shoeshop on the left, the money-changer on the right, the bakery on the left, the juice guy on the right, the falafel guy on the left and the greengrocer on the right, two of the Old City's main streets fork southwards. On the right is Khan al-Zeit, the main souk street; on the left is Tariq al-Wad, meaning Valley Road,* a thoroughfare for millennia, laid on the bed of what Roman historian Josephus called the Valley of the Cheesemakers (*Tyropoeon* in Greek, though that was probably a copyist's error, mistranslating a Hebrew word).

Today, Al-Wad still ambles along, flanked by a ridge to the west on which most of the city is built, and the summit to the east

---

* The standard Arabic word for valley is usually transliterated in English as *wadi*. *Oued* is a common transliteration in French, reflecting the vowel sounds and grammars of Arabic in North Africa, but I've wondered for years why this street in Jerusalem is called Wad with the "*ee*" omitted – especially since, in medieval times, it was known as Khatt (or Tariq) Wadi al-Tawahin, the Street (or Road) of the Valley of the Mills. I finally asked a linguist, who gave me a complicated answer that seemed to come down to three points: *al-takhfeef*, which means lightening or softening or dilution, referring to a literary technique that removes letters from the ends of words for poetic effect; colloquial Palestinian Arabic, where *wad* and *wadi* coexist; and the Quran, which has *wad* (for instance, at 89:9).

where the Jewish Temple once stood and where Al-Aqsa stands today. Like Khan al-Zeit, it is chiefly commercial – a narrow, often crowded lane, gloomy in parts – but, as well as leading to Al-Aqsa, it is also the most direct route to the Western Wall for worshippers approaching from ultra-Orthodox Jewish neighborhoods in West Jerusalem such as Mea Shearim.

Lots happens on Al-Wad, not all of it good.

One hot mid-morning I threaded a path through the lanes east of Damascus Gate to find the Spafford Children's Center, literally and figuratively a Jerusalem institution. In 1873 Anna Spafford of Chicago survived a shipwreck that killed her four daughters. Eight years later, having lost another son to illness, she and her husband Horatio, with their infant daughters Bertha and Grace, arrived in Jerusalem at the head of a Christian utopian mission that became known as the American Colony. They settled first in a house abutting the walls inside Damascus Gate before later moving to a villa outside the walls that is now the famed American Colony Hotel. As part of the group's philanthropic activities, in 1925 Bertha Spafford established a clinic in that first house that developed into the sixty-bed Spafford children's hospital – the only one of its kind within the walls, complete with a surgical wing. It remained as a hospital until 1970, since when it has refocused as a center for preventive medicine.

Today, Shahd Souri has brought UK training and qualifications back to her home city to run the Spafford Center. She told me that the center's thirty-five affiliated specialists now help between five hundred and a thousand families a year from East Jerusalem and around, offering what is a vitally needed holistic approach for vulnerable children with learning disabilities, emotional disorders or traumatic stress. Support programs range from remedial classes and speech or occupational therapies all the way up to psychosocial counselling, plugging the large gaps that exist in mental health provision and community support for Palestinian Jerusalemites.

Empowerment projects help improve self-esteem for educationally deprived women, often through business development or language learning, alongside classes in yoga, painting, drama and music, everything funded – as from the beginning – solely by charitable donations.

Souri's colleague Dr. Jantien Dajani, now retired from pediatrics, having started work at Spafford in April 1968, is still involved with the center after more than fifty years. She told me plainly: "We feel this is the right way to build a better society."

Fil-haraka baraka.

"My sons said, 'We will come here and manage the shop, you stay at home and relax,' but I said no. My life is here. I've been in this shop since 1980. I can't just sit around at home. I need to carry on here, to support my sons but also to say to them, and to everyone, that this is important. They must know how I am someone who gives, not takes." Tough-looking, short-haired, Mazen Izhiman checks to make sure I've understood, then grins.

Talking together at his shop, a prime spot at the very beginning of Khan al-Zeit immediately below the steps from Damascus Gate, we're constantly interrupted by customers. Everyone knows Mazen, because everyone knows Izhiman. In an economy where family businesses generate 90 percent or more of private-sector revenue, and employ more than three-quarters of the private-sector work-force, Izhiman Coffee is a top-drawer, gold-plated, number-one family brand. *Fil-haraka baraka.*

It also smells like heaven. Grinding machines line up on the shop counter in front of Mazen. As each customer asks for a kilo, or a half-kilo, of this blend or that, this roast, that roast, Ethiopian, Sri Lankan, dark, light, with cardamom or without, he grinds the beans on the spot. The aroma is stupefying, disabling, a kick to the back of the knees. It makes me want to pant like a dog.

The pioneer was Mazen's grandfather. Khaled Izhiman came to Jerusalem from Jaffa (the family originates in Hijaz, in western

Arabia, but they've lost track of when and where). In 1921 he got a shop just over there – Mazen points across the way to a side street off Al-Wad – and started slowly, buying Yemeni and Brazilian beans from an importer. He eventually expanded to include the current, impossible-to-beat location in 1948.

Khaled clearly had a talent for sales: not long after, he managed to buy a car, fitted signboards on the roof advertising Izhiman Coffee (in Arabic and English), then drove it around town and beyond, selling from the driver's seat. Mazen has a photo from the 1950s showing his grandfather parked up in Bethlehem making a sale to what may be one of the nurses at the children's hospital there, as crowds of kids stare and fool for the camera. "People then would only buy thirty grams, or fifty grams, just to make their own coffee, fresh. They would buy every morning," he says.

The 1967 war split the family. Everyone fled to Jordan, but though Khaled and others soon returned to Jerusalem, part of the family stayed and set up an Izhiman coffee business in Amman. Expansion followed. Now there are Izhiman factories, Izhiman shops and Izhiman cafés in both countries, but run as separate, competing concerns. Each claims rights to the name. Logos are subtly different. I'm not sure customers can tell, to be honest, but what's certain is that Mazen's little shop in the frenetic heart of Jerusalem's souk retains diamond prestige as the original.

Fil-haraka baraka.

"People here know Izhiman, they remember buying coffee from my father, and my grandfather. That's why they keep coming back to me to buy. My father – you know, he died when I was nine. It's OK, I don't really remember him, just a few things. But I do remember this: then, and afterwards, everybody passed by this shop and said 'Your father was great, a really great man.' Even if I didn't know them, or they didn't know I was his son, they still told me nobody was like him. That meant a lot. It made me want to emulate him. So I'm happy. This is my place."

5

The Stations of the Cross

STORIES FROM THE PILGRIM WAY

"I REMEMBER ONCE LATE AT NIGHT, I was coming home. It was three in the morning. The whole city was dark, quiet, you know. And as I came up this street I saw a man on his knees. He was a pilgrim. He was walking the Via Dolorosa on his knees. It looked painful, he was going very slowly, knee, then knee, then knee. On the stones. By himself. In the middle of the night. But this is Jerusalem, you know.

"I went home, went to sleep, woke up next morning, got my shop ready, and I had to get something from over near the church. So as I walked there, down this street, round the corner, all the way up the steps, across the market – and there he was, the same guy, still on his knees. It was 10:30 and he was still going. He'd been walking like that all night. This is Jerusalem, you know. People are crazy.

"Then there was the time – you know how pilgrims carry crucifixes? These big wooden crucifixes. They come along here carrying them on their back, like Jesus did, you know, all the way along the Via Dolorosa and up to finish at the church. They're heavy, but that's the point. You're copying what Jesus did, following in his footsteps. So one time there's a group coming along here and one of them is carrying the crucifix, except it's got a wheel on the bottom. Ha ha! He was just wheeling it along, this huge crucifix. Crazy people."

Jesus was brought to Jerusalem as a child. He preached in Jerusalem as an adult. Jerusalem was where he clashed with both the civil (Roman) and religious (Jewish) authorities. All four of the New Testament gospels describe Jesus eating a Last Supper in Jerusalem, being arrested in Gethsemane near Jerusalem, undergoing trial in Jerusalem, then crucifixion, death and burial just outside Jerusalem at Golgotha,* after which resurrection and ascension.

That last sequence of events, of compelling significance for believers, is known as the Passion, from the Latin *pati*, to suffer or endure: being "passionate" about something (or someone) once straddled the line between intense emotion and pain. The draw of being able to visit the same places the Son of God did on his last day of earthly suffering has sustained pilgrimage to Jerusalem for the last 1,700 years, since the Roman emperor Constantine legalized Christianity in 313 and his mother, Helena, made her pioneering visit to Jerusalem less than fifteen years later.

The focus of that pilgrimage, intimately linked to the Passion, is the Via Dolorosa. It's the most famous street in Jerusalem.

Also, it doesn't exist.

That's a typical bit of Jerusalem sleight of hand, to have a street celebrated in faith and literature, marked on maps, marked on street signs, walked on, talked about, pointed to, venerated, photographed – and yet the moment you try to define it, to say where it starts or ends, it vanishes. The Via Dolorosa isn't actually a street. It's just sections of other streets linked together. You might call it a brand.

In Latin, *dolor* is sorrow, pain or grief. The adjective, *dolorosus*, means sorrowful or painful, and its ending changes to match the noun it's attached to – in this case, *via*, meaning road or way. So the *Via Dolorosa* is the Sorrowful Road, or the Path of Pain, or the Way of Suffering (not, regrettably, the Street of the Rose, mentioned often from misheard Spanish and Italian). In Arabic, it translates as *Tariq al-Alam*; *tariq* is road, *alam* are pains.

---

* An Aramaic place name. The anglicized equivalent from Latin is "Calvary."

Tradition defines the Via Dolorosa as the route Jesus took across Jerusalem while carrying his cross. Yet nobody knows with certainty where Jesus walked, or where any of the events of the Passion took place. Early Christian pilgrims followed more or less the same route as today, entering at the eastern gate and walking a straight street that climbs westwards to the place where Pilate was thought to have condemned Christ, and where Christ was thought to have begun his final journey. The path then drops into the valley and does a left–right zigzag to climb west again. It ends at the widely – though not universally – accepted site of Golgotha/Calvary, where Christ died and was buried, now enclosed within the Holy Sepulchre church.

But this is a route mostly of conjecture, and it was often altered to suit prevailing political or logistical needs. In some periods, the pilgrimage trail was more circuitous, including sites such as Mount Zion. In others, pilgrims would start and end at the Holy Sepulchre, or follow other paths across the city. In 1422 one pilgrim measured the route as 450 paces. In 1508 another counted 500 paces. Between these, in 1479, it was said to be 1,050 paces – but the difference may stem from whether a pace was defined as one stride-length or two.

Early on, it was a continuous walk. Then the practice developed of punctuating the route with stops memorializing events described in scripture. The idea of tracing the route in the chronological order of those events only arose in the sixteenth century, after several hundred years of pilgrimage had established a firm link between Franciscan control over the holy places in Jerusalem and Franciscan devotional practice in Europe. By then, Franciscans were building replicas of Jesus's route to Calvary alongside churches and monasteries in Italy, France, Germany and across central Europe – sequences of chapels ascending a hill, each marking an event from the Passion (or from the whole of Jesus's life) where pilgrims would pause and perform specific devotions. The number of chapels would vary: small trails might have fewer than ten, large ones more than twenty, each chapel adorned with artworks and, in many cases, statuary, intended to bring the Bible – and Jerusalem – to life for those who could not travel. Many of these *Sacri Monti* (Holy Mountains) survive today.

Then the Franciscans won papal approval to install mini versions indoors, enabling worshippers to complete a devotional pilgrimage – as if to Jerusalem – station by station entirely within their local church. But still there was no common format. It was only in the 1730s that these routes became fixed with a uniform sequence of fourteen "Stations of the Cross":

1st Station – Jesus is condemned to death
2nd Station – Jesus carries his cross
3rd Station – Jesus falls for the first time
4th Station – Jesus meets his mother, Mary
5th Station – Simon of Cyrene helps Jesus carry the cross
6th Station – Veronica wipes the face of Jesus
7th Station – Jesus falls for the second time
8th Station – Jesus meets the women of Jerusalem
9th Station – Jesus falls for the third time
10th Station – Jesus is stripped of his clothes
11th Station – Jesus is nailed to the cross
12th Station – Jesus dies on the cross
13th Station – Jesus's body is taken down from the cross
14th Station – Jesus's body is placed in the tomb

Nine of these events (numbers 1, 2, 5, 8 and 10–14) are described in the gospels. The other five (Jesus's three falls, the meeting with his mother and the Veronica story) arose over the centuries from traditions of creative visualization around the Passion story.

And the locations in Jerusalem of all fourteen are made up.

That need not matter, of course. What brings pilgrims to Jerusalem is its accretion of holiness. The fact that the Via Dolorosa of Jesus's time lies some twelve meters below current street level troubles no one. Nor, you might say, should it. As in the days when pilgrims "wanted to touch, kiss and lick the stones that had once made contact with Jesus" – as historian Karen Armstrong has written – you still overhear conversations today that include things like "Jesus stepped right here!" or "Jesus touched this wall!" The urge to pin people and events to actual places is overwhelming, and also overwhelmingly distracting. You might even say it misses the point. The Stations of the Cross could be a tick-box exercise, or it could be a focus for devotional prayer and meditation. Either way it is a path full of stories – and, for this unbeliever at least, the stories matter more than the path does. You may be physically walking from station to station but the Via Dolorosa, more than anywhere, offers the opportunity to turn your journey into a metaphysical one.

The only way to know is to walk it. This chapter is about some of the stories I've found while doing so. There's not much that's metaphysical, but then again, humans have always used stories as a way to illuminate hidden truths, so maybe these tales *will* help explain the city or the world a little.

You'll find the Via Dolorosa, and the fourteen Stations of the Cross it connects on a snaking path across the city, thronged from sunrise to sunset, day in, day out. Pilgrims from every country of the world amble along, much as they must have done in centuries past, only nowadays in brighter colors, matching baseball hats and wireless headsets paired to the guide's microphone so everyone can hear without being yelled at. Many arrange in advance to carry huge wooden crosses on their backs (with or without wheels attached). Vendors along the way vie to sell you a nice map, or a refreshing fruit juice, or a souvenir crown of thorns. Meditative it isn't.

The way would be perpetually busy even without the pilgrims: the Via Dolorosa follows some of Jerusalem's busiest shopping streets. The pilgrims add a maelstrom of bewildered souls, adrift in what many of them have been told is, if not a war zone, certainly a place of danger. You see people casting about mid-devotion for anchor points of security in the crowded streets, and finding none. Most stick tight together. Some sing as they go, a wedge of fifty or more yellow-capped Nigerian or Filipino or Russian penitents shuffling along the narrow, dim-lit market lanes past displays of saucepans and toilet brushes, singing childhood-cherished hymns of praise on the journey of their lifetimes while logjammed shoppers suck their teeth and delivery boys hiss to get past.

The singing maddens me, but when I said so once to a Palestinian friend, an observant Muslim, she told me she finds it delightful, which made us both laugh with embarrassment, though not for the same reasons.

1st STATION – JESUS IS CONDEMNED TO DEATH

Jerusalem wakes slowly. If you've not been praying, or baking, there's not much reason to be up and about in the Old City when it's not yet seven in the morning.

Lying in my bed with the window open, there's only a low rumble somewhere, not nearby, to say this is a city. Inside the walls, at this time of day, it might be a village. A door is unbolted. Sparrows chirp. And honestly, a cock crows. At 6:45 a bell chimes from a steeple somewhere – not marking the time, but calling worshippers to prayer. I hear footsteps on flagstones, mixed with *tings* as the passerby gets WhatsApp messages in quick succession. Another church bell chimes, it seems a bit impatiently, at 7:00. Then again at 7:01. The bells disturb a dog. More impatient clanging at 7:03. I wonder – is a priest late? A toilet flushes with a whoosh.

Without cars, a whole other kind of city becomes possible.

Then a steady, rhythmic cooing begins. For years in this part of the Middle East – here in Jerusalem, in Amman, in Damascus, in the places in between – I've heard the same cooing in the early morning. I've heard it when it's cool, like today, and in the winter drizzle and in the dense heat of summer, when the morning is breathless even before direct sun has hit a windowsill. I never knew what was making it. I put it down to some exotic desert paradise bird, intimately adapted to the urban environment. It was grand, I thought, with a sunlit crest. It was iridescent purple, with golden flashes. Sometimes it was green. Serene in the heat, it puffed out its throat into a creamy ruff of snow-white, or charcoal-black, feathers. It bathed elegantly in dust. It watched intelligently from the shade, and built extravagant nests of pine and velvet into which it laid smooth, warm eggs of brown, or blue.

This is its call, that seductive coo, rising and falling. I loved it whenever I heard it. It was mine, my bird, it signalled warmth and life and joy.

Then, the last time I was in Jerusalem, just a few months ago, I found out what it was.

It's a pigeon.

Strictly speaking, the Laughing Dove. In Arabic, *Al-Hamamat Al-Dahika*. Otherwise known as *Spilopelia senegalensis*.

Which is a kind of pigeon.

Grey.

Dull.

Stupid.

Different from English wood pigeons, whose monotonous coo drives me bananas at home.

But still a pigeon.

I shook my head when I found out.

This morning, the cooing broke my train of thought and made me get up.

Now, standing on the roof of the convent where I'm staying, I smell *zaatar*, an aromatic blend of crushed thyme with sesame and lemony sumac that often accompanies breakfasts here, baked on top of flat bread or as a dip with olive oil.

Someone, somewhere, has a better breakfast than I do.

But it's neither the *zaatar* nor the cooing that's caught my attention. My convent lodgings stand opposite the northwest corner of the

Haram al-Sharif, which, in Jesus's day, was the Temple compound. It was exactly here, alongside the wall of the compound – or perhaps slightly separated from it – that the fortress known as Antonia stood, built by King Herod the Great around 35 BCE over the remnants of a predecessor that may have survived, in one form or another, for five hundred years before that. Herod, a puppet king, named it for his Roman boss, Mark Antony. For centuries, it was believed that the Antonia was the site of Herod's Palace, where Roman governors would stay, and where one of those governors, Pontius Pilate, passed judgment on criminals of the day, including – on the date some scholars have pinpointed as Friday, 3 April, 33 CE – Jesus. The pavement outside the palace was held to be the place mentioned in the gospels where Pilate showed Jesus to the crowd, declaring *Ecce Homo!* ("Here is the man!").

So when a pilgrimage route began to emerge in the early centuries of Christianity, it fixed the Antonia – or where it used to stand – as the first point of call.

Alphonse Ratisbonne was frustrated. Not only had he bought the wrong ticket, ending up in Rome instead of Naples, he'd run into an old school friend who was introducing him to everyone in the city. Now the friend's brother, one Théodore de Bussierre, wanted to talk to him about God. "Strange childishness!" Alphonse wrote later.

Ratisbonne had been born into a wealthy family in Strasbourg in 1814 – Jewish, but also closely assimilated into upper-class society and mostly secular. His mother died when he was four, his father when he was sixteen. Graduating in law, he was made president of the family bank. A life of privilege beckoned. At twenty-seven, before his marriage (to his sixteen-year-old niece), he embarked on a winter of Mediterranean travel. But by January 1842 he was stuck in Rome. Not only that, he was having to deal with de Bussierre, a recent convert to Catholicism, who had started pressing him to wear a symbol of Mary and recite prayers together. Ratisbonne – Jewish, atheist – gave a couple of wisecrack answers but went along with it.

On 20 January, the two bumped into each other yet again. Ratisbonne was planning to leave Rome any day, so when de Bussierre offered a carriage ride around the city, it was easy to say yes. But de Bussierre first had a matter to discuss with the priests at nearby Sant'Andrea delle Fratte. Could they go together? Ratisbonne followed him into the church and cooled his heels, wandering around a little. Then, at the third chapel on the left, something happened. Describing it later, he talked about darkness descending, then radiant light shining from a vision of Mary standing on the altar, "tall, vibrant and majestic, full of beauty and mercy." De Bussierre returned to find Ratisbonne on his knees, limp and weeping.

Ten days later, Ratisbonne was baptised. His fiancée immediately broke off the engagement – perhaps a lucky escape for a young girl betrothed to her uncle – and, after a short period of contemplation, Ratisbonne entered the priesthood as a Jesuit, taking the name Father Mary. Not long afterwards he established a new order, the Sisters of Zion. By 1855 he was on pilgrimage to Jerusalem.

When the Romans destroyed Jerusalem in 70 CE, they also destroyed the Antonia. Sixty-five years later, Emperor Hadrian rebuilt the area, creating a new street and paved forum fronted by a triple archway. The new construction overlaid the Herodian-era Struthion Pool beneath; the reservoir's name comes from a Greek word that can mean "sparrow" – did they chirp here then, as they do this morning, I wonder? Inevitably, with the passage of centuries, most of this crumbled. But a memory of the place as being connected with Christ's trial and condemnation lingered. By the time of the Crusades and later, the spot – mostly ruined, but with the central span of Hadrian's arch still standing – was known to all as Ecce Homo.

All through the autumn of 1855 in Jerusalem, Ratisbonne searched for a viable place to establish the Sisters of Zion. A tip-off from an Austrian dragoman led him to the arch, which had now absorbed the name Ecce Homo for itself. Backed by family funds and donations from Europe, Ratisbonne secured the plot. And it is from the roof terrace of the Convent of the Sisters of Zion, built by Ratisbonne directly beside the Ecce Homo arch in 1862, this cool morning at the end of summer, that I smell *zaatar*.

Formerly housing an orphanage and girls' school, and still incorporating the arch – part of which spans the street, with another part forming the apse of the Basilica of Ecce Homo – the convent now takes paying guests. I'm extremely fortunate to have found it. It's decent and very quiet, and benefits from the endlessly cheerful Nahla and Maria, who look after the keys at reception, as well as access to astonishing catacombs extending to the dank, dripping Struthion Pool and a vast stretch of Hadrianic pavement, deep below ground. It also has the single best rooftop view in Jerusalem (and I've seen a few).

I'm up there, sniffing *zaatar*, looking a few meters across the ravine of the street below to the building opposite. That's where the Antonia once stood. For the last century or so it has been a boys' elementary school, the Omariyya. Because of its traditional link to Pontius Pilate, the school is officially the First Station of the Cross, though most pilgrims make their devotions in the street outside rather than seeking permission to enter. (In any case, recent archaeological work suggests that Pilate was more likely to have done his judging far away on the other side of the city, near Jaffa Gate, rather than here, which if confirmed would – rather awkwardly for tradition – turn the whole Via Dolorosa upside down.)

Every morning I hear the Omariyya's bell ring and children yell and chatter. From the convent roof you can see into part of the schoolyard, all wire security fences against old stone arches, but today I'm instead looking down at the school's main door, located up a stepped ramp from the street. A teacher just inside the doorway, mustached, wearing a brown sweater over a collared shirt, is greeting each and every student. These are little boys, from four to ten, prancing together, their backpacks bouncing, and this man has a word for every single one, bending over to speak at their level. It goes on for ages, as kids stream up the ramp. One he shakes hands

with. Another he pats on a shoulder. I learn there's either side of a thousand boys enrolled at the Omariyya. Surely this man can't greet every child every morning. I don't know. Maybe he does.

Those pigeons are still cooing.

Thus begins the Way of Suffering, with a tear.

2ND STATION – JESUS CARRIES HIS CROSS

"*Al-hamdulillah.* Thank God."

I would see Ayman Qaisi every day. Just down the street from the 2nd Station, which is tucked within a walled complex of Franciscan churches beside Ecce Homo, Ayman runs a business selling fresh juice to tourists out of – literally – a hole in the wall. Custom is brisk: almost every Christian tourist passes this way, and he's on a pleasant downward slope, on a section of street that's fairly broad, sunlit and with no shops opposite, just a blank wall. Ayman's sell is soft, and people have good incentives to pause for refreshment.

His shop is maybe two meters by three, open to the street, placed between grand antiques emporiums and smaller souvenir outlets. Locals don't shop hereabouts. The front is a counter, on which rests a big basket of fruit and a hand-juicer. In the back is a coffee machine, a couple of blenders, more boxes of fruit. Oranges, carrots, bananas and a few other staples are always on offer; otherwise, it's whatever is seasonal – pomegranates, guavas, mangoes.

Six years he's been here. "Last two days I was on holiday, man," he says in English, handing me a banana. "Up north. Fresh air, a bit of swimming, you know. What's up, pal?" he suddenly bellows in Arabic at a friend walking past. "What's going on?"

Ayman's always slicing fruit for juicing. Always. I'd walk past in the morning, at noon, mid-afternoon – he's either slicing or juicing.

You look busy, I'd say, expecting a smile or a sigh or a what-can-you-do shrug. "*Al-hamdulillah.* Thank God," he'd reply quietly, without a glimmer, and I'd think – Check your privilege, English writer. Busyness is good. Busyness means success, dignity, hope.

Ayman sees everyone, knows everyone. He lives just a few doors from his shop, with his wife and three young kids, aged three, four and five, in a little cottage of stone that shares a wall with the Afghan Sufi lodge in the street behind. He's warm, and entertaining – it was Ayman who told me the stories about the pilgrim on his knees, and the guy wheeling his cross – but his face is lined and serious, and he's young to have a beard with white in it.

We've never really got into it, but I'm interested in his story.

"For twenty years I didn't do nothing, man. Jumping around, travelling. Italy, most of the time. I lived three years in Italy, three in Denmark." He's forty-one. His oldest child is five. He grew up between two intifadas and the Oslo peace process. I do some maths and think – You left? Really?

So why did you come back? – I say.

"I love it, man. I love my home. After all that, I said to myself I would not live outside this country." And I think – After all what?

Because all the tour groups pass his shop, and because his sell is soft, Ayman knows every guide working the city personally. Like so many in Jerusalem, he can joke idiomatically in half a dozen languages, and pass the time of day in half a dozen more. Every few minutes, another guide will greet him in one language or another, and suggest to their clients that they stop for refreshments. Maybe Ayman charges each of these customers a little extra, and then passes the extra back to the guide later. That tends to be how things work. But maybe he doesn't. I don't know. Or care. After all, price and value hardly ever match, and who's to say what this heavenly, throat-burning pick-me-up of carrot and ginger juice he's just made for me is worth? Whatever you're willing to pay, is the Jerusalem answer.

I wonder if juice is enough for him to support his family. He gestures up the slope. He's recently leveraged his connections with tour guides – and secured the requisite permissions from the Israeli-run municipality – to let guides offer clients who have limited mobility, or who are just tired, a ride through the Old City's steep lanes on an electrically powered golf cart, which he keeps tucked by the side of the street. "Juice and that. The two together," he says, and breaks off to chat with a passing friend, who's had trouble fixing his car.

A Catholic priest from North Carolina, who tells me he's studying in Jerusalem for three months, buys a pomegranate juice.

A tourist couple approach down the slope. They talk to each other in what I think is Portuguese. She wants a banana to eat.

"One dollar," Ayman says, his hands busy behind the counter. It's an outrageous price. They confer, give a hollow smile and walk away.

I'm chortling, but also thinking how they'll be grumbling to each other about Jerusalem's rip-off shopkeepers. Ayman looks at me. "I don't sell bananas. I make juice," he says. "Do you get it, man? They've already been buying drinks and everything up the street. Not here. I don't give a shit about the money, it's not the most important thing. One hundred percent you have to enjoy your work."

And I think – Pride does matter.

We're interrupted by an Israeli rental car inching gingerly down the street, only slightly narrower than the walls. The couple inside are speaking in agitated French. The driver leans out and asks directions to a hotel that is halfway across the city on a pedestrian-only alley in the middle of the market. Ayman explains she can't drive there. She needs to park and get out.

"If you want to, round this corner, you can," he says, and quotes a price in euros not much less than you might pay to park overnight in central Paris. I didn't know tourists could park here, I murmur to him. "I'll move my car and she can have my space," he says. And I walk away, laughing on the inside. Jerusalem never lets you down.

3RD STATION – JESUS FALLS FOR THE FIRST TIME

Opposite the 3rd Station, which is marked by a Polish chapel run by Armenian Catholics that was built in 1947 over the ruins of an Ottoman bathhouse, there used to be a hill. Or, at least, a big mound of dirt. This has been a busy corner for about the last 1,900 years – the point where the main street from the eastern gate (now called Tariq Bab al-Asbat) meets the main street from the northern gate (today called Tariq Bab al-Wad).

The western side of the junction is lined with shops selling trainers, biscuits and replacement TV remotes. The southeast corner has the Polish chapel, where I once watched a crew from Italian television take twenty minutes to get a three-line piece-to-camera in the can, as their gray-haired, bespectacled expert's sightline was constantly blocked by obliviously wandering pilgrims.

But the northeast corner was abandoned for centuries after the Crusades – just open land, piled with rubble. About the same time as "Father Mary" Ratisbonne was overseeing the building of the Sisters of Zion convent, emissaries of the Archbishop of Vienna were doing the same for a new guesthouse here to cater to pilgrims from their own archdiocese. This involved, essentially, moving that mound of dirt. It took three hundred laborers and fifty beasts of burden – donkeys and camels – months on end to achieve it. When the Austro-Hungarian emperor Franz Joseph visited in 1869, he inspected the result: tons of soil shifted to create the walled gardens within which the grand old Austrian Hospice still stands today.

Where did the hill go? And all the archaeological evidence it might have held? Well, that's a good question. Carted away, mostly outside that eastern gate, scattered and trampled and lost. And the hospice that resulted is one of the oddest places in the city, with its *Kaffeehaus* of glittering chandeliers and extraordinarily priced *Apfelstrudel* and *Sachertorte* (cash only; no smiling).

Requisitioned by the British army twice – first in 1918, after it had been a gathering point for German officers during the First World War, then again in 1939, despite the then-Archbishop's protestations that it was a purely ecclesiastical institution, independent of the Third Reich – the Austrian Hospice has served as an internment camp and military academy–cum–spy school. But many old-timers remember it as a public hospital, the best in the Old City. When King Abdullah I of Jordan was fatally shot at Al-Aqsa in 1951, his body was brought here first, accompanied by his fifteen-year-old grandson Hussein – later king – who only survived because the assassin's second bullet hit a medal pinned to his chest. It didn't last as a hospital, though, and stood empty for some time before reopening in 1988 as a haven for well-heeled visitors seeking coffee and cake.

Now, Israeli police with guns permanently loll a few meters from the door of the hospice compound, while a British postbox, inscribed for George V, glowers red from the hospice wall below a cluster of Israeli CCTV cameras staring in all directions, as if to remind Palestinian shoppers of the multilayered, multinational humiliations this street corner might represent for them. It makes me press my lips together and think – This city wears its history like a teenager wears school uniform, joylessly.

4TH STATION – JESUS MEETS HIS MOTHER

It's a not dissimilar story just a few meters up Al-Wad Street from the 4th Station, which is located alongside the Polish chapel in the Armenian Catholic Patriarchate. Beyond the perimeter wall of the Austrian Hospice, at a corner where steps climb eastwards into a residential neighborhood, a large, two-story building with beautiful triple windows, three atop three, spans the main street. It creates a vault beneath, framed by pointed arches. Under here in the gloom, opposite the sensationally aromatic Abu Aziz pastry shop – always with trays of sweet treats out front, *hareeseh* (moist squares of semolina cake) competing with *awwameh* (golden dough balls drenched in syrup) – hides a doorway. A few meters along, a step or two below street level, is another.

The large, two-story building they give access to once belonged to the Latin church. In 1884 Moshe Wittenberg, a rabbi from Vitebsk – then in Russia, now in Belarus – managed to buy it with the help of Vitebsk-born Hebrew linguist Eliezer Ben-Yehuda, who negotiated in French on Wittenberg's behalf. For decades thereafter, what became known as Wittenberg House was home for up to twenty Jewish families, as well as a synagogue and a religious seminary. To this day it remains a node of Jewish settlement.

Wittenberg, a business tycoon who dealt in Russian government securities, had arrived in Jerusalem two years earlier, carrying the enormous sum of 500,000 rubles, equivalent to many millions of dollars today. His legacy, paused when violent uprisings in the 1930s forced Wittenberg House's evacuation, was reinforced in 1987 when the notorious nationalist politician Ariel Sharon, then Israel's industry minister, bought one of the building's apartments, not to live in it so much as to flaunt a Jewish Israeli presence in the Old City, provoke local residents and guarantee a heightened police presence in the area. Sharon died in 2014 having sold the apartment to an extremist Jewish settler organization, but his ghost haunts this stretch of street. The activist families and individuals who live and study today in Wittenberg House – as in other, similarly occupied buildings nearby – in contravention of international law, yet privileged by the state with armed police and private security protection, drape the place in giant Israeli flags. They've mounted a huge nine-branched Hanukkah menorah (ritual candelabrum) on the roof.

As a boy, Saad al-Alami (1911–1993), later Grand Mufti – supreme Muslim religious leader – of Jerusalem, grew up on Al-Wad Street opposite. "Jews lived in the house then and we were good neighbors," he said in an interview in 1987. "But no one wants to live next to Sharon. ... Sharon wants [Jerusalem] only for the Jews."

As often here, though, there's some comfort in history. If you go back before Sharon, before Wittenberg's millions, before even the Latins, this same, large, two-story building had a life as the Mediterranean Hotel, Jerusalem's fanciest and swankiest of the 1860s. It was run at the time by Moses Hornstein from Odessa, who converted to Christianity from Judaism, and Emma Gössner, his German wife. And for two brief days in September 1867 – Monday 23rd and Tuesday 24th – Moses and Emma's acclaimed establishment, with its tiers of rooms around a paved courtyard, hosted a party of pilgrims that included the American writer Mark Twain, partway through the journey he was to publish a couple of years later as *The Innocents Abroad*.

Twain, amusingly, is often quoted by Israeli nationalists, who cite his descriptions of a supposedly barren and depopulated pre-Zionist "Holy Land" as evidence of the nonexistence of Palestinians and the non-nationhood of Palestine. They misunderstand that his book, of course, is not reportage. Before his few days being led across Palestine Twain called Greece (Greece!) "a bleak, unsmiling desert, without agriculture." And seeing as how he liked to say things like "It comes natural to [Greeks, Turks and Armenians] to lie and cheat" and "The Jews are the only race who work wholly with their brains and never with their hands," and much later, at the age of sixty-four, still apparently believed of himself, "I have no color prejudices nor caste prejudices nor creed prejudices," there may not, in truth, be very good reason to suppose the great man had any real idea about who or what he was looking at. Aged thirty-two, he was a comedian on tour.

5TH STATION – SIMON OF CYRENE CARRIES THE CROSS

But now, let's eat. Abu Shukri's, directly across the street from the 5th Station, serves amazing hummus. Amazing. You've never tasted anything like it.

OK, that's it. All done here. Move along now.

Wait, you want more? Well then, here's the long version.

A hundred-and-something years ago, a man with the family name Taha arrived in Jerusalem from Anatolia and fell in love with a local woman. They married, and had a son. Life was good, until one day war came. Taha went off to fight for the sultan, and never came back. Not long after, his widow died too, and the boy – only eight years old, and all alone – was taken in by a kindly Jerusalemite family and raised as their own, though he never forgot the name Taha and what it meant to him.

Time passed, and the boy grew to manhood, starting his own family and managing to keep his head above water in a Jerusalem that was rapidly changing. He was smart, and he kept his eyes open, and one day, even as war again came closer, he thought he could see an opportunity. What he would do is open a restaurant. Nothing fancy. Hummus had always been a staple dish, but it was difficult and time-consuming to make. All the more reason to specialize in it. He would make hummus and sell it to passersby.

In Arabic, parents often take the name of their eldest child as a nickname, prefixed by *Abu* ("father of") and *Umm* ("mother of"). If you name your son Ahmed, you become Abu Ahmed and Umm Ahmed, dignified terms that are familiar and friendly but that also denote respect and community standing.

Mohammed Taha, by then known as Abu Shukri, set up first in a tiny shop off Khan al-Zeit in the 1940s. It didn't take long for his hummus to get the kind of reputation that led to queues forming out in the street, as word spread among the crowds flocking into Jerusalem for Friday prayers about just how good it was. Every morning he would open for breakfast, do several hours of feverish business, and then close by mid-afternoon. He'd maybe see his family, grab a few hours' sleep, and then be up again at 2 a.m. to start boiling the chickpeas, draining them through cloth and mashing them by hand, ready for the first customers soon after dawn. From the beginning he was determined not to use pre-prepared ingredients, like artificial lemon juice – everything had to be fresh – and he never resorted to automation or following recipes. Every day, every batch would be made from scratch, by eye, to taste.

Quality bred success, and eventually he was able to open up in another little space, barely five meters square, on Al-Wad Street, one of the main thoroughfares leading through the Old City. For more than thirty years, Abu Shukri's hummus was the most famous in Jerusalem. And when the old man died, in 1981, his sons took over. They kept the Taha family name and the Abu Shukri branding. As tourism grew, it became more and more obvious how important location was: the restaurant, which by now had expanded to include the next-door property, was not only on the main street to and from Al-Aqsa, but it was also on the Via Dolorosa pilgrimage route, right by the 5th Station of the Cross. Word continued to spread.

Today, now in the third generation, run by Raed and Fathi Taha, Abu Shukri still opens for breakfast and closes in mid-afternoon, still has big cauldrons of chickpeas in the back boiling all night for hand-mashing, still draws as many locals as visitors. The difference is that "Abu Shukri" has become an international byword for hummus, all across Palestine and the Arab world, as well as Israel. The most famous Abu Shukris outside Jerusalem are in the hill town of Abu Ghosh, not far away – their hummus is really good, too – and in the Jerusalem suburb of Beit Hanina, the latter run by Taha cousins.

But the original is still the best. It's frenetic in there, perpetually busy, rich with steam and conversation. In the back, harried stirrers keep the chickpeas bubbling and ladle delicious goop into dozens of bowls. In the front, octopus-armed waiters make sure turbulent tides of customers stay happy. There's no menu, of course: you just say what you want. And trust me – what you want is hummus.

6TH STATION – VERONICA WIPES THE FACE OF JESUS

At the 5th Station, the Via Dolorosa leaves the main street, turning west to start the climb towards the Holy Sepulchre church. On Al-Wad, passersby breathe a sigh of relief – finally, the logjam of slowpokes is out of the way – but up here, those same slowpokes form a dense plug of pilgrims corking the narrow lane solid for prayers at the 6th Station. Here, tradition says, Veronica, a local woman, took pity on Jesus struggling with his cross up the hill to Calvary and used her veil – or handkerchief, or some other cloth – to wipe his face clean. When she took it back, it was miraculously imprinted with the image of Jesus's face.

It's an affecting story which brings up all sorts of meditative resonances about compassion and showing your true face and seeking the Face of God in all things. This lane has atmosphere to match, gloomy in parts, climbing towards uncertainty, thick with commerce and incense and puffing pilgrims. In 1883 the Greek Catholic, or Melkite, church bought the 6th Station site, which according to custom was the house of Veronica – long since canonized as Saint Veronica – and built a church to her, though there may also have been a much earlier, Byzantine, church here, dedicated to the early Christian martyr-saints Cosmas and Damian. Inside today, remote from the street and still tended by nuns from the order of the Little Sisters of Jesus, the cave-like Chapel of the Holy Face offers a haven of calm.

If Veronica was a person, perhaps her story originated with what's described in the gospels as the miracle of the bleeding woman who touched the fringe of Jesus's cloak and was healed. No details of the woman's bleeding are given, though it's generally interpreted as a menstrual disorder. She is unidentified, but a Christian text from a few centuries later gave her the name Berenice, long a name of queens (from Greek: *ferein*, to bring; *niké*, victory) – and it's a short linguistic hop from Berenice to Veronica.

But Veronica is also a thing, the cloth itself – from *vera* (Latin: true) and *icon* (Greek: image). The Veil of Veronica (or just "the Veronica") wisps through centuries of Christian history, hinted at as early as the eighth century, more concretely described from the twelfth and thirteenth, when Pope Innocent III is recorded as showing an actual cloth to the faithful in Rome. Medieval copies of the Veronica are still venerated in churches in Spain, Italy, Austria – while, inevitably, legends persist of an original, or perhaps *the* original, surviving under lock and key somewhere in the bowels of the Vatican.

Today, stuck on this narrow lane as you wait for a path to open through the crush of pilgrims, take solace in the description of how Jesus met the bleeding woman.

This is from Mark, chapter 5:

> When she heard about Jesus, she came up behind him in the crowd and touched his cloak … He turned around in the crowd and asked, "Who touched my clothes?" "You see the people crowding against you," his disciples answered, "and yet you ask, 'Who touched me?'" But Jesus kept looking around to see who had done it.

7TH STATION – JESUS FALLS FOR THE SECOND TIME

At the top of the narrow, stepped lane up from Al-Wad, under low, vaulted roofs built across the market, past the greengrocer on the left – vibrant courgettes, luscious tomatoes – you join what is now the Old City's main commercial street, Souk Khan al-Zeit.

The 7th Station directly opposite makes a perpetually packed junction of footpaths even more packed. It's marked by a nineteenth-century Franciscan chapel, built here because when the Via Dolorosa route was emerging in the medieval period, it wasn't clear to pilgrims – and, in truth, still isn't – how to tally the gospels' account of Jesus's crucifixion outside the walls of Jerusalem with the contemporary reality of a pilgrimage trail entirely within the walls. So the story arose that this spot marked the Gate of Judgment, the city portal through which Jesus passed on his way to Calvary, a hundred meters or so southwest of here in what was open country.

Today, the 7th Station is just about the busiest place in the Old City, dense with commerce. Famous brands – locally famous, that is – survive amid the frenzy. From the chapel, the friend I'm with today steers me a few steps along the greasy flagstones through whiffs of coffee, leather and drains to one particular hole-in-the-wall. She's been sent by her mum to buy a particular item from this gently smiling old man perched on a stool in a small shop open to the lane, almost concealed behind a tall glass display case.

It was 1973 when Moatassem al-Amad first started working here with his dad, whose picture is hanging on the wall beside his stool – a monochrome image of a distinguished-looking chap in suit and tie. In all that time, the main product hasn't changed, and it's piled up in front of us in that display case, gray and cream and brown blocks of it. *Halawa* – stress the middle syllable – is the stuff, and it's the sweetest thing in the galaxy, and Al-Amad makes the best *halawa* in Jerusalem, which means it's the best in the galaxy too. *Halawa* comes from sesame paste, produced by grinding sesame seeds between rough stones, mixed with hot sugar syrup or honey, dried in bricks and sliced up for sale. It keeps for months or years without refrigeration.

Normally, my friend would just exchange small talk, buy and go. Because I'm there, she's stopped to chat and Mr. Al-Amad is talking about the time he went to the US as a young man, how people

tried to persuade him to stay and set up shop there, but how he was determined to come back to Jerusalem. He speaks softly and slowly, always smiling, with long pauses to find the words. I wonder at his dedication, after a forty-six-year career, in the same cubbyhole, in the same market.

His company produces hundreds of kilos of *halawa* at a time, he says, but because it's difficult to maintain manufacturing premises in the Old City under occupation, they've moved production to Nablus. He describes the ingredients: sesame, glucose, lemon juice and – this took a bit of working out – the roots of a common local plant called *erq al-halawa*, or, in English, soapwort. Pounded and boiled, the soapwort creates a foamy cream that adds lightness to the mixture, so that when the *halawa* is dried, it takes on its characteristic crumble.

Other countries and cultures call this stuff *halva, khalva, alwa* or *halwa*. Sometimes it's made with semolina flour and ghee, or sunflower seeds instead of sesame. In homes and offices in Oman, along with dates, spiced coffee, ginger tea and crucibles of smoking frankincense, they serve you *halwa* in a bowl with a little spoon – golden, translucent, jelly-like stuff, completely different from Palestinian *halawa*, made with cornflour and sugar syrup perfumed with rosewater and cardamom and studded with cashews or pistachios.

Mr. Al-Amad has a cashew variety, too, stacked up on display. And pistachio. And hazelnut, almond, walnut, vanilla. And chocolate. And – he gestures to the counter beside him, piled with sweets and candied nibbles – he doesn't just do *halawa* anymore.

"I'm very proud," he says. "We've been open 120 years. I am the fifth generation. My children all studied at university in Israel, but now they all work here. They are the sixth generation."

And I think – *Halawa* has brought this family dignity.

Is history a burden? Knowing you have all those generations behind you, looking over your shoulder?

"The opposite," he says. "It makes me want to innovate, create these new products, build our brand by selling to other shops. I feel like I'm eighteen. I'm not old."

Later, out of earshot, my friend tells me that Al-Amad is already the number-one brand of *halawa*, and has been as long as she's known about it. Her mum wouldn't have any other in the house.

8TH STATION – JESUS MEETS THE WOMEN OF JERUSALEM

On the main market street not far from the 8th Station – just a plaque on a monastery wall recalling the gospel story where Jesus says, "Daughters of Jerusalem, weep not for me but for yourselves and your children" – sits, well, let's call her Umm Ahmed. She wears a traditional long dress, black, with embroidered decoration, and a loose, floral headscarf draping down over her shoulders. She is not alone. Every morning maybe a dozen women like her, maybe more, gather up their skirts and settle down in their own favored spots on the worn flagstones, centimeters from the feet of shoppers. They are country women, and they fill Jerusalem's market lanes to sell fresh vegetables, fruit, herbs and homemade condiments.

Umm Ahmed is in her sixties, and comes from a village outside Bethlehem, in the West Bank south of Jerusalem. She's rare among the women who sell, in that she agrees to chat. The women who sell usually give short shrift to people asking questions, because what they do is illegal. They have no commercial premises, no vendor's permit, and some – younger than Umm Ahmed – no permission to cross through the military checkpoints that ring Jerusalem to the north, east and south. But just now the Israelis are allowing women aged over fifty in. This morning, a Saturday, Umm Ahmed left her stock of chard and other vegetables, mint and thyme – all grown on her family farm – with a friend who has a car. Then she got on the bus and passed through the checkpoint into Jerusalem. Meanwhile the friend drove the greens through separately. They met up again inside Jerusalem. Umm Ahmed took possession of her stock, carried it to this spot, and is now doing good business.

She's not proud of the subterfuge, which she varies so as not to fall into a pattern. Israel's byzantine system of permits and controls forces her into it, if she wants to assert her right to move and take advantage of the much higher prices her produce can command in Jerusalem, compared with Bethlehem. Sometimes she will bring fruit and veg from her neighbor, who cannot enter Jerusalem, and sell it on her neighbor's behalf, keeping a small commission for herself. But harassment from the Israeli authorities is a headache and she runs the constant risk of being fined and having her produce confiscated. Saturdays are easier, she says, because it is the Jewish *shabbat*, or sabbath: traffic is much lighter, and the enforcement teams from the municipality don't patrol.

Jerusalem's street markets are packed on Saturdays.

Umm Ahmed has been selling here, two or three days a week, for the last thirty years, she says. Her mother sold before her. And her grandmother before that. Oh, there was her mother-in-law too. And of course also her sisters. In truth, that continuity goes back even further. Documents from the fourteenth century talk about women selling grapes, figs, pomegranates and cotton on the streets of Jerusalem. They even identify one of the traders, Fatima, who died in 1393 while, unfortunately, owed money.

Meters away from Umm Ahmed's spot the 8th Station has, by contrast, helped Ibrahim Sandouk put his sons through college. It's directly opposite his bookshop. All day long, a tide of pilgrims stops exactly outside his door to pray. Ibrahim is there, offering maps, picture books, key rings and posters. Business is good.

He's the youngest of five brothers, he says. His father came to Jerusalem from Bir as-Saba (now Beersheva), down in the desert, in 1927. Nowadays Ibrahim's hearing isn't what it was, and dental trouble makes him hard to understand. But I love his shop. In the back corner, past the tourist flimflam, where nobody bothers to look, he has a few shelves of stuff he, or his father, must have stocked up on fifty or sixty years ago. I unearthed a beautiful tourist map of Jordanian Jerusalem there, with ads for long-closed restaurants and a welcome message from the Ministry of Tourism in Amman. There was a *Guide to the Holy Land*, published by the Franciscans in 1970. And an illustrated booklet about the Dome of the Rock, excerpted from Palestinian historian (and former mayor) Aref al-Aref's

History of Jerusalem of 1961. There are magazines and textbooks from heaven knows when, and a stock of unique pirated postcards which, on the back, say "Caesarea, Israel" or "Tel Aviv, Israel," but on the front show graphics and images of Oman, Libya or Kuwait from the 1950s or 1960s, snipped neatly out of vintage magazines and hand-pasted on top. It's a goldmine.

Every time I visit, Ibrahim – who I think doesn't recognize me – is all, "From England? London? London?," and he bustles over to his desk and fishes out a fragile, sellotaped square of paper that is his son's enrolment record from University College London from fifteen years ago. He nudges me and pokes me and puffs out his chest a little. All his sons are doctors now.

I congratulate him. Are they in Jerusalem? – I ask.

He lifts his chin slightly and clicks what teeth he has – this means no – and makes a little helpless gesture with his hands.

"This shop is finished," he says.

9TH STATION – JESUS FALLS FOR THE THIRD TIME

I find my friend Khalil at a café up near New Gate. We met by chance in 2007, on a countryside walk in Turkey, and hit it off. Years later, we still crack each other up. He laughs more than anyone else I know, and has Jerusalem roots going back centuries. When I ask him for culinary advice he is unequivocal.

"You should eat Zalatimo. Come on, I'll take you." Sunbeams in flagstoned lanes split and reform as Khalil gives me the backstory. In 1860 Mohammed Zalatimo came back to Jerusalem, his home, after serving in the Ottoman army. He opened a shop selling *mutabbaq*, a sweet pastry served hot from the oven. It became so famous that, like Mr. Hoover and Mr. Biro, creator and product merged.

Along the crowded, fragrant Souk Khan al-Zeit in the middle of the city, beside a stall blaring Arabic pop music, we halt in front of an unmarked, aluminium-framed glass door directly at the foot of the steps leading to the 9th Station of the Cross. Zalatimo's dim, tiled interior, wedged under the walls of the Church of the Holy Sepulchre, holds four small tables beneath stone cross-vaults.

A family group is just leaving, their silk scarves and fancy jewelry incongruous under the dangling light bulbs. They're going back to Jordan, they tell us. When they'd arrived they'd come straight to have *mutabbaq*. They'd returned for another before departing. It's the taste of Jerusalem.

With 150-plus years of knowledge in his fingers, preparation takes Hani Zalatimo, great-great-grandson of Mohammed Zalatimo, seconds. Dough thrown and stretched by hand, and re-stretched, and re-stretched, ends up so thin you can see the speckled countertop through it. A crumble of dried Nabulsi sheep's cheese preludes four neat folds (*mutabbaq* derives from an Arabic root meaning folding and covering, also connoting layering) and, after a brush of butter on top, the little parcel goes into the oven.

While waiting, Khalil finagles a key and beckons me to join him at the back of the shop. He opens an unmarked door to a cavernous, unlit space of dirt and rubble. My eyes adjust to take in worn old columns and unplastered stone walls looming up into dimness. Broken stonework underfoot makes me stumble. There are arches overhead. It smells like secrets.

When the Roman emperor Constantine completed the first Church of the Holy Sepulchre in 335 CE, it was oriented differently from how it is now. Today, you enter the church via the south façade, located ninety-odd meters behind Zalatimo's shop. But in Constantine's day, the main entrance was from the east. And this is it. I'm standing at the original, unseen, 1,700-year-old gateway to Christendom's holiest place, concealed behind a grimy door in the back of a pastry parlor.

The ruins are connected to the excavations in the basement of the Russian Orthodox church of St. Alexander Nevsky, built on the plot of land immediately behind Zalatimo's. There, workers digging foundations in the 1880s uncovered remnants of the great staircase that led into Constantine's church, as well as earlier, Hadrianic, walls and the threshold of what's thought to have been a gateway into Jerusalem's principal Roman forum (though the legend persists that it is the threshold of the Gate of Judgment, through which Jesus passed on his way to Calvary).

After a few minutes, Khalil and I retreat, and, wonderstruck, take chairs opposite each other at one of Zalatimo's rickety tables to sample the *mutabbaq*, whisked from oven to plate. Our day becomes prayerful. Each crispy bite is both sweet and savory, the melted cheese and sugar-dusted butter pastry combining to, literally, melt in our mouths. We laugh. It's almost erotic. And over far too quickly. That *mutabbaq* might be the single most unequivocally delicious food item I have ever experienced.

But that visit – the first of many – was a few years ago, before disaster struck. In May 2019, Zalatimo's closed down. Hani just shut up shop one day, locked the doors, and hasn't come back.

Life for any Old City shopkeeper can be incredibly hard, dealing with shifting regulations on product supply or equipment maintenance imposed by the Israeli authorities, overcrowding, lack of storage or expansion space, multiple tax burdens, poor municipal services, enforcement crackdowns from the police or municipality, not to mention the wider occupation that restricts freedom of movement in and out of the city, squeezes the Palestinian economy and throttles income from tourism. But, by all accounts, nothing bad actually happened to Hani. It seems he just got bored. His immediate family runs a couple of pastry outlets in the suburbs and another in Ramallah, which are still going strong. And meanwhile, the Zalatimo name has gone global. Relatives in Jordan run two separate businesses – Zalatimo Sweets, which employs 250 people and took $11 million in 2018, and Zalatimo Brothers for Sweets, a smaller but still international concern, with revenue around $4 million. Both have outlets across the Middle East, along with worldwide distribution. (Indeed, so recognizable is the name that in 2014 a rogue outfit in Dubai started trying to sell pastries using Zalatimo branding.) But at the original Zalatimo, hidden away in the middle of Jerusalem's souk, it seems that things just got too complicated, and profits too marginal, to keep going.

Purists were horrified. There were articles in the local press. But, to be honest, Hani, known as Abu Samer, wasn't the easiest character. He came across as rather dour, unresponsive to customers and not that interested in the attention his family tradition – and its single, exquisite product – universally inspired. Every time I went, I enjoyed it despite Hani. I wanted to get to know him, to find out why he cared so little, and whether there was anything anyone could do to give him a boost.

But now it's too late. I have asked neighboring stallholders and others what happened, but they either don't know or, not unreasonably, won't tell me. One saving grace is that the owners of the building, which is a *waqf* (Islamic trust) of the wealthy Khalidi family, recently announced that the closure isn't permanent and Zalatimo's will be back. In the past Hani had said he would pass the business to his children. I can't be alone in hoping.

10TH STATION – JESUS IS STRIPPED OF HIS CLOTHES
11TH STATION – JESUS IS NAILED TO THE CROSS
12TH STATION – JESUS DIES ON THE CROSS
13TH STATION – JESUS'S BODY IS TAKEN FROM THE CROSS
14TH STATION – JESUS'S BODY IS PLACED IN THE TOMB

The last five Stations of the Cross are all located inside the Church of the Holy Sepulchre. As the culmination of the Christian pilgrimage to Jerusalem, this is a place of profound sanctity and emotion. As a church it's small, dark, noisy, confusing, a bit sweaty and there's nowhere to sit. Pilgrims expecting a cathedral on the scale of St. Peter's in Rome, say – vast, lofty, hushed, wondrous – are disappointed. But there's been a church here for nigh on 1,700 years and in terms of authenticity of experience, of finding yourself in a place where you can be confident Great Things Happened, it's the gold standard. Early morning, at four, five or six, is a good time to meditate on the spirituality of the place, if the attendants will let you in. The rest of the day, you might find the crush of bodies and ceaseless hubbub – how can I put it? – redirecting your attention to the church's status as global cultural artefact.

In Western Christianity and its languages, this is the "Church of the Holy Sepulchre," a sepulchre being a tomb. The linguistic (and architectural) focus is on the death of Jesus and the physical location of his burial. In Eastern Christianity, however – in Greek, Russian, Armenian, Arabic and other languages – it is the "Church of the Resurrection," with the focus on the risen Christ and the metaphysical mystery of life, hope, faith and spirituality that lies at the heart of the religion. One seems rather more inspiring than the other. It's best, perhaps, to hold both names in your mind as you move around, to glimpse the same place through different eyes.

Christians share the church. Today, as since the eighteenth century, three of the wealthiest and most politically powerful denominations divide the bulk of authority and responsibility among themselves: the Greek Orthodox, the Armenian Orthodox and the Latins (known elsewhere as Roman Catholics), in particular the Franciscan order. Also represented, with less influence, are the Syriac Orthodox, Coptic Orthodox and Ethiopian Orthodox churches.

It wasn't always thus: the Georgian church was once one of the most powerful denominations represented. The Serbian church was here, too, as was the Maronite. But their inability to pay taxes imposed by the Ottoman authorities in the seventeenth century saw them all ejected from the church interior. The same happened to the Ethiopians, who later installed themselves on the roof. All the Protestant churches – Anglican, Lutheran, Baptist, Pentecostal and the rest – developed too late to even have a toehold.

With so much at stake, spiritually, financially and politically, there's always been jockeying for position. With the lack of agreement between Christian denominations, for centuries the responsibility of holding the church's door keys has lain with two Muslim Jerusalemite families, in a tradition passed down the generations: the Joudeh family keeps the keys, while the Nusseibeh family turns them in the lock to open and close the church each day. (Having the keys *and* turning them was deemed too much power for one family. Most days the current custodians, Adeeb Joudeh and Wajeeh Nusseibeh, send representatives to do the work for them, anyway.) Nobody knows how long it's been like that: documentary evidence goes back only as far as 1517, but legend has it that bickering between clergy prompted Salah ad-Din to come up with the arrangement in 1192. Some say it predates even that.

An effort in 1757 by the sultan to resolve disputes at the Holy Sepulchre and assert his own power led to a ruling that codified the power relations existing in the church at that time. That ruling was restated and confirmed in 1852, but nevertheless, conflict inside the church – between France, which protected Catholic rights, and Russia, which protected Eastern Orthodox rights (and also Britain, which was setting itself up as promoter of Protestant rights) – was a leading cause of the devastating Crimean War of 1853–56. After that, the Ottoman-devised "Status Quo" (a Latin term meaning "the situation as it exists now"), as the ruling was called, was elevated to become an instrument of international law, applying to the Church of the Holy Sepulchre and eight other religious sites in Jerusalem and Bethlehem. It remains in force today.

The Status Quo effectively freezes the power balance in the church as it was in 1757, and prevents any change to it without the agreement of all. It means everything that happens in the church, from renovation works to the timing of services to who picks up litter, is governed by mutually agreed rules. Services may not over-run, even by a minute, since another denomination has an exclusive right to use that minute for its own prayers. A strict rota exists for who opens and closes the church door, and in what fashion, according to a set sequence of actions that may not be altered. The Status Quo does not allow for daylight saving time, so in summer every service in the church takes place an hour later on the clock than in winter. A representative of one denomination may, for instance, light a candle only with the express agreement of representatives of the other denominations. This is because lighting a candle implies an assertion of ownership of the candle, and thus of the candlestick, and thus of the place where the candlestick stands, and thus, perhaps, of the entire church – an issue of the utmost seriousness, with consequences that could reverberate around the world.

Yes, really.

It's easy to ridicule the Status Quo. Why can't everybody just get on, naïfs might say. But imagine the consequences. If you were to allow a rival to, say, wipe a certain ledge or sweep a certain corner or place a chair in a certain location for the comfort of a person otherwise standing, then the next time that ledge needs to be wiped, or that corner to be swept, or a person standing is said to be tired, then your rival will say that last time it was allowed so why not this time, and there will be no good argument against it. A precedent has been set. That ledge, or that corner, or that location where a chair has been placed has become the responsibility of your rival and not yourself. With responsibility, naturally, comes possession. And so your church's and your nation's sanctified heritage in this most holy of places, the solemn bequest of a hundred generations, entrusted to you for the veneration of the Savior of humanity Himself, has been forfeit in your own time. And for what? For the wiping of a ledge? It's unthinkable. It must be resisted at all costs.

Here is a perfect Status Quo story – one of the best stories in Jerusalem, untold when I first visited but now all over the internet.

If you stand outside the Church of the Holy Sepulchre and look up at the building's façade, you'll see a ladder. It's a strange kind of ladder, wooden, short (only five rungs), wide and rickety-looking, standing on an upper ledge above the church entrance and leaning against the right-hand window. Perhaps somebody cleaning the windows yesterday forgot to bring it back in.

Nope.

The ladder has been there for 265 years.

Since the Status Quo entered into force in 1757, there has been no agreement among the denominations on moving the ladder, so it hasn't been moved. In fact an engraving exists from 1728 showing it in the same place, so it might have been there longer than 265 years. Nobody knows. Some say it's a stonemason's ladder, left in position after renovation work, others that it dates from a time when the Ottomans restricted movement in and out of the church, and was placed in order to allow clerics access to the ledge for sunshine and, perhaps, to grow vegetables. Others say it was used to take food into the church when the door was barred. Nobody knows.

Some say the ladder,* the window it leans against and the ledge it stands on belong to the Armenians. Others contend that the ladder and window are Armenian but the ledge is Greek. Others say the ladder, the window and the ledge are common property, shared by all. Nobody knows.

For George Hintlian, historian of Jerusalem and formerly secretary to the Armenian Patriarch, all of it – ladder, window, ledge – is "totally Armenian." For many years, he says, the room behind the window against which the ladder rests was used by the Armenian Superior. The Superior and three colleagues would use the ladder to emerge, Hintlian told me, to take coffee together on the ledge in the sunshine, out of the gloom and damp of the church interior. But in 1980 the Superior moved premises within the church and the room stood empty. Hintlian remembers meeting around that time with an architect and the Armenian bishop to discuss renovations. He asked if they should, at long last, bring the ladder in. "But the bishop said, 'It's beautiful. Let it stay.'"

So they did.

The ladder is older than cameras. Every photo ever made of the façade of the Church of the Holy Sepulchre, over the entire history of photography, shows it in place. That, needless to say, is a lot of photos. Have a look online if you don't believe me. Add to that paintings, drawings, etchings, prints and every other form of imagery made depicting this façade, as far back as that 1728 engraving.

There are a couple of exceptions. Since the story became better known, pranksters have twice messed with the ladder. In 2009 someone moved it along the ledge from the right-hand window to the left-hand window, presumably until the church authorities noticed and moved it back. Even worse, in 1997 a tourist called Andy, who self-identified as "a Protestant believer," snuck around inside the

---

* Or a replica. The original was replaced when its condition deteriorated. That might have happened more than once. Nobody knows.

church until he located the window, leaned out, pulled the ladder in and hid it. He wanted to make a point about how ridiculous he thought the Status Quo was. The ladder was found some time later and put back (and a grille installed over the window).

Andy was a sneering idiot, of course, ignorant, self-entitled and deeply rude, but also desperately small-minded. In the ladder – once he knew to look for it – he could see only division obscuring his idea of Christianity. What he was too excited to notice was what the ladder truly represents: us. Human hopes, desires, fears and frailty have put the ladder in place and left it there. Generations of spiritual and intellectual toil in this extraordinary place. Centuries of praying, fighting and yearning. Without meaning to go overboard, I love the ladder because the ladder says people are here. It says faith is about people. It gestures around at this holiest of churches, and all of Jerusalem, and each person watching, and it says all of this is about all of us, striving for the best. The ladder, oddly, is truth.

Be less Andy.

The Holy Sepulchre also hosts a genuine, certified, annual miracle that you yourself can witness.

For Protestants, and Catholics in Western countries, Christmas is often bigger than Easter. For everybody else in the world, it's the other way round. Jerusalem is packed at Easter time: the Easter message of steadfast faith and triumph over mortal suffering resonates especially strongly here. All the markets, all the hotels, all the churches are full. The atmosphere is festive. And the biggest event – a miracle – happens at the Holy Sepulchre every year on the day before Orthodox Easter, known as *Sabt an-Noor*, the Saturday of Light.

Some camp out overnight to secure a spot. Others gather from the early hours, filling the church, the parvis (the courtyard in front of the church entrance) and all the streets around with chanting, singing and excitement. During mid-morning a delegation of officials and police pushes a path through the crowds to the church door and at around noon a ceremony of prayers begins, with solemn processing within the church. After that the Greek Orthodox and Armenian Orthodox patriarchs enter the Edicule, the shrine within the church that contains the (empty) tomb of Christ. The lights go off. Tension mounts. The Greek Patriarch then goes alone, or with the Armenian archbishop, into the inner chamber holding the tomb of Christ.

He kneels in the tiny, enclosed space, and speaks certain prayers, and waits. Unseen by watchers, Holy Fire descends. A flame emerges, miraculously, from within Christ's tomb. From it, the Patriarch lights a lamp or candle.

After a short time – a few minutes or seconds – the Patriarch emerges from the chamber bearing flame. A great roar goes up from the watchers. Bells begin to peal. Lamps around the church ignite spontaneously. The Patriarch passes the Holy Fire in bunches of candles to the Armenian and Coptic patriarchs, and then to the crowds of worshippers, who pass it from one to another, then out into the streets and across the city. The church fills with leaping flame, greasy smoke, dripping wax and beaming smiles. Assigned individuals rush the Holy Fire to Christian communities nearby, in Bethlehem, Ramallah, Gaza and beyond, where it's received with mass celebrations. Others hurry with lanterns to the airport, where planes depart immediately, carrying the Holy Fire to Athens, Tbilisi, Moscow and beyond, in time for midnight services. The whole ceremony is streamed and broadcast live around the world.

The miracle has been described since the second century, and recorded consistently since the Crusader era. It hasn't always gone smoothly. In 1101 there was no Holy Fire. In 2002 the archbishops argued, then scuffled in the Edicule: the Greek Patriarch lost a shoe and the Armenian Patriarch used a cigarette lighter to relight his candle after his Greek counterpart blew it out. Fist fights among revellers are regular occurrences, and uncounted thousands of people down the centuries have been suffocated or crushed in the frenzied crowds within the church: in 1834 hundreds died during a stampede exacerbated by panic among the Ottoman soldiery.

Some say Holy Fire is an unearthly blue. Others describe it as reddish. Many say that for a few minutes after the miracle, Holy Fire will neither singe nor burn: they hold their hand over lit candles or pass flame across their face, rejoicing.

What's that? How does Holy Fire happen?

Come on, it's a *miracle*.

One key question for pilgrims concluding their epic journey in the Church of the Holy Sepulchre is how anyone can be so sure that the church marks the place where Jesus died and was buried before rising again. If you insist on documentary evidence, you'll be disappointed. But if you'll accept contemporary accounts along with a bit of reasonable supposition, there's a story to tell.

In September 335, a church on the current site, built by the Roman emperor Constantine, was dedicated (though perhaps not actually completed for a few years after that). From then all the way until today, we are secure in being able to link subsequent churches on the same spot with that first one. We walk today where those fourth-century church-builders walked – well, we walk above where they walked, because rubble and debris have raised ground level since then, but the location is the same.

So why was that first church built there, and not somewhere else? The key period to focus on is the three centuries following the Crucifixion, when Christianity was illegal in the Roman Empire.

Jesus died in the 30s CE – some say 30, some say 33, some name other dates – at a place called Golgotha or Calvary, just outside Jerusalem. We don't know where that was. But the first Christians did. They knew the place from before, and they had seen the Crucifixion with their own eyes. It's possible they forgot exactly where, or got confused, but then again, this was the most important thing that had ever happened to them. Nothing would have mattered more. I'm as skeptical as the next unbeliever, but I'd say the balance of probabilities suggests the generation who knew Jesus in person would have, at least, tried to preserve such crucially evocative knowledge about the pivotal events of their lives as the circumstances and location of Jesus's death.

But the hundred years after Jesus died was a century of turmoil. In 66 CE Jesus's followers fled Jerusalem, shortly before the Roman destruction of the city in 70 (some historians dispute the exile). More conflict culminated in the Jewish-led Bar Kokhba rebellion, finally crushed by the Romans in 135 amid massacres and expulsions of both Jews and – as much as they were differentiated in this early era – Christians. Jerusalem was razed. Knowledge may have been lost.

Unexpectedly, the Roman emperor Hadrian can help. When he built Jerusalem anew after the rebellion, he had large temples put up on two specific sites. First, he placed a new temple to Jupiter exactly where the Jewish Temple had stood until its destruction sixty-five years earlier. The choice of location was no accident, signifying Roman victory and Jewish subjugation. So then it's reasonable to suggest it was equally no accident that he chose the location of a new temple to Venus for similar reasons. That building went up exactly over the place that was later identified as the tomb of Jesus. More victory, more subjugation.

It's circumstantial evidence, I'll grant you. Perhaps Hadrian chose that spot because it looked good, or because it aligned with his new city plan, or for some other reason. But it seems just as likely – maybe more likely – that he chose it because it was a place Jews or Christians (the difference may not have been relevant to him) already knew about and valued, and thus was ripe for erasure. We don't know whether the early Christians had managed to preserve their knowledge of the Crucifixion over the preceding seven decades, and so held this site holy, but Hadrian's choice to build a temple, a new forum and a freshly laid north–south road here suggests they may have done.

Another tasty scrap of would-be evidence comes from Melito, a bishop of Sardis (now Sart, near Izmir in Turkey). He visited Jerusalem on pilgrimage around 160–170 and wrote, in shocked terms, about the site of the Crucifixion being "in the middle of the main street, in the very center of the city." It's an odd thing to say, since it contradicts the biblical account, but he repeated it several times. Was it because when he asked to see Golgotha, he was led down a main thoroughfare (now Souk Khan al-Zeit), taken into the bustling Roman forum and shown Hadrian's Temple to Venus, thronged with people?

At that time knowledge of the Crucifixion had only just passed from living memory, handed down via a chain of transmission that continued through the early bishops of Jerusalem – James and Simeon, who knew Jesus and were perhaps related to him, to Mark, the first non-Jewish bishop, who lived just after Hadrian in the 150s, to Alexander, who assembled a great theological library in Jerusalem in the early third century, to Makarios, who became bishop in 312. All that time worshippers prayed to Venus in Hadrian's temple. It's tempting – but also reasonable – to imagine Jerusalem's tiny and often persecuted community of Christians keeping their knowledge of such a desecration of Golgotha secure among themselves, preserving the tradition for a time when the tables might be turned.

The temple to Venus was still there in 325 when Constantine, the first Roman emperor to convert to Christianity, emerged from an international conference of bishops at Nicaea (now Iznik in Turkey) fired with the idea of locating the foundational relics of the Christian tradition. He named his mother, Helena, empress, and at the advanced age of eighty she embarked on pilgrimage to Palestine to join Bishop Makarios in the search for the tomb of Jesus. In 326 or 327 Helena and Makarios found it – exactly where tradition had said it would be, under the rubble of the Temple of Venus, which they'd ordered pulled down a year or two earlier.

When news of the tomb reached Constantine he ordered the construction of a large church on the same spot. That was the building dedicated in 335 over which all subsequent churches were built, and within whose perimeter we still walk today.

Skeptics could say Helena and Makarios invented the discovery of the tomb. It's possible. However, more first-century Jewish tombs have since been unearthed within the footprint of the Church of the Holy Sepulchre, which shows, at least, that the place where the church now stands lay outside the city walls at the time of Jesus, as Golgotha/Calvary did, and that it was a place of death and/or burial, as Golgotha/Calvary was.

Constantine's church survived – with repairs and restoration here and there – until October 1009, when Caliph Hakim ordered it destroyed in a still-inexplicable spasm of hatred.* Smaller churches occupied the ruins until the Crusaders dedicated a new, entirely rebuilt structure on 15 July 1149. With some alteration, including restoration following fire in 1808, their church is what survives today. So there are gaps in the early record, it's true. But as far as it's ever possible to pin down a tradition of such longevity to one specific location, especially one in such a contested setting, it all seems pretty persuasive.

Charles Gordon, however, wasn't convinced. A fearsomely accomplished British army major-general – famous for military action in China and Egypt, and, later, Sudan, where he died in battle, earning the nickname "Gordon of Khartoum" – he spent most of 1883 in Jerusalem. This was at the height of a Protestant-led movement that said the Church of the Holy Sepulchre had been built in the wrong place, and Gordon became the best-known, and perhaps the most thunderously enthusiastic, supporter of the hunt for a Protestant Calvary.

From the 1830s onwards, as travel to Jerusalem had become easier, a tide of European and American Protestants, expecting an idealized Jerusalem and, at its heart, an idealized cathedral of contemplation, arrived in the unfortunately messy reality of a living city. They had to tangle with turbulent priests from every sect of Orthodoxy (and, perhaps worse, Catholicism) in order simply to jostle their way into the holiest church in Christendom, whose guardians had even had the audacity up to that point to require an admission fee and escort. Then they found themselves excluded from prayer services on account of their Protestant faith. Raucously undignified traditions such as the Holy Fire added insult to injury. Almost to an individual, they hated the Church of the Holy Sepulchre and everything about

---

* The church's name in Arabic is *Kanisat al-Qiyama* ("Church of the Resurrection"). Before and after Hakim, countless Muslim writers have almost reflexively called it *Kanisat al-Qumama* ("Church of the Dungheap"). Is this an innocently comic pun defusing others' sense of the sacred? A viciously derisive jibe normalizing sectarian division and persecution? Or simply a neutral descriptor of a site formerly outside the city walls where rubbish was thrown? Take your pick.

it. In a favored phrase of the time, the church, its collection of relics and holy sites and its solemn custodians were nothing more than a "pious fraud."

To find the truth, the Protestants went back to their Bibles. As Luther and the Reformers had stripped away centuries of accreted tradition to identify the true spirit of the faith, so the biblical archaeologists and "scientific" theologians of the nineteenth century sought to strip away Jerusalem's centuries of tradition to identify the true Calvary. In doing so, they also sought to recreate the life and footsteps of the historical Jesus, in the very streets they now walked themselves. The Bible said the Crucifixion took place outside the walls near a gate, in a place with a garden. The Church of the Holy Sepulchre stood inside the walls in the middle of the city, with no gardens nearby. In Jerusalem tradition it had long been accepted that the city had simply changed over time; the walls had been moved and rebuilt time and again. Construction of Constantine's church had involved quarrying of the bedrock that once formed the hill of Golgotha/Calvary and into which the tomb of Jesus had been cut. Hakim's demolition of the church in 1009 had included gangs with pickaxes literally levelling the ground. It was clear the topography couldn't have remained unchanged over all that time.

That wasn't good enough for Protestants of faith. Examining biblical sources and contemporary writings by the Roman historian Josephus, they cast about for a better candidate. "Golgotha" is an Aramaic word meaning skull; "Calvary" is the anglicized form of a Latin term also meaning skull. So from the 1840s onwards, successive visitors began to focus on a rocky, skull-like knoll that rises just north of Damascus Gate, outside the current city walls. Its pitted surface is marked by two sunken holes, like eye sockets, below a rounded summit on which stands the Muslim cemetery of Al-Sahira. To those eager for discovery, Skull Hill, as they called it, seemed like a sign. Momentum grew, particularly when some kind of ancient rock-cut tomb was discovered in the vicinity, but it was when Gordon lent his weight – "I feel, for myself, convinced that the hill near the Damascus Gate is Golgotha," he wrote – that the theory broke through into the mainstream. The Protestants had found their Calvary.

Gordon's Calvary is still there, a lovely, quiet spot now renamed the Garden Tomb. Its gardens are well-tended. Its staff – most of them volunteers for the British charity that bought the site in 1894 and still runs it – are courteous, though they do spin you some rather tall scriptural tales while you stand distracted by the honking and beeping coming from East Jerusalem's central bus station, now prosaically located at the foot of Skull Hill.

Gordon took "Golgotha'/"Calvary" to mean "a place that looks like a skull." In Orthodox Christianity, though, the term refers to an actual skull, that of the first man, Adam. A very old tradition, quoted by St. Jerome in 386 but perhaps a couple of centuries older than that, talks of Jesus having been crucified in the burial place of Adam. The story links to Jewish lore around how Shem, son of Noah, and the priest-king Melchizedek disinterred Adam's bones and reburied his skull in Jerusalem. Orthodox iconography shows Jesus's blood running down the cross onto Adam's skull beneath, thereby giving absolution for Adam's having introduced sin into the world.

Nobody takes the idea that the Garden Tomb is Golgotha seriously, or that the tomb in the garden has anything to do with Jesus (it is much older than that). But Protestant and Evangelical groups still love the place, partly because it feels so right. Much earnest praying happens there. Many tears are shed. It's an ideal spot for a sunny hour or two's reflection on colonialism, confirmation bias and other sources of Gordon's visceral disdain for the Holy Sepulchre's gloomy, tradition-heavy magic.

6

Under Stork Tower

STORIES OF BAB AZ-ZAHRA
(HEROD'S GATE / FLOWERS GATE)

MUNTASER EDKAIDEK IS ANGRY. He's seething, actually. But it's the quiet fury of the long-suffering. The angrier he gets, the softer he speaks. As we talk, I find myself craning to listen properly. By the end of our conversation, his rage is a murmur.

Edkaidek runs the Burj al-Laqlaq Social Center, a community hub in the northeastern corner of the Old City near Herod's Gate, where few tourists come. Inside the gate, Jerusalem shapeshifts. Here, it is a small market town somewhere quiet, a place on the margins where you might stop to change buses, say. Stalls sell fruit, cigarettes and cans of drink. There's a grocery with potato chips and trays of eggs, a homeware shop selling ironing boards and plastic furniture, a man frying falafel, a café with old-timers out front sipping glasses of sweet tea. The atmosphere, like the people, with their bags and their chitchat, is mild and undramatic.

Maps say Herod's Gate. But forget Herod. He only appears due to muddled Christian traditions linking the area with Herod Antipas, or perhaps Herod Agrippa, first-century successors of the Temple-reviving Herod the Great. In Arabic this gate started out being called Bab as-Sahira, which probably derives from *sahira* in the Quran (79:14), an earthly location to which resurrected souls will

one day return, long linked with the Mount of Olives overlooking Jerusalem. Directly outside the gate, now surrounded by modern streets, rises an ancient hilltop cemetery, also known as *Sahira*.

Though the tower above it is strong, the gate itself, as Suleiman the Lawgiver built it, was small and insignificant, just a narrow, right-angled pathway. This northern city wall, with few natural defenses, has always been vulnerable to attack, so people preferred to keep the gate shut: outside there was only the cemetery, and inside, this corner of the city was mostly just agricultural land. But by 1875, construction outside the walls was taking off. As the Ottoman authorities embarked on modernization projects – paving streets, installing gas lighting, laying sewer pipes – the gate's east-facing entrance was blocked up in favor of a new, wider, north-facing portal that drove a straight path through the walls, eliminating Suleiman's defensive right-angled turn. Livestock trading, which had gone on here for at least a couple of thousand years, moved away. Then after 1948, with Damascus Gate hobbled by the proximity of the international border, Jordan turned the main thoroughfare leading north from Bab as-Sahira, Salah ad-Din Street, into the city's commercial center. It's still busy today, lined with cafés, upmarket shops and offices, the heart of downtown East Jerusalem.

But as things picked up, the gate's name and its association with death made people uncomfortable. At some point *Sahira*'s S became vocalized into a Z, creating Bab az-Zahra, a much less troubling name (*zahra* is close to the word for blossom or flower and, usefully, there's a stone rosette adorning the gate tower). Herod has become a name spoken only for tourists. Nowadays, when resorting to English, Arabic-speaking Jerusalemites – and even some Hebrew speakers – will tend to call this the Flowers Gate.

Inside the gate the land is hilly, masked beneath stone and densely populated, but once hosting fruit-heavy cactus fringing earthy orchards of fig and olive. Well into the twentieth century European mapmakers called this area "Bezetha," a name culled from the Roman historian Josephus. To Jerusalemites this neighborhood is Bab Hutta (Gate of Forgiveness), named for the gateway into the Al-Aqsa compound located immediately to the south. And, as its little clusters of fancy-free shops can testify, Bab Hutta is struggling. It is the Old City's most deprived, underdeveloped area, battling poverty, overcrowding, unemployment, high education dropout rates, gender-based discrimination, poor mental health, a prevalence of drug and alcohol abuse, and significant social pressure from Israeli police and the antagonistic presence of Jewish Israeli settlers.

"Our mission is to change the situation of the people," says Muntaser Edkaidek, at the community center. "It's a long process."

Burj al-Laqlaq, or al-Luqluq (literally, Stork Tower), is the massive, squared-off fortification point at the northeastern corner of the city walls, built by Suleiman. Before 1967 the open land beneath the tower was home to the tents and shacks of the Dom people, Jerusalem's Gypsies. Then Israel expelled them and, in 1991, launched a plan to build 240 apartments in their place for Jewish Israelis to settle. The people of Bab Hutta resisted, establishing the Burj al-Laqlaq Social Center Society to save the area for the local community. Eventually, they won. Israel withdrew and Burj al-Laqlaq has gone from strength to strength. It is now a grassroots nonprofit organization utilizing what is the largest open area inside the walls other than Al-Aqsa, with halls and meeting rooms, a kindergarten, a ceramics workshop, a computer lab, playgrounds, an open-air basketball court and a football pitch with a tiered stand.

Energetic, unsmiling, Edkaidek outlines ongoing projects. After-school tutoring and university preparation run alongside psychosocial support for women and children, skills training, women's empowerment schemes, volunteering and all kinds of sporting activities from table tennis to parkour. As a journalist and sports administrator, Edkaidek worked with the Palestinian team at the London 2012 Olympics, and has brought that experience back home: one of Burj al-Laqlaq's highest-profile events is an annual month-long football tournament between Jerusalem's Palestinian families, using sport as a way to foster communication and bridge rivalries. In 2019, 158 families took part.

"This is a safe open space for children," he continues, "especially the girls of the Old City. They come here to play basketball, practice tae kwon do, also take part in drama workshops and painting, computer skills, leadership programs."

I've dropped by Burj al-Laqlaq at different times of day. It's open, a place to breathe under a wide sky and refresh your perspective. In the mornings, old folk sit outside on shady benches to gossip or play cards. One evening a Jordanian friend and I came across a football game under floodlights. ("Are we still inside the walls?" my friend goggled.) Spectators told us kids were coming down into the Old City after school from their homes on the Mount of Olives to play mini-tournaments here and hang out together. I've stumbled on capoeira classes, a hall full of shiny-muscled young guys bouncing across mats, doing stretches and back-flips and cheering each other on.

Edkaidek talks about how Burj al-Laqlaq has targeted drugs in particular. "We ran a study in 2012 on drug use in Bab Hutta. It found rates of three in five. Today, that's down to one in five – evidence of our impact." But then he mentions funding, and his voice softens ominously. "Who should run this place?" he challenges me.

The people? I hazard.

"The government," he says. "The PA [Palestinian Authority]. We fight to bring money to cover the expenses here, but it should not be me doing that."

Israel bans the PA from operating in Jerusalem. Burj al-Laqlaq's major backers include various agencies of the United Nations, the World Bank, European governments, large companies and international charities. Edkaidek is furious he is forced into the arms of such donors, who he sees as helping perpetuate the injustices inherent in Israel's occupation that mean community support organizations like Burj al-Laqlaq are so desperately needed in the first place. The damaging effects at the grassroots of an aid dependency at national level are rarely so stark.

"If I wanted to take money from Israel, they would give to me tomorrow," Edkaidek says quietly, staring at me.

And his voice drops to a murmur as he adds:

"But I will never take."

7

Everything but His Face

STORIES OF SUFI JERUSALEM

AT THE BEGINNING OF 1095 Abu Hamid al-Ghazali didn't look like a man on the edge of a personal crisis. He was a senior professor of law at Baghdad's Nizamiyya Madrasa, the greatest university in the eastern Islamic world. His recent book refuting rationalist metaphysics, *The Incoherence of the Philosophers*, had made him famous from Isfahan to Cairo. Though he was not yet forty, the Seljuk sultans sought his advice on matters of state, and he was warmly received at the court of the Abbasid caliphs in Baghdad.

But for all his learning, Al-Ghazali (the middle syllable is long) could not shake the feeling that his faith remained shallow. "What I was lacking," he wrote, "belonged to the domain not of instruction but of ecstasy and initiation." As the year wore on these doubts grew so painful that the professor was struck mute in the lecture hall. "I made an effort to teach, for the sake of my students, but I couldn't utter a word. The silence to which I was condemned cast me into despair … My health deteriorated." About six months into what we would now call a breakdown, Al-Ghazali gave it all up. He resigned his post, disposed of his wealth, and in November 1095 left Baghdad on foot. He offered colleagues the only plausible explanation – that he was going on pilgrimage to Mecca – but his real destination lay elsewhere. He sought a place of calm and simplicity, where he could reassess and rebuild his life.

After many months in Damascus, living alone in anonymity, practicing asceticism and conducting spiritual retreats within the great Umayyad Mosque, Al-Ghazali arrived in Jerusalem in the autumn of 1096. There, he spent his days secluded inside the Dome of the Rock. And it was there, in his rooms above Al-Aqsa's Gate of Mercy, that he began to develop what is considered the towering masterpiece of Sufi theology and one of the most influential books in all of Islam: a forty-volume work entitled *Ihya Ulum ad-Din*, or *The Revival of the Religious Sciences*.

There were many among Al-Ghazali's peers who didn't think religion needed any reviving. God's message to humanity was clear and final. It had been revealed to Muhammad in the Arabic language and transcribed into the immutable perfection of the Quran. The Prophet's sayings (*hadith*) had been painstakingly collected and sifted for error, and his habitual behavior (*sunnah*) had been codified into the *shariah*, a compendium of religious guidance that covered everything from the tying of a baby's umbilical cord to the washing of a dead body. This corpus of law was continually refined and arbitrated by a professional class of intellectuals like Al-Ghazali, men who gave themselves the title "knowers" – in Arabic *ulama*, from *ilm*, meaning knowledge.

But Arabic has another word for knowledge, a word that connotes not the dry, bookish expertise of the jurists but a more intuitive, mystical method of knowing: *marifa*, sometimes translated as "gnosis." Since at least the eighth century the knowers had been coming into conflict with men and women, later called Sufis, who claimed to speak from this profound and wordless recognition of God.

There were some strange characters among them. Barefoot drifters who wandered from town to town in search of enlightenment. Ascetics who dressed in woollen robes (*sufi* is an adjective perhaps derived from *suf*, meaning wool) and who slept out in the desert. Ecstatics who wept and sang for the love of God. A fringe of loner mystics might have been ignored or even tolerated, but these people were attracting followers, and in some cases preaching ideas that lay well beyond the frontiers of Islamic orthodoxy.

Exactly what those ideas were was hard to say, and it was this vagueness that most infuriated the scholars. The early Sufis refused to be pinned down to a set of beliefs that could be discussed or refuted. When jurists challenged the teaching of a Persian named Abu Yazid al-Bistami, for example, he slid effortlessly beyond their reach: "You take your knowledge dead from the dead, but we take our knowledge from the Living who does not die."

Four hundred years later we catch the same teasing, evasive strain in the poetry of Jalaleddin Rumi. "Sell your cleverness," Rumi wrote, "and buy bewilderment."

These voices emerge from a web of mystical traditions that can be traced right back to the beginnings of Islam and that is still alive across the Islamic world today. To group them under the label "Sufism" suggests a single, coherent approach to the faith, but that is misleading: the sober seclusion of a classically educated scholar like Al-Ghazali is a world away from the spinning of an ecstatic dervish at a countryside shrine, and neither has much in common with, say, the musical mysticism that flourished across the Indian subcontinent. Even the word "Sufism" is not prominent in the Islamic sources, and does not become widely used until eighteenth- and nineteenth-century British Orientalists, looking for a convenient catch-all term, threw it like a blanket across a whole variety of esoteric insights, contemplative practices and popular superstitions that had developed within Islamic cultures.

Still, woven into the Sufi tradition are patterns that surface within radically different traditions. One is the idea that Sufism cannot be caught in the net of language. Others persist, too: Jerusalem remains central to Sufi practice, and Sufi practice remains central to Jerusalem – still discernible today, even to outsiders, though you need to look hard to find it. How to trace these threads? Where do they converge? What exactly was Al-Ghazali looking for as he sat in silence beneath the Dome of the Rock, almost a thousand years ago?

"My name is Mazen Ahram. I was born in 1952. I am married, with two girls and two boys. I am an *imam* [prayer-leader] and an orator, and also a religious teacher at Al-Aqsa Mosque. I supervise all the mosques in Jerusalem – there are more than a hundred of them, including around thirty-five in the Old City. I oversee the imams, the *muezzins* who make the call to prayer, I make sure the people in the congregations are happy – that's my job.

"My family traces its origins back to Prophet Muhammad. My number is thirty-nine: when you start with me, then my father, my grandfather, you can count thirty-nine generations back to the Prophet. We came here just after the Umayyad time, from Medina to Damascus, then here. We have been in Jerusalem about 1,230 years. Most of my family have been imams in Al-Aqsa.

"I am a Sufi. To be a Sufi is to follow Prophet Muhammad in his way, very simply. As he tells us, we can grow in love. We do not hate anybody, and we do not belong to any group.

"My father used to work as a tailor. When I was young I would help him. I would split whatever money I had fifty-fifty – half would go on food, half on books. The first book I ever bought was Al-Ghazali's *Ihya Ulum ad-Din*. I would be stitching and sewing with my father, and reading Al-Ghazali at the same time.

"Let me tell you a story from fifty years ago. There was a school friend of mine. His father was imam at one of the mosques outside Jerusalem. We would talk, you know. One day my friend said, 'I'll take you to a place.' And he took me to this mosque in the Haret as-Sa'diyya neighborhood of the Old City called Madhana al-Hamra, the Red Minaret. It was built by one of the sons of Salah ad-Din.*

---

* Scholars date the minaret, built with reddish stone, to the sixteenth century, while the mosque itself is nineteenth- or early twentieth-century.

"I walked in, and there was a group of old men sitting on the ground in a circle around a *sheikh*, an old man who looked very religious. In front of him was a small table with books and a Quran and in front of that was a bag of skullcaps: everyone who entered would take a skullcap and put it on. I shook his hand, but when I reached into the bag there were no skullcaps left. Then the sheikh touched my hand and asked me to sit next to him. I was just a boy, fifteen years old. I didn't know what was happening. He moved his *hatta* off his head, took off his own skullcap, which was underneath, and put it directly on my head. Everybody there was surprised and amazed. I didn't understand what it meant at all – but they understood. He was saying I would replace him. Me, this boy, who had just walked in off the street.

"When it was time to pray, Sheikh Murtadha – that was his name – asked me to be the imam and lead the prayer. It was so hard, as a teenager, with something like eighty very devout people behind me. Such a heavy experience. Some people were jealous – who is this boy? My friend who had taken me there said, 'Mazen wants to learn the Sufi way'. I didn't even know what that meant! Sheikh Murtadha spoke to me, and told me to read certain passages in the Quran. He said, 'Remember God all the time. When you speak, in your work, in every part of life, remember God."

"When I got home that night I was so confused. I went to bed, and dreamt I saw a saint. He was dressed in rough woollen clothes with long sleeves and his hair was parted in the middle. He was very beautiful. I saw him floating above me, while I was asleep in my bed. He said to me: 'Every time you make a stitch with your needle, praise God.' I asked him who he was, and he said he was Idris. I asked him where he came from. He said he was in the fourth heaven. Then he disappeared.

"Next morning I went directly to find Sheikh Murtadha. As soon as he saw me he said, 'What did you see?' He knew what had happened before I opened my mouth. I told him my dream, and the sheikh explained. Prophet Idris [Enoch in the Bible] was a tailor. My father is a tailor, and so will I be – Idris was showing me that every stitch, every part of life, is holy. 'Just follow that,' Sheikh Murtadha said.

"So I followed! Simply this. I continued the Sufi way, and the principle of love, from then until now.

"Words cannot really explain what I feel about Jerusalem – a warm feeling every day when I wake up. The holiness of Jerusalem doesn't mean the stones. Jerusalem is from the breath of God. This is the place where people must sit together. I don't consider myself Muslim if I don't believe in the prophets of other religions – Jesus, Moses, Abraham. All the prophets are brothers, without differentiation, and we respect all human beings as a result of divine creation, including people who don't believe.

"Of course I get angry sometimes – I am human, after all – but when I feel upset I go out to the Mount of Olives and watch the sun going down behind the Aqsa mosque, and I look across in the other direction where the moon is rising, and that helps me. Because the sun is my father, and the moon is my mother. So while the sun is setting, the moon is rising – and then the opposite. A new day will come.

"Every tree, every stone, every corner, every centimeter of Jerusalem has a story. Despite the nations that come and go here, Jerusalem will remain. Our message is we want to build, and not destroy. You can destroy the biggest, tallest building in minutes, but when you want to build it takes a long, long time. As Muslims, we want to build a nation without the sickness of killing and hatred and love of money and wars.

"People change. But time is God."

Jerusalem drew the first Muslims with a field of myth and memory that linked the city with the deepest origins of their faith. Before Muslims prayed towards Mecca, they prayed towards Jerusalem; the city became known as the first *qibla* – the direction in which to pray – Abraham's *qibla*. Many believed that here, on the site of the ruined Jewish Temple, God had created Adam, Abraham had bound his son Ismail for sacrifice, and Muhammad had ascended by night through the heavens to meet the prophets who had gone before him. Other prophets in the Quran, not least David and Solomon, were known to have been associated with Jerusalem. At the end of days another prophet, Jesus, would return to the same site, and the souls of the dead would arise to face the Last Judgment here, on this mountain. When the Umayyad caliphs built the Dome of the Rock towards the end of the seventh century, they were physically grafting Islam onto the old root of Abrahamic monotheism, giving visible expression, in gold and glass and stone, to the spiritual force that was concentrated here. Cairo and Damascus may have been greater centers of politics, trade and scholarship. Mecca may have been the focus of the obligatory pilgrimage. But Jerusalem was the ground of divine illumination.

The story of Muhammad's Night Journey remains one of the most compelling and mysterious in Islam, with profound implications for Jerusalem. The Quran (17:1) tells how God takes his Messenger "by night from the sacred mosque to the farthest mosque, whose surroundings we have blessed." The "sacred mosque" (*al-masjid al-haram*) is Mecca; the "farthest mosque" (*al-masjid al-aqsa*) has been understood as Jerusalem throughout all of Islam, since the earliest scholars of Quranic exegesis in the first century after Muhammad. Traditions add detail to the story: Muhammad travelled with the angel Jibril (Gabriel) on Al-Buraq, a winged, horse-like animal. He prayed in Jerusalem with Abraham, Moses, Jesus and a company of prophets, then was lifted to heaven to meet the prophets of old and then God, before a return to Jerusalem and thence Mecca, all within one night. Thus was Muhammad confirmed as the Seal of the Prophets.

The story resonates with enigma. A common name for Jerusalem in early Islamic sources – and still today – is *Bayt al-Maqdis,* meaning "the Sanctified House," derived from a Hebrew name for the Jewish Temple. All of Jerusalem was sanctified, not one or other specific location; its holiness was unbounded. The Quranic phrase *al-masjid al-aqsa* was similarly all-encompassing. It could not refer to one specific mosque building, since none existed in Jerusalem in Muhammad's lifetime. The idea was less rigid than that. *Masjid* simply means "place of prostration." Any space – open or enclosed, roofed or unroofed – can serve as a mosque. The entire esplanade

of what we now call the Haram al-Sharif was understood to be a single mosque, *al-masjid al-aqsa*, built by Adam and renovated by the prophet Solomon.

Today, prevailing custom says that the large enclosed esplanade known in Jewish tradition as the Temple Mount is called in Arabic Haram al-Sharif ("Noble Sanctuary"), and that on – or within – the Haram stand the Dome of the Rock (with a golden dome) and, just south of it, the Al-Aqsa mosque (with a silver/gray dome). But this formula, ubiquitous in Western understanding, is not reflected in everyday usage. To Palestinian Jerusalemites, and Muslims world-wide, the term "Al-Aqsa" refers to the entire esplanade, all of which is a mosque, including its many courtyards, colonnades, steps, free-standing buildings, minarets and open spaces. In this conception the silver-domed building known by outsiders as Al-Aqsa is only one of the prayer spaces within the Al-Aqsa compound, and is commonly called *Al-Masjid al-Qibli*, the Mosque of the Direction of Prayer, or *Al-Jameh al-Qibli* (*jameh* is another word for mosque, implying a main or congregational mosque). "Al-Aqsa" is in any case a much older name for the esplanade than the Ottoman term "Haram al-Sharif."*

When a Muslim army conquered Jerusalem in 637/8, its famously ascetic commander, Omar ibn al-Khattab, refused to

---

* This linguistic inconsistency was exploited by US and Israeli negotiators drafting Israel's 2020 agreement with the UAE and Bahrain. The document excludes non-Muslims from praying at "the Al-Aqsa Mosque." That means one, uncontroversial thing in Arabic – that the entire esplanade is reserved for Muslim prayer – but another, potentially explosive thing in English and Hebrew – that only the silver-domed building is reserved for Muslim prayer, and that non-Muslims may pray anywhere else on the esplanade. This formulation codifies a long-held desire on the Israeli right to divide Al-Aqsa into Muslim and Jewish prayer zones as a prelude to total takeover. It has yet to be tested.

don finery or ride a horse: he arrived to accept the city's surrender on camel-back, wearing rough clothes of camel hair. He was met by the Christian Patriarch of Jerusalem, Sophronius, who led him around the city. At prayer time, Omar declined Sophronius's invitation to pray in the Church of the Holy Sepulchre, for fear that Muslims after him would seize the site and turn it into a mosque, and instead prayed outside on the steps. The mosque his followers built on that spot is now gone, but his action is commemorated by the still-functional Mosque of Omar beside the church, dating from 1193.

Sophronius also showed Omar the former site of the Jewish Temple. The way this momentous story is usually told, the two men have to pick a path through mounds of rubbish, thrown there by generations of Christians to spite the Jews and negate the site's sanctity. Rubbish – so the story goes – almost blocked the gateway into the compound, forcing Omar and Sophronius to crawl on hands and knees. Historians and tale-tellers variously describe this mess as filth, trash, a garbage dump, even a dungheap, conjuring ever more distasteful images to reinforce the narrative of Christian desecration. Omar is shocked and orders the area cleared.

But hold on. Should we imagine the ordinary people of Jerusalem climbing the hill of the Temple Mount, generation after generation, to dump their rubbish within the city walls? Centuries of dung, piled summer after stinking summer? Rivers of ordure flowing down with winter rains into the streets, contaminating cisterns?

What seems more likely is that this was a field of ruins. The future site of Al-Aqsa had been abandoned – or, at least, neglected – since the Roman destruction in 70 CE of the Jewish Temple and the Christian destruction in the 330s of the Roman Temple to Jupiter that replaced it. It makes more sense to see the desecration as spiritual, and to envisage the rubbish as rubble.

Having cleared the area, Omar built Jerusalem's first structure for Muslim prayer almost immediately, in 637/8, on the south side of the esplanade. Just over fifty years later, near the center of the esplanade, came the Dome of the Rock. In its internal and external decoration of paradisal mosaics, this shrine – not a mosque, strictly speaking – expressed the developing theology and philosophy of Islam, while also embodying the political ambition of the Damascus-based Umayyad caliphs in shifting the base of power in the Islamic world away from Arabia, asserting Jerusalem as a focus for pilgrimage to rival Mecca. It is a uniquely complex building.

In form, the eight-sided Dome of the Rock draws from the octagonal shrines, churches and mausoleums of Byzantine Christianity, yet in conception it is deeply anti-Christian, built in part to counter the aesthetic influence of Constantine's Church of the Holy Sepulchre. It was inscribed with verses from the Quran that specifically reject the divinity of Jesus, and it was positioned over the Foundation Stone – central to Jewish practice – in order to reach back beyond Christianity for older sources of sanctity.

It was also shatteringly, Islamically original. The Quran's account of the Day of Judgment (69:15–18) speaks of the heavens splitting open and eight angels bearing God's throne to the place of judgment, the Rock in Jerusalem: this ethereally beautiful building, compellingly, was nothing less than an evocation of the octagonal Throne of God itself. Façade-less and focus-less, it has no main entrance and no interior direction: function and form are one. Multiple axes of symmetry and ratios of harmony soothe and inspire. An octagon of columns inside the building carries the dome, hidden, leaving the external walls as curtains of beauty to bear decoration – mosaics of glass originally, blue tiles today. And the dome itself, rather than being an external consequence of interior design, as at, say, the Holy Sepulchre, has its own dynamic, designed as a visual magnet to draw attention from afar.

Nothing like the Dome of the Rock had ever been built before. Very little approaching it has been built since.

In the same decade or shortly afterwards, Omar's first, plain mosque on the same esplanade was reimagined and replaced by the grand, multiple-aisled Masjid Al-Aqsa. The tangible link Al-Aqsa thus represented to the Quranic story of the Night Journey persists to this day. Holiness suffused Jerusalem.

Yet even from the fragmentary records of the eighth century it is clear that Islam's first mystics were marginal characters in the life of Jerusalem. They practiced extreme forms of piety – fasting, weeping, vigils – and often seem to have arrived from the eastern edges of the Islamic world: Ibrahim bin Adham, from Balkh in Afghanistan, who was born a prince and gave up fabulous wealth to live as an itinerant farmhand in Palestine; Sufyan al-Thawri, from Kufa in Iraq, who wore black and wept as if in mourning, and spent his days reading the Quran inside the Dome of the Rock (charmingly, Sufyan declared life's greatest pleasure to be eating bananas* in the shadow of the dome); Rabia al-Adawiyya, from Basra on the Persian Gulf, the first great female saint of the Sufi tradition, who slept on a reed mat and used a brick as a pillow but who, despite the many traditions about her in Jerusalem, may never have visited at all.

As well as a dedication to poverty, Muslim ascetics shared with their Christian contemporaries the idea that humans could enter into a kind of intimacy or friendship with God. The Christian path towards this kind of sainthood ran through the wilderness, but Sufis, by contrast, began to develop spiritual disciplines that were based more often on communal prayer than extreme isolation.

The most important of these practices, and one that can still be seen in Sufi gatherings today, is chanting or singing the names of God, sometimes for hours on end. This is a discipline called *dhikr*,

---

* Bananas were new in Palestine. Even two centuries after Sufyan, in 985, the geographer Al-Muqaddasi ("the Jerusalemite"), when describing the produce of his native city, still felt the need to offer a gloss on bananas: "a fruit of the form of the cucumber, but the skin peels off and the interior is not unlike that of the watermelon, only finer flavored and more luscious."

or *zikr*, meaning "remembrance." It remains the most distinctive ritual that sets Sufis apart from other Muslims.

The Quran contains hundreds of verses urging believers to "remember" or "invoke" the presence of God, and it was this Quranic sanction that gave Sufis the license to develop forms of *dhikr* based on the rhythmic repetition of sacred names and phrases, usually "Allah" or one of Islam's ninety-nine names of God, or the first line of the Islamic declaration of faith, *la ilaha ilallah* ("There is no god but God"). There are Sufis who practice *dhikr* alone, silently counting their repetitions on strings of glass or wooden beads, but more often the words are chanted in a shared ritual that includes physical movement and can also draw energy from flute and drums.

The addition of music marks the point at which *dhikr* begins to blur into a more controversial practice called *sama*. *Sama* literally means "hearing" or "audition," but the Sufis used the word to describe a spectrum of song and dance whose purpose was to intensify the invocation of God and to awaken a kind of spiritual yearning in the dancers. "*Sama* rouses hearts," said the ninth-century Nubian-Egyptian master Dhu'n-Nun. "Whoever listens as is intended attains realization." From this pitch of longing the music could even carry the seeker into that obliterating union with God that was the goal of the Sufi quest. At the most profound depths of listening, the listener disappeared. The Sufis of the Mawlawiyya order developed the best-known form of *sama*, the distinctive turning ritual that gave them the name "whirling dervishes" and which they practiced in Jerusalem throughout the Ottoman period.

Whether or not these rituals transgressed the *shariah* depended on who you asked. At its edges *sama* strayed into frenzied sessions of whirling and drumming that drew hostility even from other Sufis. The twelfth-century Persian mystic Ruzbihan Baqli poured scorn on the pretensions of the unschooled masses who joined the *sama*: "A group of the delirious dance, recite poetry, perform the Audition, clap their hands and tear their clothing, imagining that, having achieved this, they have found the states of God's friends. What nonsense!"

But *dhikr* and *sama* were always more than just song and dance. Rhythmic chanting, with or without music, deepened remembrance, wearing away at the ego until it evaporated into the oneness of the divine. Rumi came at it with his characteristically light touch: "If you could get rid of yourself just once, the Secret of Secrets would open to you."

I really wasn't sure what to expect. I knew this was the right place, and I knew it was more or less the right time, so I just opened the door and walked in.

I needn't have worried. Sufis are lovely people.

Jerusalem's seventeenth-century Qadiriyya lodge, named for revered Sufi scholar Abd al-Qadir al-Jilani (1078–1166), stands on a back street just a few steps off the northwestern corner of the Haram al-Sharif. The single entranceway, under a plain pointed arch, gives onto a large, irregularly shaped courtyard, open to the sky, decorated with a central fountain and filled with olive trees and vines. Overhead run strings of lights between the trees; underfoot frolics a tribe of marmalade cats. Eleven simple ground-floor cells line the far sides of the courtyard, while a two-story building serves as a meeting hall and upstairs mosque. After a decades-long association with Jerusalem's community of Afghans – pilgrims who decided to stay on – the lodge is now known as the Afghaniyya and has shifted from the austere Qadiri order to the more worldly Alawiya branch of the Shadhili order.

And, as far as I know, it is the last place in the Old City still to hold a regular *dhikr*, two (or more) evenings every week.

That old grump Ruzbihan Baqli, besides scorning truth-seekers, wrote how *dhikr* and especially *sama* "excite human nature ... For some it is a seduction, because they are incomplete. Those who are alive through nature but dead in the heart should not listen, for it will bring destruction down upon them."

Being incomplete, I find *dhikr* hugely seductive. Once, before the Syrian war, I was lucky to be invited to a *dhikr* in Aleppo led by several of Syria's best-known Sufi musicians and vocalists. Perhaps fifty men packed into a small, unremarkable room somewhere behind the

500-year-old Bab al-Hadid gate, swaying to the rhythmic amplified chanting of "Allah, Allah" fed through an echo machine to create a booming, reverberating wall of sound. Percussionists clashed tiny cymbals, drummers kept a pounding beat and soloists performed vocal pyrotechnics as devotees splashed perfume on their skin, filling the air with heady fragrance. I saw old men rocking, their eyes closed, I saw faces lifted in rapture and brows knotted in fevered intensity. Every sense was stimulated to bring each individual closer to God – then the lights went off. We stood, a mass of bodies chanting, shouting, swaying in the pitch dark together as the music seemed to crescendo, but just kept on crescendoing. Then it was all over. The music ended, the echoes died away, the lights flicked on, men rubbed their eyes, shook hands with each other and left.

So in that secluded courtyard at Jerusalem's Afghaniyya I wondered what might happen. It was an ordinary midweek evening. Attendants were laying out three rows of chairs in a V shape facing a table, set in front of a low stage. A steady trickle of men were arriving, deferential and welcoming to me, the stranger, and for the thousandth time in such situations, I didn't know – and couldn't reasonably ask – whether I could sit where I was sitting were I not a man. At different times, in different places, women have joined the *dhikr*, but I have never witnessed it.*

After the sunset prayer, there was an extra crackle of atmosphere as all present rose to greet a very old man, dressed in a beige gown, waistcoat and suit jacket, his head under a white skullcap. This was the venerable Sheikh Abd al-Kareem al-Afghani, Sufi master and spiritual leader of this community, making his entrance after having prayed at Al-Aqsa. He was escorted slowly into the courtyard to

---

* Religious orthodoxy and/or social conservatism have often restricted women's presence in the public sphere, yet from its earliest origins Sufism regarded all people, irrespective of gender, as equals on the spiritual path. Camille Adams Helminski, a Sufi master in the US, has written: "Within some Sufi circles that developed over the centuries, women were integrated with men in ceremonies; in other orders women gathered in their own circles of remembrance and worshipped apart from men. Many of the great masters ... had teachers, students and spiritual friends who were women ... [Rumi] himself had many female disciples, and women were also encouraged to participate in *sama*, the musical whirling ceremony." Ethnographer Moyra Dale identifies many Sufi orders of today where women participate or lead, including the Naqshabandi, Chishti and Mawlawi.

take the seat of honor facing the rows of chairs, in front of the table which had been laid with books, papers and glasses of tea and coffee. He sipped, listening, as his son beside him greeted us and embarked on a lecture and discussion. My Arabic wasn't nearly good enough to follow it all – it was a debate of theology and philosophy, and as the evening drew on, a few yawns arose among the listeners. Then debate gave way to teaching, everyone leaning forward to catch the sheikh's whispered words, then to rounds of communal call-and-response singing. Finally the sheikh rose, and we all rose with him. The men on each side of me linked their fingers with mine, and their singing blurred into rhythmic chanting of the name of God in pairs – "Allah, Allah; Allah, Allah" – two notes falling, two notes rising, an infinite iambus repeated over and over in unison, each stressed syllable a growling exhalation. It became trance-like very quickly.

And when it ended, and men smiled and shook my hand and wished me well before stumbling out into the night, the continuity was the thing. The Secret of Secrets had eluded me again – at least, I think it had – but the chain of human tradition that had produced this group of people, at this time, performing this ritual together, in this place, felt both a privilege to share and a treasure to cherish.

By the tenth century there were many among the intellectual elites of Islam who, despite their hostility to the unlettered and unruly edges of mysticism, recognized that there was something profound in the Sufi tradition – something that, as Al-Ghazali would point out, gave life and beauty to the practice of the religion. And it was within this educated class that a more moderate asceticism began to gain ground, a model of Islamic behavior that rejected extremes of hunger and solitude for a less ostentatious simplicity: modesty in dress, restraint of appetite, generosity to the poor.

Social justice was just one element in Sufism's growing popularity. It was becoming a mass movement across the Islamic world, and it's not hard to see why. Here was a tradition that talked more of God's gentleness than of his severity, that had developed celebratory, musical forms of worship, and that spoke a dialect of Islam in which love sounded louder than prohibition. Its leaders turned away from the corruption of political power, but instead of retreating from the world they engaged in teaching and charity. Many became respected figures, passing on not just mystical insight but also intellectual instruction and moral guidance to thousands of students.

The Sufi fraternities of the tenth and eleventh centuries still had a fluid and informal character, meeting in a corner of the mosque or in the home of the sheikh, and it was still common for Sufi students to wander, seeking wisdom from many different teachers. But a more structured approach was emerging, and the influence of the Sufi teachers now extended far beyond a narrow circle of mystics. It had become a culture within Islamic culture, a way of being Muslim that appealed across the social spectrum.

In the villages around Jerusalem, these holy figures continued to attract followers even after they had died, and their tombs became the focus for local Sufi cults and rural pilgrimages. Between an illiterate, vulnerable peasant class and the remote, unknowable God of Islam, these country saints inserted themselves as intermediaries, intercessors who might be petitioned to bring rain to the fields or cure a sick child. The charismatic mystics of early Islam provided a focus for patterns of thought that had flourished for thousands of years across the pagan, Jewish and Christian Mediterranean. This is the world of amulets and rags tied to trees as a marker of prayer, of spirits and incantations at the water well, the world in which a few ears of newly reaped wheat were buried in the corner of a field as insurance against the harvest yet to come. A network of shrines and tombs grew, places to which villagers felt an emotional attachment.

By the time Al-Ghazali arrived in Jerusalem in 1096, Sufism could no longer be dismissed. It had to be accommodated within Islam, to be recognized as a legitimate interpretation of the faith. The problem for the religious elites was how. How could they absorb Sufism without giving sanction to the wilder, boundary-pushing ideas it also encompassed?

This is what Al-Ghazali was working on when he started to write *Ihya Ulum ad-Din*. He wasn't the first to take on the task: the effort to integrate Sufi insights into mainstream Islamic thought was already under way in Baghdad. Nor did he put an end to the debate: controversies over Sufism's legitimacy still fester across the Islamic world. But it was Al-Ghazali, with his tremendous intellectual prestige and his mastery of Islamic law, who articulated a version of Islam in which mysticism could flourish while at the same time insisting that the pursuit of illumination remain within the limits of the *shariah*. Conservative and dismissive of scientific rationality, it was Al-Ghazali more than anyone else who made Sufism respectable.

But at the exact moment Al-Ghazali was seated, writing, in his rooms at Al-Aqsa, another, bloodier movement was gathering pace on the far side of the Mediterranean. On 27 November 1095, in what is now France, Pope Urban II had given a speech urging Christian knights to seize Jerusalem from Muslim control by force of arms. The idea spread like a virus. Only three and a half years later, in June 1099, a Frankish – meaning French, or, more broadly, Western European Christian – army arrived outside the walls of Jerusalem.

By then Al-Ghazali had already returned east. When news of Jerusalem's fall reached him in Persia later that summer, many of the scholars and mystics he had known there were already dead, hacked to pieces on the carpets of Al-Aqsa. The few Muslims who survived were expelled from Jerusalem and a cross was mounted over the Dome of the Rock.

The Crusades destroyed the Islamic Jerusalem that Al-Ghazali had known. But their violence also changed the terms of the debate about what was and was not acceptable within Islam, clearing the way for the great flourishing of Sufism that would follow.

No one knows exactly how many people died in the massacre that was the Crusaders' first act within Jerusalem's walls, in July 1099.

"None was left alive," wrote Fulcher of Chartres, a Frankish priest who witnessed the carnage. "Neither women nor children were spared." As the knights stabbed and looted their way through the city, thousands of terrified Muslims gathered in the precincts of Al-Aqsa, hoping the sanctity of the site might offer protection. They were quickly disabused. Frankish accounts of what followed exult in ever-gorier hyperbole, from Fulcher ("If you had been there you would have seen our feet colored to our ankles with the blood of the slain") to Godfrey of Bouillon ("Our people had blood up to the knees of their horses") to Raymond of Aguilers ("Men rode in blood up to their bridle reins").

Initial Muslim reports express fear of the invaders' brutality and contempt for their lack of civilization, but crucially show no insight into their motivations. No one reflects on *why* the Franks had come. They simply arrive, a barbarian horde as inexplicable as the bedouin raiders who would suddenly appear without warning, take what they could and then vanish again into the desert. The Franks, though, did not vanish. And when they had been in the Levant for a generation and more, the Muslims understood these were not mercenaries after gold or even settlers seeking land. They were monks and pilgrims as much as they were soldiers, and they had come to claim a place – Jerusalem – which held for them a magical, redemptive power.

No one grasped this more purposefully than Salah ad-Din al-Ayoubi (often anglicized as Saladin), a Kurdish general who, almost a century after the Franks arrived, managed to galvanize the Muslim armies into a decisive counterassault. When he finally expelled the invaders from Jerusalem in 1187 – waiting deliberately to do so until the deeply resonant twenty-seventh day of the Islamic month Rajab (Friday, 2 October, that year), which marks the anniversary of Prophet Muhammad's arrival in Jerusalem on his Night Journey – Salah ad-Din took possession of the city with an act of purification: he had the sacred rock over which the Dome of the Rock stands washed with rosewater, sanctifying Jerusalem in the name of Islam. This was not mere ceremony. He understood that if the city were to be defended over the long term, Muslims would need to match the Franks in their devotion to Jerusalem, publicly as well as in private.

An emotional connection to the city had been a cornerstone of Sufi mysticism since the earliest days of Islam, expressed, as we've seen, by chains of traditions that linked legendarily pious individuals. Now, attachment to Jerusalem began to be harnessed to the urgent need to consolidate Palestine's status as a Muslim holy land. Piety had become a political project, and the more established Sufi orders began to receive public endorsement and financial support.

Salah ad-Din died only five years after taking Jerusalem, but within that time he converted the palace of the Latin Patriarch, directly beside the Church of the Holy Sepulchre, into a mosque and lodge for Sufis, named after himself – the Khanqah Salahiyya, which survives today – and then transformed the Crusader church of St. Anne into the Madrasa Salahiyya, a school of Islamic law that flourished for the next six hundred years.

His program of religious building and endowment created colleges, convents and hospitals that contributed to the city's renewed Islamic character. By the time the Mamluk sultans took control in 1250, Jerusalem was becoming a center of Islamic learning that attracted scholars from across Egypt and Syria.

Over the eighty-eight years in which Jerusalem had been under Christian rule, an Islamic literature had emerged which lamented the loss of the city, celebrated its sanctity and sang the praises of the holy figures who had prayed or died there. This genre, known as *Fadail Bayt al-Maqdis* (the "Merits of Jerusalem"), continued to grow after Salah ad-Din's reconquest. Now, though, the veneration of the city's Muslim saints was not confined to the pages of books. The shrines of Jerusalem's holy men and women were restored as centers of pilgrimage and prayer, places where the Sufis could gather for rituals that survived right through to the Nakba (1948) – and, in truncated form, even after that. In springtime vast crowds would make their way over the hills east of Jerusalem to the desert tomb of Nabi Musa (Prophet Moses) for days of festivities that included fire and feast alongside prayer – as well as, in later accounts, snake-charming, sword-juggling and body-piercing. In summer similar crowds would congregate west of Jerusalem on the coast, at the shrine of Nabi Rubin (Prophet Reuben), by a brook south of Jaffa, and at the seaside shrine of Sidna Ali ("Our Master Ali," an eleventh-century saint), on cliffs overlooking the beaches north of Jaffa.* A network of lesser tombs and shrines, each the focus of its own local cult, emerged in villages across the country. Sufism had become a permanent part of Palestine's – and Jerusalem's – cultural life.

The visual impact of entering the Al-Aqsa compound can be over-whelming. The Dome of the Rock is so imposing, the surrounding architecture so striking, the open space so expansive after the constrictions of the city, it can be easy when walking there to lose your way, and find yourself thinking only about art, or God, or nature, or politics, or nothing. Visitors sometimes miss that Al-Aqsa is a human place, still suffused in the person-centered spirituality that Al-Ghazali sought to revive.

"The cats recognize me as soon as I walk in," said Ghassan Yunis. "They try to get other people to pay attention to them but nobody does. But when I arrive they all come after me."

Cats are special in Islam. Prophet Muhammad is said to have cut the sleeve off his robe one morning, rather than turf his sleeping cat Muizza off – what a lovely name for a cat! – so he could get dressed. It's even reported he owed his life to a cat that saved him from being bitten by a snake. That particular kitty's owner was one of the early fighters of Islam, a man named Abdulrahman ad-Dowsi (603–681) who was so attached to cats, always stroking them and playing with them, that since childhood he'd been nicknamed "Abu Hurairah," or, loosely, "The Kitten Guy." Islamic sources reveal plenty more foundational cat stories. The upshot is that in mosques, homes, schools, cities, villages, pretty much everywhere, cats get a universal free pass. "Love of cats is an aspect of faith," the Prophet is reported to have said.

---

* Nabi Rubin no longer functions, but the mosques of Nabi Musa and Sidna Ali still thrive.

"So if the Prophet ordered us to honor cats when they mew, and feed them, how can I not comply?" With his cotton-wool beard and crinkled smile, Ghassan Yunis was one of Al-Aqsa's best-loved characters – known in his community as Abu Ayman but widely recognized by regulars at the mosque as a twenty-first-century Abu Hurairah. For years he came into Jerusalem several times a week from his home in a village south of Nazareth, carrying meat he'd prepared for the constellations of cats that roam the compound. "I started with one cat, then a second, a third, a fourth. Some days there might be forty cats around me."

You could recognize him by the forest of raised tails that would scamper after him when he walked across Al-Aqsa's flagstones – and by the cawing and cooing that draped behind him like a fluttering train. It wasn't just cats. Abu Hurairah also brought food for Al-Aqsa's pigeons, crows and other feathered defenders. "God is the provider, not me. I am only an instrument."

And it wasn't just animals. "Anyone who enters Al-Aqsa gets a sweet, or for children I carry toys and trinkets – whether I know them or not, from babies to old folk, they all get special presents, and I tell them to remember God. I put a smile on their face."

Ghassan Yunis died of COVID-19 on 18 January 2021, aged 72.

By the thirteenth century, with Jerusalem battered and depopulated after the ousting of the Franks, there came a concerted effort to encourage Muslim pilgrimage and settlement. Sayings of the Prophet referring to the sanctity of Jerusalem and the merits of praying there circulated widely. The idea of the *ziyara* ("visit") to Jerusalem grew; this deliberately chosen term, denoting a religiously inspired journey, gave the Jerusalem pilgrimage special status while still preserving for purists the sanctity of the obligatory, and uniquely Meccan, pilgrimage, the *hajj*.

Strange tales arose, to entice the mystically minded: one scholar published the story of Abu Zahir, who said that one evening he lingered in Al-Aqsa after the night prayer, managing to dodge the

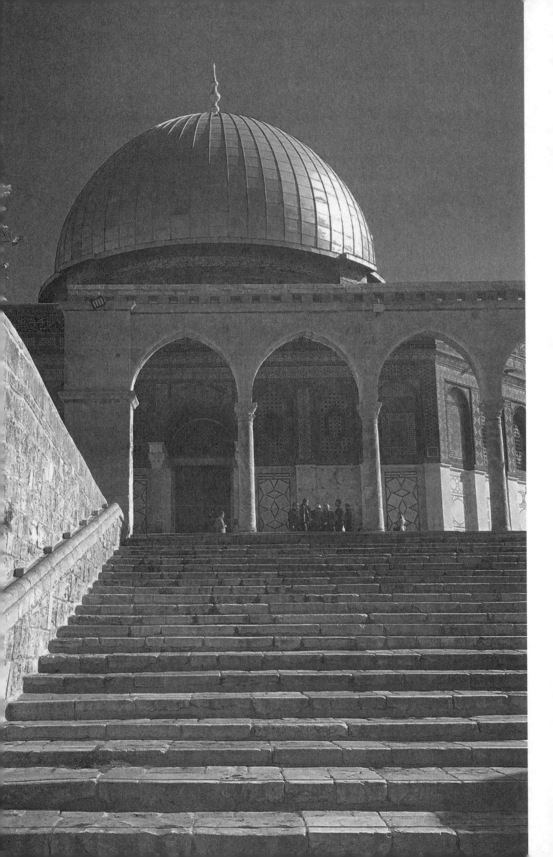

guards until the lamps were extinguished and the doors locked. Alone, in the silence of the small hours, he suddenly heard the beating of wings and a voice calling praises to God. Then more wings, and more praises, until he realized the mosque was filled with angels. "Are you human?" one of them asked him. "Don't be afraid!"

Sufis poured into Jerusalem, encouraged by the Mamluk sultans. Many came from Morocco and North Africa, founding a new quarter beside the western wall of the Haram, close to Al-Aqsa. The Bistamiyya order targeted its spiritual practice on fostering reconciliation between followers of different religions. The Qadiriyya emphasised community engagement and humanitarian relief for the poor. Then there were the Tuluniyya, the Khatniyya, the Salahiyya, the Wafa'iyya, the Shaybaniyya, and dozens more, each centered at its own lodge, most built in the lanes and alleys clustering around the gates of the Haram. In the southeastern corner of the Haram itself was built a domed prayer-hall evocatively named *Suq al-Marifa*, the Marketplace of Mystical Knowledge. (It appears in written accounts and on drawings, maps, photographs and models from 1486 to as late as 1927, but no longer exists.)

Many of the Sufi lodges were – and still are – called a *zawiya*, some a *khanqa* or *takiya* and others a *ribat*. These words have different etymologies, from Arabic, Persian or Turkish, and shades of meaning, but in practice, in the Jerusalem context, they can be used more or less interchangeably to mean a Sufi building, large or small, where people gather for study, prayer and spiritual retreat, where pilgrims lodge and where students and teachers reside.

One of the most architecturally striking of medieval Jerusalem's new institutions was a *madrasa* (college), the Ashrafiyya, on the Haram al-Sharif. This magnificent building, part of which still stands, exemplifies the transition that Sufism was making from the margins to the mainstream of Islamic intellectual life. It was built in 1482 by the Mamluk sultan Al-Ashraf Qaytbay as a college of law. Covered by its endowment was support for lawyers, students, professors – and a stipend for sixty Sufis. Remarkably, the jurists and the gnostics were now living together under the same roof, a law lecture proceeding in one hall as the *dhikr* was performed in the next.

But it would be a mistake to imagine Sufism had been tamed. Islamic mysticism retained its wild edge. Mendicant dervishes, or *fakirs* (from Arabic *faqr*, poverty), had wandered the byways of the Muslim world for centuries, particularly the pilgrimage routes. Jerusalem was no exception. From the fourteenth century on, these Qalandars, as they were known, would congregate in the Mamilla cemetery and roam the city, praying and begging "as naked as the day they were born," wrote a shocked French Franciscan in 1646. "One of them," the monk continued, "more than sixty years old, wore on his penis an iron ring the size of his little finger, to prove he was living in chastity."

The same era saw the arrival in Jerusalem of another – clothed – Sufi wanderer, Uthman Beg, who came from Istanbul to marry the governor of Jerusalem's daughter. Uthman was a master of the Naqshabandi, a Sufi order established in the fourteenth century that remains one of the most prominent in the world today, characterized by its principles of mindfulness through controlled breathing and its uniquely silent *dhikr*.

The lodge he founded in 1616 long catered to pilgrims from the Uzbek city of Bukhara and neighboring Turkmen, Tajik, Kyrgyz, Kazakh and Uyghur lands. Named variously as the Bukhariyya, or the Uzbekiyya, or the Naqshabandiyya – and often, over the years, affiliated with the Afghaniyya lodge, founded a few years after on an adjacent plot – it flourished under Bukhari sheikhs right through to the twentieth century, when multiple blows – colonial rule, restrictions on travel out of the Soviet Union, British diversion of funds, Israeli occupation – combined to undercut its viability. Part of the building was unaccountably demolished in 1983.

Many in Jerusalem still talk fondly and respectfully of its last head, Sheikh Abdulaziz al-Bukhari, a strong advocate for non-violence who worked publicly with Christians and Jews to promote interfaith reconciliation. He returned in the 1990s after twenty years in the US to rejuvenate the lodge, not least as a cultural center for the thousands of Palestinians who have Uzbek roots.

But since his death in 2010, the *dhikr* is no longer performed, the lodge's upper levels have been turned into residential apartments, and its manuscript library and museum remain in limbo. There's still a sign marking the building's entrance, opposite the Ecce Homo convent on the Via Dolorosa, but I've never seen prayers held in the small street-level mosque. Most days its doors are propped open with wire racks of paperback Qurans in multiple languages, printed in India or Saudi Arabia, for the Via Dolorosa's tourists to take for free. I browsed once, while an attendant tried to evangelize me.

"It's getting harder to think of God," Sheikh Abdulaziz said in 2004. "Myself, I am thinking of God and then the phone rings."

Sufism continued to thrive in Jerusalem. In the middle years of the seventeenth century the great Ottoman traveller Evliya Çelebi counted more than seventy Sufi lodges inside the city walls, and described how dervishes from one or other of the orders would perform *dhikr* every night.

But by the nineteenth century colonialism was upending the traditions and institutions of the Islamic world. Old routes of pilgrimage were fragmenting. In the aftermath of the First World War, France and Britain drew borders across the region for the first time. To some Muslims, Sufism began to appear an anachronism, a superstitious relic that could serve no useful purpose in an age of industrialization and social progress. In 1925 Turkey's secularist president Mustafa Kemal Atatürk closed Sufi lodges across Anatolia, imprisoned the dervishes who dared to whirl in public and even banned the *ney*, a reed flute that is emblematic of the Sufi musical tradition.

Below the surface of such nominally progressive repression lay the age-old fear of Sufism as wild and uncontrollable, a liberating and therefore subversive threat to the politically authoritarian power structures that were emerging in the twentieth century. That fear persists. From Mali and Morocco to Pakistan and Saudi Arabia, shrines of the saints have been destroyed by puritanical militias and national governments alike (the two are often indistinguishable), who condemn Sufi traditions as idolatrous.

Yet Sufism survives, in Jerusalem too. At Al-Aqsa, at noon, six days a week, every week, Mustafa Abu Sway, dean of Islamic Studies at Al Quds University and first holder of Al-Aqsa's Jordanian-endowed Chair for the Study of Al-Ghazali's Work lectures on *Ihya Ulum ad-Din* to public audiences of sixty or more. On Sunday mornings a women's study group convenes at Al-Aqsa to analyze Al-Ghazali's theology. At the Afghaniyya, Sheikh Abd al-Kareem presides over *dhikr* – small, midweek affairs like the one I attended, and big, festive gatherings with hundreds of participants. Jerusalem's built infrastructure of the Mawlawiyya, the Bukhariyya and other lodges persists, and memory of their centuries-long role lingers, even if the buildings themselves have now lost their Sufi communities.

That memory remains deeply embedded in place. In days gone by, each Sufi lodge would have sat an imam beside the tomb of its founder within the building to recite continuous prayers for the dead, their voices part of the soundscape of Jerusalem. Today, even though the tombs are silent, if you pause, as I've done, by the Qiramiyya lodge, now a private home but still housing the tomb of the fourteenth-century Sufi scholar known as Al-Qirami, you may see each pedestrian, as they pass the barred window behind which Sheikh al-Qirami rests, making a small gesture of supplication and offering a few words of prayer to the memory of the Sufi saint and his Sufi son, who lies beside him. Most don't even break stride.

Like the Afghaniyya, the Qiramiyya stands on a back street. It is easily missed. And that's also the case with one of the city's largest and most important Sufi lodges – still functioning today, after eight hundred years. This is a rich and surprising Jerusalem story, with interlinking threads that span centuries and continents.

The saga starts with a Sufi saint we've already met – Ibrahim bin Adham (roughly 718–782), a high-born prince of Balkh, in northern Afghanistan, who gave up his wealth to live simply on the land. One of his followers passed on the master's wisdom to another generation, as did that generation to the next. Some time in the early tenth century, or perhaps the late ninth, the inheritor of the tradition, a man named Abu Ishaq ("father of Isaac") – known also as Al-Shami, the Syrian – set out in search of wisdom. Maybe it wasn't a coincidence that he, too, ended up in northern Afghanistan, in the village of Chisht, east of Herat. There, he used the knowledge he'd been bequeathed to tell his followers of a new path towards enlightenment. He eventually returned to Damascus, and died there around 940, having adopted the name Al-Chishti. The Chishti order he established flourishes today worldwide as one of Sufism's largest and most prominent traditions.

Hold on to that: we'll come back to it shortly. And bear in mind that these chains of transmitted knowledge from master to student are vital in Sufism and also in orthodox Islamic theology, studied down the generations and preserved as confirmations of doctrinal and/or spiritual authenticity.

Next we have Moinuddin, born in Herat, or Isfahan, or somewhere along the Persian-Afghan border, in 1136, though some say 1142. After losing his parents while still in his teens, Moinuddin became withdrawn and meditative in his grief. While wandering he met a Sufi master who traced six generations of transmitted knowledge back to Abu Ishaq al-Chishti. After years of travel and learning with his master, Moinuddin saw a vision prompting him to spread the Chishti way to India. He settled in Ajmer, where followers gathered to perform *dhikr* and *sama*. He died in 1236, impossibly old, and his shrine today is one of India's most important, drawing millions of visitors each year, Hindus as well as Muslims.

The Jerusalem connection comes next, through Fariduddin Masoud, who was born around 1175 near Multan in the Punjab region of what is now Pakistan – as close to Ajmer, across the desert, as Madrid is to Barcelona. As a young man, Farid learned theology and the esoteric lore of Islam from a disciple of Moinuddin's. Legends of miracles had always surrounded him: after he had prayed so hard one day as a small boy that sugar had appeared as a reward under his prayer mat, his mother called him Shakar Ganj ("Treasury of Sugar"). The nickname stuck, and, over time, Baba Farid – *baba* is a term of respectful endearment for elders – became revered for his wisdom and learning. He was a natural successor as spiritual head of the Chishti order.

Baba Farid is still revered today as one of the greatest of religious scholars and mystics, a golden link in the chain of transmitted knowledge back to Abu Ishaq (and beyond, to Ibrahim bin Adham and, ultimately, the Prophet himself). His reputation crosses boundaries: Farid's poetry, composed in Punjabi – which up to then had not been considered a literary language – is included in the Guru Granth Sahib, the holy scripture of the Sikh religion, forming a bridge between Islam and Sikhism. Cities, schools and universities in India and Pakistan are named for him; his shrine in Pakpattan, south of Lahore, hosts continuous concerts day and night of *qawwali* devotional singing, and hundreds of thousands of pilgrims mark the anniversary of his death each year with a festival of prayer and music.

So, Jerusalem?

It was as a teenager in Multan that Baba Farid would have heard about the road to Jerusalem reopening following Salah ad-Din's victory over the Crusaders in 1187. News was already spreading of the resurgence of Islamic observance in the newly liberated Holy City, and the welcome the Sufi orders were receiving. It seems he resolved to visit. We don't know when he arrived in Jerusalem, or how long he stayed, or exactly what he did. In truth, we don't know for sure that he was here at all, but stories quickly arose that he lived humbly at Al-Aqsa, and that he spent forty days secluded in a tiny cave at the edge of the city, fasting and meditating. After he had returned to Punjab, and the legend of his sainthood had grown, a new tradition arose. "Indian Muslims passing through Jerusalem on their way to Mecca wanted to pray where [Baba Farid] had prayed, to sleep where he had slept," as one writer put it.

Eight hundred years after Baba Farid, in a whitewashed room empty of furniture or decoration, I gingerly lower myself into a narrow gap in the floor. Instantly, I wish I were alone. The cubby-hole below is bare, crumbling, dusty with old plaster, unappealing in every way bar the silence, and the associations. For this is the focal point of the story of Baba Farid in Jerusalem – the shrine to his sainthood and the cave where legend and memory says he meditated. The thought enters my head that I would happily take some time – say, the rest of the week – to sit down there alone, in peace, just to see what, if anything, might happen.

But in the room above I've left Nazer Ansari, eldest son of the venerable Sheikh Munir Ansari, ninety-three-year-old head of Jerusalem's Indian Hospice. Jovial and accommodating, Nazer is heir to the custodianship of the shrine and the pilgrim lodge that has grown up around it. Just now he's taking a moment to vape, and I can't realistically keep him hanging about on the off-chance the Secret of Secrets might be about to reveal itself to my overstimulated ego.

He helps me brush off once I'm back at ground level.

"It all started with an underground cave," he grins. "By the way, the Indian ambassador's wife went down there, too."

As you enter Jerusalem at Herod's Gate/Flowers Gate, steps to your right rise to a grand entranceway marked "Indian Hospice," shielding Baba Farid's shrine and its associated pilgrim lodge.

The hospice is a place of blissful serenity behind its pine-shaded walls and gates. It is as big as a football pitch, set around a courtyard of lemon trees and palms. There are guest rooms, offices, a mosque, a small library, the *chilla* (spiritual retreat; from Persian *chehel*, meaning "forty") from which I'd just emerged, but also residences: almost the whole Ansari family – Nazer, his brother Nazeer, two of their three sisters Najam and Nourjahan, plus their spouses and children and elderly parents, Sheikh Munir and his wife, Ikram – live within the compound.

The family's arrival in Jerusalem is a story in itself. In his intimate account of the hospice *Indians at Herod's Gate*, diplomat Navtej Sarna gathers evidence to show that Jerusalem long had more than one Indian hospice. Aside from the current buildings, there were Indian properties documented at Bab al-Ghawanmeh and around the city, serving pilgrim communities from different parts of the subcontinent. Each was run by a sheikh – a man garnering respect

for religious observance and administrative skill, often Indian but not always. Over the centuries some hospices survived, many did not. In 1824, an Indian hospice in the North African quarter, by Jerusalem's southern gate, was sold to enable the current compound, consisting at that time of little more than Baba Farid's cave and the small mosque over it, to expand. In 1846 there was another expansion, apparently concentrating all of Jerusalem's remaining Indian property holdings on the one site. By the time of the tumult at the end of the First World War, the hospice comprised a substantial plot of land but lacked any money to rebuild.*

At that time Jerusalem's Islamic authorities, facing growing threats from Zionism and the imposition of British colonial rule, were searching for allies, and naturally looked to the country which, at that time, held the largest Muslim population in the world – British-controlled India. In late 1923 the newly appointed Grand Mufti of Jerusalem, Hajj Amin al-Husseini, sent a delegation to India to fundraise for the restoration of Al-Aqsa. This was partly a logistical move – the buildings needed work – but also represented a political effort on Hajj Amin's part to channel worldwide Muslim opposition to Britain through himself. As part of the delegation's discussions with the leaders of India's Khilafat movement, the derelict state of the Indian Hospice came up. Would the Khilafat committee like to help develop the hospice for the benefit of Indian pilgrims to Jerusalem? Did they know of a reliable figure who could run it? The committee selected one of their most active members, Nazer Ansari.

The man later to become father of Sheikh Munir and grandfather of my host Nazer arrived in Jerusalem in 1924 and set about fixing the hospice, parts of which were, in his words, "a pile of stones." Hajj Amin's delegation had gathered the impressive sum of £22,000 – more

---

* The Indian Hospice's last Sufi head was a sheikh of the Qadiri order named Abd al-Rahman Riyazi al-Din Babur bin Riyazi al-Hind. He lived a remarkable life. Born in India in 1881, he opposed Britain's colonial occupation as a young man and was forced to flee. He studied in Baghdad, then Cairo, and arrived in Jerusalem before 1912. As head of Jerusalem's Indian Hospice he fought the British again, and so had to escape Palestine with the Turkish army in 1917 in advance of British invasion. He ended up in Istanbul, where after imprisonment and torture (by the British, once again), he lived a long life as a scholar and translator, and died there in 1966.

than a million today – some of which perhaps went to the hospice. There was also money from the British authorities, and the Jerusalem Waqf department. Ansari travelled to and from India several times over the next decade or more, soliciting funds from the likes of the Nawab of Rampur and the Nizam of Hyderabad, then the richest person in the world. Both sponsored a wing.

"All the residents [of the hospice] were Indian. I felt as if I was living in India," Sheikh Munir has said of his 1930s childhood. "At that time people came by ship. They used to bring food, rice, even their salt. Salt! All from India. As soon as you entered the gate, the smell of Indian food, they were washing their clothes, hanging them here in the courtyard." After the hospice hosted Indian troops during the Second World War, and Palestinian refugees following the Nakba, Munir took over on his father's death in 1951. The 1950s and 1960s, he's said, were "golden years ... the place was full of spirit, full of joy, full of pilgrims all the time." But then, catastrophe.

During the war of June 1967 Israel bombarded the hospice, apparently in retaliation for fire from nearby. "I remember it perfectly," says Nazer, who was fourteen at the time. "Thirty-five, thirty-eight bombs. All the rubble came down on us. I was hit on my head" – he leans forward and makes me feel under his hair for the scar – "and my father was burned. He was pulling us out from under the rubble as bombs were falling. Each and every member of the family was injured. I lost my grandmother, my aunt and my cousin."

After burying the dead, surviving family members spent, in some cases, months recovering in hospital before emerging to pick up the pieces. Pilgrims were few and rebuilding work was complicated by the lack of diplomatic relations between India and the occupying power, Israel. Until India opened an embassy in 1992, allowing formal support to be reinstituted, Sheikh Munir got by on rental income from properties outside the compound, including twelve shops owned by the hospice inside Herod's Gate and residences nearby whose longstanding tenants include members of Jerusalem's Gypsy community, the Dom.

Uniquely for East Jerusalem, where most Palestinians are effectively stateless, the Ansari family, including Nazer – who has just retired after thirty-six years working for Britain's Ministry of Defense in Saudi Arabia – hold Indian citizenship. The hospice, as an Islamic *waqf* (endowment), nominally falls under Jordanian administration, but in fact comes under the protection of India – though it flies the Indian tricolor only when somebody important is visiting, Nazer says, so as not to provoke the neighbors. Yet its days as a lodge, open to pilgrims and the spiritually curious, seem to be over. The only guests the hospice receives now are those approved by India's embassy in Tel Aviv – parliamentarians, diplomats, official visitors. To all others, and to casual passersby, the gates are closed.

Nazer tries to explain the reticence about having inquisitive strangers wandering around. "We are surrounded," he says, and takes me up on the roof to point out where militantly nationalist Jewish Israeli settlers are encroaching into the neighborhood, house by house. Then he mentions the difficulties over the years with Palestinian neighbors: one who "annexed" a room, another who illegally added a window. "We are looked upon as foreigners, which they think gives them the permission to swallow us," he says.

The family's staying power is one of the most intriguing aspects of the story. In Sarna's book, Sheikh Munir reveals that his father, by then a Bombay-based scholar and political activist, was about forty-five when he arrived in Jerusalem, and left behind a wife and two daughters in his home village, north of Delhi. I try to imagine the depth and permanence of such a rupture; it's almost inconceivable. Nazer Ansari's dedication to his cause must have been all-consuming. Yet was he being used? Soon after arriving in Palestine he agreed to a local marriage arranged by the mufti, Hajj Amin.

"The mufti did not want him to go back to India," Sheikh Munir told Sarna. "He was afraid that if he went back, even to get his wife, he may not come back at all. Or his wife may join him and not like it here and then force him to go back. So he hatched a plan to find a Palestinian [wife] for him and keep him in Jerusalem forever."

Hajj Amin, vile, Machiavellian political operator that he was, seems to have viewed Nazer Ansari as a useful tool with which he could bind India to the Palestinian cause. But the marriage he set up did not last. After thirteen years, the couple separated. At each point in the tale's telling, Sarna elicits stories of heartbreak and resentment that continue to reverberate down the generations.

What stands out is how remote the hospice's links with religious practice have become. Unlike the Afghaniyya, or the Bukhariyya, or Jerusalem's other institutions rooted in Sufi traditions, this *zawiya* – preserver of the Chishti flame and Baba Farid's spiritual legacy – shows little evidence of worship. After its long line of Sufi sheikhs, it changed direction in 1924 with my host's grandfather, a political appointee. Its survival since then reflects the skill of Sheikh Munir in treading a delicate line of self-preservation between competing interests – Indian, Palestinian, Jordanian, Israeli; Muslim, non-Muslim and anti-Muslim – but I wonder at what cost. When I ask Nazer, who has a degree in Islamic theology from Cairo's Al-Azhar University, if he or the family call themselves Sufi, his response is unequivocal.

"No, no, no," he says quickly. "We are moderate, liberal, we are not fanatics at all. In order to be religious you don't have to knock your head five times a day, and have a beard reaching your belly button. This is not religion. If you'll ask me to define religion, I would tell you it's the fear of God in your heart. We have the fear of God in our hearts."

That sets me back, and I'm silent for a second.

So does the Indian Hospice maintain any sort of living connection today with Baba Farid? – I ask.

"No," says Nazer. But then he adds, quietly: "I mean, it's possible to rekindle the candle, but that's a headache."

I ask what he means, and he continues: "There are Sufis in Jerusalem. I have never got involved with those people, they are against my concepts in life. But they gather, they get together ... They asked to come here, but my father stood like a mountain. We don't want to go down this road ... We don't want to start something here, we don't want to provoke any side. We want to live in peace and we want to keep the place. It is extremely, extremely sensitive."

Nazer's meaning lies between his words. It makes me wonder what kind of horrific pressure this embattled family has been put under, and from how many different sides, that has made them conclude they cannot host spiritual seekers who wish to chant at the shrine of a saint, and must instead keep their doors closed for fear of dispossession. They have already been the targets of geopolitical game-playing once, in the 1920s and 1930s. Then in 1967 they were caught, literally, in deadly crossfire. Now they face hostility from acquisitive neighbors. No one could blame the Ansaris for wanting to keep their heads down for another generation or two. It is tragic that the eight-hundred-year remembrance of Baba Farid in Jerusalem has become collateral damage, atrophied now to a mere story of words heard only by visiting diplomats and inconstant journalists.

What a heartbreaking city this is. I thank Nazer and am shown to the gate. Outside, I sit on a low wall and dip into Navtej Sarna's book again. Baba Farid died at a grand old age, at his *zawiya* in 1266. Sarna quotes the words of Farid's successor Nizamuddin Auliya, one of India's greatest Sufis. "The door to his hospice was never closed. Silver, food and blessings due to the kindness of the Almighty Creator – all were distributed from there to all comers. Yet no one came to the sheikh for material assistance since he himself possessed nothing. What a marvellous power! What a splendid life!"

Ideas can be condemned, shrines abandoned. But Sufism has never been dependent on buildings or patterns of worship, the external expressions of a human experience that can be neither outlawed nor eradicated. Such forms simply serve as pointers towards what Sufis themselves might call a living reality that is not subject to the tides of human history, a presence that does not come and go.

And I remember a line of the Quran (28:88) that has always been cherished by Islam's mystics: *Everything will perish but His face.*

8

From the Women of Dom

STORIES OF BAB AL-ASBAT/LIONS GATE

THE GIRL DROPPED OUT OF SCHOOL when her mother died. It was a heart attack, they said. So young, only thirty-seven. The girl was about seven, and didn't understand what a heart attack was. Suddenly her father had become a widower, taking care of nine children – five boys and four girls. The girl's grandma helped raise her. Grandma was very kind, but she died only three years later, and after that it was much harder. The girl was sad. All of them were sad. It left a big impact. This wasn't the life they wanted.

The girl is grown. Her name is Amoun Sleem. She is from the women of Dom, born into a family that has lived in Jerusalem for more than two hundred years. In English she chooses to call herself a Gypsy, even though that word is emotive and can sometimes carry offensive overtones in Europe and elsewhere. But "Gypsy" is her preference and her prerogative. Dom is what Amoun's people call themselves. Their roots, like the roots of almost all the Gypsies, lie in India. In that country, a low-status caste of people who travel, and who earn a living from music and craft-making, was – and still is – known as Domba.

In irregular waves of migration beginning roughly 1,500 years ago, some Domba people began to move westwards. Some reached Armenia and the Caucasus around the eleventh century. They are the Lom, who now speak Lomavren. Some continued on into eastern and central Europe, and some of these kept moving, reaching northern and western Europe in the fifteenth and sixteenth centuries. They are the Rom (or Roma),* who now speak Romani. And some stayed in Turkey and Iran and Central Asia and the Arab lands of the Middle East, travelling independently or forcibly relocated from place to place by rulers or invading armies. They are the Dom and they speak Amoun's language, Domari.

Down the centuries the Dom reappear here and there, always on the edge of things. Brought to entertain the Shah of Persia as dancers and musicians. Exiled first to the Mediterranean coast, then to the islands of Greece, to be kept well away from power centers in Damascus and Baghdad. Employed as acrobats, fortune-tellers and bear handlers in Constantinople. Scraping a living in Cyprus selling nails and handmade belts.

Today there are maybe two million Dom, most in Turkey and Iran. There are sizeable communities in Jordan and Egypt, and there used to be many in Syria, before the war. Roughly twenty thousand Dom live across Gaza and the West Bank, Amoun estimates, plus maybe 1,000 or 1,500 in Jerusalem, about half of them inside the Old City. The Dom are Muslim (bar a very few Christians) and speak Arabic, and live within Palestinian communities, but Amoun is very clear: they are neither Palestinian, nor Israeli. They are Dom.

Almost everybody calls the Dom "Nawar" but Amoun clicks her teeth at that. "Nawar" derives from the Arabic word for fire. It has pejorative connotations of fire-worship. Perhaps that's because, before, people were envious of Dom blacksmithing skills, she says. Or maybe they just mixed up Dom with Zoroastrians. Nobody knows. But the word also has older meanings connected to deceit and witchcraft, and has come to stand for people lacking decency and civilized values. People who are dirty, living in filth, begging from others. Some translate it as "black," suggesting it refers to the Dom's often darker skin color. It's a racist slur that deliberately ropes together lots of different minorities, not only the Dom. But few peo-

---

* The English thought they had arrived from Egypt, hence the term "Gypsy."

ple consider the disrespect. They just say "Nawar" and spit. They don't recognize the Dom as part of society, Amoun says.

There is a lot of discrimination. Israelis dismiss the Dom as Arabs. But Arabs dismiss the Dom as "Nawar." Socially, politically and economically these people are at the bottom of every heap. Almost no Dom children leave school with qualifications. Perhaps two-thirds of Dom men are unemployed. Many of the rest earn a living as sanitation workers, clearing drains and sewers.

Amoun grew up among the Dom community that lives in the north-east corner of the Old City inside the Lions Gate,* in one room in a house right by the old city wall. People still call that area *Haret al "Nawar,"* the Gypsy Quarter. It's very precious to her. She thinks of it as her bolthole, her hideaway. Those streets were her home, and the compound around the Church of St. Anne, a few steps from her house, was her favorite place in the world when she was little. Whenever things got too much, she would retreat into those shady gardens to find peace and privacy, or sneak inside the church to listen to the pilgrim groups singing hallelujahs.

Amoun's parents couldn't read or write, so when the family got a letter, she'd be sent out to find a neighbor who would read it for them. It was so humiliating. She could see nobody really wanted to help, and it made her angry and ashamed to be put in the middle

---

* Jerusalem has pretty much always had an eastern gate, opening to the Kidron Valley and its water sources as well as to long-distance routes eastwards over the Mount of Olives into the desert towards Jericho. It's had a multitude of names – Valley Gate, Mount of Olives Gate, Jericho Gate, St. Stephen's Gate (the relics of the Christian martyr Stephen were moved near here in the twelfth century). It's also called the Gate of Our Lady Mary (*Bab Sittna Maryam*), after a tradition placing the birthplace of Jesus's mother – sanctified in Christianity, revered in Islam – nearby. The most common Arabic name is now *Bab al-Asbat*, Gate of the Tribes – which, confusingly, is also the name given to the gateway inside the walls fifty meters to the south that leads into Al-Aqsa. Early last century the British rebuilt the gate to create direct access for motor vehicles. Even today you can drive into the Old City here, all the way to Al-Wad Street. In English it's almost universally known as Lions Gate, after the stone-carved beasts (actually leopards) that were attached to the exterior wall during the gate's construction in the sixteenth century; they are the symbol of the Mamluk sultan Baybars – whose name means "noble leopard" – retrieved from an earlier building.

like that. She's never forgotten how abusive the teacher was to her at school when she was little. The teacher would stand her up in front of the whole class and shame her, calling her names like "Nawar" and "street urchin." Sometimes the teacher would hit Amoun. She would call her worthless, or say there was no point her being at school because she'd just grow up to be a prostitute and a beggar, like all "Nawar." When Amoun's mother died that was the last straw. Amoun ran away from school, and stayed away, for two years.

Finally, she did go back – but the very first day, the teacher pulled her by the ear so hard she lost her earring. From then on, she and her friend Latifah, another girl with dark skin, agreed that whatever the teachers did to them, they were going to laugh. At every punishment, Amoun and Latifah laughed and laughed. The head teacher called Amoun an insect and said she should be exterminated.

Amoun remembers her school uniform. Blue and white it was. Like prison clothes, she says. The day she graduated, she tore it to shreds. But she refused to see herself as a victim. Quite the opposite. She led a gang of girls in her neighborhood who fought back against boys who would bother them. She saw herself as someone who would never do what is expected.

She was always open to the world, always talking to foreigners and the tourists at St. Anne's church, selling them postcards. Maybe that's why her language skills are better than some other people's, she says. During and after school she worked as a cleaner at a Dutch guesthouse on the Mount of Olives. The money helped her through three years of college, where she qualified with a diploma in business administration.

She owes that spirit to her wonderful dad, she says. He was strict, but also kind and patient. He spent all his life trying to be a father and a mother, in one. Every year, Amoun would rename Mother's Day as Father's Day, and hunt around for some small gift she could afford for him. Socks are cheap, but useful. He got a lot of socks.

Her father would talk to Amoun about the skills the Dom brought to Jerusalem, like weaving reeds into mats, working with metal to make cutlery and sieves or fix cooking pots, or training horses. Amoun remembers watching her father's Gypsy guests carefully cutting at the bamboo that grew beside the house, then crafting bamboo flutes by hand and playing beautiful music.

Her father also gave her a lot of freedom from social traditions, including marriage. The usual Gypsy model, Amoun says, would be to marry his daughters off at fifteen or sixteen, but he let Amoun say no. The neighbors reckoned he thought he was better than them, that he had ideas above his station, but he didn't, Amoun says – he was just open-minded and wanted the best for his children. So he let Amoun choose. And she chose to stay single. She still is today, in her late forties. She doesn't feel sorry about it one bit, she says. Quite the opposite: her freedom and independence to decide her own path, are the most important things in her life.

Thanks to the kind and supportive staff at the Dutch guesthouse, Amoun had the chance to visit Europe – that first trip was more than twenty-five years ago now – which helped open her eyes to new possibilities. But still, she lost many friends, at school and afterwards, when they realized she was "Nawar." All her siblings have faced the same thing. Her three sisters also never married, and two of her five brothers married women who are not Dom. This comes from the open-mindedness of her father, she says. But other Dom people don't like it. Some ask Amoun why her brothers didn't take wives from within the community. She says she doesn't care what people say and neither do her brothers. They are happy with their choices, she says, and so is she. She loves all of her nieces and nephews.

This leads to what has become the major work of Amoun's life, trying to improve the situation for the Dom in Jerusalem. So often they've given up, she says. They have no hope to make a better life for their children, or to create change by finding new doors to open. But she has long been committed to trying to show her community that misery and poverty need not continue unbroken from generation to generation. The future can be new, she says. Her father understood the importance of education, and she wants to pass that on.

At the beginning, in 1999, she would just try to help people by distributing clothes and blankets, and by running informal classes to boost literacy and job skills. Her office was her bedroom. That was where the nonprofit Domari Society of Gypsies in Jerusalem began. Then, by meeting people from outside the community, she slowly started to develop wider networks. Volunteers arrived to help out. Small amounts of funding began to trickle in from donors. By chance she found a building available to rent in Shuafat, a low-income neighborhood north of the Old City, and the Domari Society moved there in 2005, expanding to become a community center, offering more classes and more support.

Now she and her team of volunteers offer Dom women access to vocational training and fresh sources of income from craft skills like embroidery and jewelry-making, hairdressing or cooking. Women – and even some men, she says – take literacy classes, to improve their reading and writing. The idea, she insists, has always been to try to help the Dom help themselves.

Amoun remembers her father speaking the Domari language sometimes, but it's hardly heard anymore. Everyone speaks Arabic, and Domari is getting lost. It's poorly documented. There are maybe as few as ten or twenty individuals left who are still fluent. That's another motivation for the society, to help keep Domari alive and support scholars who are able to study it.

So Amoun got the last laugh on those awful, sadistic teachers. Now she calls herself a warrior for education. Discrimination in school isn't as bad as it was when she was young, she says, but it still exists, and it still dissuades children from completing their studies. Amoun has put more than a hundred Dom children through the Domari Society's after-school program since it started, giving them support with homework and one-to-one tutoring for extra study in Arabic, mathematics and English. Some of those children have gone on to university. At the moment she has fifteen students enrolled, and two teachers coming in to help them.

But, equally importantly, she's taken on the role of changing minds about the Dom. She says too many Palestinian people stick to old stereotypes about the Gypsies being a closed community, unwelcoming to strangers. It's not true, she says: she'd welcome anyone willing to help or support. But nobody comes. In twenty years, Amoun says, not one official from the Palestinian Authority has knocked on her door to ask about the Domari Society or see if they can help. She gets some interest from Israeli academics and journalists, and she receives them because she says people need to know the hardships the Dom face, but she is adamant she doesn't want to take anything from them.

A key concern is raising awareness internationally about the situation of the Dom. There have been exhibitions and lectures, and Amoun has travelled abroad to collect awards. She always says yes to interview requests from the media, she says, because before the Domari Society few people even knew that the Dom existed. Her community was unseen and unheard. Now it has a voice. With the help of friends and supporters, in 2014 Amoun published a book in English called *A Gypsy Dreaming in Jerusalem*, to tell the story of her life and family, but also, she says, to help readers around the world understand Dom perspectives from the inside. Tourism is another way. Amoun has started hosting international tourist groups at the center in Shuafat. They eat, and talk. And hopefully buy some crafts. All of it helps take her message about the Dom to the world, as well as generating income for future sustainability.

But despite all this, she's faced huge opposition, not least from within the Dom community itself. Some say that she's trying to change Dom culture, or that she's seeking power and money for herself. She knows that people don't like how she's broken down gender barriers and challenged the community's patriarchal leadership. Some accuse her of corruption. They shun her and slander her. But, as she wrote in her book, she did not seek the pain of being a Gypsy, the pain of being a woman or the pain of people attacking her.

And there are still lots of attacks and violence within her own community. Things sometimes feel desperate to Amoun. But she tries to walk tall, she says, to live her life decently and honestly, to bring no disrespect to her two cultures, the Arabs and the Gypsies, and to encourage children and adults to be proud of their identity. That was missing for many years here, Amoun says. She is proud she's been able to help bring it back.

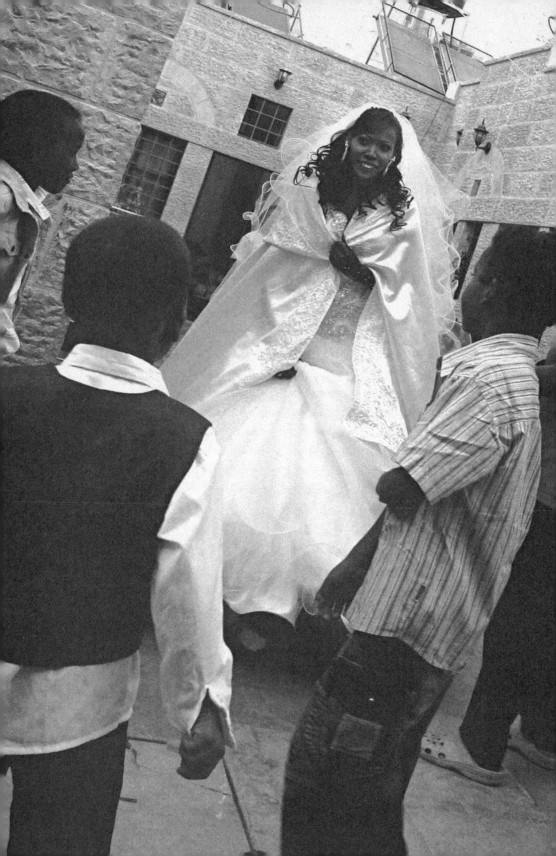

9

Aladdin Street

STORIES OF SLAVERY AND FREEDOM

THERE WAS ONCE A BLIND MAN called Aladdin who loved animals. Aladdin was special all his life, and even after he died people never forgot him. When he was still young and sighted he was trusted with dangerous, clandestine missions. When he got older and settled into a position of authority, he wielded his power so wisely and generously people began to talk about him as a sign of divine intervention, so determined was he to make life better for all. Folk even gave him a new, gently ironic (but religiously inspired and deeply respectful) nickname: "Someone who Sees Things Clearly."

You can give a nod to Aladdin today, if you'd like to, because he was real, and he's still sleeping the big sleep, more than seven hundred years on, behind a window looking onto the flagstoned street in Jerusalem that carries his name.

It's an old, complicated name, and an old, complicated street. I want to tell you about it.

"Aladdin" is formed of two parts in Arabic – *ala*, from a root meaning elevated or excelling, and *deen* with a long vowel sound, meaning religion, which carries the definite article *al* (in this instance, elided into its noun as *ad-deen*). It translates as "the nobility of faith," or "devout," or "excelling in religion," and is more usually transliterated with its two parts separated, as Ala ad-Din, or Alaa Ed Deen, or a dozen other spellings.

We in the West know Aladdin from the legend about the lamp, the genie and the princess. And that – Hollywood notwithstanding – is down to a rather amazing man you probably haven't heard of, named Hanna Diyab. A poor boy from Syria, only nineteen or twenty years old, Diyab had been working as a guide and interpreter for a French expedition to the Middle East. It had involved lots of scrambling around, exploring strange caves in the desert, unearthing magical treasures: one time, near Idlib, he'd watched a goatherd being sent into a hard-to-access tomb-cave and then emerging shortly after with a ring and an old lamp. He'd accompanied the charismatic expedition leader Paul Lucas across North Africa, then to Livorno, Marseilles and finally Paris, where in 1708 he'd been introduced to the French king Louis XIV at the dazzling royal palace in Versailles.

In late March the following year, on the hunt for a new job, he was introduced to an old man – Diyab never names him – who was engaged on some project translating ancient works from Arabic into French. The man, a librarian, asked him for help, and wondered if he knew any stories. Stories? Ha! The old man was in luck. Diyab was born and raised in Aleppo, famed for its coffeehouse culture, its literary cosmopolitanism and its professional storytellers. He could spin yarns till his tongue grew hair.* The old man was delighted. They met every few days for a month or so, and Diyab gave him story after story, including, on 5 May 1709, one about a poor boy from the East who gets wrapped up in all sorts of adventures to do with a charismatic sorcerer, a ring and an old lamp unearthed in a strange cave in the desert, and a dazzling royal palace.

That much we know. Where the Aladdin story came from (we have no prior record of it, orally or in manuscript) and how much of the first printed version came verbatim from Diyab and how much from the old librarian's editorial embellishment, we can only speculate.

---

* An idiom in Syrian Arabic, meaning talking at length regardless of whether an interlocutor is paying attention or not. The phrasing is mine, not Diyab's.

Shortly afterwards, perhaps tired of seeking favors in Paris, Diyab went back home to Aleppo. He got married, raised a family and lived a full life trading fabrics in the souk. It's not certain if he ever knew that the old librarian he'd met in Paris, Antoine Galland, was archaeologist, scholar and antiquary to Louis XIV. By 1709, when they met, Galland had already won wide acclaim for the eight volumes of stories derived from Persian and Sanskrit folk tales that he'd translated from medieval Arabic manuscripts. They had been published in French as *Les mille et une nuit** (*The Thousand and One Nights*, a rendering of the Arabic title *Alf layla wa layla*), translated almost immediately into English under the exoticized title of *The Arabian Nights Entertainments*. They were an international success. But after a decade of slog, Galland was running dry. For Volume 8, his publisher filled the gaps with stories translated by a rival from a different, Turkish collection, which had annoyed Galland. Meeting Diyab put more fuel in his tank. Galland wrote up "Aladdin" and other tales that came direct from his Syrian source (including "Ali Baba and the Forty Thieves"), eventually publishing four more volumes, the last posthumously in 1717. All the stories, but particularly Aladdin, caused a sensation, and have colored cultural and political contacts between the West and the Arab world ever since, fuelling prejudices and stereotypes galore.

Shamefully, Galland never credited Diyab once. (Incidentally, neither did the expedition leader Lucas in his memoirs.) For more than a hundred years no one even knew Diyab existed. For another hundred, after the discovery of Galland's diary in 1880, which mentions Diyab but only in passing, scholars wondered if Galland had made him up. Then, in 1993, historian Jérôme Lentin unearthed Diyab's own memoir in the Vatican library, where, since the first few pages had been torn out, it had been miscatalogued as anonymous. It is, as you might expect, full of color, character and vivid dialogue, written – or, more likely, dictated – by Diyab when he was about seventy-five in the form of an extended series of traveller's yarns reflecting on his adventures more than half a century before. It has been published only very recently (2015 in

---

* Singular *nuit* in eighteenth-century French; plural *nuits* today.

French, 2017 in Arabic, 2021 in English). *Nights* scholar Paulo Lemos Horta highlighted Diyab's role in his introduction to Yasmine Seale's sparkling new English translation of Aladdin, which came out in 2018. Only now, in our own generation, is the world beginning to understand just how important Hanna Diyab (and, by extension, Syria's vast oral literary tradition) really is for Western conceptions of Arab culture.

See? A cracking tale. But Aladdin, whether the story rightfully belongs to Diyab or not, is just a name. Countless people today, and for centuries past, have been called Aladdin, Ala ad-Din, Alauddin, Alaa Al Din, Ala Edin, Alaeddine and many other renderings of the same original. Who does Jerusalem's Aladdin Street commemorate?

Our Jerusalem Aladdin, the governor, the blind man who saw clearly, was probably born in the early 1220s, named Ala ad-Din Aydughdi. He was a Mamluk, and the Mamluks – who controlled Jerusalem and, more widely, Syria until 1517 – entirely changed the face of the city. Jerusalemites today live with the built legacy of Mamluk culture.*

"Mamluk" literally means "one who is owned," but the Mamluks shouldn't be understood as slaves in the usual interpretation of that word. The origins of the term lie as far back as the ninth century, when Islam's early political and military elites began searching beyond the borders of their empire for resources, particularly human resources, to help shore up their rule. Over two or three centuries, they fostered the growth of a human trafficking network, which was focused on non-Muslims from the frontier regions of eastern Turkey, the Caucasus and Central Asia who had been captured in battle or on raids against resistant tribes or, as the system developed,

---

* There were two Mamluk governors called Ala ad-Din Aydughdi in Jerusalem in the thirteenth century. The other one ruled Safad and Aleppo before a bout of jail time and then retirement to the city. He was known as Al-Kubaki and his tomb, the Kubakiyya, still stands in Jerusalem's Mamilla cemetery, west of the Old City. He's not the same Ala ad-Din Aydughdi as our Ala ad-Din Aydughdi.

simply sold direct to traffickers. These *mamluk* boys and young men were brought to the centers of power – notably Damascus and Cairo – in service of their owner, to be converted to Islam and schooled to peak performance in military skills. They formed elite protection units of highly trained individuals who, crucially, lacked any social or communal loyalties in their new homes, other than to their masters and each other.

Beside the issue of gender, race was also a factor: Mamluks, though nominally enslaved, had much higher social status than the millions of Black people trafficked at this time from Africa to the Middle East for agricultural labor or to perform menial duties. Such enslaved individuals could not carry weapons, as Mamluks could, and were invariably dismissed in speech as *abd* ("slave"; plural *abeed*), a term still freighted with racism across the Arab world today.

The Mamluks became renowned as mounted archers. As their military skill grew, their prominence in the army and throughout society also grew. They became a dominant caste of enslaved warrior knights, deployed everywhere from Egypt to India. By 1250, when the Ayyubid dynasty, which had ruled since Salah ad-Din's victories over the European Crusaders, was splintering, Turkish Mamluks were perfectly positioned to assassinate the son of the Ayyubid sultan and seize power across Egypt and Syria for themselves. The state they established lasted over 250 years.

After having been a focus of conquest, Jerusalem gratefully stepped back from the frontline. The city was of little strategic or political relevance to the power brokers in Cairo, and their unchallenged military dominance provided longed-for stability. Merchants, scholars and mystics started returning from all over the Muslim world, and Jerusalem's restoration as a focus for spirituality led to a parade of notables lavishing it with patronage. Islamic schools and colleges, markets, fountains, bathhouses and other public and private buildings went up, rejuvenating and reconsecrating the city after the aberration of Crusader rule. Much of this new building survives today.

The economy boomed: local production of textiles and olives, including olive-oil soap, was enhanced by imports such as leather from Portugal, cloth from Venice, Persia and North Africa, and rugs and blankets from Turkey and Yemen. Rights of minorities were protected: Christians and Jews lived freely, and visited as pilgrims. Jerusalem became an early Florida – a choice posting for Mamluk retirees, and also the perfect backwater where those who had fallen out of favor with the biggest of big cheeses could be sidelined.

Viceroys ruled Jerusalem, appointed initially from Damascus then direct from Cairo. They were mostly military officers, but also included a number of religious judges, yet decisive power often lay with an oligarch class of princes. This is where our man Ala ad-Din comes in. He was trafficked most likely as a young boy in the late 1220s. Going by Mamluk history and his family name, which is of Turkic origin (it means "son of the rising moon"), it's possible he came from Crimea or the Caucasus. He would have been brought to Egypt and installed in the military barracks at the hilltop citadel overlooking Cairo, cut off from wider society and trained intensively hard. We know little of his early life, but following the Mamluk coup in 1250, he moved into the service of famed military commander Baybars – also a Mamluk, who had been trafficked to Cairo from somewhere around Astrakhan in the modern Russia-Kazakhstan borderlands. Baybars excelled, rising to the highest echelons of the army and eventually, in 1260, to the throne as sultan.

It was soon after 1262, when he was sent by Baybars on a secret mission to arrest the governor of Damascus, that Ala ad-Din's life changed forever. We don't know how, but he lost his sight. No record of his personal anguish survives. He next appears as one of the oligarchs, shunted off to Jerusalem. There he served as governor, taking the title "Superintendant of the Two Noble Harams": a *haram* is a holy sanctuary and the title refers to Haram al-Sharif and Haram al-Ibrahimi – that is, Al-Aqsa in Jerusalem and the Ibrahimi mosque in nearby Hebron, built over the burial place of Abraham (Prophet Ibrahim, as he is known in Islam).

This period – the 1260s and the couple of decades following – was a time of plenty: trade was flourishing, as was the reputation of Jerusalem as a center of religious study. Governor Ala ad-Din appears not to have let his disability hold him back. In Jerusalem he had the platform around the Dome of the Rock paved and may also have renovated Al-Aqsa's ablutions facilities as part of a wider scheme fixing public water supplies in the city. In Hebron he secured food resources by building new ovens, mills and storage warehouses, and increased distribution of welfare to the poor. He seems to have had a special affinity for animals: he was trained on horseback as a young man, but even into old age he held particular renown as a breeder of horses. It was said he loved his animals so much he was able to recognize each individual by its distinctive smell and gait. People gave him the tender nickname *Al-Basir*. That means "All-Seeing" when used as one of Islam's ninety-nine names of God but is perhaps better translated in this context as astute or clear-sighted.

Governor Ala ad-Din also established endowments for public institutions, including, in 1267/68, soon after his arrival in Jerusalem, a *ribat* (pilgrim hospice) for impoverished men and women arriving to pray at Al-Aqsa. The Ribat Ala ad-Din still stands today as one of the city's oldest Mamluk buildings, an array of cells around a central courtyard just a few steps from the entrance into the Al-Aqsa compound known as Bab al-Majlis (Council Gate) or Bab al-Nazir or Nadhir (Inspector's Gate). When the governor died, in the late summer of 1294, he was laid to rest in a side room within that same hospice. And there he still lies, behind a barred window looking out onto *Tariq Ala ad-Din* (Aladdin Street) – named not for the man but for his tomb, which over the centuries became venerated as the mausoleum of a saint. Pray beside it and God answers your prayers, wrote the Jerusalemite historian Mujir ad-Din in 1495.

But that's not the end of this story, or of the curious links between this one modest building on this one short street – only ninety meters from end to end – and the long history of enslaved people in Jerusalem. Fifteen years after the Ribat Ala ad-Din opened its doors, another hospice – similar, but larger – was completed directly across the narrow lane. It was named Ribat al-Mansuri for the new sultan, Al-Mansur Qalawun. Both *ribats* flourished, and by the sixteenth or seventeenth century they'd gained a new function, converted into permanent lodgings for people described as *Takarna* (also spelled in English as Tukarneh, Tukarina and in other ways).

Who the Takarna are takes us into a story of Africa.

War Jabi (or, in some readings, *the* War Jabi – it may be a title rather than a personal name) was the first ruler in the West African Sahel to adopt Islam, in 1035. He had authority as king of Takrur, an independent state established in the semi-arid country that flanks the lower Senegal River, on the border between modern-day Senegal and Mauritania.

Mass conversion of the king's subjects quickly brought Takrur new links of culture, politics and trade with the wider world of Muslim Africa to the north and east. In the years after, Takrur became prosperous enough and confident enough to challenge and eventually subdue the great Ghana Empire, for several centuries the regional superpower, founded on dizzying wealth from gold and salt.

Takrur faded, but its Muslim status had already propelled it into the consciousness of Arab and Muslim geographers and historians, observing from beyond the great sandy expanse of the Sahara (*sahra* is the Arabic word for desert). Some even visited Takrur, to write reports and compile maps. Interest in the region grew rapidly, and the name of the country became an Arabic shorthand for West Africa as a whole. The adjectival form *Takruri* (plural *Takarir*) or *Takruni* (plural *Takarin* or *Takarna*) morphed into a broad-brush descriptor for any Black, Muslim person with origins in West Africa – or, in some usages, central or eastern Africa too. That looseness persists to this day: some will hazily place Takrur in the deserts and arid highlands of Darfur, where modern-day Chad and Sudan meet, thousands of kilometers distant from Senegal.

African Muslims may have been visiting Jerusalem from the earliest days of Islam, but the tradition of coming to the city after completing the *hajj* to Mecca only really took off in the fifteenth century. And, as always, some pilgrims chose to settle. During the Ottoman period, as also in Mecca and Medina, Africans – or "Takarna" – resident in Jerusalem found jobs as police enforcers and security guards for the colleges and residential courtyards that clustered around the edges of the Al-Aqsa compound, and also as gatekeepers ensuring that non-Muslims did not enter the compound itself. These loyal employees needed somewhere to live, and the Ottoman authorities selected the two *ribats* of Ala ad-Din and Mansuri (the former now known as Ribat al-Basiri, after Ala ad-Din's nickname). This small section of a small street became a center of African settlement in the very heart of Jerusalem. As under the Mamluks, social stratification gave the free Muslim "Takarna" higher status than Jerusalem's many enslaved non-Muslim Africans, who lived where they did without choice.

More changes swept through the narrow street in the last century. It's not clear where the "Takarna" had been relocated, but by the time the British displaced the Ottomans in 1917 the two *ribats* had been converted into a prison, to cope with fallout from the growing Arab resistance to Ottoman rule. Ribat al-Mansuri had become a holding pen for those with short sentences or awaiting judgment, while Ribat al-Basiri housed lifers and those condemned to death, thereby gaining another name along the way – *Habs al-Dam*, the Prison of Blood. Soon after taking power, the British moved the prison away to the Russian Compound outside the walls of the Old City.

"At that time you know, Amin al-Husseini – he would become the mufti of Jerusalem – his six bodyguards, they were Africans." Musa Qous, tall, glasses pushed up on his forehead, quick to smile, is standing in a room within Ribat al-Mansuri, a long hall of rough stone divided into five bays by four squat columns. Notwithstanding the new tiled floor and a bit of touching up here and there, the structure of the interior is pretty much how it would have been when Ala ad-Din Aydughdi stood here. "The mufti was in conflict with the British then. They chased him inside the mosque [Al-Aqsa] and shot dead one of his bodyguards, a man called Jibril, but the others helped him escape to Silwan and then outside the country."

Musa is talking, I think, about 1920, when Amin al-Husseini was implicated in fomenting violent protests. The British authorities tried him *in absentia* and sentenced him to ten years in prison, before upending their own policy by issuing a pardon and appointing him mufti the following year. "In return for the help from the bodyguards, the mufti used his influence with the Waqf.* Since then, Africans have lived here in these two courtyards. We are protected, and we pay a [nominal] rent to the Waqf."

It's an extraordinary connection, and an unlikely chain of events, that nonetheless helped ensure the continuity of Jerusalem's centuries-long African presence in what's commonly called the Bab al-Majlis neighborhood, right at the gates of Al-Aqsa.

Musa is a journalist, working the late shift at *Al-Quds*, translating English news reports into Arabic for the morning edition. He's lived all his life in Bab al-Majlis as part of the *Jaliyya al-Ifriqiyya*, the African Community, that won the right to settle a hundred years ago. He also volunteers to help run the African Community Society, a grassroots local organization founded in 1983 that punches far above its weight in terms of social impact and visibility among the wider Palestinian community.

"More than two hundred people live here, most of them kids. There are about twenty-eight families," Musa says, referring to Ribat al-Mansuri. Slightly fewer live in Ribat al-Basiri, he adds, estimating that something like 450 people form the whole community.

These two Mamluk *ribats* are full of life, with children and mothers and shouts and laughter and cooking. Both courtyards, formerly large open spaces, are now crammed with modern housing, built with support from Taawon, a Palestinian NGO that draws international funding to help restore Jerusalem's buildings. Few people here can afford renovation costs themselves: estimates suggest around three-quarters of Palestinians in Jerusalem live below the poverty line. Within the *ribats*, narrow alleys now thread

---

* The Muslim religious authority that controls property endowments.

between unmarked doors and walls of stone or concrete for only a few meters before reaching a dead end: the pressure on space doesn't allow for throughways. Every corner is occupied, rising three and four stories overhead. "We consider ourselves Afro-Palestinians," says Musa. "We are Palestinian, but we have African roots. We have built here in order to keep our residency rights in Jerusalem."

There are African Muslim communities of varying backgrounds and histories outside Jerusalem – in Gaza, Jericho, Haifa, Jaffa – but the families living in the two *ribats* originate from four specific areas: Senegal at the westernmost edge of the continent, and Nigeria, Chad and Sudan* stretching towards the east. Many came after performing *hajj*, some then choosing to volunteer with the Syrian-led Arab Liberation (or Arab Salvation) Army in 1948 and staying on after defeat. They are, and, as Musa emphasizes, always have been, free. Other African communities in and around Jerusalem may have roots in slavery, he says, but not the people of Bab al-Majlis.

"Our older generation used to get in fights with people about this," says Musa in his easy, soft-spoken way, crow's-feet crinkling the corners of his eyes. "My father came from Chad. People would say *abeed* ["slaves"] and call this place *Habs al-Abeed* ["Prison of Slaves"] or *Haret al-Abeed* ["Slave Quarter"] and [my father's generation] would have to say no, we came here voluntarily, as pilgrims. Now we rarely hear this word *abeed*. Because of our activity in the Palestinian community, in the last ten or twenty years we succeeded in changing this name. If you ask anyone about this place now, they will say *Jaliyya al-Ifriqiyya*, not *abeed*."

That activity – open and accessible to all – is a source of pride. Manar Idris, from the African Community Society, describes a children's club run for under-twelves, designed to combat high drop-out rates among Palestinian students by offering help with

---

* There may be confusion over nomenclature. Palestinian researcher Husni Shaheen in 1984 identified the four areas as Senegal, Nigeria, Chad and "French Sudan," a distinct colonial term which equates more or less to modern Mali. A related term in Arabic, *Bilad as-Sudan*, meaning Lands of the Black People, is vague, referring to a sub-Saharan region stretching all across the continent from west to east. "Sudan" may not always refer to the modern-day republic, and might be better understood as western/central Africa. For more, see the notes to this chapter.

homework, emotional support from a social worker and space for leisure activities and social interaction. She outlines programs to strengthen bonds of identity between Palestinian young people living inside and outside Jerusalem, as well as mentoring schemes, skills courses such as sewing workshops for women, and grassroots projects to build links between neighborhoods across the Old City. The hall in Ribat al-Mansuri was recently renovated to serve as a community hub, hosting exhibitions and arts events as well as seminars and workshops. It draws outsiders to Ala ad-Din Street, raising the community's profile and providing an independent source of income.

But the respect shown by wider society to Jerusalem's African community also stems from political action. Several individuals have played significant roles in Palestinian resistance to Israel's occupation. Nasser Qous, Musa's brother, heads the Jerusalem section of the Palestinian Prisoners Society, supporting Palestinians in the Israeli justice system. Fatima Barnawi, of Nigerian descent, served ten years in Israeli jail for a failed bombing attempt in 1967 before joining the Palestinian national movement and becoming the head of the Palestinian Authority's women's police force in the 1990s. She died in 2016. Mahmoud Jaddeh and his cousin Ali Jaddeh both served seventeen years in Israeli jail for a 1968 bomb attack when they were members – Mahmoud aged twenty, Ali aged eighteen – of the secular, left-wing Popular Front for the Liberation of Palestine. Both, now in their seventies, are freelance political tour guides, explaining Palestinian perspectives to visitors, and have become well-known Jerusalem characters.

The community's location, steps away from Al-Aqsa, also plays a role. Afro-Palestinian youth see themselves as a line of defense for the whole Old City community and are often first on the scene when there are clashes inside the mosque compound. This makes them the targets of Israeli police. Many have served prison terms, which, as Musa explains, often rules out decent jobs thereafter. "We are not very compliant people," he says. "Most of the youth are unemployed." He recalls how, at one point, he and his three brothers were all in prison at the same time. "Every Friday, my mother would come to visit us all," he says, rubbing the stubble on his chin and chuckling. "It's not funny, but we are used to laughing at these stories, because we have nothing else. They are difficult times, but they pass."

Mahmoud Jaddeh, born in 1948, remembers growing up in one of the original cells around the edge of the Mamluk courtyard of Ribat al-Basiri, his family of eight occupying one room. "I believe at that time I was happier, much more, than this time," he has said. "We were living as one family. We can share everything together. We have condolences that we all share. If somebody got married we all shared. I remember my father, when he used to come from work, he used to ask my mother if she cooked that day. We rarely cooked because we were very poor, but if she said yes, then the second question was: 'Did you send something to our neighbors?' Because if we cook, for sure our neighbors would smell it, and maybe they don't have food. How could we enjoy our food if at the same time our neighbors are hungry?"

Mahmoud's cousin Mohammed, who came to Jerusalem in the 1940s, spoke of the same era in a 1997 interview. "When I arrived there was a big war going on between Germany and England," he said. "But it didn't affect us much." His family's journey began before that, and far away. Mohammed was born in the Chadian capital N'Djamena, then known as Fort-Lamy. His family was Hausa – Africa's largest ethnic group – and as a young boy he spent five years studying the Quran at schools in northeastern Nigeria. Around the age of fifteen, he and his uncle started walking. They walked east for two months, across Chad and Sudan, until they reached the Eritrean coast. They found passage across the Red Sea to Yemen. Then they started walking north, to Mecca for the *hajj*, then to Medina, then to Jerusalem. If you add it up, it must have been five thousand kilometers altogether, maybe more.

"I was married [in Jerusalem] when I was about twenty," he said. "My wife had been born here. But her father was Fulani, born in Nigeria. He did as I did, marrying an Arabic-speaking woman."

Today, all these lines are getting blurred. A hundred years of intermarriage, along with cultural and political assimilation, means that many in the Afro-Palestinian community, now in its third generation, freely recognize a complex layering of identity. "I'm an Arab and I'm an African," says Mahmoud Jaddeh. "At the same time, for example, my mother has two sisters, one is a villager, one is a bedouin – so I am from the city, the village and the desert. I live these three things." Musa Qous speaks even more plainly. "I am Black, and Arab, and Muslim," he says. "The Jaddeh family and the Qous family are both from the Salamat tribe in Chad. The first generation [who came to Jerusalem] used to speak [Hausa and other] African languages. But because our mothers are Palestinian, we – the second generation – didn't learn these languages, only Arabic. With the intermarriage with the Palestinian community, little by little in fifty years' time you won't find a Black person here."

It strikes me that of all the many migrations into pre–Second World War Palestine, the African migration has been studied the least. Why, for instance, has the twentieth-century experience of two marginalized Muslim communities of color – the Africans and the Dom – been so different? The Dom, like other disempowered groups in Jerusalem, are taking concrete steps to try to preserve their cultural heritage, but the African community has lost much of theirs in the space of fifty years, apparently without regrets.

British writer Nikesh Shukla helped develop the thesis of the "Good Immigrant." It says that immigrants are automatically assumed to be bad people – bad for society, bad for the economy and/ or just bad in general – until they somehow "earn" the right to be called good and treated fairly by the majority population. For mainstream Palestinian society, it seems, the Dom – despite having been present for centuries, settling, speaking Arabic, sharing community – haven't reached the mark and so remain "bad," still ostracized and dehumanized with racist slurs. By contrast, the immigrant African community – also settled, also Arabic-speaking, also community-oriented – is deemed to have done enough to merit acceptance. Much, or all, of the difference seems to rest on each community's engagement in acts of resistance to Israel. The Dom try to withdraw from political engagement to occupy a tiny space *between* Palestinians and Israelis, suffering grievously from both sides as a result. The African community has thrown itself wholeheartedly into Palestinian national politics, also suffering hardships, injustices and bereavements but able to claim a moral standing that has overcome antipathy.

It's a point not lost on the Israeli authorities, who have tightened their control over Bab al-Majlis in recent years. In addition to the checkpoint at the street's eastern end by the Al-Aqsa gate, armed police now also stand ninety meters away at the street's western end, where it meets the market thoroughfare Al-Wad Street. They effectively seal off the neighborhood. Only residents, and sometimes older Muslim Jerusalemites, can pass, usually after questioning. Others must show permission, or be escorted. Tourists are barred from entering what is a public street.

The extra checkpoint raises tensions and has had a devastating impact on the street's half-dozen small businesses, who now see no tourist traffic and instead must rely on selling knickknacks to worshippers passing to and fro between prayer times. The community's social programs, workshops and after-school clubs – reliant on ease of access – are often suspended for months at a time. Even from within Palestinian society, historian Yasser Qous notes how slurs such as *abeed* remain "oddly frequent," as does generic labelling of Black people as "Sudanese" or *Takarir*. "Other Palestinians perceive them as a single entity [but Jerusalem's] West African descendants are far from constituting a homogeneous group," he writes.

Faced with the extra stress and overcrowding, Musa says, some in the community are moving away, to the suburbs or to towns such as Ludd and Ramla, west of Jerusalem, and Rahat in the south. Dispersal is helping to forge links with other Black communities. Musa describes cordial relations between the Afro-Palestinians and Jerusalem's Ethiopian Christian congregations, as well as with a group known as the Black Hebrews, founded by African Americans in the 1960s in the Israeli town of Dimona. But he draws a sharp contrast with Israel's substantial Ethiopian Jewish community, who – like all Israelis – serve in Israel's army. "We don't have any relation with them at all, because of their military connection," he says.

Why does Musa stay? He offers a familiar Jerusalemite metaphor. "If you take a fish from the sea it will die. Jerusalem is my sea. I can't live outside it. There's a special feeling you get when you walk in the Old City. When I leave my work at the newspaper around midnight, and arrive back at Damascus Gate, quite often I just stop and look. You feel secure, even though there are many settlers, and soldiers. It's a feeling I can't describe. I can't live anywhere else."

Lots of Palestinians express *sumud*, a hard-to-translate word that is often rendered as "steadfastness," particularly in the face of hardship – the willingness to persist against the odds, to take the long view, to keep your eyes on the prize. Musa's attachment to Jerusalem is the very definition of *sumud*.

Back outside the two *ribats* again, I pause once more at Ala ad-Din Aydughdi's window to give him a quick nod, and to reach back across the centuries for a second to ask him what home really means for any of us. (There's no reply.) Children are scampering to and fro across the lane. I peek through the Bab al-Majlis gateway at the glorious open expanse of the Al-Aqsa compound beyond. A woman, having just left the mosque, pauses to buy a juice.

Next to Ala ad-Din's window, I rest my hand on another monumental chunk of Mamluk architecture sandwiched between there and the gate, a school founded around sixty years after Ala ad-Din by a particularly adept fighter and political operator named Saif ad-Din Manjak al-Yusufi. The Manjakiyya, as it's known, straddles the edge of the Haram: entry is from a relatively narrow south-facing frontage on Ala ad-Din Street but it extends a long way back and its upper rooms are built on top of the beautiful portico that runs along the western side of the Haram.

For something like 550 years the Manjakiyya functioned as a *madrasa* (school), but after a remodelling in 1921–22 it now houses the offices of the Department of Islamic Endowments in Jerusalem, known for short as the Waqf. This bureaucratic body, which in theory has sole authority to administer the day-to-day running of the Al-Aqsa compound, is independent of Palestinian or Israeli control and instead is affiliated with Jordan's

Ministry of Awqaf and Islamic Affairs. Jordan expanded the Waqf's ruling council in 2019, and again in 2021, to include represent-atives of the Palestinian Authority and Jerusalemite community leaders, in an effort to boost the body's legitimacy. Its presence here reflects the historic claim of Jordan's Hashemite monarchy to be custodian of Jerusalem's holy places, even though, in reality, the affairs of Al-Aqsa are administered by a delicate balance of trade-offs between a welter of competing interests, the Waqf only one among them.

The Manjakiyya is not open to the public and the Waqf is not the easiest office in the world to contact, but there's a good reason why you might want to try. All the gates giving public access into the Al-Aqsa compound are guarded on the external (street) side by Israeli armed police, and on the internal (Haram) side by Waqf officials. If you are Muslim, and you have already gained access to Jerusalem – a near impossibility for many Palestinians – you may enter at any time through any of nine gates ranged around the northern and western walls, subject always to Israel's rigid control over each gate's opening hours and its often arbitrarily imposed temporary restrictions on admittance by age, gender or other factors. If the Israeli police on duty suspect you of not being Muslim – which they judge by appearance – they may demand you show ID and/or submit to the humiliation of proving your religion to them by reciting the *Shahada* (declaration of faith) or *Fatiha* (first chapter of the Quran) before allowing you to pass.

Guidebooks and the internet will advise that non-Muslims may enter Al-Aqsa only via a tenth gate, Bab al-Magharba (Gate of the North Africans) – and then only on a limited schedule, usually for three hours in the morning and one hour in the afternoon, five days a week. These periods are often tense, less for the straggles of tourists that show up than for the presence of roving bands of religious Jews, often escorted by Israeli security, who enter the compound for political and ideological reasons.

Dictating non-Muslim admittance like this is an Israeli policy, instituted unilaterally in 2003. From the Jordanian period until 2000, when the Waqf controlled admittance under the Status Quo, non-

Muslims could also enter via other gates. *A Brief Guide to al-Haram al-Sharif, Jerusalem*, published by the Supreme Muslim Council in 1927 under British rule, states: "Admission may best be gained by the gate known as Bab al-Silsileh." Under Jordanian rule in the 1960s, the Supreme Awqaf Council published *A Brief Guide to the Dome of the Rock and Al-Haram Al-Sharif*, a stapled handbook whose back cover is numbered, with the top corner obliquely perforated, as if to be torn off: presumably it doubled as brochure and ticket. It doesn't specify any gates for tourist entry. Six more guides from 1954 to 1984 follow suit, while later guidebooks identify several gates open to non-Muslims under Waqf auspices – the *Rough Guide* (1989), for example: "Entry to non-Muslims is permitted only through four of the gates – Bab al-Ghawanimeh, Bab al-Naazir, Bab al-Silsileh, Bab al-Magharebeh."*

The Waqf's official stance remains that non-Muslims may enter the compound only under their auspices, and that entering via the Israeli checkpoint at Bab al-Magharba is a violation of the Status Quo. So you can, in theory – indeed, the Waqf say, you *should* – ask the Waqf for advance permission in writing to enter the Haram via another gate. In practice I've never managed this, and the last time I tried I was met with incredulity. Even if you succeeded, you'd have to run the gauntlet of Israeli police at whichever gate you choose, who are likely to be disbelieving. Novelist Ahdaf Soueif tells of how, in 2010, she secured Waqf permission for herself and a group of visiting writers to enter at Bab al-Asbat, only for them to be barred by Israeli police at the gate, notwithstanding intervention by a Waqf official. Before and since, Soueif's literary groups have been forced to enter only via the Israeli checkpoint at Bab al-Magharba. "That's the gate the settlers come through with the soldiers," Soueif reports a mosque official telling her. "Trouble comes through that gate."

A man is sitting on the shaded steps of the Manjakiyya, smoking, while I'm taking my time looking up at the three-story façade of

---

* See the notes to this chapter for full details of all the guidebooks cited here.

stone blocks opposite it. This is what was once called the Wafa'iyya, a Sufi lodge related to the religious order founded here by the Abul-Wafa family in the 1380s, but which in the eighteenth century became the property of Sheikh Mohammed ibn Budeir, a prominent scholar. It is very old, probably built soon after the Crusaders were ejected. One of its doorways, narrow, with a pointed arch, has a plaque over it noting the presence of the Budeiri Library, "established in 1180 H" (H denotes *hijri*, meaning the Islamic calendar; 1180 equates to 1766–67 in the Gregorian calendar). The library is one of Jerusalem's most important private manuscript collections. I've never yet had the chance to see it. Just along from it, another door, tucked almost out of sight immediately beside the gate into Al-Aqsa, is marked "Al Budeiri House, built 572 H [1176–77]."

"Go on," the smoking man says, watching me. "She's alright."

Sorry? Who's alright?

"The lady. They live upstairs. It's a huge house. Go on, you can ring the bell. She's alright."

I ring the bell.

An ancient entryphone crackles. "Ye-es?"

And that, amazingly, is how I meet Al-Shaima al-Budeiri, speed-talking matriarch of one of Jerusalem's grand families, and her cats. At least, it's amazing to me. In truth it was a very Jerusalem thing to happen.

"This one thinks he's a lion," she says upstairs, as a ginger ball of fluff meows like a toad and stretches full-length before me on a vast, well-stuffed sofa in a vain attempt to melt my cold, cold heart. Others sashay across the decorative floor tiles as we chat, rubbing themselves against curlicued table legs of dark, solid wood. I wonder to myself what it took to get all this furniture up those stairs.

Nobody I've ever met talks faster than Al-Shaima al-Budeiri. When I listened back to the recording I'd made, I had to check that I hadn't selected double speed by mistake. Cats and coffee, I thought. Cats and coffee.

Mrs. Budeiri sits me down to explain she is the sixth generation of her family to live here. "Al-Shaima, Abdullah, Tawfiq, Hamid, Abdullah, Sheikh Mohammed ibn Budeir." She reels off the names between herself and her forebear, turning over a finger for each generation. Then she tells me the story of how Mohammed ibn Budeir had been a *sheikh* – in this sense, a learned scholar – at the great Al-Azhar University in Cairo for more than eighteen years, how he'd returned to Jerusalem to teach at Al-Aqsa and had bought this house, how he would present his best students with certificates like doctoral diplomas. She tells me how the house had once been a Sufi lodge, and how the Syrian mystic and spiritual guide Mustafa al-Bakri had holed up in one of the rooms to withdraw from the world and meditate, but nobody knew which room. And she adds that before the Sufis, this had been the home of Fatima, sister of Muawiya, fifth caliph of Islam. That last bit sounds apocryphal to me – Muawiya's sister was called Ramla and she died in the 660s before even the Dome of the Rock had been built – but I don't press Mrs. Budeiri on the details.

All the while she talks rattlingly fast, each phrase emphasized with a little clap of the hands. After a bit she stops doing that and gently slaps the cushion beside her for emphasis. "I feel with the souls of my grand-grand-fathers," she says. "All the stones of the Old City speak with me. When I leave Jerusalem, when I leave Palestine, I am nothing, I feel nothing. When I come back, I am everything."

She is divorced, she tells me. As well as administering her own family library she also works part-time at the famous Khalidi Library nearby and at the contemporary art gallery Al-Mamal, over by New Gate. She leads me to her home's enclosed rooftop courtyard, whose upper rooms overlook the whole of the Al-Aqsa compound. From up there, she says, you could walk over the rooftops in broad sunshine beside the glittering Dome of the Rock to Bab al-Qattanin, the Cotton Merchants' Gate, 150 meters to the south – well you *could*, she says, but just now it's the quiet hour after lunch and her son is sleeping up there and she doesn't really want to disturb him by waking him up just to show me the view.

Of course, I smile.

"He doesn't feel the same about all this," she says. "This generation. They want to be able to park their car in front of the house, but here there are no cars and no parking. They don't want to carry everything from there to here. The police are outside our door all the time, because of the [Bab al-Majlis] gate. There are cameras. It's terrible. For me, I will stay here forever. While I'm alive I will do my best, but when I'm gone, that's it. What else can I do?"

Down in the street, the man on the steps had finished his cigarette and departed. Again I stood with my back to the Bab al-Majlis/Bab al-Nazir gateway, facing west along Ala ad-Din's narrow lane. Again I thought, what you see in this place is never what's actually going on.

A gate in this location and a street running more or less like this one have been here for a very long time. Mujir ad-Din, writing in 1495, said the gate here used to be called Bab Mikhail, which suggests it was the same as what the Crusaders had called Michael's Gate. "Aladdin" is theophoric, a name within which is embedded a reference to the divine. Standing there, I thought about how "Michael" is theophoric too: "*mi*," "*kha*," "*el*" literally asks the – presumably rhetorical – question "Who is like God?"

Playing with words makes me grin.

But there's more to this than just words. According to a pilgrim chronicle from 1229, a tradition at that time said that the street along which Jesus was led to crucifixion passed from the Temple directly, in a straight line, to Calvary. This street, the one I'm standing on, is the only one that forms a straight line between what was the Temple and what is now the Church of the Holy Sepulchre, built atop Calvary. Were I to begin walking west along Ala ad-Din Street and its arrow-straight continuation, Aqabat at-Takiya, I would, in maybe ten minutes of mostly uphill puffing, reach the church.

So where did that tradition originate?

An earlier pilgrim account from 1187 says the same thing. It adds another note that after Jesus passed through what it calls the *Porte Dolereuse* (Sorrowful Gate) from the Temple, he crossed a stream, "and in that place there is a church."

Was the Sorrowful Gate the same as Michael's Gate? It could be. But what's this about crossing a stream?

It takes me less than a minute to walk along the whole of Ala ad-Din Street, past the two *ribats*, to its western end. Where the lane meets the main thoroughfare Al-Wad (the Valley) now stands an ornate, stone-carved public fountain, set into the wall as a recessed niche, created in 1537 from chunks of Crusader architecture. The fountain, now disused – and blocked from view most days by Israeli police, who stand in front of it behind metal barricades – was formerly served by a small hidden reservoir and cistern, but the reservoir's water source is unknown. At least one scholar asks whether the fountain's presence here may be related to whatever long-lost stream it was that that twelfth-century pilgrim was referring to.

And then there's Mujir ad-Din again, who wrote of a church that formerly stood on this same corner, directly opposite where the fountain is today. Architectural scholars investigating the building currently in that location have suggested that it may be from the Crusader period.

So *if* it's a church, *if* the fountain channelled a stream, *if* those ancient stories about a direct path from Temple to Calvary were passed down reliably and not invented, *if* the whole thing stacks up, then this could be where Jesus carried the cross.

Jerusalem's Aladdin is a very old, very complicated street.

10

Do Not Be Frivolous

STORIES OF BAB AR-RAHMA/GOLDEN GATE

THE GOLDEN GATE – which is not golden, unless you see its east-facing stonework illuminated by the rays of the morning sun – is the easiest, and hardest, of Jerusalem's gates to understand.

If you want the easy version, the gate is bricked shut, and has been for the last four-hundred-and-something years. That's it. It's not a gate at all, it's just a fancy bit of wall. But the backstory could fill a book. Because this, to many, is not merely a gate, but a transition point between our earthly realm and the theater of divine illumination. How apt, some think, that it is closed.

When Suleiman the Magnificent rebuilt it in the sixteenth century, the gate was already several hundred years old, and perhaps older than that. Jewish tradition holds that the Divine Presence entered the Temple (thought to have been built by Solomon three thousand years ago) through its eastern gate. Every day, later Muslims said, Solomon would gather leaves of silver and gold from two trees that stood beside this gate and use them to beautify the Temple. The prophet Ezekiel declared that when the Messiah returned, it would be through the same, eastern gate – and that the gate would, until then, remain shut.

Unfortunately, we have no evidence linking the current structure with that unnamed and unlocated gate, nor with the subsequent

Shushan Gate of the Second Temple, built in the sixth century BCE. Shushan was a capital of Persia, far to the east, from where the Jews had just returned after the Babylonian exile, and the Shushan Gate was special, used only by the Jewish high priest and attendants during annual rituals of Temple purification.

Christian tradition holds that Jesus rode a donkey into Jerusalem on Palm Sunday via this gate, thereby fulfilling Ezekiel's prophecy, and that Jesus's grandparents learned of their daughter Mary's Immaculate Conception here. It may also be that this is the "Beautiful Gate" mentioned in the New Testament, where Jesus's disciple Peter performed a miracle. If so, the name "Golden Gate," which is of medieval Christian origin, could derive from "beautiful" – *oraia* in the Greek of the Bible, mistakenly transcribed as *aurea*, Latin for golden.

Either way, the gate was (probably) destroyed by the Romans during their sack of the city in 70 CE. But that's only the start. When did the current structure originate? Historians argue over whether its foundations date from the (Christian) Byzantine era, when the gate may have been built as part of the celebration of victory over Persia after 629, or the (Muslim) Umayyad era, when the gate may have been built as part of the rededication of the entire esplanade around 640–90. Other scholars date it still earlier, or later.

At some point, perhaps the ninth century, Jerusalem's Muslim rulers had the gate sealed shut; nobody is sure why, but it may have been an attempt to undermine Christian attachment to the site and/or to thwart Jewish traditions of prayer at the gate's entrance (non-Muslims were barred from entering what was, by then, the compound of Al-Aqsa, so Jews would instead gather by the gate, as near to the site of the Temple as they could get). Or perhaps the closure was to associate the physical reality of Jerusalem with a metaphysical passage in the Quran describing how a gated wall will separate believers from hypocrites, with mercy inside the gate and torment outside it. It was around this time that the gate became known as the Gate of Mercy – *Bab ar-Rahma* in Arabic, *Shaar ha-Rakhamim* in Hebrew.*

---

* Strictly speaking, the name *Bab ar-Rahma* refers only to the southern of the two sealed archways forming the gate. Its neighbor to the north is *Bab at-Tawba* (Gate of Repentance). Some, though, say that the twin (sealed) arches facing east are *Bab at-Tawba*, and the twin (open) arches facing west into Al-Aqsa are *Bab ar-Rahma*.

In the twelfth century, the Crusaders reopened the gate for royal pageants and Palm Sunday re-enactments of Jesus's triumphal entry. In the thirteenth, the Ayyubids sealed it shut again. When the Ottomans rebuilt the gate in the sixteenth century, it still had wooden doors – described as being plated with gilded copper – though they were falling apart and jammed shut by earth and debris. The likelihood is that the gate was finally sealed with masonry at this time, around 1540. It remains now as it was then.

However, the Golden Gate is not just an entryway, or even just a fortification in the city wall. It comprises a substantial two-story building, still in use and accessible from the Haram al-Sharif. At ground level (reached by steps dropping six meters from the level of the Haram pavement) is a multi-columned hall, entered via a double-arched portal. Originally the throughway for the gate, then used as a mosque, then as a space for religious teaching and an exam room for students, this hall has recently been subject to political claim and counterclaim: in 2019 Palestinians restored access to it after sixteen years of Israeli-enforced closure and it is now a mosque again, one of the prayer spaces of Al-Aqsa. Upstairs from it are domed rooms that may have served as the residence of eleventh-century scholar Al-Ghazali and a retreat for Sufi mystics.

No survey or archaeological investigation of the Golden Gate or its foundations has ever been done – and that's unlikely to change any time soon, what with the sensitivity of the site, Al-Aqsa on one side, Jerusalem's oldest Muslim cemetery on the other. Almost everybody who has ever visited or written about Jerusalem mentions it, yet almost everything we know about it is guesswork. Why is it so grand, when other comparable structures – such as the now-sealed gates on the south wall of the Al-Aqsa/Temple compound – are plain? In fact, why have a gate here at all? The land to the east falls away steeply; there have never been major population centers there.

The only reason can be solemn observance, the ceremonies of Jewish Temple ritual that a gate here first facilitated subsumed into Christian ceremonies surrounding temporal and spiritual victories in battle, in turn absorbed into Islamic ceremonies of resanctification of the same site in preparation for the fulfilment of prophecy on the Day of Judgment.

A gate that is not a gate. A gate through which no one can pass. A gate that, in three thousand years of human history, has only ever been open for momentous encounters with the divine. The Golden Gate is irresistibly mysterious. Legends in all three religions talk of its stones shifting and reforming themselves into portal or barrier, depending on who was attempting to seek passage, and for what reason. Do not be frivolous or lighthearted when you are near it, warns the Mishnah, the third-century CE compilation of Jewish law that forms the basis of the Talmud. Prepare yourself for the fateful day it opens again.

11

Suddenly I See Everything

STORIES OF REMARKABLE WOMEN

ONCE UPON A TIME, long, long ago on the darkest of nights in the city of Basra, which carries the mingled waters of the Euphrates and the Tigris to the sea, when the air was warm and dense as woven reeds and if you listened hard you could hear the water lapping against the mud, a baby's cry startled the roosting birds. A daughter is born! A daughter! The girl's father, who worked as a ferryman on the river, earning barely enough to keep hunger at bay, thanked God for the arrival of the child, but then he was ashamed, because he knew there were no swaddling clothes to give his wife to wrap their baby, who would be named Rabia, because she was their fourth daughter,* and there was no lamp in the house on this darkest of nights and not even any oil with which to light a lamp.

The girl's father was even more ashamed when his wife asked him to see if their neighbor might lend them a cloth in which she could swaddle the child, and a lamp, and some oil. He obeyed and he went out on this darkest of nights, but he was trembling and he hid his emotion from his wife, for he had already sworn an oath to seek all he ever needed in his life from God alone, and never to ask anything of any person, neither sustenance nor gifts nor charity. So he did not knock on their neighbor's door, but instead hid himself

---

* Rabia means "fourth" in Arabic.

in the shadows before returning home to his wife and his daughters empty-handed and sorrowful.

That night, feeling conflicted and guilty for having betrayed his family's needs, even while keeping his personal vow, the girl's father slid into a fitful sleep. There, in the place we know but cannot name, he was visited by the Messenger of God, the Compassionate One, the Seal of the Prophets, the Lamp That Gives Light, Muhammad, peace be upon him. First the Prophet told the girl's father to calm himself and be happy, for his daughter just born would become a great saint and comfort to believers. Then he told the girl's father to write a letter on his behalf to the prince of Basra, reminding the prince of his obligation to offer one hundred prayers every day and four hundred every Friday, and telling him that as penance for neglecting his prayers this last Friday he was to give four hundred dinars to the father of the girl just born.

The girl's father awoke next morning, his face wet with tears. He wrote the letter, and after the chamberlain had handed the letter to the prince, the prince blanched, for the letter was a sign. He instructed his vizier to distribute two thousand dinars to the poor of the city and then to give four hundred dinars to the father of the girl just born, adding that he did not consider it right to summon to the palace such a holy sheikh as the father of the girl just born and instead sought the holy sheikh's permission to come and humbly pay compliments at his door.

Years passed, Rabia grew, but her father and mother died and she was left an orphan. Away from her sisters one day, walking alone, she was seized off the street by a man who sold her in the market as a slave. She wept and prayed and sought comfort from God, but her new master worked her hard. All day she fasted while she worked, then all night she would pray.

On the darkest of nights in the city of Basra, which carries the mingled waters of the Euphrates and the Tigris to the sea, when the air was warm and dense as woven reeds and if you listened hard you could hear the water lapping against the mud, it happened that Rabia's master could not sleep. He got up and wandered to the window, disturbed by a strange light that was filling the house.

There, down below, he saw the slave Rabia standing in prayer. Suspended above her bowed head by no chain he could see hung a lamp, shining brightly with the radiance of a saint's presence.

He retreated and spent the rest of the night in prayer. Next morning, he gave Rabia her freedom. She left, and journeyed out of the city into the desert, seeking a place of solitude for contemplation.

And so her story continues.

"Rabia? Oh, Rabia is wonderful," Salwa tells me, juggling room keys at the front desk of the hotel where I'm staying. "Nai Barghouti – you know, the singer? – she did a song of Rabia's poetry. You can find it on YouTube.* It was Rabia's poem about the two kinds of love. Do you know it? Oh, I love it so much!"

> *I love you with two loves:*
> *Desire*
> *And a love that is worthy of you.*
> *In my desire, all I do is think of you.*
> *In that other love, I see you and suddenly I see*
> *Everything.*

That's a loose translation, but it gets the gist. It doesn't matter that Rabia was born and died more than twelve hundred years ago: literally everyone in Jerusalem I asked knew her name and her status as the first female saint in Islam, mystic, poet, celibate and proto-feminist. Not one person had never heard of her.

That's partly a reflection of the kind of people I asked, but also of the value that Arab popular culture places on poetry. People love it. And since classical Arabic hasn't changed, anyone can understand a 1,200-year-old poem in the original. (Try that with *Beowulf*.)

It is also down to religion. Rabia – Rabia al-Adawiyya after her family's clan name, or plain Rabia Basri ("of Basra") – is often named

---

* See the notes to this chapter.

as one of the few women who attained spiritual perfection in Islam, alongside Asiya, foster mother of Prophet Musa/Moses; Maryam/Mary, mother of Prophet Isa/Jesus; Khadija and Aisha, wives of Muhammad; and Fatima, daughter of Khadija and Muhammad. Many traditions exalt four women from this list of six, though opinions vary as to which. The meaning of Rabia's name – "Fourth" – gains added symbolism in such traditions. But whereas the other five achieved their saintliness through association with revered men, Rabia earned her respect and sanctity through her own piety and uncompromising ascetic practice. That she also firmly rejected every irritating man who pestered her to marry in favor of pursuing her ideals by herself adds further zing.

One of the most famous stories tells of Rabia marching through the streets carrying a bucket of water in one hand and a flaming torch in the other. When challenged, she said she wanted to douse the fires of hell and burn down paradise, because both stand in the way of truth. We should act not from fear (of punishment) or from desire (of reward), but through love alone.

Now there's an idea.

But Rabia's popularity in Jerusalem is also because she is buried here. When I got on the 275 bus at Damascus Gate, I just asked the driver for "Rabia al-Adawiyya" and he nodded. It's like getting on a bus in Sunderland and asking for The Venerable Bede.* Her tomb lies on the Mount of Olives, just east of the Old City, in a building beside and partly beneath the Chapel of the Ascension, a church-turned-mosque that shelters a rock bearing the footprint of Jesus. The chapel had crowds of tourists – Filipino, German and Spanish – but round the corner, where Rabia sleeps, I was on my own. You enter a small mosque – renovated, but likely twelfth- or thirteenth-century – and go down some steps to a burial chamber that is older, perhaps fifth- or sixth-century, about five meters by three.

There lies Rabia, in a stone sarcophagus covered by a tasselled cloth of pinkish velvet. Only, probably not. Sources on Rabia's life

---

* I haven't tried this. It might work. "Bede" is a stop on the Tyne and Wear Metro, not far from where Bede (the monk) lived and wrote.

are scant, but nothing we have says she left Basra before she died there in 801 (or some say earlier), aged in her eighties.

The trouble is, Rabia is a figure of literature – or, perhaps better, of cultural memory – rather than history. Virtually everything we know about her was made up by writers and commentators, almost always male and often long after her death. That includes the story at the beginning of this chapter, which retells two famous episodes. Rabia's life comprises parables, archetypes, mystic morality tales. A series of dialogues between Rabia and the Sufi master Hasan of Basra, celebrated for showing a woman besting a man in spiritual and intellectual rigor, have profound value in Islamic study but never happened. The poem attributed to Rabia about the two kinds of love has different words depending on whether the source prefers to emphasize Rabia's pious orthodoxy or her heterodox mysticism. The poet herself shimmers, out of reach.

Rabia has become a wish-fulfilment figure, a screen on which generations have projected their own ideas and hopes, a prism through which onlookers clarify filters of gender, class and ethnicity.*

---

* Since Islamic law forbids Muslims from enslaving Muslims, scholars have suggested that Rabia may have been Christian or Jewish, later converted to Islam. Others theorize, from her tribal origins, that she was Persian rather than Arab.

That continues today: movies are made about Rabia, songs are sung about her, and she is frequently cited in academic discussions of gender relations in Islam and feminist theory. Her name has even become associated with infamy, for it was in Cairo's Rabia al-Adawiyya Square on 14 August 2013 that Egypt's army and police killed a thousand people or more in a single day, citizens who had gathered there to protest the previous month's military coup. The crime, as yet unpunished, has become known as the Rabia Massacre. Saints, like all of us, weep.

Who, then, lies in Jerusalem's decorated tomb?

Well, there was another Rabia, named Rabia bint Ismail ("daughter of Ismail"). She lived in Damascus and reportedly died in Jerusalem about 850. This Rabia, called al-Shamiyya ("of Syria") and al-Badawiyya ("the bedouin"), had a very different background – she was extremely wealthy and twice married – but stood comparison with her namesake in Islamic piety. "When I gaze on her face," said her Sufi husband, Ahmad, "I sense a higher level of enlightenment and devotion to God than when I am with my friends performing the *dhikr*." Perhaps people mixed up Rabia al-Adawiyya with Rabia al-Badawiyya? Confusion reigns.

But before either of the Rabias, Christians would visit the selfsame tomb to venerate another remarkable person – Pelagia, who made a living as a dancer (or, depending on who's telling the story, a sex worker) in the city of Antioch, now Antakya on Turkey's Mediterranean coast. Pelagia performed under the stage-name Margarita, until a visiting bishop refused to condemn her for immorality, as all others had. The bishop's acceptance drove Pelagia to repent, and she asked to be baptised. Claiming a new identity as a eunuch, the now-religious penitent dressed as a monk and travelled to Jerusalem, living as the hermit Pelagius in this cell on the Mount of Olives. Having died in about 457 from emaciation caused by extreme ascetic practice, the hermit was entombed in the same cell and later canonized (but as Saint Pelagia).

We also know of a Jewish tradition a bit later, from 1322 onwards, which said that the same cave in fact held the tomb of Hulda, who lived in Jerusalem in the seventh century BCE. Hulda taught law and morality to the women of the city – as her cousin, the prophet Jeremiah, did to the men – and she is named in the Old Testament as a prophet who foresaw the destruction of Solomon's Temple.

There's even a nineteenth-century account of Muslims, Christians and Jews descending the steps together to pray at this one tomb side by side, some invoking Rabia, some Pelagia, some Hulda. (That doesn't happen anymore.) Pilgrims would challenge each other to tests of piety by trying to squeeze through the narrow gap between the tomb and the wall. Only honest people of faith could manage it. Sinners would get stuck. Jews even held that if you could squeeze through seven times, all your sins would be forgiven and you would achieve prosperity. I tried it, just for fun. Then I took some time to sit by the tomb. There was no chair, so I sat on the ground. The only other visitors while I sat there were some Turkish students, whose guide told them Rabia's story. The women lingered longer than the men.

One thing's for sure: this little cave has resonated for many, many centuries, across multiple cultures and traditions, as the final resting place of some extraordinary woman, whatever her name was and whatever she did. I found it one of the most memorable, thought-provoking places in the city. And it turns out the truth of the place may be more mysterious even than Rabia herself. "Courage, Domitilla. No one lives forever," reads an inscription on the wall in Greek, discovered in 1853 but since erased. Domitilla? Nobody knows who she was.

Back inside the walls again, it's possible to trace an unexpected and almost entirely overlooked architectural legacy left across Jerusalem by other remarkable, but often unknown, women.

In any other city, the Palace of *Sitt* ("Lady") Tunshuq would occupy a prominent location in its own grounds, with a grand approach and sightlines carefully manufactured to impress. This is the largest civic – that is, nonreligious – building in the Old City. But Jerusalem is crowded, and constricted by its walls. Up until the nineteenth century – and arguably beyond – there was never enough space. So this lofty, six-hundred-year-old mansion stands crammed in on the narrow, steep lanes just west of Al-Aqsa, too large to take in at a glance, impossible to photograph, neglected and mostly ignored.

Again, we know almost nothing about Tunshuq, other than that she lived in Jerusalem for barely ten years at the end of her life, before her death here in 1398. We don't even know her name for sure: it may have been copied wrongly from "Tansuq," an old Turkic word that can mean "precious." She is also called Al-Muzaffariyya, which may mean she was related by blood or marriage to – or perhaps had been owned by – one of the Muzaffarid princes who ruled in southern Iran, around Yazd and Kerman, from 1314. One theory is she fled for safety to Jerusalem when Tamerlane overthrew the Muzaffarids in 1387. All we can surmise is that when she got here, she was rich, because she built what was, for Jerusalem, an eyeful of a house to live in. It extends from a large hall at ground level to a cross-vaulted mezzanine and formal reception area above with a courtyard, its twenty-five rooms linked by four staircases.

Turning off from the souk and walking down Aqabat at-Takiya, once known as Aqabat al-Sitt ("The Lady's Hill"), brings one of the airiest street-level views in the otherwise densely enclosed city core. Breezes drift from the Mount of Olives, in sight a mile east. This was where the Lady built her palace, on the side of the hill facing Al-Aqsa. But the palace is now a school and generally closed to the public: all we can admire from the street are its three grand doorways, with their red, black and cream striped *ablaq* stonework, arches and stalactite-like *muqarnas* decorative vaulting. The main door is highest up the slope, beside a porthole window. The middle door, the widest, opened directly into the main hall, while the final doorway is the most elaborate, thrumming with striped marble and topped by a carved panel that once sparkled with multicolored glass inlay. When Tunshuq died, in the summer heat of 1398, her body was placed in an ornate mausoleum across the lane from this doorway; she lies there still, in what is now a private home.

But her palace remained significant. When another rich and powerful woman came along a hundred and fifty years later, she chose to – literally – build on Tunshuq's legacy.

We don't know the birth name of the woman nicknamed Roxelana, but that term shows she came from Rus, or Ruthenia – modern Ukraine. She was born near what is now called Lviv around 1502, kidnapped as a young girl and bought at an Istanbul slave market by the wife of the Ottoman sultan as a gift for her son, then in his early twenties. That young man, eight years her senior, acceded to the throne shortly afterwards as Suleiman the Magnificent. Roxelana's rise within the confines of Suleiman's harem was meteoric, from his slave to his favorite concubine, then in 1533/34 his legal wife. She became known as Hurrem Sultan (from a Persian term connoting laughter), and was granted the imperial title Khaski Sultan, roughly "The Sultan's Own." Throughout her life she exercised influence on political affairs, advising Suleiman on matters of state and wielding unparalleled power at court. As well as inspiring art, music, literature and TV series galore, her life marked the start of what's known as the Sultanate of Women, a period of a century or more when royal women dominated Ottoman politics.

Roxelana built charitable institutions around the empire, in Istanbul, Mecca, Medina – and Jerusalem. Beside and behind

Lady Tunshuq's palace stands what is formally named Al-Imara Al-Amira ("The Flourishing Edifice") or the Takiya, which in the Jerusalem context means a public kitchen. It's almost universally known, though, as Khaski Sultan, after the woman who built it, and is famous for having served hot meals to all comers, free of charge, no questions asked, every day since 1552. At one time it had dozens of employees and fed hundreds of families; that is somewhat reduced now, but it remains vital to many Jerusalemites and cherished by many more, though essentially invisible to outsiders. The kitchens and the palace alongside have long since merged to form the interconnected complex of Dar al-Aytam al-Islamiyya, the Muslim Orphans' Home, a dense cluster of buildings comprising a school, vocational training center with carpentry and print workshops, dormitories and a mosque. Owned and run by the Waqf, it's the largest charitable institution in Palestine – and must surely be the world's oldest continuously operating soup kitchen.

All from a traumatized Ukrainian victim of sex trafficking who was known for laughing.

Jerusalem has many more such stories, everywhere you turn.

In Baghdad in 895, an enslaved Greek woman given the slave-name Naima ("Gentle") bore the caliph a son. She was freed and renamed Shaghab ("Tumultuous"), and became hugely influential when her son acceded to power. Much intrigue ensued, including torture and executions, but, like Roxelana, this powerful Queen Mother – whose birth name remains unknown – also sponsored public works, in this case renovation of the Dome of the Rock.

Turkan Khatun (*khatun* is an honorific) was an Uzbek aristocrat who had apparently made the long journey to Jerusalem, presumably on pilgrimage, when she died in 1352 or 1353. We know of her only from the stone-carved inscription on her mausoleum, a domed building beside the Bab al-Silsila gateway into Al-Aqsa, drenched in ornately carved panels.

Across town, two unnamed women from the Turkish city of Mardin, freed from slavery, founded around 1360 the Ribat al-Mardini, a residential complex for women pilgrims from their hometown. One poor soul named Bulghar is recorded in 1392 as having died in the building, which now houses a souvenir shop.

Around the same time, 1380, a woman named Isfahan Shah completed a residential school overlooking Al-Aqsa. Construction had begun twenty-five years or so earlier by a noblewoman from Baghdad, possibly Isfahan's mother, whose tomb still lies within the building. The Khatuniyya, as it's called, stands close to Al-Aqsa's graceful Uthmaniyya school, built around 1440 by a Turkish princess and now a grand residence.

Then there are women whose lives tantalizingly emerge from the anonymity of history with a line or two in the archives.

Aysha the Moroccan, who died alone in Jerusalem in 1391, owning eighteen hats and twenty-one pairs of boots, even though her husband, mother and son were all in Damascus.

Shirin, who in 1382 used her own money to buy an enslaved (and unnamed) African woman from another woman named Bayram – evidence of wealthy women managing their own business affairs.

Qutlumalik, a Muslim woman, who in 1394 lived in an apartment she owned in a house in the Jewish Quarter where Jews also lived and worked – evidence of coexistence.

Qamar, who also in 1394 is recorded as owning five gowns, including two lined with fur, one blue, one red; seven shirts; a blue coat; a cloak of wool; a wrap; ten handkerchiefs; a pair of silver anklets; two pairs of gold earrings; four silver bangles; a copper kettle, cups, flasks and lamps; two frying pans; boxes, jars, trays and wooden boards; a silver scale; a mattress, bedcovers and cushions, and plenty more. She was single.

There's the unschooled fifteenth-century prodigy Bayram, who spoke with authority to the sages at Al-Aqsa and lectured on Islam to the women of the city. But then she married and, her biographer concludes cryptically, "her life changed."

The no-nonsense eighteenth-century grandmother Amna, who knew the law and wasn't afraid to stand up in court to help her granddaughter, Khadija, get a divorce because Khadija's husband hadn't paid the agreed amount.

Maryam, who was courageous enough in 1656 – aged sixteen, yet confident in the rule of law, even as a Christian – to publicly reject Ibrahim the blacksmith, the husband chosen for her by her father, and demand that her marriage contract with him be annulled. She won.

And that's not even to mention women such as Armenian-born Melisende, who ruled the Crusader kingdom of Jerusalem for thirty years until her death in 1161. Or Tarafanda bint Najmaddin, who in 1787 gathered several hundred manuscripts that formed the core collection of the Khalidiyya, Jerusalem's greatest library. Or Hind al-Husseini, who in April 1948 found huddled in the street fifty-five young children who had fled the killing of their parents at Deir Yassin near Jerusalem by Zionist paramilitaries. She took them in, established an orphanage and school in her family's home named Dar al-Tifl, the Children's House, and devoted the rest of her life to advancing girls' and women's education. Dar al-Tifl still functions today, located beside the American Colony Hotel in East Jerusalem.

12

The Fig Tree of Maslohi

STORIES OF BAB AL-MAGHARBA/DUNG GATE

IN JERUSALEM, THERE'S A DOOR. It's not a grand door. It's small and ordinary and made of metal, under a stone archway on a narrow footpath. Attached to the wall beside it is an entryphone, dented and damaged, with ten buttons. Most of the names beside the buttons are illegible. But this isn't a hidden door, down some back alley. Hundreds of people each day, maybe thousands, pass this door. Sometimes they queue up outside it, chatting and laughing and waiting patiently, shuffling forward every so often. But they're not waiting to go in. None of them ever goes in.

Remember the door. It's important.

In Jerusalem, the main axes of movement across the Old City – the whole city, as was – are the same today as when they were laid out by the Romans in the early second century. There's a main east–west *decumanus* road that, unusually, is split because of the topography: to pass from city gate to city gate you have to do a dog-leg around the hilltop platform where the Temple once stood and where Al-Aqsa now stands. From north to south the Romans, again unusually, laid two roads, both originating at the northern entrance (now

Damascus Gate): a western *cardo*, following what is now Souk Khan al-Zeit, and an eastern *cardo*, now called Tariq al-Wad or "Valley Road." Al-Wad marks the Tyropoeon Valley, now mostly filled in, which rises in Jerusalem's northern hills and flows southwards. Damascus Gate is the mouth where the Tyropoeon enters the Old City. From there it passes all the way through. Though the valley has actually been dry for, who knows, millennia, imagine it like the guts of the city, winding its way through and channelling all of the unwanted waste away into the larger encircling valleys, Kidron and Hinnom, further south. At the point where this alimentary channel exits the body of Jerusalem on its southwards rush, there's a small opening in the walls of the city.

This exit – or an older one in the vicinity – was named the Dung Gate or Rubbish Gate (*Shaar ha-Ashpot* in Hebrew) as far back as the Old Testament because this was the direction Jerusalemites would carry their waste for burning in the valleys to the south. It's also been called the Silwan Gate, in reference to the village of Silwan that clings to the slopes below the city walls here.

That covers its Hebrew and English names.

Arabic, though – not for the first time in this book – sees things entirely differently. The common Arabic name for this gate encodes a memory of the global reach of Islam, of a place now destroyed and a people now dispersed.

This is a long, difficult and eye-opening story that doesn't get told nearly enough. But we have time, and it matters.

It all begins nine hundred years ago in a small village called Cantillana, northeast of Seville in Muslim-ruled Al-Andalus, where a boy named Shuayb, son of Hussein, was born into a poor family. Some say Shuayb was orphaned at a young age and brought up by his cruel older brothers, who beat him. Others say he learned to weave, to help his family. Either way, the boy knew his destiny lay elsewhere and eventually managed to find his way to the great Moroccan city of Fes. There he learned Islam, fasting and praying

THE FIG TREE OF MASLOHI

with a string of ascetics and Sufi mystics until he, too, by then known as Abu Madyan, became recognized as a Sufi master. People called him *Al-Ghawth*, the Helper, a special title indicating a cosmic level of spiritual enlightenment. He established a *zawiya* (Sufi lodge) in Bijaya, a city of culture and trade on the Algerian coast, where multitudes would gather to hear his sermons, delivered with a characteristic mix of scholarly analysis, proverbs, storytelling and emotion. Even before his death in 1198, Abu Madyan was being hailed as one of the most influential teachers to spread Sufism across North Africa. Pilgrims still flock to his tomb today.

It was when he was already renowned as an ascetic that Abu Madyan is supposed to have made the pilgrimage to Mecca. Dates and details are hazy, but the story goes that he was in Damascus in early 1187, on the long journey home, when news of a call to arms from Salah ad-Din, commander of Muslim forces against the Crusaders, reached him. Perhaps improbably, Abu Madyan, who was already in his sixties, is said to have joined up and helped defeat the Crusaders in the Battle of Hattin (where he lost an arm) before going on with Salah ad-Din to Jerusalem, helping to liberate the city.

Is it true? Did the famous Abu Madyan bring his distinctively North African style of Islamic esotericism to Jerusalem? Many believe so. But the best we can say is that his grandson was here.

By then Jerusalem's North African presence was burgeoning. Salah ad-Din's son, Al-Afdal, gained power in Damascus in 1193 and almost immediately established a *waqf*, a property endowment, for the benefit of North African Muslims of all backgrounds, "male and female, old and young, the low and the high," across an entire district of Jerusalem beside the great wall that supported the southwestern corner of the platform of Al-Aqsa. This site has huge significance in mystical Islam: the stretch of wall had been identified since at least the tenth century as the place where Prophet Muhammad tethered the winged horse-like creature Buraq during his supernatural Night Journey from Mecca, and the Buraq Mosque still exists today as a prayer space secreted within the structure of the wall here.

The North African community that established itself beside Al-Afdal's seminary the Afdaliyya, and in front of the Buraq Wall, was strong enough a century later in 1303 for Omar al-Masmudi, a pilgrim from North Africa, to found a *zawiya* nearby for his compatriots. By then the Jameh al-Magharba, a congregational mosque for the community that had been consecrated soon after foundation of the Afdaliyya, was already open in the southwestern corner of the Haram beside Al-Aqsa; it survives today as the Islamic Museum. We know that one of the teachers at the Afdaliyya in 1326 was a man named Abu Abdullah Muhammad, dubbed "Al-Gharnati," the Granadan (this was when the Muslim-ruled Emirate of Granada was flourishing in what is now southern Spain).

On Saturday 2 November 1320, Abu Madyan, grandson of the Sufi master Abu Madyan al-Ghawth, put his name to a document endowing another *zawiya* in the same neighborhood. A fourth *waqf* followed in 1352, when the King of Morocco donated to Al-Aqsa a copy of the Quran he himself had written, to be read in the mosque; it is still there today. Jerusalem's *Haret al-Magharba*, the North African (or Moroccan) Quarter, founded in Abu Madyan's name, had become a reality.

Hold on, brief time out needed. Arabic can be confusing, and I'm afraid this is another example.

Gharb means west. *Maghrib*, a noun derived from it, means "a place in the west" (and, relatedly, "evening," and therefore also the daily prayer recited at sunset). But, separately, the same word *maghrib* is also used for two different geographical concepts – on the one hand Morocco, and on the other all the Arabic-speaking countries of North Africa to the west of Egypt (so Morocco, Algeria, Tunisia, Libya, Western Sahara and Mauritania). It has even passed into English: the Maghrib, or Maghreb, is a familiar general term for Arab and Amazigh – that is, Berber – North Africa.

For our purposes relevant adjectives are *maghribi* (singular) and *magharba* (plural) – these can mean Moroccan/Moroccans if used narrowly, or North African/North Africans in a wider sense. Unless a speaker clarifies which meaning is intended, there's no real way to be sure which it is. This linguistic ambiguity, coupled nowadays with a false conflation of this Muslim community's history with unrelated Israeli narratives around Moroccan Jewry, means that Jerusalem's *Haret al-Magharba*,* which might best be translated as "North African Quarter," is usually given as "Moroccan Quarter." The adjacent gateway into Al-Aqsa, which became known as *Bab al-Magharba* ("North Africans' Gate"), is mangled on street signs into "Morocco Gate." And to add another layer of confusion, the southern gate in Jerusalem's city walls here was also given the name *Bab al-Magharba*, despite keeping "Dung Gate" in Hebrew and English. It's all a bit of a muddle.

Now, in order to understand what happened here later, we need to widen the scope a little.

When the Romans destroyed the Second Temple in 70 CE, it caused a rupture in Jewish devotional practice that, for many, remains stark to this day. What did Judaism mean, if the Temple – humanity's interface with the Divine Presence, the focus of all prayer – no longer existed? What even was the purpose of prayer, when the Holy of Holies had been desecrated?

Such questions have consumed two millennia of spiritual and intellectual exertion. That's too much for us to get into here, but we can look at how it affected Jerusalem's religious geography. For centuries after the Romans, Jewish worship became refocused on two sites outside the city walls (not least because for long periods Jews were barred from entering the city). First was the Mount of Olives, which has a direct view down onto the Temple platform, and where important rituals of Temple purification were performed. Then, in the desire to recall the Temple and to pray as close as possible to its former location, Jews would also gather outside the Gate of Mercy/Golden Gate, the portal through which Temple priests had passed on the route to and from the Mount of Olives.

---

* Also rendered *Magharbeh*, *Maghariba* and in other ways. Grammatical niceties may also produce *Mughrabi*, *Moghrabi*, *Mugraby* and other variations.

Within the city, by contrast, the long western retaining wall of the Temple platform, so central to Jewish prayer and spirituality today under the name "Western Wall," didn't mean much. It had survived the Roman destruction and had assumed spiritual significance in Islam and become part of Al-Afdal's Moroccan *waqf* – but it is barely referenced in Jewish sources. Its first mention is by an Italian poet in the eleventh century but not, it seems, in connection with prayer.

That changed five hundred years later. By then, most of Jerusalem's Jews were using the thirteenth-century Ramban synagogue for everyday prayer – but public prayer became redirected by two actions of the Ottoman sultan Suleiman (the Second, or the Lawgiver, or the Magnificent). As a carrot, Suleiman opened access to a part of the Haram al-Sharif's western wall, creating a blind alleyway three or four meters wide between the last row of houses in the Haret al-Magharba and the wall itself, accessed from the north and closed at the south; and as a stick he established a Muslim cemetery directly outside the Gate of Mercy, which he also had sealed. The combined effect was to shift Jewish public observance away from the Gate of Mercy and Mount of Olives on the eastern side of the Haram, over to the Wall on the western side.

Why there? When Solomon's Temple and its replacement the Second Temple stood, their western wall, as far as we can judge, defined the innermost boundary of the east-facing Holy of Holies. Jewish traditions from the seventh or eighth centuries onwards have named the western wall of the Temple as being the place where the Divine Presence resided. In the aftermath of expulsions of Jews from all over Christian Europe (Spain 1492 was just one of many), Suleiman wanted to demonstrate his – and Islam's – hospitality to Jewish refugees for political as well as economic reasons. He wanted to counterbalance Christian intolerance while also benefiting from an influx of skills. Jerusalem, and the wider empire, he decided, was to be made attractive to Jews. Opening access to this wall would signal a willingness to embrace the return of Jewish public observance to the heart of its holiest city.

It's of little importance that that particular wall was not the western wall of the Temple but, rather, an outer wall that supported the western side of the mountain-top platform upon which the Temple once stood. Suleiman was setting in train a creation of memory, and history is no match for memory. Sure enough, since his intervention, Jewish tradition has effortlessly transferred its age-old reverence for the western wall of the Temple to a newfound reverence for the western wall of the Temple Mount. That's been achieved because a wall is not the object of prayer. The Divine Presence is the object, and a wall is where the Divine Presence is said to choose to reside.

Should we read such traditions literally? Should we really locate the transcendent Godhead in one precise spot in physical space? Whether we do or not, four centuries of Jewish exegesis, experience, mysticism and emotion have combined to imbue the Western Wall of today with profound sanctity.

A word about nomenclature. English calls it the "Western Wall" because that is a direct translation of the Hebrew term *ha-Kotel ha-Maaravi*, first used by that eleventh-century poet but which only entered general usage in the sixteenth century, after Suleiman.

The more usual name in English and other European languages was once "Wailing Wall" or "Wailing-Place of the Jews." This derives from an Arabic name common throughout the medieval period – *Ha'it al-Mabka* (Wall of the Place of Weeping) or just *Al-Mabka* (Place of Weeping), which in turn originated from onlookers' observation of Jewish prayers of lamentation for the destroyed Temple. Jerusalemites also knew the place as *Hosh al-Buraq* (Buraq Courtyard) for its associations with Prophet Muhammad's Night Journey, the creature Buraq and the proximity of the Buraq Mosque. That is how British cartographers labelled it on their 1865 Ordnance Survey map.

Today, *ha-Kotel* persists in Hebrew, but "Wailing Wall" has fallen out of favor, partly because Israel's militant nationalism says there's nothing to wail about anymore and partly because "Western Wall" raises the juicy possibility of an Israeli claim on the entire 488-meter length of the Haram's western boundary, rather than just the currently exposed sections (58 meters today, 28 meters before 1967).

In a similar way in Arabic, *Al-Mabka* was superseded a hundred years ago amid an upsurge in Arab nationalism by the name universally used today, *Ha'it al-Buraq* (Buraq Wall), which emphasizes the site's Islamic sanctity.

Back to the story.

Until Jewish immigration to Palestine took off in the years after 1881, greatly increasing demand for space at the Wall, sources show little discontent with Suleiman's readjustment. A request in 1840 by Jerusalem's Jewish community to pave the alleyway in front of the Wall at their own expense was officially denied, but images from not long afterwards show the alley as paved anyway.

Things changed as sectarian tensions rose in the years either side of the First World War. The Wall became a focus for Zionist ambition in Jerusalem, and thus also a corresponding focus for Arab and Muslim defense of rights. Traditions surrounding Al-Buraq were circulated with new zeal in an effort to entrench Islam's presence, even as wealthy figures from European Jewish society tried several times to buy the Wall and the area in front of it, without success.

For the Ottoman authorities the Wall was *waqf* property, endowed in perpetuity and unsaleable (at least that was the official line: Jamal Pasha, the Ottoman governor of Syria, tried and failed to sell the Wall to a consortium of Palestinian Jews in 1916). For the British, any deviation from the intercommunal status quo threatened the overall stability of their rule in Palestine. That status quo extended to denying Jews attending prayers at the Wall any infrastructure that could conceivably be used to justify a claim expropriating the space. The British banned chairs, benches, sun shades, bookcases, partitions to segregate the sexes, and so on. (That said, it's not difficult to find photographic evidence of such items in use.) After Britain's colonial governor ordered police to remove chairs and a partition during prayers on the Jewish holy day of Yom Kippur in 1928, months of escalation by community leaders resulted in full-blown civil disorder the following summer in which more than

240 people died, many Arabs killed by British soldiers, and many Jews killed by Arabs.* The year 1929 became one of the bloodiest stepping stones on the path to war in 1948.

In 2017 Mahmoud al-Mahdi, a former resident of Haret al-Magharba, told an interviewer that between 1948 and 1967, "he sometimes spotted Jewish worshippers at the [Western Wall], mixed in with the tourists." Elmer Berger, an American rabbi (and vocal anti-Zionist), visited the Jordanian-held Wall in 1955 as part of a fact-finding tour that also took in Cairo, Baghdad, Beirut, Damascus and Amman. US author Iris Keltz, who identifies as Jewish, has described how she

---

* The police inspector sent in to handle the Yom Kippur situation in 1928 was the notoriously brutal Douglas Duff, who inspired the phrase "to duff someone up," meaning to beat them mercilessly. Duff spent nine years in Britain's Palestine Police, exulting in violence with impunity, writing later: "We scarcely regarded these people [the local populations] as human." He was finally dismissed in 1931 for torturing a prisoner. In retirement he became a TV game-show panellist.

visited the Wall in May 1967, under Jordanian rule. "No one stopped me from leaning my forehead against the cool stones," she wrote.

Their testimony goes against dozens of published sources which assert that Jews were barred from Jordanian-controlled Jerusalem and that Jordanian officials would demand tourists show baptismal certificates to ensure no Jews could enter.

Some context. Between 1948 and 1967 the border between Jordan and Israel was sealed, and could be crossed only at the Mandelbaum Gate checkpoint in Jerusalem, a short way north of the Old City walls. This was the sole route between the Israeli- and Jordanian-controlled parts of Jerusalem. UN officials and other religious and diplomatic VIPs could secure visas allowing them to cross both ways unhindered; some went back and forth several times each day. A military convoy passed to and fro every two weeks, and there were special arrangements allowing cross-border family reunifications, medical consultations and repatriations to take place, as well as religious excursions for Christians at Easter and Christmas.

Tourists from Europe and North America wanting to visit Jordanian-controlled East Jerusalem (which included the Old City) had several options. It was possible under certain circumstances to arrange to cross the Mandelbaum Gate from Israel into Jordan, though Jordanian officials would then not allow you to cross back. Wealthier folk could fly via Beirut, Cairo, Kuwait and other regional cities – in Rabbi Berger's case, Damascus – to Jerusalem's airport, located in Qalandia on the Jordanian side; direct European service began from Rome in 1959, then Paris and London in 1966 (international flights were halted by the 1967 war, and the airport was permanently closed in 2001). But most tourists – including Iris Keltz – reached Jordanian Jerusalem overland from Amman, applying there for a permit to enter the West Bank, then either returning to Amman or departing via the Mandelbaum Gate into Israel for onward journeys to Nazareth, Tel Aviv or other destinations.

Not everyone was welcome. A 1962 Jordanian government guidebook states: "Persons professing the Jewish faith are not admitted into Jordan." Similarly, an Israeli guidebook from 1960 says: "To enter the Old City you need a permit from the Israeli

District Commissioner of Jerusalem who gives it in accordance with the instructions of your consul. Each permit has to be acknowledged by the Jordanian authorities, who have never accorded it to anyone of the Jewish faith."* Jordan's discriminatory policy formed part of the wider refusal in the Arab world to grant recognition to the Israeli state. It violated the terms of the armistice agreement and UN Resolution 194 assuring free access to the Old City's holy sites. However, it has also been widely, and wrongly, interpreted as having been designed to deny Jews access to the Wall. As scholar Kimberly Katz has pointed out, that stemmed from Jordan's linkage of the issue with another clause in Resolution 194 that called for Palestinian refugees to be allowed to return to their homes: Israel denied (and still denies) the latter, so Jordan denied the former.

Jordan certainly barred Jewish Israelis and Jews of any nationality seeking to cross from Israel – with which it remained in a state of war – and Jordanian policy, along with repressive measures under Israeli martial law, which persisted until 1966, also had other consequences, such as stopping Muslims living in what became Israel from praying at Al-Aqsa. But Jews *did* visit Jordan and the Western Wall, as Keltz's and Berger's presence and Al-Mahdi's anecdotal account testify. As Katz observes: "Jordan did not ban all Jews ... Some Jews from other countries travelled to Jordan's holy places in Jerusalem during this period." Even an Israeli government official, a former deputy mayor of Jerusalem, acknowledges that "a few Jewish tourists from western countries" freely visited the Wall under Jordanian rule.

That said, the atmosphere of suspicion and political tension must have dissuaded many. A 1959 account by Linda Zackon, a Jewish woman from South Africa who hitchhiked to Jordanian Jerusalem from Rome, via Aleppo and Beirut, includes the line: "I knew I couldn't go up and touch [the Wall] or kiss it because I didn't want people to know I was Jewish." Numbers of Jewish travellers willing to run the very real risks of a visit to Jordan at this time must have been tiny.

---

* But see the notes to this chapter for why things may not have been so clear-cut.

Meanwhile life in Haret al-Magharba, clustered within meters of the Wailing Wall, continued. Jerusalemite historian Nazmi al-Jubeh, born in the Old City in 1955, has described how the neighborhood "became part of my daily adventures and explorations" as a young boy. "I was fascinated by the Moroccans' colorful traditional clothing," he has written. "My favorite was a hood that hung over the shoulders and back ... My vocabulary was enriched with new terms and phrases as my ears became familiar with the Moroccan dialect ... I learned a lot about Moroccan food ... The strong aroma of spices coming out of the quarter's kitchens became a familiar fragrance to my nose."

"I explored thoroughly all the alleys in the quarter, and I believe now they were the smallest and narrowest in the Old City," al-Jubeh says. "I recall the numerous small home gardens, and the many fig and pomegranate trees, more abundant [there] than in other neighborhoods ... I will forever remember the large fig tree that leaned over the high gates of al-Maslohi's garden on Abu Madyan Alley."

More than fifty years later, her hands neat in her lap, Maysoon al-Maslohi wears the broadest smile as she explains to me how both her grandfathers arrived in Jerusalem as pilgrims after *hajj*, and both chose to stay. Not only that, both men happened to find work as security guards at important mosques – her paternal grandfather at Al-Aqsa, her maternal at Nabi Musa, the shrine of Prophet Moses in the desert east of Jerusalem.

"Protection is in our genes!" she grins.

Maysoon's father, Mahmoud Ahmed al-Maslohi, a house decorator tracing his family origins to Marrakesh, and her mother, Nawal Qasem al-Daraji, from a family originally Algerian, both grew up in Haret al-Magharba. "Even now my mother will close her eyes and remember what life was like in the neighborhood," Maysoon says. "How they would make soap, or how she and her friends would stay up all night making *shariyeh* [a kind of vermicelli] and early in the morning go to the market to sell it, or how they would sit and weave baskets. All the community was together."

But then life changed forever. War broke out in June 1967, and it soon became obvious that the Israeli army had seized the Old City from Jordan. On 11 June, a Sunday morning, Nazmi al-Jubeh ventured out to investigate. "What we saw ... was indescribably horrific. Right there, at the bottom of the stairs, we saw soldiers, so many of them, heavily armed from head to toe, dancing and singing in a language that we did not understand, and behind them – emptiness. The Moroccan quarter no longer existed. The fig and pomegranate trees were gone, and so were the alleys I used to walk and play in ... Maslohi and his fig tree were not there; the only thing visible under June's hot sun was a cloud of dust hovering over a heap of rubble. Bulldozers, which I had never seen before in my life, were roaring along their metal chains to the tunes of victory music."

Israel's idea to take possession of the Western Wall by purchase or expropriation, and then to facilitate Jewish prayer in front of it by destroying an entire 700-year-old Muslim neighborhood and displacing its population, was not new: it had bubbled below the surface since the mid-nineteenth century. Chaim Weizmann, later Israeli president, had suggested it. So had philanthropists Moses Montefiore and Baron Edmond de Rothschild, and British planner Patrick Geddes. It had helped fuel fear, resentment and violence in Jerusalem throughout the 1920s and 1930s, inflamed by community leaders and exacerbated by colonial misrule. Then Jordan's destruction of Jewish neighborhoods in the Old City in 1948 and displacement of the Jewish population inspired an unfulfilled desire for revenge, which had festered for nineteen years. On 8 June 1967, the morning after Israeli forces seized control, Israel's former prime minister David Ben-Gurion visited the alleyway that Sultan Suleiman had opened at the "Wailing-Place of the Jews" four hundred years earlier. He was accompanied by the Israeli mayor of Jerusalem and the head of the Israeli parks authority.

In the way this tale's been told ever since, disgust plays a central part. One story says Ben-Gurion watched as a boy emerged from one of the houses and urinated on the Western Wall. Another story – by far the most prominent in Israeli sources, and repeated widely to this day – is that Ben-Gurion and the men with him were horrified to discover that the Jordanian authorities had built a public toilet against the Wall. The theme of righteous revulsion at non-Jewish desecration goes back a long way, to Psalm 79's "the heathen have … defiled your holy temple." Hebrew poet Hayim Bialik had in 1928 famously described the Wall's alleyway as "a public latrine bespattered with dung of man and animal." (Tales from that period speak of neighborhood residents leading donkeys to and fro, which was interpreted as provocation.) Over decades, Israel developed a narrative centered on Arab soiling of the Wall, which was used – and still is used – to justify what followed.

I've been unable to verify the existence of a public toilet. Acts of aggression or disrespect by individuals notwithstanding, it's unclear when or why the Jordanian authorities – if it was them – might have built a latrine against the Wall, or connived at one being built, since its presence would have desecrated a Muslim holy site. There were latrines only a hundred meters away, at the Haram's ablutions place, Bab al-Mathara. It's also unclear whether public toilets (rather than mosque ablutions) existed anywhere in the Old City in this period, Jordanian or British. Maybe there was a toilet here – in 2017 one of the Israeli contractors from 1967 said he remembered being "surprised" by the "stench" at the Wall before the demolition – or maybe men had just informally adopted some other structure for public urination.*

---

* Where would this public toilet have stood? The alleyway in front of the Wall was a narrow, enclosed area. On the east was the Wall itself. On the north was a wall at right angles to the Wall, punctuated by a doorway looking south down the alleyway; behind the doorway was a courtyard with fig trees and other foliage beside the Tankaziyya building (a former college and law court, also the mufti's office). On the west were the walls of the last row of houses in the Haret al-Magharba, two of which had stepped doorways opening onto the alleyway. On the south was another wall at right angles to the Wall and a short blind alley serving private family houses, one of which was converted into a *zawiya* after 1929. At least one of the houses (or, perhaps, the *zawiya*) did have a toilet in or near it. Was this what Ben-Gurion was so disgusted by? Others, too: army officers present in 1967, and Chaim Herzog, later Israeli president, also spoke of it. Or was it that the building identified by the Israelis as a public toilet had originally been something else and fallen into neglect? The citadel moat, the guardhouse adjoining Lions Gate and the entire Suq al-Qattanin market are all documented as having been used by men for public urination before their restoration around 1920. Disrespect may also have played a part, as it did at Ain Karim west of Jerusalem, where Israelis used an Ottoman mosque as a public latrine after 1948. Curiously, considering the controversies that followed, Avigdor Hameiri's 1934 Hebrew novel *Tnuva* includes a scene featuring a Jewish man urinating at the Wall. He is observed by other Jews – recent Zionist immigrants – who then beat him unconscious and run away.

Regardless, Ben-Gurion insisted the whole area be razed and the Wall exposed. Within twenty-four hours a plan had been cobbled together. No written orders were issued. "Best to do it and not ask questions," said the head of Israeli army central command. "Whatever has to be done, do it fast," said the Israeli justice minister.

Next day, 10 June, after dark, Israeli soldiers stormed through the neighborhood, shouting and banging on doors. Residents were given two hours – or, in some reports, three; others say only fifteen minutes – to leave their homes. That same night, around 11 p.m., men with sledgehammers went in first. Bulldozers followed, working through the night and into the next day. "In two days it was done – finished, clean," said Jerusalem's Israeli mayor, infamously.

After the area had been levelled, it was discovered that a woman had been killed in the rubble of her home. One source names her as Rasmiyyah Ali Tabaki; Maysoon tells me she was called Amina, and that she died because she was deaf and so didn't hear the warning calls.

Some thirty-two years later an Israeli army engineer who oversaw the operation spoke of having found several "Arab corpses" that night, some of which, he says, were simply bulldozed into the dirt in front of the Wall. Presumably they lie there still, trodden by the observant.

When it was all over, 138 buildings had been destroyed. Shrines, lodges and two mosques had been reduced to dust, including the ancient Afdaliyya. A long list of families were suddenly homeless – Zawawi, Jarbi, Dakali, Fassi, Marrakshi, Shawi, Filali, Teeb, Madyoni, Tazi, Tijani, Halafawi and dozens more. Later excavations here revealed possessions and even money discarded as people fled.

Their home is now the vast, paved plaza in front of the Western Wall. Bedecked with Israeli flags and floodlit after dark, much-visited, much-admired, much-photographed, the plaza is big enough to hold sixty thousand people at once. The Israeli army uses it to stage mass swearing-in ceremonies several times a year. It hosts memorial services on Israel's Remembrance Day, gala festivities on Israel's Independence Day, vast crowds celebrating every Jewish religious holiday. A demarcated area close to the Wall has been defined as an Orthodox synagogue and reserved for Jewish prayer. Every entrance to the plaza has a checkpoint with airport-style security. No sign or plaque recalls the presence of the Haret al-Magharba.

"I can still trace exactly where my grandfather's house was," says Maysoon.

If you search online, it's not hard to find a photo, taken from the German airship *Graf Zeppelin*, that shows the "Moroccan Quarter" from above in 1931. It's a grainy old image, but clear enough. You can see figures praying in the alleyway by the Wall (it was a rainy *Shabbat*, Saturday, 11 April), houses, trees, domes, courtyards, fields, stretching as far as Dung Gate.

One day I saved the photo on my phone and went down to the Western Wall plaza to see if I could use it to pace out the neighborhood. I imagined myself walking along phantom alleyways on that bare expanse of hard, shiny paving, pushing at ghostly doors, peering over vaporous walls into spectral gardens, sniffing at smells of long-eaten food in long-demolished ovens.

It didn't really work. A phone's too small. You'd need to print the photo out large, as a poster. And even then. New buildings block the space where the Afdaliyya used to be. The synagogue area by the Wall is for solemn prayer, not psychogeographical game-playing. Maybe you could do it if you were clever with GPS, but there are no physical reference points, other than the Wall. I couldn't place myself.

Remember the door at the start of this story? The one where people wait but no one goes in? That door stands at the head of steps leading up from the Western Wall plaza, the same steps twelve-year-old Nazmi al-Jubeh clattered down in horror in 1967. Every day, lines of people stand outside that door, but they are not waiting to go in: they are waiting to be frisked at the Israeli security checkpoint before walking down the steps into the Western Wall plaza. Beside them just happens to be a door, unmarked and private.

Maysoon al-Maslohi grew up in the building behind the door. It is almost the only standing remnant of the destroyed Haret al-Magharba, located on the very edge of the former neighborhood, where it merges into what used to be called Haret al-Sharaf, now part of the Jewish Quarter. But it's not only a home. Remarkably, behind that door stands the Zawiya al-Magharba, a Sufi lodge and mosque that has somehow survived the centuries.

A line of people are queuing for the checkpoint. Maysoon and I run the gauntlet of twenty pairs of watching eyes as she unlocks the anonymous metal door under the old stone arch and shows me into an enclosed space with plants and doorways, and steps leading to a rooftop courtyard. There, in an upper room at the back of a small mosque, behind another door bearing a Moroccan pentagram, virtually overlooking his old, old neighborhood-as-was, stands the plastered tomb of Abu Madyan himself, draped in green, unvisited and, for all intents and purposes, forgotten.

I don't think it's the famous Abu Madyan al-Ghawth, even though the hand-embroidered drape over the tomb says it is – his burial place in Tlemcen, in western Algeria, is pretty well attested. But it may be his grandson, the Abu Madyan who signed *waqf* papers in Jerusalem in 1320. Maysoon, though, is insistent about the Islamic *hijri* date 703, which is 1303 in the Gregorian calendar – and 14 November 1303 is precisely when Omar ibn Abdullah al-Mujarrad al-Masmudi signed *waqf* papers endowing a *zawiya* in the Haret al-Magharba. I wonder if this tomb is his, if this whole *zawiya* is his.

"My family, the Maslohi, is trying to keep this place," Maysoon says. "Israel wants to take the building so we keep everything locked and we don't annoy the neighbors by calling the prayer." She explains that five families live in the building – so, around thirty people – supported by the Moroccan Waqf. A Moroccan charity helped several years ago to renovate the building, which is in poor condition, and there have also been welcome expressions of support from Moroccan Jewish organizations and the French government, the former colonial power in Morocco.

We chat for a while, circling around the elephant in the room, then jointly agree to face it.

Do you remember 1967? I try to ask diplomatically.

"I was born in 1971," she replies, gently. "But my father was thirty-five in 1967. He always tells the story, about how nobody knew what was happening, how there were no announcements, just destruction. He didn't flee the country, he stayed. This was his home, he felt Jerusalemite, Palestinian. He said it was better to die here. My mother was younger; her family took her to Jordan but they came back a month later. [My parents] got married in '68."

All through her teenage years, Maysoon lived with her family in the *zawiya*, walking to and from school nearby, celebrating her sister's wedding here. Though she now lives in the Jerusalem suburbs, she keeps one property in the building, meeting any visitors who arrange to see the mosque and sometimes staying here over Ramadan. She tries to research the families of 1967, to keep Jerusalem's North African past from disappearing. "This is the only part of the Haret al-Magharba that is left," she says, describing how one or two other houses survived nearby: the Jibli home – where the family of her aunt's father lived – is now an Israeli police post.

And I think – What must the stress be like, to live with those stories looming over your childhood and a checkpoint literally outside the front door? The site of destruction is very close.

Do you ever try and pass through the Israeli security to walk across the plaza, to envisage how it used to be? – I say.

It's not an easy question to ask, and it shines a spotlight on the layers of privilege that separate us.

"I don't want to. They took it by force, and I have no power to take it back," Maysoon replies matter-of-factly.

The community of the Haret al-Magharba is now dispersed. A few families remain within the Old City; others live outside the walls or abroad, many in Morocco. A group of the survivors still meets every so often in Jerusalem, keeping contact with each other and with the younger generations, who grew up hearing the stories without ever knowing the quarter themselves. Of the institutions of study, learning and prayer established all those centuries ago in memory of Abu Madyan, only this *zawiya* under Maysoon al-Maslohi's protection remains, with its silent tomb. The lane it stands on used to be called Abu Madyan Alley. It is now Western Wall Street.

And of the thousands who tread the Western Wall plaza daily, and the millions who have trodden it since its creation fifty-five years ago, how many are aware of what happened where they step?

So today, entering at the mundane Dung Gate – rebuilt by Israel after Jordan had widened it to take vehicles, and now commonly known in Hebrew by the ahistorical name *Shaar ha-Kotel* (Western Wall Gate) – Jerusalem becomes an echoing field of absences. The sky is wide open. To the left is an unused piazza, created in the 1990s when Israeli archaeologists reopened the small Tanners' Gate beside it, a misshapen hole in the wall that may correspond to a Crusader fixture here. To the right are skeletal fragments of stone exposed at the foot of Al-Aqsa's walls, from when this used to be the main approach to the now-erased Temple courtyards. In front is a structure like a mini-airport terminal, built by Israel in 1988 as a security barrier in the absence of security. Beyond lies the vast, thronged, stone-paved lack of the Haret al-Magharba, with its dearth of acknowledgment, devoid of uncertainty. Flags mark a want of thought. Signs show no Arabic. Al-Wad Street ran here; there is no street. Women wove baskets here; there are no baskets. Abu Madyan's ghost drifts invisibly. Here, as everywhere in Jerusalem, what you see is never what's really going on.

I look up at the broad, tall, blankly enigmatic focus of all this drama, in front of which I myself was bar mitzvah one hot day long ago.

Wall.

Wall is the absence of Temple. Revenge is the absence of compassion. Wrong compounds wrong, bulldozing right into dust.

13

A Just and Happy Place

STORIES FROM THE JEWISH QUARTER

WE'VE TALKED OF THE FOUR QUARTERS and how little sense they make. How you can't tell when you cross between the Christian Quarter and the Muslim Quarter, while the Armenian Quarter is just an amorphous scattering of streets around the Armenian convent. It's the same with the older traditional quarters: Haret Bab Hutta merges invisibly into Haret as-Sa'diyya. It doesn't really matter which is which. Enter Jerusalem's Jewish Quarter, though, and you enter a place apart. It's unmistakable. You hear no Arabic. You smell no cumin. You see no checkpoints staffed by armed police.

And everything, or almost everything, is new. The ruptures of 1948 and 1967 had a greater impact on the urban fabric here than anywhere else – 1948 for the destruction in war and subsequent years of neglect under Jordanian rule, and 1967 for the Israeli government's reinvention of the area as a gentrified, Westernized, upmarket residential enclave, rebuilt in such a way as to distance it from what went before in both architecture and population. The stone cladding used here has had only decades, rather than centuries, to weather – edges are sharper, tones are brighter. Taxes paid here are, unusually for the Old City, put to good use: the municipality supplies services that are generally lacking in other neighborhoods, such as cleaning, lighting and street maintenance. Sky-high property prices put the area out of reach for all but the wealthy or the subsidized. The difficulties of access, pressure from tourism and the overwhelming dominance of religion in daily life further narrow the quarter's demographic profile. And then there's Israeli law, which forbids non-Jews – defined as such by the Chief Rabbinate, an office of the Israeli state – from purchasing property here.*

It's also a place where the catastrophe of 1948 – celebrated in Israel, of course, as anything but a catastrophe – feels entirely unbridgeable. In May of that year, immediately after Britain withdrew from Palestine, the Arab Legion – the army of Transjordan, later Jordan – joined volunteer fighters in the Old City in an effort to dislodge Zionist paramilitaries holed up in the Jewish Quarter. As the country continued its collapse into war, ten days of intense fighting left the Jordanians in control of the Jewish Quarter, but under devastating circumstances. The Legion advanced – as one historian put it to me – "meter by meter, by dynamiting, not by shelling." By the end whole neighborhoods had been flattened. Several landmark synagogues, used by Zionist paramilitaries as defensive fortifications and stores for weapons and ammunition, had been damaged in the fighting or, in some cases, destroyed by the Legion.

"Most of the Jewish quarter is now a complete ruin," wrote the *New York Times* correspondent on 28 May. That afternoon, a Friday, the leaders of the Jewish community inside the Old City surrendered to the Jordanian commander, Abdullah al-Tal. Al-Tal ordered all fighting men to be taken as prisoners-of-war and everyone else to be expelled to the Israeli-held part of the city, west of the walls.

Present throughout was the British-American photojournalist John Phillips. He had been granted accreditation by the Arab Legion and wore its uniform, so was able to work unhindered. It's largely thanks to his photographs, published initially in *Life* magazine and widely reproduced thereafter, that the surrender has become such an iconic episode in the Zionist narrative of the 1948 war.

---

* The precedent arises from a jaw-dropping 1978 decision of Israel's Supreme Court, which ruled that Muhammad Burqan was indeed the rightful owner of a residential property in the Jewish Quarter from which the government had evicted him, but that the area had a "special historical significance" for Jewish people which overrode his rights and the rights of all non-Jews.

Most of what happened in 1948 – massacres, expulsions, attacks, destruction – went unphotographed, preserved only in written and spoken (or, often, unwritten and unspoken) memories.

As the sun began to set that Friday, ushering in Shabbat, the Jewish day of rest and prayer, Phillips turned his lens on the Jewish Quarter's roughly 1,200 civilians as they were expelled from their homes. All had spent the previous six months besieged and under fire. Phillips immortalized scenes of hopelessness and despair amid the rubble. An old man sits cross-legged in the dirt, lost. A mother clutches her infant, blank-eyed. A young girl in a throng of soon-to-be-refugees flowing out of the Old City through Zion Gate turns back in fear or anguish, screaming. Phillips reports that a Spanish UN official beside him remarked: "It was just like this at Malaga during the civil war."

An account of the flight speaks of several people who had never before left the Old City. One man had been beyond the walls only once, as a young boy ninety years before. It is unimaginable. But even then, at the very point of victory and defeat, Rivka Weingarten, daughter of the mayor of the Jewish Quarter, Rabbi Mordechai Weingarten, who had just signed the surrender document, remembered how, "the first thing the [Jordanian] soldiers did was to give us all cold water to drink. They gave out bananas to the children and cigarettes to the soldiers and I also saw them carrying old men and women in their arms to help them reach Zion Gate."

An American and a French journalist who interviewed Abdullah al-Tal years later even recorded the victor's emotions as mixed. "His happiness that he had held Jerusalem's walls was mingled with the compassionate thought that 'so many Jews had lost their lives for nothing,'" they wrote, oddly uncritically. In his memoirs Al-Tal was less ambivalent: "Old Jerusalem was cleansed of the Jews, and not a single Jew was left for the first time in more than a thousand years."*

By the time the fighting was over, some two thousand Jewish people had been displaced from their homes in the Jewish Quarter

---

* Al-Tal used the word *taharat*, from a root meaning to clean, purge, sterilize or purify. He was wrong: a few – very few – people who identified as Jewish, or part-Jewish, remained; and the last expulsion of Jews from Jerusalem had been by the Crusaders, less than 850 years before. But still.

and elsewhere in what became known as East Jerusalem. Around twenty-eight thousand Palestinian people had been displaced from their homes in the Arab neighborhoods of what became West Jerusalem. Many of the former were given the homes of the latter. Thousands of the latter took refuge where the former once lived – a "charred and burnt-out shell" as Phillips described the Jewish Quarter the day after the surrender. They were joined, over the years, by new arrivals, particularly from Hebron, encouraged by the Jordanian government. Conditions were terrible. Water and electricity supplies remained intermittent. Rubble lay uncleared. Buildings were ramshackle, with blankets draped across windows and doorways. One friend, a teenager in 1960s Jerusalem, talked to me of what Jordan called the "Ex-Jewish Quarter" as "an ugly space, an area you never wanted to go through."

When Israel defeated Jordan in 1967 and occupied the Old City, the people who returned to the Jewish Quarter after nineteen years tended to do so for ideological reasons rather than for the desire to pick up the pieces of former lives. As far as I can establish very few – one study says "no more than a handful" – of the expelled residents, all of whom were resettled outside the walls, came back. I've tried to find if anyone living in the Jewish Quarter today is from a family that lived in the quarter before 1948, just to see if it's possible to trace any personal histories that might bridge that nineteen-year gap. Rivka Weingarten would have been perfect. As we'll see later in this chapter, she returned and opened a museum in her home. I'm sorry I never got the chance to talk to her before she died, in 2013. There may be others, too. I'd love to know.

At this point it's important to recall that Israeli law encourages the right of return not only for displaced Jewish Israelis but for all people the state defines as Jewish. It facilitates the reclamation – or, often, seizure – of property by Jews, while denying the same right to non-Jews and rebuffing their claims. Not one Palestinian family has regained their pre-1948 home in West Jerusalem, many of which still stand.

Israel had undergone a sharpening of political and cultural clarity over those nineteen years. Social stratification that produced an overwhelmingly dominant Ashkenazi* establishment and active suppression of Sephardi and, especially, Mizrahi – and, of course, Arab – cultures negated much of the desire to preserve heritage in the Jewish Quarter, other than in commodified form for tourist consumption. "Should ... keeping [the Jewish Quarter's] traditional Islamic–Middle Eastern character be the fulfillment of our dreams of a unified Jerusalem?" wrote one Israeli architect in outrage in 1968.

Faced, too, with the discovery of Jordanian desecration of Jewish cemeteries on the Mount of Olives, the urge was to erase, expressed literally, as we've seen, in the immediate razing of the North African quarter in front of the Western Wall. Soon afterwards, the Israeli government confiscated all land in what it defined as the Jewish Quarter – a larger area than previously – and created the Company for the Reconstruction and Development of the Jewish Quarter (which still exists) to direct the work. Postwar triumphalism drove a desire to break with the relatively recent past, where Jews had lived together under Islamic rule with Jerusalemites of other religions and ethnicities, sometimes accepted by them, sometimes not. Israel instead preferred to create links with periods of Jewish ascendancy in the Second and First Temple periods, fabled eras when David and Solomon ruled in wisdom and warrior heroes such as Judah Maccabee won glorious victories.

This is in part why Israel focuses so intently on King David, and why most excavations in the Jewish Quarter (and beyond it, notably the "City of David" project in Silwan) leapfrog the last 1,500 years to concentrate on showcasing ancient history. Enlarging and reinventing Jewish Jerusalem became a project of national assertiveness, in deliberate opposition to the old models of coexistence. It was, as two historians have written, "not only about heritage and tourism, but

---

* "Ashkenazi": Jews with origins in northern and eastern Europe. "Sephardi": Jews with origins in Iberia and southern and southeastern Europe. "Mizrahi": Jews with origins in the Arab and/or Muslim-majority countries of the Middle East, North Africa and Central Asia. These umbrella terms can overlap and are not universally accepted – especially "Mizrahi," since it originates in Zionist attitudes of discrimination against people from the deprived Jewish communities of eastern Europe, reinvented and redirected after 1948 against people from the Jewish communities of the Arab world. Also, geography is not the only consideration: religious, cultural and communal practices vary widely within as well as between these groupings.

also a political and religious statement to the world." The intent was to shape the future character of the Israeli state.

The way Esther Weiss talks about the Jewish Quarter in 1967, it seems like it must have been a place where the jubilation of victory and possession tussled daily with fear and hardship.

Esther knows the quarter. She knows the people, the places, the stories. And she'll tell you it all. All. But she's not a tour guide, or anything like that. Esther has lived it, to her fingertips. She was one of the first Jewish people to settle the neighborhood after Israel occupied (though she wouldn't use that word herself) in 1967, and fifty-five years later she still lives there. Her shop, selling jewelry and Judaica – artworks, silver candlesticks, paraphernalia for prayer – is on the quarter's main market street. Everyone stops in.

Esther was born in Netanya, a town on the coast north of Tel Aviv, in 1950. Five years earlier, her parents had been liberated from the Nazi death camp at Auschwitz. They'd made their way back home to eastern Czechoslovakia, but left for good as soon as they heard about the new State of Israel. "They said they'd had enough *goyim* [non-Jews] in their lives," Esther sniffs. "They didn't want to live with them anymore." Then she clarifies that she was actually born in a tent outside Netanya, since "that was where Israel put all the newcomers. There was no housing at that time."

The first time Esther saw Jerusalem was on a school trip for her bat mitzvah, aged twelve. Teachers took her and her classmates to Mount Zion, right on the border with Jordan. They stood on the roof of King David's Tomb and craned their necks to catch a glimpse of where the Western Wall lay.

It was in 1967, immediately after the war, that she walked into the Old City for the first time. She talks about it in a tone of wonder. "The Jewish Quarter was all ruins, piles of ruins, no sign of houses, nothing. Jewish people were afraid to go there alone. When we walked to the Kotel [Western Wall] the first time, we went in a group, and we avoided going through the quarter."

What was she afraid of? Esther leaves that unsaid.

All of Jewish Israel was caught up in the atmosphere of triumph. "Crowds of people were streaming down to the Western Wall every day," one observer noted. "It seemed like the Messiah was just around the corner. There was such euphoria. The joy, and the feeling that we were involved in some superhuman process, was indescribable."

Esther fell in with a group of Israeli soldiers who had been charged with re-establishing a Jewish presence in the Old City. They operated under a government program that mixed military service with vocational training in trades such as carpentry, metalwork, electrical engineering and printing. Termed Nahal – a Hebrew acronym standing for "Fighting Pioneer Youth" – this particular cooperative, including graduates in Jewish religious studies, was code-named "Moriah," after Mount Moriah, the Temple Mount that dominated the Old City.

In August 1967, only a couple of months after Israel's victory, the first Nahal Moriah members moved into a ruin on Gal'Ed Street in the Jewish Quarter and began clearing rubble. By the following February the building was deemed habitable. More settlers followed.

It was around this time that Esther, barely eighteen, signed up to study art at the Hebrew University of Jerusalem. But her mind was elsewhere. "I started to come in and out with those soldiers. They brought girls to serve, together with them. It was so exciting. Everything was very fresh and very new. Exotic. These soldiers had to walk around in uniform and show there was a Jewish presence, but they were working professionals too. It was a wonder."

Teams began fixing up tiny half-ruined apartments around the Nahal Moriah settlement. "It wasn't comfortable, but nobody complained. There was a feeling that that's what we have to do, this is our time." She remembers the quarter's first wedding. "There was no furniture to sit on, so we rented benches from Arabs in the *shuk* (Hebrew: market). It was very exotic. Our Arab neighbors, at the beginning, were not so violent. They had to adjust to the new situation. They were afraid."

Everyone was afraid. Of each other, it seems.

When Esther married David, one of the soldiers, they lodged with his buddies at first, but then were given a little apartment of their own on a high slope overlooking the Western Wall, in 1969. They and four other couples were the first Jewish families to set up home in the postwar Jewish Quarter. "It was amazing to live there, like being the captain of a ship," Esther remembers. "The view I had, it was phenomenal. I'm a curious person, and we walked all the little alleys. So many layers of history. The mix of *muezzins*, church bells, listening to the Jewish study groups at the Wall on Shabbat afternoon. Everything coming to your home."

How were relations with Muslim neighbors at that time?

"We had Arab families living downstairs, and soldiers protecting us on the roof. Some people made friends with the Arabs. We didn't so much. They were compensated and moved out anyway."

That's where the story of Muhammad Burqan comes from.

Even for Esther it can't have been pleasant. Aged twenty, she was living in semi-ruined housing under armed protection as a beneficiary of the state's colonial settlement policies, in sight and sound of all the diverse communities and crowded markets of the Old City but cut off from them by language and culture. And politics.

"We didn't have a grocery for three or four years. We had to go to a shop in Mamilla [outside Jaffa Gate] to get whatever we needed. Our old houses were damp and needed lots of work, but it was a struggle to find materials in the Old City. Being newly married was not easy. Having a little baby was not easy. You don't have anyone around to help you, advise you, take care of the baby for five minutes if she cries. We had a very nice window with a bench that opened up to the Kotel, so if she was crying and I didn't know what to do with her anymore, I used to lay her on a pillow and put her in the window and say, 'God, here she is, please take care of her.'"

Eventually family life settled. Esther and David got a new house in the quarter in 1973 and after finding work as an art teacher, in 1988 Esther opened her Judaica shop in a building alongside. It's still there today. She's adamant that despite all the hardship early on, she never yearned for comfort, or even better conditions. She is still filled with wonder at the privilege of watching the Jewish Quarter rise around her over five decades, seeing archaeologists unearth remnants of the past, watching artists decorate the newly built synagogues, feeling communities grow. The changes have been huge, she says, but some things haven't progressed much.

"We still have very poor services. We have a clinic, some schools and nurseries, but real shops and services for the local people? Very few. It's more for tourists. You have so many here now, it's crowded. You have to push your way through a mob." And lots of people from the heady days after 1967 didn't stick it out. "They wanted to go back to their modern houses in their cities," she says. "They weren't attracted to this place. You needed a special feeling to be in all this mud."

Ah, so that's why you stayed, I laugh. You had that special feeling, right?

"Probably, looking back. But we were not so aware of history, these big moments. We were young and busy and living our lives, you know."

That's the thing about Esther. Knock on someone else's door if you want rose-tinted nostalgia.

In some cases, Israel's break with the past after 1967 was unavoidable. The most famous of Jerusalem's grand synagogues is the Hurva (Hebrew: "Ruin"), its high dome, rebuilt in 2010, standing above the Jewish Quarter as a visual parallel to the domes of Al-Aqsa and the Holy Sepulchre. It got its nickname in the early eighteenth century, when a synagogue on the site was abandoned half-built – and then perhaps demolished – after works failed due to debts and disputes within the Ashkenazi community of the time.

The Ruin lay undisturbed for a century. Before it, there was a church here in the Crusader period, though traditions suggest that a synagogue stood here earlier still, as far back as the second century. By the 1810s Ashkenazi immigration was spurring plans to build afresh on the Hurva site, and a new synagogue was finally dedicated in 1864, square, domed, fully twenty-four meters high, with graceful window arches. It flourished until 1948, when it was reportedly dynamited by the Jordanian army to flush out Jewish paramilitaries hiding within, and then reduced to rubble. (Some say the initial damage was caused by the ignition of ammunition the paramilitaries had been storing inside the synagogue.) Arguments among Israeli planners and architects after 1967 over whether to replace it like-for-like or design anew delayed rebuilding until the 2000s, when the traditionalists eventually won out.

The Hurva, rebuilt in whitish limestone to its nineteenth-century design, now overlooks a large, open piazza ringed by new apartments, like a European suburb. Women push their strollers, men push their sunglasses, kids push each other, tourists suck on milkshakes at café tables set out under the trees, flags fly, cyclists cycle, buskers busk, and it's as if the world is a just and happy place.

In other cases, Israel's break with the past was a conscious policy.

Compare a current map with a pre-1967 map and it's clear that the streets of the Jewish Quarter do not match. Part of the reason is war damage, exacerbated, say many here, by Jordanian demolition. Only about a third of the buildings in what had been the Jewish Quarter are reported as having been habitable after 1948 – and throughout the Jordanian period they were overcrowded with refugees and the otherwise unhoused. By 1965 Jordan had started evacuating people to the suburbs ahead of redevelopment plans that were cut short by the 1967 war. When Israel occupied, displacing remaining residents, it could bulldoze with impunity and plot new streets without reference to preexisting structures.

Multiple quarters with mixed populations once filled the zone that Israel now defines as the Jewish Quarter. From long before the nineteenth century Jews had lived in a small area on and just beside the main north–south market street, known as *Haret al-Yahud* ("Neighborhood of the Jews"). To the east were Muslim quarters known as *Haret al-Sharaf*, after Sharaf al-Din Musa, a Jerusalemite official of the fourteenth century,* and *Haret al-Magharba*, the North African quarter. To the west were Armenian, Maronite and Syriac communities, grouped around their church buildings, and clusters of Muslim settlement.

---

* This name survives on the trilingual street signs marking an alley that branches off St. Mark's Street. The English and Hebrew on the signs call the alley Bikur Holim Street, named for the Bikur Holim Jewish hospital that operated here from 1864 to 1947. But the Arabic on the same signs names the alley as Tariq Haret al-Sharaf ("Sharaf Quarter Road"), somehow having evaded Israeli erasure. Multiple histories overlay each other, often heedless of each other's presence. The fifteenth-century historian Mujir ad-Din records that before Haret al-Sharaf the same neighborhood was known as the Kurdish quarter.

There has been a concerted effort to expand the Jewish Quarter westwards by expropriating buildings around the Syriac, Maronite and Armenian churches and, as the political scientist Michael Dumper writes plainly, "evicting the Palestinian tenants and replacing them with Israelis." After 1967 the Jewish Quarter became critical to the Israeli government's stated aim of preserving a demographic balance in Jerusalem of 70:30, Jews to non-Jews. (The current ratio, citywide, is between 65:35 and 60:40.)

Israel's current Jewish Quarter has already subsumed both Haret al-Sharaf and Haret al-Magharba: their populations have been dispersed and their streets erased. What replaces them is a simulacrum of what they once might have been, infused with the hollow spirit of 1970s and 1980s European urban design. A defensive warren of alleys, linked by stairs and covered passageways, holds the ambience of intrusion into a gated community: you wonder if this walkway leads only to someone's front door, or if you should ask permission before climbing those steps to find your way. Yeshivas rear up like corporate offices. Memorials to Jewish fighters nestle in corners like water features decorating the privatised plaza of a bank. An iron gate separates the rebuilt Israeli-owned art galleries in the Cardo from the old Palestinian-owned shops in the adjacent souk, ready to be clanged shut and locked tight.

Still, stories survive here and there. There's Udi Merioz, who runs a gallery selling Judaica and sentimental paintings on Jewish and nationalist themes; the most famous shows a group of armed Israeli soldiers at prayer. He's developed a line in tale-telling from the time when, as a nine-year-old boy, he accompanied his artist father, Elyada – formerly of the Irgun, a Zionist paramilitary terrorist group – as one of the first Jewish Israelis to settle the Jewish Quarter immediately after the 1967 war, even before Esther Weiss and her husband (though Merioz initially stayed less than a year, establishing the business some time later).

Then there's the Muslim-owned Abu Sneineh bakery that has survived in the heart of the Jewish Quarter by securing a *hechsher**– apparently the only such enterprise in the city to do so. Thirteen Muslim families still live on the edge of the neighborhood, I was told, having clung to their properties since before 1967. I haven't yet been able to meet them.

Both of the Jewish Quarter's surviving mosques, empty for many years, were reportedly refurbished in 2019. One is a fifteenth-century building near Zion Gate, where the Jewish and Armenian quarters merge, named for the Disi family. The other, a few steps from the Hurva synagogue, is the Sidna Omar, whose minaret, rising above the trees, is very old, first built perhaps soon after Salah ad-Din retook Jerusalem from the Crusaders and recorded as having been restored some time after 1397. It's not yet clear what the renovations portend.

Directly beside the Sidna Omar mosque – the two share a wall – is the Ramban Synagogue, named for the Hebrew acronym RMBN, which stands for Rabbi Moses ben Nachman. Despite the bloodbath that was the Crusader invasion, Jews had started to resettle in Jerusalem even before Salah ad-Din ejected the Crusaders in 1187. Nonetheless when the Catalan rabbi Moses, also known by the name Nachmanides, arrived in 1267, he found only a few individual Jews, who prayed together at home. The synagogue he established, whose presence fuelled a strengthening of community, was closed by the Ottoman authorities in 1586 and was only restored and reopened in 1967.

I've rambled around this neighborhood of latte bars, yeshivas and souvenir galleries often, from the Sidna Omar mosque to a preserved section of the sixth-century *cardo maximus*, a colonnaded street exposed to the sky three meters below street level, and over to a ruined Crusader church known as St. Mary of the Germans, now surrounded by the Jewish Quarter's new building. Its

---

* A frequently renewed notice of certification from a rabbinical authority that a food outlet, or a specific product, is kosher – that is, compliant with Jewish dietary laws. Observant Orthodox Jews will not buy or consume foods that do not bear a *hechsher*.

preserved ruins were once open for sightseeing but, amid objections from religious authorities and disputes over ownership, the site has been closed and overgrown for some time.

Overlooking an exposed section of the Cardo stands the Tzemach Tzedek synagogue, built in 1856 during the same settlement drive by Ashkenazi Jews that resulted in the Hurva synagogue, a few meters away. This group of families, though, belonged to the *Habad* (or *Chabad*) ultra-Orthodox movement, and they named their new building after their *rebbe* (Yiddish: spiritual leader) based in Lubavitch in Russia, Menachem Mendel Schneersohn, known as the Tzemach Tzedek (Hebrew: Righteous Branch).* Take a step back and you can see how the original synagogue, with its mismatched arches in stone, is below: the community added the upper, archless storey in 1879, when additional funds came through.

This synagogue plays a role in the "who was the first Jew to settle the Jewish Quarter after 1967" story. Moshe Segal – a "Lubavitcher" rabbi then in his sixties, famed as a paramilitary fighter and for resisting the British before 1948 – rushed to the Old City as soon as Israel occupied and talked his way past the sentries guarding the Jewish Quarter. The one synagogue he found intact was Tzemach Tzedek. Leaving his family (his wife said she didn't want to live around Arabs, and only joined him the following year), Segal set up house that night in the building alongside, fixing damage and restoring the synagogue in a matter of months. He lived in the Jewish Quarter almost until his death in 1985.

The Lubavitchers are the nearest Judaism has to evangelicals, stopping passersby in the street to ask "Are you Jewish?" and trying to persuade anyone who says yes to join them in prayer. The more Jews fulfilling the *Habad* idea of observance, the more likely it is that the Messiah will return, they say.

That their synagogue stands on the Jewish Quarter's busiest corner seems apt.

---

* A complex phrase that is a quote from his writings, sourced from Zecharia 3:8 and 6:12. See also Jeremiah 23:5 and 33:15.

Down a quieter alley nearby I thought I might unearth some stories at the *ha-Ari* synagogue, birthplace of the sixteenth-century rabbi Isaac Luria, a founder of the Jewish mystical tradition Kabbalah. The complex housing the synagogue, just across the blurry line where the Jewish and Armenian quarters overlap, was the home – indeed also the birthplace, in 1922 – of Rivka Weingarten, who we met earlier on. Her family arrived in Jerusalem from eastern Europe in the early nineteenth century, the first Ashkenazim to settle in more than a hundred years. They were prosperous people, silversmiths and property magnates, who before 1948 enjoyed the rarity of a telephone line and the only radio in the neighborhood. After 1948, and nineteen years of displacement in West Jerusalem, Weingarten returned in 1967 only to find part of the building destroyed and the family's possessions gone. "The Arabs looted everything," she told a reporter in 2008. "But I don't mind, I am not angry at them. Jews looted, too. That is the way it is in war."

By 1976 Weingarten had renovated the building and converted part of it to house an absorbing five-room museum documenting the Old Yishuv, the term denoting Jerusalem's Jewish community – or, more accurately, communities – that existed before Zionism and the late nineteenth- and early twentieth-century waves of Jewish immigration. I've spent hours there. One exhibit dwells heavily on the 1948 surrender, showcasing John Phillips's photographs. Others detail social history, down to bed linen and kitchenware. The old maps they've pinned on the wall are pure catnip. The last time I was there I stayed so long they had to throw me out in the end so they could close up – but still, I couldn't find a living link to the present that would help me bridge the catastrophe of 1948.

Then I happened to come across the oldest active synagogue in Jerusalem. It's an outlier, overlooked by almost everyone, tourists and the Israeli state included. To find it, you need to squirrel around in the lanes behind the big square in front of the Hurva synagogue. Old buildings don't guarantee human interest, of course, but this is not your average old building. "In 1989 one family returned and lived here, but they were old and they left. Another family came and they also left. Now it's just me," Avi Yefet, the caretaker, said, before startling me with his next sentence. "My family came from Egypt, but before that my great-great-grandfather used to be the chief *hakham* [rabbi] of Jerusalem."

What followed was an unexpected glimpse into a world of Jews who kneel on carpets and touch their foreheads to the ground to pray, Jews who do not light candles on Friday night, Jews who do not celebrate Hanukkah, Jews who are told they are not Jews at all.

Mainstream Judaism accepts two sources for the religion, both of which are believed, in Orthodox traditions, to have been transmitted from God to Moses at Mount Sinai. First is the Written Law, which strictly refers to the first five books of the Torah from Genesis to Deuteronomy, but which can encompass all twenty-four books of the Hebrew Bible (what's commonly called in English the Old Testament). Then there's the Oral Law, a set of statutes, commentaries and interpretations that was passed verbally down the generations until being codified between roughly 200 and 500 CE as the Talmud.

The large majority of believers treat the Written Law and Oral Law as having equal, divinely endowed force. They accept the authority of rabbis (Hebrew: "teachers") to interpret the Torah and are thus known as Rabbinic or Rabbanite Jews.

Others, though, differ. They say religious authority derives solely from the Torah, the Written Law. They reject the idea that the rabbinical Talmud, the Oral Law, has equal authority and instead emphasize the capacity of each Jewish individual to interpret the texts for themselves. They are the Karaite (or Qaraite) Jews, from a Hebrew word meaning "readers."

"We are not Mizrahi, not Sephardi, not Ashkenazi. We are Karaite. We have another tradition. And the *haredi* [ultra-Orthodox Jews] don't like us," says Avi Yefet with a grin. Young, T-shirted, slow to speak, Yefet is the live-in caretaker for Jerusalem's Karaite synagogue, which, apart from a few gaps here and there – the

Crusaders, the Jordanians – has been open the last 1,200 years, give or take. It's small, and the synagogue itself is now below ground level, but around it has developed a little compound: the rooms where Yefet lives alone, a couple of guest apartments and a museum, all overlooking a shady courtyard.

"We have a few families in Jerusalem, outside the walls, but most of the community is in Ramla and Ashdod," Yefet says, naming two cities forty or fifty kilometers to the west. "Today is quiet, but last week two hundred people came here for *Sukkot* [the Feast of Tabernacles, a Jewish harvest festival]. It's the same for *Pesach* [Passover, a spring festival commemorating the Exodus]. And every week another group asks to stay here over Shabbat."

Karaite Judaism is usually said to have been founded by Anan ben David, an eighth-century anti-rabbinical dissident from Babylon in modern Iraq. Some, though, date it long before: Judaism hosted similar movements as early as the second and first centuries BCE. But it was amid the political and ideological ferment thrown up first by the promulgation of the Talmud from the sixth century onwards, and then by the arrival and rapid spread of Islam in the seventh, eighth and ninth centuries, that Karaite philosophy took hold. "Search carefully in the scriptures, and don't rely on my opinion," Anan said, in a provocative foretaste of Martin Luther's words 750 years later, and Muhammad Abduh's 350 years after that.

He may even have drawn inspiration from Islam. After having been jailed by the caliph of Baghdad for opposing the appointed leader of the Jewish community, Anan – so the story goes – met a Muslim scholar in prison. They discussed their different outlooks, and the scholar advised Anan to focus on clarifying the teachings of the Torah, even if they ran against traditional interpretations. That scholar was the Persian jurist Abu Hanifa, founder of the Hanafi school of Islamic law, himself jailed for having stood up to the caliph.

After talking himself out of jail, Anan took those ideas with his followers in exile to Jerusalem, where, perhaps around 770–790 CE, they established the synagogue that Avi Yefet watches over today. For several centuries thereafter, Karaism spread around the Levant and into southeastern Europe, establishing itself particularly in Egypt, Constantinople and Crimea.

Some of Karaite practice is astonishingly like Islam. Worshippers leave their shoes at the synagogue entrance. They kneel on the floor, prostrating themselves during prayer and touching their forehead to the ground in forms of worship mainstream rabbinical Judaism now explicitly prohibits. All of it is drawn from biblical verses: Exodus 3:5 ("Take off your shoes, for the place where you stand is holy ground"); Daniel 6:10 ("Three times a day [Daniel] knelt down and prayed"); Joshua 7:6 ("Joshua fell to the ground on his face before the ark of the Lord"); and so on.

I ask Avi whether observers make the visual connection with Islam.

"Everybody says it," he says flatly, adding, perhaps predictably, though also perhaps not wrongly, "But the Muslims came later. *They* copied *us*. You can read about the old Jewish traditions of kneeling. The Rabbinic Jews don't want to pray like Muslims, but look – now they build their synagogues like a church. Have you seen the Hurva, with its pews?" He snorts, but then adds more thoughtfully: "Even if Islam does the same as us, it's OK. It doesn't matter."

Karaite prayer also involves raising the hands, and the eyes. The Amidah, a prayer at the core of rabbinical Jewish liturgy, recited three times a day for the last two thousand years or more, is absent from Karaite worship, since it is absent from the Written Torah. The festival of Hanukkah is not celebrated, since it originated after the Torah. Karaism accepts patrilineal descent, not the matrilineal descent of mainstream Judaism, yet – unlike Orthodox Judaism – in Karaism women and men are equal, and women can take active roles in prayer services. There are many more differences of doctrine and identity.

It's a compelling idea, to reject tradition and the accumulated wisdom of sages and revert to the purity of a source text. Many other religions and traditions, including Christianity and Islam, have undergone their own versions of it. But Karaism shouldn't be mistaken for an anti-intellectual fundamentalism. Reasoning and analogy lie at the core of Karaite grapplings with meaning in the Torah, and Karaite literature is full of debate; indeed, it has inspired much opposing argument from rabbinical scholars defending their own traditions.

Yet mainstream hackles are permanently up. Israel's Chief Rabbinate will still not authorize Karaite marriages, and in 2015 had to be forced by the courts to certify Karaite ritual slaughter as kosher. It has openly decreed: "Israel is a Jewish state and Jews have superior rights. But the Karaites are not Jewish." In a polity which only functions because of sharp – and strictly enforced – ethno-religious divisions between in-groups and out-groups, such a statement has serious implications.

I spent a long time in Jerusalem's Karaite museum. One display reproduces an account of a visit to the city in 1641–42 by a Crimean Karaite, Shmuel, describing how he approached the subterranean synagogue via a flight of twenty steps leading down from the courtyard. Avi unlocked a door off the courtyard and showed me a flight of twenty steps leading down to the synagogue (plus three new ones added at the top to reach current ground level). But he said I couldn't go down: non-Karaites may only view the synagogue through a window. So I viewed the synagogue through a window. Its carpeted floor was clear of obstacles. Thick pillars of stone sprouted typical Jerusalem cross-vaulting. Pewter lamps hung on chains, each with a Star of David dangling beneath. I thought about the tyranny of majorities, especially religious ones, but what rang loudest in my head was the hunch that Judaism and Islam share more, superficially and at their spiritual cores, than either is prepared these days to acknowledge – and more, it seems to me, than either has ever shared with Christianity.

Avi and I chatted for a while, me looking over Avi's elbow as he scrolled through his family tree on his phone. He pointed at an image of an old gray-bearded face, head tilted and eyes weary.

"My great-great-grandfather, Moshe al-Qudsi, or Moshe Yerushalmi," Avi said. "He was chief *hakham* in Jerusalem and Cairo a hundred and fifty years ago. He moved from here to marry

in Egypt but then came back with his wife as an old man because he wanted to die in Jerusalem."*

The couple's dates show that they died within six months of each other, in 1905 – Moshe first, aged about ninety-five, then his wife Biana, eighty-five – though Avi didn't point that out. They are buried in Jerusalem's small Karaite cemetery, outside the walls.

"They left three sons behind in Cairo," says Avi, explaining that his grandparents were also born there but his parents and he were born in Israel after the family fled Egypt in 1950. But then he starts scrolling the other way on his phone. First he shows me his three-times-great-grandfather Abraham ha-Levi al-Damaski

---

* Avi didn't say "Musa al-Qudsi," which would be the Arabic equivalent of the Hebrew "Moshe Yerushalmi" (both terms mean "Moses the Jerusalemite"); instead, he mixed elements of both languages. Many Karaite religious leaders prefer to be called *hakham* (feminine: *hakhama*), a Hebrew title meaning scholar or sage, rather than "rabbi."

(1776–1830), then, above him, his four-times-great-grandfather Moshe ha-Levi al-Damaski (1735–1820). What is the family's Damascus connection? Avi doesn't know. He tells me he can count back eight generations altogether, then shrugs and puts the phone down with an air of finality. I try, gently, to elicit something from him. What does it feel like, to have that connection with the past? Does it make you proud?

He's quiet for a moment, and when he replies he wears an unreadable expression. "It doesn't change anything," he says, slowly. "Eight generations, ten, a hundred – I don't care."

There's a pregnant pause. I wait for something to emerge. Nothing does. Well OK then.

We chat a bit about safer subjects, like politics – "I don't think you can believe in God and be a leftist," says Avi, which makes us both smile, though for different reasons – and I leave him spraying glass cleaner on the windows, keeping the old place looking good.

I should
like to
see any
power
of the
world
destroy
this race,
this small
tribe of un..
important people,
whose wars have all been fought and
lost, whose structures have crumbled, litera..
ture is unread, music is unheard, and prayers
are no more answered. Go ahead, destroy
Armenia. See if you can do it. Send them in..
to the desert without bread or water. Burn
their homes and churches. Then see, if they
will not laugh, sing and pray again. For when
two of them meet anywhere in the world,
see if they will not create a New Armenia.

William Saroyan

14

When I Speak in Armenian

STORIES OF BAB AN-NABI DAWOUD/ ZION GATE

I'D PICKED UP BITS AND BOBS of Apo Sahagian's output online, both his alternative folk-rock band and his solo material, all of which I loved. I found out he was born and brought up, and still lived, in the Old City. Then I came across a video he'd posted of himself on stage. He'd begun by talking, in English, about his community, the Armenians of Jerusalem, and – well, this is what he said:

> We daily juggle with languages, and I realized I'm a different person in each language I speak. When I speak in Armenian I'm chill, as if I'm at home. When I speak in English I'm confident and I can go on for hours and hours. When I speak in Arabic I'm shallow, because when it comes time to use the deeper words, I forget the deeper words. When I speak in Hebrew I'm defensive, because it's always in a confrontation, it's either at the airport, the bank, the checkpoint or Misrad Hapnim [the Israeli interior ministry, which issues passports and ID].

So I realized music is actually a good platform to approach these languages in my own way. I started to sing in English, for years, but nobody really cared because everybody sings in English and there's nothing special about it. Then I started a band called Apo & the Apostles, in Arabic, and it became a hit – but I still stayed a shallow person when I speak Arabic. Then I started to song-write in Hebrew – it went well, but the confrontations go on.

But being an Armenian in the diaspora, and from Jerusalem especially, it's the Armenian folk songs that come with passion for me. I'm dealing with dialects that are almost dead now, a hundred years after the genocide. This is my way of reconciling with part of my heritage that is on its death-bed. So what I do in my small corner of Jerusalem, I try to rebuild the stories, the tales, the songs of our villages, our towns, our history that we've left behind. I put them online so that the generation that comes next will discover them, and appreciate our culture that I'm trying to preserve.

Then he sang a gorgeous, plaintive old Armenian folk song about a girl who reassures her mother that the boy she loves may not be tall, but he's still beautiful.

Interesting, right? How many quadrilingual rock stars into cultural heritage do you know? And he *is* a rock star – Buzzfeed picked up on Apo & the Apostles' local popularity and named them as one of the Middle East's most exciting new bands. Their channel on YouTube has millions of views. They've already played in several European cities and are getting a reputation on Europe's summer festival circuit. They turn out cheerful, good-time music that makes you want to dance, and people respond.

So when I met Apo – he cut quite a figure, tall, skinny, in a red plaid shirt, his dark hair loose, striding towards me through the dithering tourists – I wanted to ask him about the band, about his folk roots, all sorts of stuff. He doesn't drink coffee but we sat in a café anyway and ended up talking for two hours straight. As it turned out, almost none of it was about music.

But first, the place. Apo was born, brought up and still lives just inside what's known in English as Zion Gate. This is probably the least used of Jerusalem's city gates, and has become a bit of an anomaly. The communities inside – chiefly Armenian and Jewish – tend to have their attention directed elsewhere, looking either east to the Jewish Quarter or north to the Armenian convent. Immediately outside Zion Gate are only the holy places and cemeteries on Mount Zion.

The gate used to be in a more logical position at the southern end of the main street that carves through the city from Damascus Gate, but it was shunted slightly west during Sultan Suleiman's rebuilding work in the sixteenth century to create better access to Mount Zion. The old story runs that Suleiman was so furious when he heard this stretch of wall had been built on the "wrong" side of Mount Zion's summit, excluding the holy places, that he had his chief architects beheaded. That's dramatic, but apocryphal, as we'll see later.

Then again, it's not half as apocryphal as the tale about Mount Zion told by Benjamin of Tudela (1130–1173), a Jewish traveller from what is now Spain, who visited Jerusalem a few years before he died. He got talking here to an old rabbi named Abraham al-Constantini, who spun him a yarn about what had happened while workmen were fixing an old church on Mount Zion. As Benjamin recounts it, the men came upon a cave which opened to a shrine with marble pillars, a golden table, a crown and scepter, treasure chests and tomb after tomb. They were about to enter the room when a violent blast of wind struck them both down. Then another gust swept through, whispering at them to stand up and leave. They fled in terror and told the Patriarch, who declared that the tombs must be those of David, Solomon and the kings of Judah. But his intent to explore the cave was called off, as the workmen took to their beds and refused to return to the site. The hole was sealed and the place closed up.

Now, there *is* such a tomb on Mount Zion (no crown or golden table, mind). Unfortunately it isn't King David's, though such claims had circulated in Islam and Christianity for a couple of centuries even before Benjamin, first noted by the tenth-century polymath

Al-Masudi. Back in the early centuries of Christianity the building housing the tomb may have been a church, or a synagogue, or some kind of hybrid of the two, but the tomb chamber itself has been a mosque dedicated to Nabi Dawoud (Prophet David) for most of the last five hundred years.

This building took on extra significance between 1948 and 1967, when Suleiman's city wall became an international border here: Zion Gate was sealed and Mount Zion fell under Israeli control. The tomb was the closest Jewish Israelis, or anyone approaching from the Israeli side, could get to the Western Wall. Pilgrims would gather on the roof to pray towards the Wall, and the tomb chamber itself was turned into a synagogue dedicated to King David. Since then, all traces of Islam have been expunged.*

What makes the situation more fraught still is that upstairs from the tomb chamber, within the same building, is a (probably) twelfth-century hall, later gothicized, that is traditionally the place where Jesus and the disciples ate the Last Supper. A short walk away stands the House of Caiaphas, the high priest who tried Jesus, now an Armenian church; the Abbey of the Dormition, as in the "falling asleep" (that is, death) of the Virgin Mary; and the Church of St. Peter in Gallicantu, where the apostle denied Christ just before the crow (*cantus*) of a cock (*gallus*).

Truly, the density of Jerusalem's holy sites can be exhausting.

There's no refuge in words. Even Zion. Nobody is sure where Zion came from or what it means – it goes back to the Old Testament, and perhaps before – but for millennia it has stood for Jerusalem, or Israel, or the Jewish people as a whole or, metaphorically, in multiple cultures and traditions (not least Rastafari and many Black churches in the US), for a utopian haven of harmony and freedom. People who lived far from the Promised Land took the biblical stories of Jews' oppression and exile and mapped them onto their own lives, reinventing the ancient Jewish yearning for Zion as a yearning for their own freedom from enslavement and return from exile.

---

* The Israel Antiquities Authority recently ruled that seventeenth-century Ottoman wall tiles lining the tomb chamber, every one of which was diligently smashed to pieces by persons unknown over two nights in December 2012 and January 2013, just before CCTV was to be installed, should not be replaced.

Adding insult to injury, the name "Mount Zion" has shifted around, at one time referring to the hilltop on the eastern side of Jerusalem where the Jewish Temples stood and where Al-Aqsa stands now. Today, Mount Zion is on the other, southwestern side of the city, named as such roughly since the Roman destruction of Jerusalem, when it began to be linked with King David. Zion Gate, in front of the mount and still riddled with bullet holes from the fighting in 1948, preserves that link in its commonest Arabic name Bab an-Nabi Dawoud ("Gate of Prophet David"). It's also known as Bab Sihyun (*sihyun* is Zion).

Inside the gate, you feel like you might have made a wrong turn: Jerusalem has become a suburban industrial estate. Facing you are the high walls surrounding the Armenian convent, topped with a chain-link fence. Traffic passes on a one-way circuit, marked with no-entry signs. Following the cars round the corner reveals apartment blocks and a large Israeli-run car park. It's like some other city altogether. Perhaps it's not a coincidence that, for hundreds of years up to the late nineteenth century, this area inside Zion Gate was where Jerusalem's lepers lived, dubbed *Dar al-Masakeen* ("Miserable Place," or, euphemistically, "Abode of Poverty"). Next door was the city abattoir.

Today, these rather pleasant back streets form the edges of the Armenian Quarter.

"When I was young, the Armenian Quarter was Jerusalem and Jerusalem was the Armenian Quarter," says Apo. "My family lives inside Zion Gate and my friends and I, we stayed in the quarter, we didn't really go out of it. But wait, do you get the difference? People think the Armenian convent is the quarter. It isn't. The quarter is public space, you can walk through it, but the convent is like a city within the city, with its own door. You have to be Armenian to go in. By 'quarter' I mean both of them."

A brief bit of explanation. Armenia is traditionally named as the first nation to have accepted Christianity, in 301 CE, though there were contacts between Armenia and Palestine before that, even before Christ. Armenians lived in Jerusalem long before the Armenian Cathedral of St. James first went up in the fifth century, and they've been here ever since. The cathedral, much rebuilt, still stands as the focal point of the convent which has grown up around it, now walled, comprising multiple courtyards, houses, churches, a museum, seminary, clinic, library, school, youth clubs, refectories, guest quarters and offices of the Armenian Patriarchate, the body managing the community's religious and social affairs. All of it is hidden from public view.

Where is better to live, I ask Apo – in the convent or outside?

"Oh, by far the preference is to live outside in the quarter, because the convent door closes at twelve. It used to close at ten, but the younger generation, eighteen- to twenty-four-year-olds, asked the patriarchate to extend it, because a lot of them work in retail in the Mamilla Mall [in West Jerusalem] and the shift ends at eleven, so they need to make it home. There's only twenty priests in the convent, but maybe two hundred, you know, civilians." Apo laughs. "And not just old people. Families. Guys with earrings. Girls with skirts. A lot of sins happen every night behind that door."

He reveals some. My lips are sealed.

We talk about the three big waves of Armenian migration to Jerusalem. The first came with the Crusaders, whose route to the Holy Land passed through Cilicia in southern Turkey, which at that time was an Armenian kingdom. All the Crusader queens of Jerusalem in the twelfth century were wholly or partly Armenian. The second wave was prompted by genocide: Turkey killed more than a million Armenians after 1915 and expelled millions more, creating waves of migration across the Middle East, as well as to Europe and North America. Tens of thousands of refugees arrived in Jerusalem, seeking safety inside the convent.

"Most of the community here are descended from genocide survivors, from that second wave," says Apo, who tells me the story of how his family fled Sebaste, now Sivas in central Turkey, in 1921. They were aiming for France, he said, but in the chaos of Constantinople Apo's great-grandfather heard that his brother was alive and had made it to Jerusalem. "The economy wasn't so bad here

because of the Brits, so they came here," Apo shrugs. Then there was 1948, the Nakba for the Palestinians, when Israel declared its statehood. "That's when my grandmother came," Apo says. "She was from Jaffa. They built a whole new building in the convent for the Armenian refugees from the '48 war." It all forms a dizzying tale of trauma and dislocation. Apo refocuses on sources of joy.

"Growing up as an Armenian, music is always around you," he says. "We have a very musical culture, stemming from the church liturgy. At the Armenian school here, Srpots Tarkmanchatz – it means the Holy Translators, perfect for a multilingual community – I'd have to go to church every Sunday, and the liturgy is based on folk songs. Whenever my friends hear an Armenian folk song they think it's a prayer – I have to tell them, no man, it's a love song. That's my solo project separate from the band, focusing on folk music. My mum says I sound better in it, more emotional."

Rock stars' mums, guardians of bitter truth.

Then Apo talks about the cultural isolation of knowing every Armenian folk song but none of the tunes your Palestinian friends spent their childhoods singing. That leads us into the question of identity, and whether the community is Palestinian or not. Israel treats Jerusalemite Armenians the same as Jerusalemite Palestinians – they are deemed to be residents of Israel but effectively stateless, and can apply for temporary travel documents that give their nationality as Jordanian. I know people for whom the identity is a given. "Of course, we are all Palestinian," a politically active Armenian friend from an older generation once told me.

Not Apo.

"Armenian, that's my only national identity," he says with a smile. "My local identity is Jerusalemite. I'm not Palestinian and I'm not Israeli. [Political scientist] Benedict Anderson has this theory about nations being 'imagined communities' based on a myth, how you're supposed to feel this affiliation to people you'll never meet just because you live in the same place. I decided a while ago, if nation is imagination, then there is only one imagination I want to subscribe to in this lifetime, and that is the Armenian imagination. I feel more of an affiliation to the people I will never meet who live in Armenia than to the people I will never meet who live in [the Palestinian city of] Tulkarm or [the Israeli city of] Ashdod. I have a *human* responsibility towards people near to me, but not a national responsibility."

And I think – That's hard, to raise a barrier around your everyday life like that.

How does Jerusalem fit in? – I ask.

"Armenia is the homeland," he says, before immediately interrupting himself. "Actually in Armenian we say it's the "father-motherland" – we're a sexist society but we have one of the least sexist languages in the world." Grinning, he carries on. "But Jerusalem is the home of our spirituality. Armenians amount to only ten million people around the world. In Jerusalem we are less than eight hundred, yet we have a quarter, an area – that's very important to us, and to the Armenian nation. We need to keep it."

And I think – See? Quarters do matter sometimes.

Then I think – So you've been born and brought up in a place you don't feel a part of, but nevertheless you'll stay here all your life for the sake of people you'll never meet? My god.

"It creates a lot of problems for Armenian Jerusalemites, especially the people of my age," Apo explains, adding that he was born in 1990. "Every day we struggle with the question of where is home, Jerusalem or Armenia. For decades we were raised on the idea that we have to go back to the homeland, we have to make *aliyah** – but then you realize that the value to the Armenian nation of [the community in] Jerusalem is greater than the value of [other Armenian communities in] Beirut or California or wherever. Jerusalem has religious value, national value. It's part of Armenia, so you have to take care of it."

---

* *Aliyah* (Hebrew: ascent) is a Zionist term extolling Jewish immigration to Israel from the diaspora, perhaps derived from a pilgrim's uphill approach to Jerusalem. Apo was using it sarcastically in his own cultural context. It made us both laugh.

15

This Original Man

A STORY OF LIBERATION

SOMETIME IN THE SPRING OF 1853, an American traveller named David Dorr rode a camel out of the deserts of southern Palestine. "At one o'clock we were passing over rolling mounds adorned with olive trees," Dorr wrote. "One was higher than the rest, and from its summit I saw Jerusalem only half a mile ahead. The [Dome of the Rock] glittered in the sun beam, above all the other buildings. I made my way straight to [the Church of the Holy Sepulchre] and fell upon [its] marble slabs."

The French invasion of Egypt five decades earlier had sparked a wave of outside interest in Arab culture. Political reforms in the 1830s prompted many Europeans and Americans to explore – and write about – the territories of the Ottoman Empire. Palestine was a favored destination. Huge growth was to follow Dorr's visit, partly inspired by Mark Twain's witty, much-celebrated travel memoir *The Innocents Abroad*, published in 1869, which helped fuel a Western fascination for visiting (as well as shaping and colonizing) the "Holy Land" that has never abated. By contrast, Dorr's own memoir of his three-year journey around Europe and the Middle East, self-published more than a decade before Twain's, is virtually forgotten outside academia. Its title gives a clue as to why this might be. He called it: *A Colored Man Round the World*.

African American social reformers including Harriet Jacobs, William Wells Brown and, most famously, Frederick Douglass had travelled to Europe before Dorr, lecturing and publishing. Others had been as far as Egypt.

But as far as we know, David Dorr was the first African American person ever to visit Jerusalem.

He did not travel of his own free will. In this period before the American Civil War, and before the Emancipation Proclamation of 1863, Dorr – like some four million of his compatriots – was enslaved. He was brought to Jerusalem by his owner.

David Dorr was born in New Orleans in 1827 or 1828 (he had no birth certificate, but we can deduce the date from later evidence), enslaved to a white business-owner named Cornelius Fellowes. He described himself – and was described by others – as a "quadroon," a now-archaic term meaning that he was one-quarter Black, with one white parent and one parent who was of mixed white and Black background. He refers to his mother also being enslaved in Louisiana, but doesn't name her and we have no way of identifying either her or Dorr's father. Significantly, Dorr's skin color seems to have been pale enough for him to "pass" as white.

Although Fellowes legally owned Dorr, the practical nature of their relationship, and how it was expressed, seems to have had more nuance than that suggests. Dorr says that Fellowes treated him "as his own son" and "as free a man as walks the earth" – though we should naturally be wary of taking such words at face value.

When Dorr was in his mid-twenties, Fellowes brought him on an extended world tour. They left New Orleans probably in early 1851, most likely taking ship from New York. Dorr records his and Fellowes' arrival in the English port of Liverpool on 15 June that year and, after visiting London, the two men crossed to France and then meandered for more than two years through Europe and into Turkey, Egypt, Palestine, Syria and Lebanon, often with long stopovers. Paris was a favorite haunt. Their return ship, the US Mail

Service steamer *Franklin*, departed Le Havre in northern France on 2 September 1853.

Back home in New Orleans later that year, everything changed. As Dorr writes: "When we returned, I called on this original man [Fellowes] to consummate a promise he made me in different parts of the world because I wanted to make a connection, that I considered myself more than equal in dignity and means. But as he refused me, I fled from him and his princely promises."

In other words, Fellowes had vowed to free Dorr, but then went back on his word. Astonishingly for an enslaved person in the mortally dangerous surroundings of the Lower South, as it was called then, Dorr escaped, "reflecting on the moral liberties of the legal freedom of England, France and our New England States, with the determination to write."

Perhaps helped by the Underground Railroad, a secret network of guides and safe houses for fugitive slaves, Dorr made it north to Ohio, where slavery was illegal. There he lived as a clerk, lecturing and, in 1858, paying to publish his book. During the Civil War (1861–65) he enlisted but was wounded in battle. He returned to New Orleans in failing health and died there, probably in 1872, aged in his mid-forties.

But for his book, we wouldn't know Dorr at all. We have nothing from Fellowes to corroborate his account, and the purpose of their long journey is never made clear. Nonetheless, in a literary act of deep resonance, considering the erasure of Black perspectives and Black lives in America before (and after) the Civil War, Dorr almost entirely erases Fellowes from his narrative. The journey is described as if it were Dorr's alone. He is the one dining grandly, selecting itineraries and ordering transportation. "I went down to have my bill made out," he says of his Liverpool hotel. In Germany: "I declined all invitations and got a carriage." In Italy: "Having arrived and hoteled myself, I ascertained where the races were." Quietly but deliberately, Dorr claims the agency denied to him.

Moreover, where Dorr includes Fellowes, it is generally only to poke fun at him, as clumsy or socially awkward. Dorr's writing shows acute sensitivity to power relations, yet he subverts those relations not through righteous anger – as many campaigners after him would – but subtly, by recreating himself on the page as a refined and tasteful gentleman of leisure. He invents and inhabits a persona able to wield the cultural capital that he himself, back home in New Orleans, cannot.

In this way, Dorr created a genre. "*A Colored Man Round the World* appropriates the forms and structures of Anglo-American travel writing so completely that what we have is a superb case of literary doublespeak: the blackest of texts in whiteface," literary scholar Malini Johar Schueller wrote in 1999, in her introduction to what is still the only modern edition of Dorr's book.

In contradistinction to "blackface," a theatrical tradition where white performers wear clownish makeup to caricature Black people, Schueller's idea of "whiteface" has Dorr deftly adopting a privileged air of urbane sophistication to mock and undermine his owner and other wealthy white American travellers. The veneer may be jokey, but the purpose is sharp. Dorr is "writing for an American audience, mostly a white audience, and fashioning a self that is radically different from perceived ideas about African Americans, especially slaves," says Schueller. By assimilating – or even by just affecting assimilation – Dorr becomes able to quote Shakespeare and Byron. He can speak French. He can comment with insight on the social issues of the day.

Most of Dorr's book is devoted to his travels in Europe, where he encounters social contexts radically different from those back home. One example: "26th of September [1851] and I am at the capital of Holland. I just dined with a king. The father of the Queen is putting up at [my hotel]. He is going out – he bows to me."

The significance of a king bowing to a slave – and a white man bowing to a "quadroon" – would not have been lost on Dorr's readers. It is one of many such anecdotes throughout *A Colored Man Round the World*, whose very title reflects Dorr's gleeful deconstruction of power and privilege. Amid overwhelming disadvantage, and between the covers of what is ostensibly a travel diary, this self-confident – sometimes cocky – young man offers a pointed commentary on American racial prejudice.

Dorr also seems to have had a whale of a time, flirting with (presumably white) hotel maids, attending high-class balls, viewing fine art, hobnobbing with nobility and having a hundred other adventures that would be barred to him in America.

But then he reaches the Muslim world, and a harder, more judgmental tone takes over, as Dorr's manufactured identity coalesces. In Constantinople (modern Istanbul) – whose "immense number of steeples, towers and minarets [made] the fairest sight I ever beheld" – Dorr adopts a common Western literary trope in describing the Ottoman sultan Abdulmejid as "a weak-looking man … surfeiting on the fat of the world."

His internalization of a Western notion of supremacy deepens in Egypt. In Alexandria he is disgusted by the food. Cairo he describes with a back-handed compliment as "a still magnificent city for its age." He scoffs at local guides' descriptions of sights ("I could plainly see that his information was merely traditionary, without the least shadow of history for support") and he rails against the crew on his Nile river boat and others when they ask for tips. There is even outright racism: "To believe what an Arab says when trying to sell anything would be a sublime display of the most profound ignorance a man could be guilty of."

Later, however, in a lengthy evocation of Egyptian prowess in civilization-building, Dorr reflects on historical context and Black identity. He discusses Alexander the Great, the Ptolemaic dynasty and biblical history, painting one particularly stark picture: "In going to these Pyramids, one walks over a pavement of dead bodies. I sunk in the sand … and my foot caught in the ribs of a buried man … The whole plain from the Pyramids to Cairo, some six or seven miles, is macadamized with dead Egyptians."

It was a pivotal moment. He sees the ancient Egyptians as "the ancestors of which [I am] the posterity … Egypt was a higher sphere of artistical science than any other nation [and] the Egyptians [were] men with wooly hair, thick lips, flat feet and black."

His horizons had expanded massively. In America, he was enslaved and discriminated against as Black. In Europe, he not only encountered social equality but was not seen as Black at all. Then Africa presented a social context where Black achievement and Black cultural pride were the norm. He felt a deep affinity.

But extended travel seems also to have undermined Dorr's debonair literary persona. After Egypt, it's as if something breaks in his literary resolve. Having devoted more than a hundred and eighty pages to the journey thus far, he rushes through the remainder of his trip in a bad-tempered eight pages.

Following the long camel ride across the desert into Palestine, Dorr harrumphs when authorities in Hebron refuse entry to the town's mosque. Lodged in a Jerusalem convent – tantalizingly, he doesn't identify which one – he offers a wry, Twain-like comment, years before Twain, on the economics of pilgrimage and the hierarchies of power between traveller and host: "They make no charges against a pilgrim, but no pilgrim can come here unless rich, and no rich man will go away without giving something to so sacred a place."

He calls a local guide "impudent." Jerusalemites are "ignorant." Then there are factual discrepancies: Dorr says he rides from Jerusalem to Bethlehem – that is, southwards – but then discusses the tomb of Lazarus (which is in Bethany, east of Jerusalem) and Bethel (which is north of the city). Was he lost, mistaken or misled?

Finally, "having stayed seventeen days, I leave [Jerusalem], never wishing to return." By then, in mid-1853, tension was rising between the Ottoman Empire and Russia. "The Turks all through Palestine [are] preparing for war," Dorr writes, and hostilities did indeed break out only a few weeks later (that conflict, the Crimean War, ground on for more than two years). Dorr says he "hurried on to Damascus," but then unaccountably leaves the city undescribed, speeding through Lebanon to reach Acre and then Jaffa, where he departs for home.

Near the end of this rushed sequence comes an apparently minor episode outside Jerusalem that encapsulates Dorr's extraordinary style. He writes, of a rural excursion: "The same evening I camped at Jericho. We took a bath in the Jordan [River], and tried some of its water with *eau de vie*,* and found it in quality like Mississippi water."

Centuries of yearning in African American poetry and song evoke a remembrance of "Zion" in exile, often centered on the liberating experience of flowing water. Countless images link biblical baptism with spiritual freedom from enslavement. Here is Dorr, literally enslaved, presumably alongside an older man who claims legal ownership over him, surrendering his body, Christ-like, to the flowing water of a river that holds profound significance for his culture, religion and political identity – and he calls it merely "taking a bath."

Then he drinks the very water of liberation, intoxicating himself and, with a devastating comparison, anchoring his own emancipation to the emancipation of his readers in America, who live lives of enslavement beside another flowing river. In one line Dorr winks at his white audience, who might grin (or tut) at the irreverence, and simultaneously broadcasts a message of solidarity and hope to African Americans.

He also, perhaps unwittingly, exposes the contradictions within his literary affectation. Dorr, Schueller observes, "claims an authority over the landscape that he, as a Black person with origins in Egypt, [feels he] can claim," yet he vilifies the Arab people who live in it.

If "cool" began with African Americans assuming a front of ironic detachment as personal rebellion against overwhelming oppression, concealing the emotional impact of terrible injustice behind a persona created to disarm, David Dorr is a pioneer of cool. He asserted his authority to speak, despite enslavement. He shamed white Americans by demonstrating the abnormality of what they took as normal. Laconic, funny, literate, sharply observant – and also arrogant and prejudiced – Dorr speaks as loudly to our century as to his. We should know his name.

---

* A colorless fruit brandy or other alcoholic spirit. Perhaps Dorr was sipping *arak*, an anise-flavoured spirit distilled in the countries of the Levant that is traditionally drunk slightly diluted.

16

The Invisible Clocktower

STORIES OF BAB AL-KHALIL/JAFFA GATE

IT WAS THE BEST OF TIMES, it was the worst of times. Modernity was in the air. You could *taste* it. Jerusalem was on the up. There was new street paving, new lighting, new water systems. New schools. New hospitals. New libraries. Tourism was through the roof. Money was begging to be made. New books being written, new philosophies being talked about. New newspapers being printed. People had a spring in their step. Outside, in the countryside, railways were being built. New links of trade and culture with the grand cities of the empire, the East, Europe, even America. There were threats, too; of course there were. Lots of new people walking around. Lots of dangerous ideas. But you got a sense that the direction of travel was forward.

Take the clocktower, for instance. What a symbol. The Turks loved their clocktowers. Abdulhamid II, the Sultan in Constantinople, had been telling everyone for years to build clocktowers. Part of it was about improving accuracy: it's always been important in Islam to be able to tell the time, so as to call the five-times-daily prayer correctly. Mosques had had sundials for centuries, and big cities across the Ottoman Empire had been putting up fancy public clocks since Safranbolu, north of Ankara – *Saffron-polis*, City of Saffron, what a name! – got theirs in 1798.

And of course, Abdulhamid wanted to project his mighty and benevolent power into the farthest-flung provinces. Building symbols of authority had always been a good marker of that.

But it was also about modernity. As in Europe, ideas of public space and the public good were starting to have an impact. From 1863 Jerusalem had had its own municipal government, charged with defending and improving public space, the city for all. The idea of collective purpose, beyond the self-interest of sect, was gaining traction. Part of that – as Europe was finding, too – was public time. If time could be taken out of the hands of clerical gatekeepers, it would place new power in the hands of every individual in the city (who then, of course, would thank the sultan). Idiosyncrasies of tradition, old-fashioned and divisive, could be ironed flat, for the benefit of all. What could be more modern? "The clock bell rings but it is the sound of the state," read an inscription on the clock-tower installed in Adana in 1882.

As 1901, the twenty-fifth anniversary of Abdulhamid's accession, approached and passed, more than a hundred clocktowers went up in towns and cities all over the empire, from Istanbul, Ankara and Smyrna to Mosul, Beirut and Jaffa. Jerusalem, being small and out of the way, came late to the party: the municipality only got round to approving a clocktower in 1907. The result, a florid hybrid of Turkish and European Baroque designed in local limestone by municipal architect Pascal Seraphin, was unveiled in 1909 soaring into the sky directly above Jaffa Gate. Tall, fluted, with a balcony just below the clock face, it cost the astronomical sum of twenty thousand francs – perhaps as much as a million dollars today – raised entirely by donations from city residents of all faiths. It had four faces. The eastern and western ones showed standard time as Europeans would recognize it, the northern and southern ones Ottoman Islamic time based on sunset, for prayer purposes (every day at sunset the hands would be reset to 12:00).

Jerusalemites, it seems, on the whole liked the tower – not least because they had paid for it. But then the British invaded.

Almost from the day in 1917 when General Allenby announced British rule over Palestine after a stage-managed march in through

Jerusalem's Jaffa Gate, Britain's colonial administrators took against the sultan's clocktower, so obvious looming behind Allenby in every photograph of the momentous event. One archaeologist called the tower "ultra-hideous," a "perfect eyesore" and said it "utterly spoilt" the view. The planner Patrick Geddes decreed it a "vulgar modern decoration" and "probably the most dreadful piece of architecture in existence." To the governor, Ronald Storrs, it was a disfigurement that looked like a cross between "the Eddystone Lighthouse and a jubilee memorial." Storrs's sidekick Ashbee, whom we've met already, detested it, obviously. The visiting writer G.K. Chesterton weighed in, too, calling the tower "unnaturally ugly." Geopolitical triumphalism became dressed up as an issue of taste.*

Abdulhamid's symbol of modernity, cultural assertiveness and progressive communalism was no match for such a blast of colonial disapproval. In 1922, the British pulled the clocktower down.

The outcry surrounding the demolition disturbed even Storrs. It seems he hadn't considered that Jerusalemites might actually have been proud of the tower and what it represented – let alone wanting to be able to tell the time. "A certain degree of sentiment attaches to the clock," he murmured to one of his officials. One rumor said the news reached the ears of Atatürk himself, whose objections finally swayed the governor.

The British brought the clock back. They could not, of course, countenance sullying Jaffa Gate again, so they instead had the mechanism installed in a new tower they built themselves in 1926 opposite Jerusalem's new municipality building, outside the walls. Abdulhamid's clock now rose above an L-shaped parade of shopfronts, designed in a bizarre hybrid of European modernism and Arab pastiche, complete with arches and domes. "The Ottoman Victorianism of the old tower was replaced by the British Orientalism [of the new]," one study has noted.

It didn't last long. The British demolished the tower again, in 1934, and permanently this time. To improve traffic flow, they said.

---

* British disdain persists. In 2011 author Simon Sebag Montefiore wrote that the clocktower "looked as if it belonged in a suburban English railway station."

So rest in peace Jerusalem's municipal clocktower, born, lived and died in the space of twenty-five awful years. The clock mechanism was apparently shipped to the British Museum in London; maybe it's still there. *Tempus fugit*. No flowers.

Whenever I pass Jaffa Gate I look up at the gap in the sky where the clocktower stood and give a nod to the age of possibility, and remember its destroyers.

The clock marked a temporal, as well as a physical, transition. Almost as soon as it had started ticking, political ambivalence in Palestine towards Ottoman rule began to coalesce into discontent. The Young Turk revolution of 1908 had installed constitutional government and multiparty politics; calls began to emerge for social freedom and Arab self-rule. War and forced conscription caused desperate hardship, hardening grievances. There was famine, disease, genocide – and then the arrival of the British threw everything up in the air. Relief in Palestine at Britain's ouster of the Turks soon evaporated along with the prewar sense of collective purpose. Britain's colonial administrators, with their self-image as Christian conquerors of the holy city, their imposition of rigid social stratification and their support for the Zionist aspirations of European Jewry, preferred to foster sectarian factionalism. They ruled by playing powerful interests off against each other, incubating hatreds and provoking violence. The ethno-religious divides they encouraged led directly to the international community's adoption of the horrifying idea of partition, more war and the grinding injustices Jerusalemites to this day struggle with.

"The ensuing military occupation brought ... three discrete processes – the emergence of Zionism, Protestant millenarianism and British imperialism – to Palestinian shores as a powerful fusion of ideologies that destroyed the country and its people over the next thirty years," one historian has written. Jerusalemite author John Tleel breathed life into the same idea: "In 1917 [when they arrived,] British troops distributed to the Jerusalemites sugar and chocolate. When they left [in 1948], they spread chaos and bitterness."

Jaffa Gate is still a good place to get a flavor of that colonial legacy. It's not a happy place, for me the most disquieting corner of a disquieting city. It's where those coming from outside, seeking to dominate, have most often chosen to intrude into the lives of Jerusalem. One nickname for it is "Invaders' Gate."

Stand outside the gate with your back to the city walls and a road passes in front. To the right (north), it climbs the slope and bends west, continuing, eventually, to Jaffa on the coast. To the left (south), the same road drops to the valley floor and extends southwards to Bethlehem, Hebron and into the desert.

In European languages and Hebrew you turn right: this gate is seen as the entry-point to Jerusalem – and also the exit-point – from the west, from Jaffa and thus the wider world of the Mediterranean and beyond. It is called Jaffa Gate, *Porte de Jaffa, Jaffator, Shaar Yafo.*

In Arabic, though, you turn left: this gate binds Jerusalem with hinterland communities closer at hand, in the city's immediate social and cultural orbit. It is called *Bab al-Khalil,* Hebron Gate,* previously Bethlehem Gate and, in older times, *Bab Mihrab Dawoud,* the Gate of the Prayer-Niche of David, referring to a tradition that associated King David/Prophet Dawoud with the three-towered citadel beside the gateway.

The contrast in conceptual understandings of the gate is instructive.

That citadel, a work of Suleiman's, stands at what's been a fortification point for two thousand years, back to the second century BCE. Herod reinforced it, Rome's Tenth Legion camped beside it, and it was most likely where Pontius Pilate judged a Jew named Jesus. Today the citadel holds an Israeli history museum that

---

* *Al-Khalil* ("The Friend") is the Arabic for Hebron, from that city's status as burial place of Abraham/Ibrahim, who is called *Khalil-Allah* ("Friend of God") after a line in the Quran (4:125): "And God took Abraham as a friend." Bab al-Khalil, the gate, is named for the city rather than the prophet.

tells instead of shows: its blandly uninformative signage, uncritical regurgitation of state narratives and an overreliance on illustrations, figurines and contextless models eventually drove me up to the roof, where I could, at least, lean on the battlements and feel some cobwebs blow away.

The Israeli authorities call the citadel the Tower of David; David wasn't here, but the idea arose in the Byzantine era that he had been. Nowadays, people look up at the massive fortifications, floodlit at night, and – because of the name – imagine the cylindrical seventeenth-century stone minaret of the citadel's now-deconsecrated mosque rising above the walls to be some kind of Tower of David. Israel doesn't disabuse them. It could call this place the Citadel. But David, the biblically lauded Jewish monarch of a united kingdom of Israel, with all his evocative associations as shepherd, poet, conqueror and Goliath-killer, is central to how Israel's heritage industry projects Jerusalem to Christian and Jewish visitors. So the state transubstantiates a symbol of Islam – the minaret – into a symbol of Judaism – King David – before your very eyes.

British colonial planner Charles Ashbee was besotted with King David, too. He called Jerusalem "The City of the Great Singer," reflecting how perfectly the lyre-strumming psalmist of old epitomized the linkage of art and holiness in his absurdly idealized Jerusalem. Ashbee is why today, in English at least, we know the main market alleyway leading east from Jaffa Gate into the heart of the city as David Street: as Civic Advisor he chose to restore the street's medieval name *Khatt Dawoud*. For a century or more before Ashbee, David Street was – and, in Arabic, still is – called *Sweiqat Alloun* in its upper part (*sweiqa* means little souk; Alloun is a local family name), and *Souk al-Bazaar* further down.

Tourists enter Jerusalem at Jaffa Gate, as they have done for a hundred and fifty years. I first came in 1980, and I remember the buses and shared taxis on the road by the walls which turned the gate into a hub for public transport, connected. Now that road has been dug down into a tunnel, the roof of which forms a pedestrian plaza linking with the upmarket shops and car parking of West Jerusalem's Mamilla Mall alongside. The plaza facilitates a flow of mall people and mall culture in through the gate, bringing the voracious consumerism of Israeli Jerusalem into the Old City. It also showcases a view of the "Tower of David" rising above the battlemented walls that is familiar from promotional imagery. The municipality bedecks the plaza and walls here with Hebrew banners and flags, celebrating Israeli holidays and events.*

And because this is the easiest access point direct from West Jerusalem, enveloped, unlike Damascus Gate, in the semiotics of familiarity – Hebrew signage, Israeli urban visual culture – many ultra-Orthodox Jewish Israelis also enter here on foot, on their way to pray at the Western Wall. Their preferred route avoids the potential hostility of the souk for a cut-through via the friendlier lanes behind the Armenian convent. On their left hand stands the Israeli government tourist office. On their right is the headquarters of the Israeli police, insinuated into a former Ottoman barracks and prison known as the Kishle.

That route also takes them straight past (but never into) Christ Church, the oldest and oddest Protestant church in the Middle East. Founded in 1849 alongside what was, until 1914, the British Consulate, Christ Church was built ostensibly to serve the handful of Protestant individuals in the city at that time, in reality to promote British interests and evangelize Jews.

It is still run by an Anglican missionary society, the Church's Ministry Among Jewish People. The society espouses pro-Israel political views, operates independently of the Bishop of Jerusalem and offers support to Messianic Jews, who observe elements of both Judaism and Christianity and are ostracized by the religious establishments of both. Inside Christ Church you'll find no crosses, but

---

* Just west of Jaffa Gate is a formerly open area of caves and an ancient reservoir that fed Jerusalem's water supply. It's been associated with death since Persian invaders massacred Jerusalemite Christians there in 614. Its name, Mamilla, perhaps derives from an unknown Roman benefactor (*mamilla* or *mammilla* is a Latin diminutive from *mamma*, meaning "breast," but the association is opaque), or a Christian saint, or from the Arabic term *ma'man allah*, translated most often as "Sanctuary of God": Mamilla was a Muslim cemetery, in use from at least the eleventh century until 1927. Since 1948 Israel has bulldozed most of the cemetery to create a public park, luxury residences (named David's Village, naturally), hotel, shopping mall and, believe it or not, a Museum of Tolerance, due to open in 2022.

there is a menorah, and the altar shows a Star of David and inscriptions in Hebrew.

It's impossible to understand Christ Church (or, indeed, Israeli policy in Jerusalem) without understanding Christian Zionism, a political ideology resting on the evangelical imperative that Christians must encourage Jewish immigration to the "Holy Land" and the conversion of Jews to Christianity in order to hasten the Second Coming of Christ. It contends that the founding of the Israeli state was a fulfilment of Bible prophecy. Christian Zionism is too big a can of worms to open here, but it is now an integral part of America's political establishment, Republican and Democrat. It is key to the political prosperity of the Israeli right, as well as the economic prosperity of the Israeli tourist industry (almost two-thirds of visitors to Israel identify as Christian), yet its origins lie in Anglican missionary activity in the nineteenth century and, specifically, the people and ideas behind Christ Church.

Britain wasn't the only country with a foothold inside Jaffa Gate. Beside Christ Church was the Austrian post office, the Banco di Roma and the American consulate. When the German emperor Wilhelm II said he would be visiting the Ottoman Empire in 1898 and wanted to ride into Jerusalem, Sultan Abdulhamid – incredibly, looking back – knocked down part of the city wall beside Jaffa Gate and filled in a section of the citadel's moat to accommodate the Kaiser's white charger and carriage. Stand by the gate today and you can see where the edge of the moat used to run, marked by a shallow groove snaking across the paving underfoot.

Post-Kaiser repairs were never done, and this remains the only breach in the entire circuit of walls, now developed by Israel into the start of a one-way system for vehicles that enter the Old City here, proceed around the Armenian convent to the car park by Zion Gate, then continue beside the Jewish Quarter to exit the Old City near the Western Wall.

What's worse, though, is the fate of the two large nineteenth-century hotel buildings that overlook the square inside Jaffa Gate, across from the Citadel. Since 2005 Palestinians have been fighting to retain control of them, in the face of a legal battle with an extreme nationalist and religious Jewish Israeli settler organization seeking to take them over. In 2019 Israel's Supreme Court ruled in favor of the settlers and issued an eviction order to the hotel owners. If that order is enforced, and the buildings seized, Jaffa Gate would become Israeli, one Palestinian friend said to me. Can you imagine all the flags and the religious zealots and what would happen to the place when these hotels become a huge yeshiva? my friend added. He was smiling with his teeth, but only to mask his emotion.

Twenty-odd years ago, when US president Bill Clinton tried to broker an Israel-Palestine peace deal, his plan sought to divide the Old City along the lines of the four quarters. The Muslim and Christian quarters would become part of Palestine, while the Armenian Quarter was to be joined to the Jewish Quarter and given to Israel, thus forming a corridor between West Jerusalem and the Western Wall. Such horror boggles the mind, but, fortunately, the deal was never done. Nevertheless, I've heard the fear from many Jerusalemites – not just worried Armenians – that everything Israel has done at Jaffa Gate since then has been intended to bring about the same result.

See? Jaffa Gate is relentlessly upsetting. The invisible clocktower casts a long, long shadow. In addition, all the tourist activity around the gate means it takes concerted effort to connect with people and place in ways that aren't transactional.

I was lucky to sit here once for a whole afternoon with Judge Fawaz Attiyeh of the Ramallah Appeals Court – not on official business, thankfully – who gave up his time to ply me with coffee and tell story after story from his family tree, intimately linking his forebears and himself with the urban history of Jaffa Gate. The potted version includes Nasreddin ibn Dabbous, who created a property endowment here in 1437, and Nasreddin's grandson Ibrahim Safouti (roughly 1519–1592), a merchant and property trader, who added to his grandfather's *waqf* with more land at Jaffa Gate, shared equally between two sons and four daughters. Then came a story of how damage caused by heavy snowfall in the winter of 1735 prompted a sale of land to an Armenian trader shortly before the family became known as Zreiq, and then Attiyeh. Thanks to peculiarities of inheritance law, Judge Attiyeh said, the 600-year-old *waqf* at Jaffa Gate is now hopelessly atomized, split 1,630 ways between relatives.

But it wasn't just stories. The judge walked me from building to building – all of them shops now – showing me small plaques that have been put up by the family to record their history, even here, in the maelstrom of the most touristy street market in Jerusalem. Every plaque was concealed by T-shirts, cashmere scarves and Jewish prayer shawls hung for display by shopkeepers, but you can find them, at David Street 26 and 30, for instance. There's another on St. Mark's Street, just behind the souk, where the family still owns a house – a lovely house, with a beautiful upper courtyard, now unfortunately loomed over by a high-walled extension built onto the Maronite church next door.

Judge Attiyeh was particularly keen to show me the two Ottoman tombs, one decorated with a rather splendid marble turban, that survive just inside Jaffa Gate, in a small courtyard open to the street between buildings. Tour guides will tell you these are the graves of two architects, as mentioned previously: Suleiman the Magnificent, they say, was so furious to learn that Mount Zion had been excluded from his new city walls that he had his architects executed and buried here as a warning. Or, they add, he was so delighted with the new walls that he executed his architects to stop anyone else commissioning them to produce even finer work. "Cruel old Suleiman," you're supposed to respond. "So irrational, so bloodthirsty."

The stories don't stand up. If this was a burial of disgrace, why decorate the tombs? If this was a burial of gratitude, why not in a sanctified cemetery? Suleiman's walls followed previous walls, and Mount Zion had never been walled. Considering its natural defenses – steep slopes on three sides – and its (then) minor status, there was no need to divert to include it. By the time the wall-builders reached this point, with resources running low near the end of the project, building work needed to speed up, not slow down.

The real story is this. The tombs didn't exist in 1590, because that's when Judge Attiyah's forebear Ibrahim Safouti made his endowment

covering three adjoining homes and a bakery on this exact spot. But some years ago, Jerusalem historian Yusuf Natsheh unearthed a document dated 1656 that does refer to the tombs, under the name "Al-Safadiyya" – that is, related to the town of Safad in northern Palestine.

So at some point between 1590 and 1656 – at least fifty and perhaps a hundred years after Suleiman's city walls had been completed – this small part of the Safouti endowment was given over for the burial of, most likely, two scholars or nobles from Safad. And there they lie still.

Maybe Jaffa Gate's tour guides could retire the myth of the executed architects, and call these the Safadiyya tombs again? The judge and I shook hands on that.

Another day, beside a large crowd of, I think, Spanish tourists, who were being overtaken impatiently by a line of four ultra-Orthodox Jewish students in white shirts and black trousers, walking at pace with black hats tilted back, I ducked up one of Jaffa Gate's side alleys to look for a once-famous literary café.

Jerusalemite writer, educator and political activist Khalil Sakakini, born in 1878, first came to prominence for his progressive teaching style at the school he founded, which replaced grading, prize-giving and corporal punishment with music, storytelling and outdoor activity. From 1919 he developed a journalistic career, gathering around him a circle of writers, publishers and newspaper editors who would meet at *Qahwat al-Mukhtar*, the Mukhtar's Café.* Sakakini's circle became the core of the Vagabond Party, a group of dissident writers and agitators backing Arab nationalist causes against British and Zionist interests, even fighting the Greek clerical establishment. For a few years *Qahwat al-Mukhtar* became *Qahwat al-Saaleek*, the Vagabond Café, as Sakakini and his disciples espoused an epicurean philosophy rejecting religion, convention and social hierarchies in favor of idleness and merriment. Then in 1926 Sakakini took a job as government inspector of education, later becoming a leading public intellectual, and the cultural atmosphere in Jerusalem shifted under increasing political tension. The Vagabond Café faded away.

But people still know the name and where it stood. I've tried everything to see the place, but it's been closed up for years, sealed

---

* A *mukhtar* is a community representative. This café was owned and run by Issa Michel Toubbeh, a writer and publisher who was the *mukhtar* of Jerusalem's Greek Orthodox Christians. Ink is in the blood: one of Toubbeh's grandsons, Michel Moushabeck, also a writer and publisher, founded the US publishing house Interlink in 1987 and still runs it today.

tight with metal shutters. I keep thinking it should be a cultural shrine, Jerusalem's version of Cairo's Café Riche, the Deux Magots in Paris, the Cabaret Voltaire in Zurich, Vesuvio in San Francisco, open, celebrated, busy. Instead, it's ignored. Fifty years before Saka-kini this street was an open field, one corner of which was used to dump livestock carcasses. A hundred years after him, the café now hides beside a kebab diner and deli, across the way from the Gloria hotel, once also the municipality building, where on 29 June 1967, after victory in war, an Israeli army officer told the mayor of (East) Jerusalem Ruhi al-Khatib that his services were no longer required.

One sunny Friday lunchtime at Jaffa Gate I wander past the closed-up café again. It's a day when the Israeli management team at the Citadel have rented out the ancient fortress to a private party: crassly triumphalist dance music smothers the old streets, obscenely intrusive, so powerfully amplified its bass is rattling windows two hundred meters away. Down in the souk, where it isn't any quieter, beside a shop selling T-shirts that read "Super-Jew" and "Don't Worry Be Jewish," I press a button and push a heavy door open. As it swings shut the hubbub softens. I have an appointment.

Nora Kort has one of those minds fearsome in its clarity. She has devoted herself the last five decades to good works in the Palestinian community through her directorship of the Arab Orthodox Society, an NGO set up by a group of women in 1926 to serve the underprivileged of Jerusalem. From a background in sociology and psychology, and years of experience in community development – not to mention unparalleled networking skills and pin-sharp recall for names and faces – Nora has raised literally millions of dollars for projects supporting Palestinians in Jerusalem and the West Bank.

Over tea served in china, and with impeccable English diction exoticized by a hint of French in the vowels, Nora regales me for more than an hour with memories, sometimes decades old, of conversations at receptions and conferences with the heads of regional and international donor bodies, and the checks that resulted. She explains how society premises near New Gate support as many as five hundred families by providing workshops and retail space for self-employed women producing handicrafts such as embroidery and pottery, as well as the much-loved *Bint al-Balad* ("Daughter of the City") café-restaurant. The Society's medical center, the first in the Old City to offer mental health services, recently celebrated its fortieth anniversary.

We are meeting at Wujoud, a museum and cultural center opened by the Society in 2010 amid the souvenir floggers just down from Jaffa Gate, in a building – once a grand family home – donated by the Greek Orthodox Patriarchate. "I couldn't believe it [when they offered it]," Nora says. "They take buildings, they don't give them out." The structure is more than 650 years old, but had been empty since 1967 and needed extensive work. "The architect said to me, 'This will cost millions.' I told him, 'We don't have millions. God will provide,'" Nora recalls. And it seems He did, in the form of fat donations from a representative of the French government – "*Such a nice man*" – and the Kuwait-based Arab Fund for Economic and Social Development, among others. "I was so appreciative. This place [embodies] a religious message of love, faith, compassion and hope," Nora adds, to make sure I understand.

The money funded a truly beautiful interior restoration. The house looks magnificent, from its vaulting and skylit atrium to its rugs and inlaid furniture. It holds an absorbing collection of historic craft items from around Palestine and displays dozens of photos of pre-1948 Jerusalem, as well as an Arabic New Testament handwritten in 1820 that was donated by Nora's own family. There are artworks and examples of embroidery, and the rooftop lounge has epic views down into the adjacent Pool of the Patriarch's Bath-house, also known as Hezekiah's Pool. This 73-meter-long reservoir behind the souk, perhaps 2,700 years old, once fed by the Mamilla Pool outside the walls but now dry, is otherwise completely hidden among the surrounding buildings.

Nora's stories of the abuse, legal challenges and violence she faced early on from her neighbors in the souk, who were suspicious of a newcomer undercutting their sales, left me open-mouthed in shock. But I get the unmistakable feeling that this coiffed, diminutive figure is considerably tougher than she looks. Things tend to go her way.

So Wujoud has thrived, hosting groups of tourists, women's charities and support organizations, outreach meetings, parties of Christians, Muslims and Jews from Israel, Europe and America seeking engagement with Palestinian society – but its purpose remains pleasingly indistinct, on the one hand to present a positive message of interfaith reconciliation, and on the other to reinforce the Palestinian character of Jerusalem. *Wujoud* means existence, or presence; the museum came about "to say we exist, we are here to stay, nobody can deny our presence in this city," Nora says, with passion. "I don't say I'm a Christian, I say I'm a Palestinian, but I stay in Jerusalem because of my faith, because I think I can do something to change the reality. And to say *we* can, the Palestinians can."

Jerusalem's Israeli-run municipality wants to get its hands on the historic reservoir out back, a vast chunk of unused real estate that it envisages nicely paved over as a plaza for staging music shows. It has so far been thwarted by Al-Quds University and the Islamic Waqf, who own the site. Municipality staff apparently came to Wujoud not long ago, to try to survey the area and assess access routes. They met Nora but, the way she tells it, they may not have realized exactly who she was, or exactly who they were dealing with. It seems they ended up departing unexpectedly soon after having arrived.

17

On the Champs-Élysées

STORIES FROM CHRISTIAN QUARTER ROAD

MARCH IN THE DUTCH CITY OF ROTTERDAM can be bitingly cold. Winds whip in off the sea, and the all-enveloping drift of the Nieuwe Maas, one of the waterways carrying the Rhine to its outflow, exacerbates the chill. That March of 1884, Rotterdam was abuzz with change. The city was growing. Grand plans were afoot. Less than five years before, a big new bridge had opened over the river, named Willemsbrug for the king, Willem III. But it all meant little to the anguished man trying to keep warm in the plain Hotel Willemsbrug, opposite the bridge's northern end, on the boulevard known as De Boompjes. It must have been a noisy place to stay. Elevated railway tracks ran within meters of the hotel, steamboats departed from the adjacent quay and people, horses, carts and trams would have been moving to and fro constantly. Perhaps the anguished man slept fitfully that dank early March. Would spring never come? Maybe the hotel staff whispered to each other about the dark circles showing under his puffy eyes.

So when, on Sunday 9 March, the police were called to the hotel because the anguished man had not been seen for two days, and Inspector Cramer broke down the door of the room only to see that the man had shot himself in the head, perhaps it wasn't such a big surprise. The police spoke to the hotel proprietor, Mr. Van Wiekera, recorded the dead man's name as Shapira and moved the body to the Drenkelingenhuis (House of the Drowned), where the corpses of unidentified sailors were stored before burial. Nobody knew anything about Shapira, or where he came from, so shortly afterwards they buried him in a pauper's grave, unmarked.

It had been less than a year since Moses Wilhelm Shapira had arrived in London from his home in Jerusalem, ready to shake hands on a million-pound deal that would have changed the world.

Jerusalem would probably exist even without commerce; such is the legacy of holiness. That said, buying and selling have long defined the place. George Hintlian has written of the markets in Shapira's day:

> On the street [at Jaffa Gate are] charcoal merchants. As we [enter the souk] we find shops filled with choice fruits and sweets. Further down are the polyglot money-changers. In Christian Quarter Road they sold buttons, thread and ribbons – it was common practice for cloth merchants to hire pedlars to sell clothes by transporting them on their shoulders. Behind the vegetable bazaar, which teemed with villagers in embroidered dresses, lay the market of the tanners and dyers, easily identified by their blue hands. Just beyond lay the triple market reputed to have been founded in the twelfth century by Queen Melisende. The first is the Butchers' Market; at its northern extremity were coppersmiths, tinsmiths and leather-workers. The middle street was the Market of the Apothecaries, who sold spices, saddlery, herbs, ropes, gunpowder and hunting materials. [The last housed] goldsmiths and drapers.

Another historian, Nicola Ziadeh, wrote of his experiences as a teenager in 1921 walking the same markets:

> Suq Khan al-Zeit, which had all sorts of shops, smelled of olive oil, sesame oil, soap, fresh bread, grilled meat, sweetmeats,

leather goods and rosewater. [In] the Christian Quarter, shops catered for salted cod, pickled fish and the fresh smell of bread. Another lot of shops sold "souvenirs" from the Holy Land, olive-seed rosaries, mother-of-pearl rosaries, crosses and candlesticks. Candles, to be used on festival occasions at the church, were available. [Then] we came to a small market Sweiqat Alloun where various kinds of cheeses, labaneh [cream cheese], laban [yogurt], eggs, butter and chocolates were sold.

Jerusalem, obviously, has changed. I don't remember cheese in Sweiqat Alloun, but I do remember newsagents and bread. Today, that stretch is pretty much all T-shirts, sparkly gewgaws and Judaica. But there are stories to be found.

Since a mutual friend introduced us a couple of years ago, I've often stopped to chat with Suha Alami. She is a genuine rarity – a single woman who owns and runs her own shop, a broad, brightly lit space partway along Christian Quarter Road. This is one of the busiest tourist streets in all of Jerusalem, flanking the west wall of the Church of the Holy Sepulchre. It's never quiet. There must be a couple of hundred shops, lining both sides: it's a strip mall, and it's always full of people from everywhere except Jerusalem. Virtually every Christian pilgrim will pass this way, to or from the church.

But that doesn't mean things are always easy for Suha. She suffers from high blood pressure. She gets overcome by fatigue. Once, she told me, she was sitting on a bus worrying about her mother – this was not long before her mother died, a few years back – and when she stood to get off she suddenly fainted. Someone helped her, but it was a big shock. It happened in the shop, too; she was holding a box full of glass pieces at the time. Somehow nothing broke.

Christian Quarter Road is big on souvenirs, everything from cheap imported knickknacks all the way up to handmade furniture, specialist crafts, art pieces, religious icons, even genuine antiquities. One of the bestsellers is ceramics – cups, jars, tiles, ashtrays, coasters, bowls and other glazed kitchenware, produced with the distinctive blue-and-white floral designs originated by Armenian artisans a hundred or more years ago. The proper, expensive, handmade Armenian stuff is elsewhere: what you find on Christian Quarter Road is factory-produced, but that doesn't mean it's bad. On the contrary. It's attractive, plentiful and distinctively Jerusalem – perfect for low-priced souvenirs. Some places will import from China, but Suha has been in her shop thirty years, and her father before her, and they have a long-running relationship with a manufacturer in Hebron who brings her ceramics as well as fancy decorated glassware – some cheaper glass that is painted, and also authentic smoky Hebron glass, whose colorful designs are swirled in during production. All of this stuff you can find, for better or worse, at shops up and down the street, but Suha's stock is nice and I like to chat with her.

The life that ended in Rotterdam in 1884 began near Lviv in what is now Ukraine, where Moses Shapira was born into a Jewish family in 1830. It seems his father emigrated to Palestine when Moses was small, leaving the boy – and, perhaps, the rest of the family – behind. At the age of twenty-five, Moses made the same journey, but while holed up for five months with missionaries in Bucharest he converted to Christianity, later taking German citizenship and the new name Wilhelm. On arrival in Jerusalem, he settled with the tiny community of converted Protestants who worshipped at Christ Church, marrying German nurse Rosetta Jukel there in 1861, preaching to passersby and developing his trade as a bookseller, alongside studying the Talmud – for historical as well as religious reasons – and deepening his language skills.

Then a headline-grabbing discovery changed everything.

In the summer of 1868, as Protestant-led efforts to prove the historicity of the Bible were reaching fever pitch, a German missionary was travelling in the wild backcountry of Transjordan. Near Dhiban, now a small village but once capital of Moab, bedouin showed him a large basalt stone inscribed with strange characters. The missionary informed the German consul in Jerusalem, who made arrangements to buy it. Then the British found out and made inquiries. A French archaeologist secured an imprint of the text. The Ottoman government stepped in, ordering the bedouin to give the stone to the Germans, so the bedouin did the obvious thing: by heating the stone over a fire then pouring cold water on it, they managed to shatter it, enabling them to sell off each valuable fragment to the covetous foreigners one by one.* Meanwhile, scholars in Europe were studying the imprint of the text, which turned out to be a record of the achievements of Mesha, a ninth-century BCE king of Moab mentioned in the Old Testament. The discovery was hugely significant – the first evidence confirming events that had been described in the Bible. The French eventually recovered all the bits and put the reassembled Moabite Stone (or "Mesha Stele") on display in the Louvre, where it remains today.

The furore got Wilhelm Shapira thinking. He changed direction, diversifying into souvenirs and antiquities and beginning to work with a local guide, Salim al-Khouri, who had excellent contacts with the notoriously difficult and aloof bedouin of Transjordan. Al-Khouri's skills are key to what followed.

Throughout 1872, the Jerusalem market was suddenly flooded with Moabite antiquities. Shapira was stocking – and selling – large quantities of Moabite stone heads, clay vessels and figurines, many inscribed with the same characters that had described Mesha's battles. British scholars again took interest, with reports and sketches passing between Jerusalem and London. By May 1873 Shapira had sold a collection of 1,700 Moabite pieces to the Prussian government for display in Berlin, for the equivalent in today's money of perhaps as much as half a million pounds. It was an astonishing coup. Shapira bought a new house in Jerusalem on the proceeds, and became known as a host of high-society parties.

The first suggestions that the Moabite pottery was not what it seemed began to circulate soon afterwards. By 1877 it was clear to all: the Germans had been swindled. Every last one of Shapira's "Moabite antiquities" was a forgery. That could have signalled the

---

* Another interpretation is that rural people destroyed antiquities in order to avoid unwelcome attention. Holding items that foreigners and the government considered valuable could bring inspectors to the locality who might then impose new tax demands or enforce military conscription.

end for Shapira. But the anguish of Rotterdam was some way off. This wily character had another trick up his sleeve.

"Syria is the second country in the world that is expert in textiles."

That takes me by surprise. Second? Who's first, then?

"Go on, guess."

I don't like to be a smartarse. Palestine?

Gales of laughter. By his reaction that's the funniest thing Ibrahim Abu Khalaf has heard all day.

"India," he says, after he recovers. "They have 1.5 billion people. In that population you'll have maybe 300 million people who know and love textiles. They have the skill and the creativity. But brocade like this? Syria is the number one expert in brocade."

We're standing in Ibrahim's shop on Christian Quarter Road, in front of a bolt of shimmering, iridescent silk brocade that is beyond words. Beyond my ability with words, anyway. I can't describe the colors because they keep changing. I can't describe the pattern because it keeps moving. Ibrahim calls it the Tail of the Peacock. It's a talisman, it opens a portal to some other realm of existence. It is like nothing I've seen before or since, let alone actually handled.

"I don't sell much of this," Ibrahim says. "It comes from Syria, but the factory doesn't exist anymore because of the war. Mouzannar. They are experts for brocade, handloom. Ordinary brocade sells for a hundred shekels a meter, say twenty-five or thirty dollars. A meter of this is at least five hundred dollars. It is art, it is museum-quality."

As Ibrahim shows me more stuff – silk scarves that Mouzannar puts out as a form of promotion for their brand quality – he explains how Syria's textile firms may be headquartered in Damascus, but the real skill lies in Aleppo, the center of production. "I bring from where Israelis can't reach. Half my shop is from Syria and Morocco. I got new cotton, triple jacquard, last month from Aleppo, from a friend of mine who kept stock from before. It comes through Turkey."

Ibrahim is part of a dynasty, the Abu Khalaf family – originally Kurdish – that came to Jerusalem with Salah ad-Din in the twelfth century to fight the Crusaders. He is the third generation of his branch and has been forty-two years in this shop, taking over from his father Taher and his grandfather Abd al-Rahman, who look down from framed photographs hung on the back wall. "Even now, the electricity and telephone bill are still in my grandfather's name," he laughs. "My grandfather started selling on his shoulder. Then he got one small shop, then it grows, you know."

Now, there are forty shops under the Abu Khalaf name, all around Palestine and Jordan, but the family has separated and most are run by relatives. Ibrahim has three shops in Jerusalem – including one a couple of minutes' walk away, run by his brother Bilal – and one in Amman with another brother.

One big seller is liturgical robes. The Greek and Armenian patriarchs, neither of them short of a penny or two, are good customers of Ibrahim's. He also has stories of supplying the highest echelons of Jordanian royalty. One time I was in his shop when two ultra-Orthodox Jewish men came in to discuss pure white silk, to be made into kaftans for use on Yom Kippur – another strong seller.

The shop is crammed, literally to the ceiling, with hundreds of varieties of linens, cottons, silks and cheaper polyester fabric, on two floors. There's just enough space between upright bolts of cloth to squeeze up the stairway. But there's so much variety, from all over the world, I wonder if most people have any clue what they're looking at. "They don't know," Ibrahim says. "I explain for them."

I, too, have no clue what I'm looking at, but it's a pleasure to be persuaded by Ibrahim, to sense yourself in the hands of a master. He knows that you know that he knows he's leading you by the nose, but there's never any condescension. From the first moment I stepped into his shop, this expert knew me inside out. He knew what I might buy, and he knew what I would never buy, and all the chat was part of the dance. By the end I *wanted* to give him my money.

In the souk, as long as you move you're essentially invisible, because almost everyone is moving – two-dimensional figures in a constantly scrolling backdrop. People who move are inconsequential. The story of the souk is the story of the people who have stopped moving. Maybe you saw something you liked, or thought you did. Maybe you stopped to catch your breath or to look at the sky or for some other reason, but stop and it's as if you materialize. You solidify from vapor to customer. Or potential customer. Or, perhaps, threat.

Stopping to make notes in the souk, for instance, is a bad idea, because shopkeepers think you are from the municipality, or the customs authority, or some other governmental body planning to impose some new regulation that will make their lives even harder, or their rent even higher, or their taxes more burdensome. Stand typing on a phone and nobody cares. Stand writing in a notebook and you must be CIA. In the words of Ahmed Dajani, who sells rather beautiful embroidered gowns on Christian Quarter Road: "We are not only merchants. We are watchers. We sit all day long, we see everybody, we talk to everybody, we know who everybody is and is not."

The souk that you and I experience is not the same souk that insiders, the people who don't move, experience. A long-in-the-tooth Jerusalemite friend, sober and serious, not prone to fancy, once called the Old City "a place of spies and torture and death." That's a Jerusalem mostly out of reach to me, but I can sense it when people are unaccountably wary of my presence or reluctant to interact, or when I watch Israeli police checking Palestinian people's IDs on the street and turning out young men's pockets. It's ever-present in the CCTV cameras that stare from every wall, fixed on every corner. Torture need not involve pulling fingernails; continuous hostile surveillance can have the same effect.

One evening I was walking with that long-in-the-tooth friend and we stopped to talk to a shopkeeper and some other guy, and afterwards my friend asked if I'd noticed how the other guy had surreptitiously taken pictures of me on his phone during the conversation. I hadn't. That's because they're good, my friend said. Who's good, I said. The Israelis will have recruited him to keep an eye on the neighborhood, my friend said. That's his patch. He's interested in who you are and why some English writer is out walking with me.

My friend may be paranoid, but then again Jerusalem is rock-solid proof of the old adage: just because you're paranoid doesn't mean they're not out to get you.

Kevork Kahvedjian had gentle eyes. Known in English as George, he was one of the most respected figures in the souk, and everyone knows his shop, "Elia Photo-Service," off Christian Quarter Road. It was named for his father, Elia, one of the cohort of Armenians who led the development of photography in Jerusalem for a century or more. The first was Essayi (or Issay) Garabedian, who set up a studio and workshop in 1857 to teach photography. Before then the new science had been the preserve of European visitors; they still dominated, but Garabedian coached many of the region's pioneering local photographers. His protégé Garabed Krikorian opened his own studio in 1885, and one of Krikorian's students was Khalil Raad, famed as the first Arab photographer in Palestine.

Elia had fled the Armenian genocide as a young boy, having seen his family murdered in front of him. When he was picked up with thousands of other orphans and brought to Palestine, he didn't know his own surname. All he could remember was his father having traded coffee (*kahve* in Turkish), so he was called Kahvedjian – "son of the coffee-seller." He started carrying equipment for a teacher who dabbled in photography, then went to work at a studio in Jerusalem, then, in 1930, bought out his bosses and set up by himself.

Jerusalem had dozens of photographers during and after the 1930s, but Elia Kahvedjian's particular skill lay in street photography. He was able to capture personalities and atmospheres others missed: Dom women dancing, men huddled at a table eating hummus, souk scenes galore. Of his thousands of images, going through to the 1970s, one stands out for its backstory.

All over the souk (and the internet) you'll see a vintage poster of Jerusalem showing an evocatively hand-drawn view of the Dome of the Rock, seen from afar. The city is framed in the foreground by the curving trunk and suspended foliage of an olive tree, like Hok-

usai's wave, above the slogan "Visit Palestine." Since its rediscovery in 1995 the poster has become a symbol of Palestinian nationalism, even though it was designed in 1936 by graphic artist Franz Krausz for a Zionist development agency. Yet Krausz, who himself only arrived in Palestine in late 1934, may have adapted the image from a photograph by Elia Kahvedjian. Some time ago, Kevork showed me a picture his father had taken as a teenager in 1924 of a rural scene of sheep and goats beside the curving trunk and suspended foliage of an olive tree. He pointed out the parallel between the tree in the photo and the tree on the poster. But is there a way to prove that it's basically the same tree, creatively transplanted? No. Did Krausz know of Kahvedjian's work before he designed the poster? We don't know. It's pure speculation.

Before and after Elia Kahvedjian died in 1999, Kevork was careful to protect his father's legacy, selling framed photographic prints and publishing a large-format book *Jerusalem Through My Father's Eyes* that is so sought-after that unauthorized distributors have been shut down and pirated versions seized. My signed copy is a treasure.

Thousands attended the funeral of Kevork Kahvedjian in 2018. The business is now with Kevork's son Elia, who told me not long ago: "This shop is bigger than me. It's history through pictures. If I close it, a big part of Jerusalem will be gone. It has to go on."

I was on Christian Quarter Road once, chatting, when I spotted a friend. Dawoud Manarious must be Jerusalem's hardest-working tour guide. Alert, knowledgeable, fluent in several languages, he leads only Christian pilgrim groups sent by one particular British company. Yet he works full-time, week after week, month after month, morning till night, virtually the whole year round.

Dawoud takes pride in being a member of the Coptic Orthodox Church, which was founded in Egypt soon after Christ and is still centered there ("Copt" derives from the Greek word for Egypt). Only about a thousand Copts remain in Jerusalem, roughly 250 of whom live inside the walls – which is where Dawoud was born and raised.

His church has an exceptionally long history in Jerusalem, going back to the fourth century, and before. For the last fifty years, though, it's been embroiled in one of the most intractable of Jerusalem's inter-communal disputes, centered on Deir al-Sultan, a set of buildings claimed by both the Copts and the equally ancient (and much larger, though less powerful) Ethiopian Orthodox Church. For centuries, these were one – or, rather, the Ethiopian church came under the authority of the Coptic. In 1959 it won a degree of autonomy.

Their dispute is phenomenally complicated. Who started it, when and why, depends on who you ask. Over the sixteenth and seventeenth centuries the Copts built churches, a hospice and an episcopal residence on the roof of the Holy Sepulchre church, also taking over two chapels that lie on a stepped path between the rooftop and the church proper. Slightly later, the Ethiopians lost rights within the Holy Sepulchre due to accumulation of debts, and retreated to a knot of ramshackle huts in Deir al-Sultan, a courtyard on the Holy Sepulchre's roof beside the Coptic complex. The two communities shared the whole space (or, some say, the Copts hosted the Ethiopians) until 1948, when the process of separating the two church administrations began. Unanswerable questions started to be asked about who owned which bit of property.

Things came to a head over Easter 1970, when the Israeli police either initiated or connived at the Ethiopian clergy changing locks in order to take (or, some say, retake) control of Deir al-Sultan and the two chapels beneath. Resentment has festered ever since, the Copts angling to regain a toehold, the Ethiopians implacably assertive. Arguments occasionally escalate into violence. Geopolitics plays its part – Israel has warmer relations with Ethiopia than with Egypt – and accusations of discrimination fly.

Tour groups passing across the courtyard get little sense of the tension and miserable poverty the Ethiopian clergy live with, and tend to think it's all rather picturesque, having Africans on the roof. Dawoud tells me plainly he sees no resolution to the Deir al-Sultan dispute. It'll just rumble on. That day on Christian Quarter Road, though, his harried expression spoke of more pressing concerns. He was leading a group through the souk. Mostly Canadian, on their way to the Holy Sepulchre. He'd been with them on the Sea of Galilee the day before, and was taking them to Bethlehem that afternoon. He couldn't stop. He'd catch me later.

It took an age for the crocodile of baseball hats cramming the market lane behind Dawoud to pass. There must have been fifty at least. People think Dawoud's job is easy. He's just a tour leader. But tour leaders are also project managers. Educators. Facilitators. Negotiators. Linguists. Sociologists. Psychologists. Comedians. Magicians. Friends. Dawoud has to be everything to everybody.

Scholars have long debated who was responsible for the Moabite pottery forgery, Shapira or his sidekick, Salim al-Khouri. Al-Khouri – nicknamed Al-Kari or Al-Qari, "the reader" – seems to have been a middleman between Shapira and the bedouin, who controlled access to the desert, and also between Shapira and the potters of Jerusalem, who were able to produce sufficiently convincing work. Nowadays the pieces are seen as crude, not least because their inscriptions are meaningless strings of characters copied from the Mesha stone. But at the time, many scholars were persuaded (though, significantly, not experts in Semitic languages, who immediately smelled a rat).

Yoram Sabo, a dedicated Shapirologist, has discovered that much later, in 1902, Abraham Yahuda, a Jerusalemite scholar who would become an eminent collector of manuscripts, had by chance been approached by a guide named Salim who offered to procure Moabite "antiquities." Yahuda played along. When the artefacts appeared he saw they were fake, but realized "Salim" was Shapira's Salim al-Khouri. The two apparently struck up a friendship, and Al-Khouri eventually led Yahuda to a kiln hidden in a cellar off Souk Khan al-Zeit where he claimed to have fired the figurines, also showing him sketches he had drawn for the potters.

Scholars who exposed the fraud had been careful not to accuse Shapira, instead piling all the blame onto Al-Khouri. Shapira, too, protested his innocence and publicly denounced his assistant as a cheat. In 1878 Al-Khouri was reported to have fled to Alexandria. But Shapira, innocent? Ha. Not a chance. He was a con artist. It's impossible he wasn't in on the deception. He is known to have led clients into the desert for exploratory digs where they just happened to unearth "Moabite antiquities" that had been buried there by Al-Khouri with the connivance of the bedouin. Shapira was no dupe. So why did he throw his friend under the bus?

Ostensibly, Shapira dumped Al-Khouri so he could retain his international standing as a dealer in antiquities. That fits with what came later. Also, Shapira had been a target for the Hebrew press, who had gleefully denounced him both as an apostate and a forger. Prejudice from Shapira – and from European scholars – against Al-Khouri as Arab and poorly educated may have played its part.

But think again. Al-Khouri and Shapira were buddies. Not just buddies. Their lives were intertwined. I wonder if Shapira, in his indignant outrage, wasn't really just playing games, throwing sand in the eyes of the world by declaring he had made a definitive break with the past, whereas secretly he and Al-Khouri were preparing for the heist to end all heists, the one that would change the world.

The stakes couldn't have been higher.

Christian Quarter Road is bad for phone reception. It's just about the worst in the Old City. There's an OK patch at one end, near Ibrahim's shop, but a bit further along you move into a dead zone where you get no reception at all.

I stood there once, playing with my settings, when I mentioned it to a shopkeeper who was watching me from nearby.

"What network are you on?" he said.

Cellcom, I said, naming an Israeli company. All mobile networks in Jerusalem are operated by Israeli companies. Palestinian providers are restricted to the West Bank and Gaza.

"Only Pelephone works here," he said, naming another Israeli firm. "Because of the police. All the police, all over Israel, have Pelephone. So they make coverage everywhere."

He showed me the difference on his two phones: the handset showing Pelephone had full bars, whereas another – Cellcom, he said – had no service, the same as mine.

I have no way of verifying whether every Israeli police officer's phone operates on the Pelephone network or not. It sounds plausible. Since 2012 Cellcom has had the exclusive contract to provide mobile phone service to the Israeli army.

The occupation demands complicity.

Suha often mentions – always with a weary smile – how rude tourists can be. Stingy, she calls them sometimes. She tells me how she watches some guides lead their groups straight past her shop, telling their clients that everything in there is rubbish from China. When she cleans she finds sweets wrappers dropped into the bowls for sale. Her shop isn't a rubbish shop. It's pressure inside you, she says. That's one of the reasons I get all dazed and dizzy.

She was a child when she would come and help her dad in this very shop. She would work half a day or so to start with. Her dad started as a tailor, but after he'd got the shop, he told her if she didn't take it over there wouldn't be any income. She had to work.

She started at eighteen and everyone saw she was a fast worker, even though she was a girl. She got to know everybody by going with her father to the factory. She would open the store at six or seven in the morning, and stay until evening. Her dad would ask why she worked so late and she'd say I'm busy, I'm working with customers. He could see how good at business she was. Before he died he told the whole family that this shop was for Suha.

But now things are hard. Her father made her promise she wouldn't sell the shop, but some of her relatives keep telling her the time has come. That's more pressure. But she knows she can't just sit at home doing nothing. She'd be sick. She has to fight for herself and for the people with her. It was for them I did everything, she says. It was for mum and dad. But tourists can be so rude sometimes.

Head up some steps behind Christian Quarter Road and you'll usually find a Harley-Davidson parked outside a shop. Both bike and shop belong to Wassim Razzouk, the founder-president of the Holy Land Bikers Motorcycle Club and the twenty-seventh generation in his family business. Twenty-seven is a lot of generations.

Wassim has presence. Long hair frames grayish stubble above a black T-shirt, but it's an intensity behind the eyes that holds you. "I am religious in my own way," he tells me. "I go to church every time I ride my bike. I talk to God on my bike. When you're riding with a group of people, you're entrusting your life to them. It's fun but it could be dangerous. Slowly you start feeling like it's a group that has a code which bonds the brothers together. There's nothing you have to do. You have to become. It's like being a knight. It makes you a better person."

Coincidentally – it didn't have to dovetail so well – Wassim's long-running family business is tattooing. In Jerusalem, tattooing is a Christian thing. Barring henna, which is temporary skin decoration, and bedouin cultures where women have face tattoos, most Islamic and Jewish practice prohibits body art. But some Christian communities nurture long traditions of tattooing. Wassim is Coptic. Having faced intolerance that veers often into murderous persecution, Copts have long recognized each other by a small cross tattooed on the inside of their right wrist (or on the forehead in the Ethiopian Orthodox church). This marker of identity remains almost universal. Without it, strangers may even be barred from entering a Coptic church.

For centuries Christian pilgrims – not just from the Coptic church – have sought tattoos to commemorate their visits to the holy places. And nowadays, decorative tattooing for fashion or as a declaration of countercultural identity crosses every social division: traditional attitudes are changing in Jerusalem, as anywhere.

Other shop signs might proudly declare "Established 1961" or "Founded 1889." The sign above Razzouk Tattoo says "Since 1300." Beat that. Wassim's family, which comes from Minya, a center of Coptic culture on the Nile in Upper Egypt, have been tattooing for seven centuries. Something like five hundred years ago, he says, his ancestors travelled on pilgrimage to Jerusalem. "They discovered a tattooing tradition already existed here, so they stayed, and started tattooing pilgrims. We still have the old stamps."

As customers cram into his shop – a church rector from Connecticut is having the Annunciation on her arm; a trio of tough guys from France want a banana on their ankles – Wassim points me to display cases lined with carved medallions of wood, which would be inked and pressed onto skin to serve as a template for tattooing. Many are originals, used by Wassim's forebears for centuries past, including a Jerusalem cross – an equal-armed cross with four crosslets in each quadrant, associated with Jerusalem since the thirteenth century – and a dragon being skewered by St. George, who was first venerated, and perhaps martyred, in Palestine.

"I see it like baptism," says Wassim. "Baptism with water is a physical process, but it's not your body that is baptised, it's your soul.

When we tattoo people, it's a very deep spiritual connection that you cause people to feel what they are and who they are. I tell them: 'You'll take this with you.' The tattoo is a reflection on your body of a mark on your soul."

Wassim was already riding motorbikes and had turned his back on the family tradition when he was caught by a pang of conscience, and came back to his father to learn. And the women of the family also learned the trade: Wassim's wife, Gabrielle, is a tattoo artist in her own right. Now their teenage sons Anton and Nizar – generation twenty-eight – are involved.

"By me being here, present, with my children, not wanting to emigrate, doing this, I'm keeping Christianity alive in a way that nobody else can. It's a Christian presence, in Christian Jerusalem. And if we don't do it, there would be an Israeli tattoo artist who would do it instead – but then it wouldn't be the same, like buying a fake Rolex. You come to Jerusalem as a pilgrim, you want to be tattooed by a Christian who has been doing it forever. This is why I see our family is important. Jerusalem gives me my identity."

Every chat I have with Wassim reveals new depth. The motorbike element is really interesting, especially that line of his: "It's like being a knight." Those medieval knightly orders – the Knights Hospitaller in particular, but also the Knights Templar and Teutonic Knights – were established in Jerusalem during the Crusades partly or wholly in order to protect pilgrims. The idea was that the knights' moral codes and fellowship would facilitate the spiritual advancement of others. The parallels with what Wassim says about spiritual marking are plain. Of all the places where you might think you'd hear an echo of medieval chivalry, I wouldn't have considered a back-street tattoo parlor, loud with Led Zeppelin.

Even as the Moabite pottery scam was being exposed, Shapira was on the rebound. In 1876 the influential Baedeker guidebook named Shapira's shop on Christian Quarter Road the best in Jerusalem for books and souvenirs. Starting in 1877 the British Museum began buying genuine manuscripts from him, including 145 Karaite texts that are still of global significance. That's not to say Shapira was on the level. On a trip to Yemen in 1879 he deceived Jewish elders there by posing as a rabbi, then pressured them to sell manuscripts. When they refused, he bribed the local governor to send in soldiers, who forcibly seized the scrolls and handed them to the visiting "rabbi." The European thirst for biblical antiquities was driving Shapira – and other unscrupulous tricksters – to strip whole communities of cultural heritage for profit. Then it was time for the big one.

On 21 July 1883, Shapira arrived at the British Museum bearing fifteen strips of ancient leather inscribed with text from the Book of Deuteronomy. He said the bedouin had discovered them a few years before in caves in Wadi Mujib, a canyon on the east shore of the Dead Sea. But this wasn't the same Deuteronomy as in the Bible: there were significant differences, suggesting that Shapira's scrolls could demonstrate the human process of editing and compilation that had gone into the Bible as we know it. And they included an eleventh Commandment: *Thou shalt not hate thy brother in thy heart.*

It was a sensational discovery. Scholarly understanding of the Bible would have to be rewritten. Religious practice for individuals and communities around the world would never be the same again. It could precipitate schisms, even wars.

Shapira coolly stated his price. One million pounds. It was an astronomical sum, like demanding a hundred million today. Controversy erupted immediately. The press bubbled with the story. When Shapira allowed the British Museum to exhibit two of the strips, the prime minister, William Gladstone, came to see. But then things started to go pear-shaped. First one scholar declared the strips to be forgeries. Then another. The British Museum refused to buy. The press quickly turned against Shapira. *Punch* magazine printed an anti-Semitic caricature of him captioned "Mr. Sharp-Eye-Ra."

Shapira tried to brazen it out by playing the innocent dupe again: "You have made a fool of me," he told the British Museum, "by publishing and exhibiting things you believe to be false. I do not think I shall be able to survive this shame." Incredibly, this manufactured image of the honest dealer deceived by his own suppliers seems to have worked. The British Museum continued to buy from him – just small items, in October 1883, and again in January 1884, their greed clearly outweighing their scruples. But the bottom had dropped out. Two months later, in Rotterdam, Shapira killed himself.

That, though, is still not the end. Sixty years on, in 1946/47 at Qumran, barely a day's walk from Wadi Mujib on the cliffs over-looking the northwest shore of the Dead Sea, bedouin found what came to be known as the Dead Sea Scrolls – ancient manuscripts showing biblical texts, some of them written on strips of leather, including many copies of Deuteronomy. More discoveries followed in nearby caves. To this day the Dead Sea Scrolls, unquestionably genuine, are studied intensively, and have completely changed how we understand biblical history.

The question soon arose: in light of the discovery of the Dead Sea Scrolls, shouldn't we reassess Shapira's scrolls? Perhaps we've all made a terrible mistake. Perhaps they weren't fakes after all.

There are conversations to be had up and down the souk. Elie Kouz, who sells ceramics like Suha, has a thousand stories from the fifty-seven years he's been in his shop – from the disappointment of his mother that this boy, top of the whole school in maths and sciences, didn't follow her to become a doctor, to the days when, aged eight or nine, he and his brother would smoke a packet of cigarettes between them in the cinema. Or that period when he got married five times in the space of twenty months. Or how his family's fashion, jewelry and philately business, spread between Amman, Damascus, Beirut and Jerusalem, flourished until Elie's father lost virtually everything in the wake of the triple blow of war in Jordan in 1970, war in Syria in 1973 and the outbreak of war in Lebanon in 1975.

Elie belongs to Jerusalem's tiny Syriac community, only a hundred and twenty families, roughly five hundred people alto-gether. The Syriac Orthodox Church is one of Christianity's oldest, claiming its origins in first-century Antioch from the apostles themselves. English has often confused "Syriac" with "Syrian" and long knew this church as "Syrian Orthodox." But though the church is now headquartered in Damascus, for centuries until 1932 its seat was at Tur Abdin in Turkey: it is named not for a place but for the Syriac language that is used in the liturgy and in everyday communication. Syriac is a dialect of Aramaic, which was a lingua franca across the Middle East before Arabic arrived. Jesus spoke a variety of Aramaic.

To confuse matters even more, while some Syriacs claim a unique ethnic identity, many identify as ethnically Assyrian, a pre-Arab people indigenous to Assyria, which comprises the northeast of modern Syria and adjacent areas in Iraq and Turkey.

St. Mark's, where the Jerusalem community prays, is an old and beautiful twelfth-century church on a hard-to-find alley behind the souk. An inscription discovered there says a church existed in the same place as early as 73 CE. It's a strong candidate for the site of the Last Supper. I was lucky once, several years ago, to hear an impassioned Lord's Prayer sung in St. Mark's in Syriac by an apple-cheeked nun named Yostina al-Banna. "My mother told me I was always hungry as a baby, so she would sing to me to help me sleep," Yostina told me, as an explanation for how she acquired her extraordinary vocal power. She had come to Jerusalem in 2000 from the Assyrian heartland of Ninawa (that is, Nineveh), in northwestern Iraq, and her singing slid a hot knife between my ribs. I want to find Yostina again – once heard, never forgotten – but each time I've visited recently, the church has been closed due to renovation work, with the courtyard full of rubble and nobody about. I'll go back.

Round the corner from St. Mark's hides the shop of Sami Barsoum, the Syriac Orthodox *mukhtar*, or community representative. Groomed, debonair and entertaining, Sami looks and acts at least twenty years younger than his grand age. Of all the people I spoke to in the souk, many of them spinning out family traditions decade after decade, Sami outdoes them all. After a few teenage years in Baghdad, learning his trade of tailoring, Sami came back to Jerusalem and opened his shop in 1959. We sat and talked in the same shop in 2019. Sixty years open for business. With the same chairs, too.

As you'd expect, Sami has developed a nice line in patter over that time. He told me the one about his five nationalities.

First, he feels Turkish: the Syriac church accepts patrilineal descent, and Sami's father was born in Turkey in 1908, fleeing to Jerusalem with his family in 1915 during the genocide.

Then, he feels British: he was born in British-held Jerusalem in 1935, and to this day remains proud of his British birth certificate.

Jordan gives him a passport.

Israel gives him an identity card.

And he identifies as Palestinian, born in Palestine, and part of Palestinian society.

"Five nationalities, one person, one city. I didn't seek any of it. They all came to me," he said. "Just wait. If we tell them the right stories China will invade Jerusalem one day. Then I'll have number six." And he roared with laughter.

I meant to talk to him about the Syriac community, but we got distracted. By his grandmother, for instance. He remembers her, even though she died when he was only six or seven. She would always talk to him in Aramaic. And by what happened to his father, who worked as a shoemaker on Jaffa Street in West Jerusalem. In 1948 the poor man lost everything – his house, his shop and then his mind. His mother had to work to feed the family. "I told my mother I will not leave Jerusalem," Sami said. "My father came here as a refugee – why do I want to be a refugee somewhere else?"

Sami was long Jerusalem's leading tailor. Mayors, diplomats, officials of all kinds, from all over the world, came to be fitted for a suit. Clerics, for liturgical robes. But no more. "No, my children have good positions, not like their father. My grandchildren too – doctor, engineer, chef, teacher. I will not let them be a tailor. In the past there was a job called tailor. Now it's finished. This shop? Let it go to hell. Am I going to take it with me? My children can sell it or make it a home. They are not interested in shops."

Sami showed me his library – "a tailor, with a library!" – which includes the memoir he published a few years ago. It was highly praised by the late Albert Aghazarian, one of Jerusalem's most eminent historians.

"Jerusalem is my country," Sami said. "Everyone who passes this shop says, 'Hi, Sami.' That's enough, really. That's enough."

Why did Wilhelm Shapira kill himself?

Let's say the scrolls were a forgery. A carefully planned heist, years in preparation and immaculately executed, had failed. Shapira had been able to bounce back once, after the Moabite pottery fraud, but how could he carry on now? For a man who'd got used to hobnobbing with diplomats and nobility, being ridiculed in the London press would have hurt. Maybe he tried to imagine his future, and could only see himself scraping a living selling trinkets in Jerusalem. That might have seemed bleaker than March in Rotterdam.

Indeed, that's how most people tell this story.

But there's a possibility often overlooked. Shapira was a crook, obviously. But a very plausible, skilled and erudite crook. We can never know the depths of another's despair, but it doesn't quite ring true to me to imagine such a resourceful, resilient man feeling so irretrievably downcast at – what? a mere loss of face? – as to have no option but to abandon his wife and young daughters and end it all.

What, instead, if Shapira had realized he'd made the worst mistake of his life, and had boxed himself in with no means of escape? After a career of wheeling and dealing, and of carefully lying to preserve his friendship with his partner behind the scenes, what if he'd turned out to be the luckiest loser in history? What if the two chancers had hit paydirt for real? What if Al-Khouri had come to Shapira bearing not crude bits of clay, but something even the bedouin had thought might be valuable when they'd found it?

What if the scrolls were genuine?

Just along from Ibrahim's shop, and Suha's shop, and Elie's shop, there's a place on Christian Quarter Road that, as far as I know, is doubly unique. First, it's the only commercial art gallery in the souk. Then, it's the only British-owned* shop in the whole of the Old City.

Its owner, Karen Mann, a copy-editor with a degree in law, has lived in Jerusalem for thirty-four years. Her husband Mohammed Salhab runs a jewelry shop a few doors down from the gallery and spends his day popping between the two premises, reacting to customer demand.

They met in Jerusalem, spent several years on Merseyside, where Karen is from – Mohammed drove a taxi in Chester – but then came back home. When the children grew up and their son chose not to follow his father into business, retaining the lease on the second

---

* That is, the lease is British-owned. Almost all property in the Old City is rented. Most land is owned or controlled by the Greek Orthodox Church and the Islamic Waqf. In the gallery's case – as with all commercial premises – the shop owner rents the space from the church.

shop looked doubtful, but then Karen had an idea. "The Old City was losing its voice, particularly in art. Everywhere you go you see the same stuff. I felt there was a need for the local Palestinian voice to be given a look-in. We wanted to have a space that would serve local artists and allow them to show their work to a much wider audience than they could otherwise. Here, we're on the *Champs-Élysées* of Jerusalem."

So Karen has forged links with twenty-five Palestinian artists from Jerusalem and around the West Bank and Gaza,* sometimes purchasing artworks from them outright, sometimes agreeing to take a commission on sale. With the quantity of footfall, and Karen and Mohammed's skills as salespeople, the shop has developed a healthy turnover of both prints and original works, aimed squarely at foreign visitors: views of the Old City predominate, alongside domes, churches, rural scenes, small sculptures and photography, by a mix of lesser-known and more prominent artists, costing from a few shekels to several thousand dollars. Karen is clear about the wider aim – and her feet remain firmly on the ground.

"This is a commercial gallery," she says. "The point is to sell, to give the artists an income. Many of them feel this pressure to create big conceptual pieces with deep meanings. I'm saying to them, 'Look, just go and make me some nice pictures about things you love about Jerusalem. It doesn't have to be deep.' Then people have bought them and loved them and sought the artists out later to say thank you. For them, that's huge that they can have fun with their art as well. They still have their deep conceptual projects, but this allows them to make money."

It's easy to dismiss the Shapira scrolls as a forgery. With their editing and reordering of the Commandments they present a Christianized version of Deuteronomy that rather too neatly mirrors Shapira's

---

* They include Shehab Kawasmi, whose panoramic drawing of Jerusalem graces the cover of this book.

own Jewish-Christian identity. They were written on strips of leather that were straight at the top and ragged beneath, exactly as if they had been sliced from along the bottom of a genuine ancient scroll. Scholars even noticed perpendicular scratch-lines in the leather that would have acted as margins for text in the original scroll; the forged text ignored these margins. In 2016 Shapirologist Chanan Tigay discovered a manuscript collection in San Francisco once owned by Shapira that included genuine ancient leather scrolls, with perpendicular scratch-lines, that had had large sections sliced out of them along the bottom. All the circumstantial evidence points to forgery.

Or, almost all. Some onlookers have doubts. No manuscripts up to that point had been discovered on leather: a forger would have been more likely to have worked in stone. Until the later Qumran discoveries, scholars even doubted leather could survive two thousand years in the Palestinian climate. Some of the genuine Dead Sea Scrolls are also straight at the top and ragged at the bottom. Shapira said the bedouin told him they found the scrolls wrapped in cotton or linen that had been smeared with pitch, an outlandish detail that was unheard of in archaeology at that time. Two of the first Dead Sea Scrolls that were discovered sixty years later were wrapped in linen that had been smeared with pitch. And so it goes on, with epigraphic analyses and even doubts raised about the process by which the forgery was exposed in 1883, and the personalities – and geopolitical maneuvering – behind the exposure.

The next step is clear. The only way to settle the matter is to reexamine the scrolls using modern technology.

Unfortunately, they've disappeared.

After news of Shapira's death broke, Sotheby's auction house sold the scrolls in 1885 for ten pounds five shillings (roughly £800 today) to London book dealer Quaritch, who sold them for almost double that in 1888 to Philip Brookes Mason, an antiquarian living in the Staffordshire town of Burton-on-Trent. On 8 March 1889, – five years to the day since Shapira pulled the trigger – Brookes Mason showed them to his local archaeology society as part of a lecture. That's the last we know. When Brookes Mason died in 1903, childless and without mentioning the scrolls in his will, it seems his widow disposed of his possessions. The scrolls have gone.

Then again, one thing's for sure. Right now, today, as I am writing these words, folk will be out on the trail somewhere, poring over records of auction sales in the English Midlands, or typing unfamiliar addresses into Google, or maybe already sitting on chintzy sofas, holding cups of milky tea, trying to control their excitement as they say, "Do you happen to know if your great-grandfather ever bought some scraps of old leather with strange writing on them?" In March 2021 the *New York Times* published a breathless four-thousand-word feature on the work of biblical scholar Idan Dershowitz, whose new analysis, undermining the dismissal of the scrolls as forgeries, has lent the seekers fresh energy.

I doubt this is the last we've heard of Shapira.

But why this long story about him here?

Shapira's first property in Jerusalem, which included the shop from which he conducted all his business, outside which he once hung a sign reading "Correspondent of the British Museum," stretches across three modern-day shopfronts on Christian Quarter Road. One of them, I discovered only recently, after I'd already completed my research for this book, is now the shop of Suha Alami.

It's mind-boggling. All that time, I was chatting away to Suha in the very place where Shapira worked.

I haven't been back yet to see Suha. I can't wait to tell her.

18

A Voice Coming Out from Jerusalem

A STORY OF BAB AL-JADID/NEW GATE

JACK IS TELLING ME SOME HISTORY. "On my father's side, the family came from Turkey, most probably a place called Marash. Apparently my great-grandfather was a baker on a ship in the Ottoman navy. He came to Palestine around 1896 and settled in Nablus. He brought his wife and child, then they had three more kids – one of them was my grandfather. Around the time of the British Mandate, 1918 or 1920, something like that, they moved to Jerusalem. That was a period when people were hopeful. My father, Hanna, was born here.

"One day, when he was a kid, my father was out in the street and a horse-drawn cart ran him over. It was bad. They had to amputate his leg. So from a young age he was disabled. What are your choices at the age of thirteen with one leg, at that time? The family was poor. They told him you can either be a tailor or a bookbinder – that was it. Luckily, he opted for bookbinding."

Jack's neighborhood is the hill inside the northwestern corner of Jerusalem's walls. This, the Crusaders believed, was where David swung his slingshot and felled Goliath. When Suleiman rebuilt this wall in about 1539, over preexisting foundations, some knew the

fortification marking the corner as Tancred's Tower (Tancred was in the Crusader army that attacked Jerusalem in 1099). Others knew it by a name that preserved the old legend: *Qasr al-Jalut*, Goliath's Palace. The tower's foundations lie today within the premises of the Collège des Frères, a famous old school established in 1876 that helped educate many celebrated Jerusalemites – including my host, the artist, gallery owner and museum curator Jack Persekian.

Jack was born, lived, grew up and still works in his family's premises right here, inside the walls, one minute from the gates of Frères college, perhaps a hundred meters from New Gate. We met there, on an afternoon that shifted from sun to rain and back again while we talked. But this is not another parochial story of tireless toil in a family business, a father handing a baton of dedication to a son down the generations. At least, not in the usual way.

This is really a story about liberation and sustainable futures.

Hundreds of years ago Jack's neighborhood was Jerusalem's Serbian quarter, clustered around Deir as-Sarb, a Serbian Orthodox monastery near a postern in the walls known as Bab as-Sarb, the Gate of the Serbs. The gate probably disappeared with Suleiman's rebuilding, and by the time the Collège des Frères went up, more changes were afoot. French pilgrims were flocking into Jerusalem, and in 1885 building work began on the huge Notre Dame de France hospice to accommodate them, just outside the walls here. But at that time the quickest way into the city to reach the holy places meant walking all the way round to Jaffa Gate. With European power in Jerusalem on the rise, the French consul put in a request with Sultan Abdulhamid to create a new entrance into the walled city opposite Notre Dame, near where the old Bab as-Sarb had been, to ease the pilgrims' passage. Heedless of heritage, but also aware on which side his diplomatic bread was buttered, Abdulhamid gave his approval to take a sledgehammer to Suleiman's handiwork. In 1889, the year after Notre Dame hosted its first pilgrims, workers completed punching a hole in the walls that came to be known as New Gate; in Arabic *Bab al-Jadid*.

As long as you're not there around 7:45 in the morning, just before school starts, or between 2 and 3 in the afternoon, when lessons end, New Gate is a lovely, peaceful way into the Old City. (Even then, the hubbub with all the kids streaming to and fro is fun. Or you could choose a Friday or a Sunday: the school operates a split weekend for its Muslim and Christian students.) Tourists rarely come this way, and cars are restricted to residents only. There's a tiny Ottoman mosque and Islamic school wedged into the corner inside the gate, opposite a back entrance to the Franciscan monastery, but otherwise the west side of New Gate Street is mostly given over to the Frères college. The east side is lined with small shops – a barber, a grocer, a ceramicist, a patisserie. And facing the end of the street stands Gallery Anadiel, owned and run by the bookbinder's son, Jack.

Persekian's reputation spreads wide. The founding director of the Sharjah Art Foundation in the United Arab Emirates and a visiting professor at London's Royal College of Art, he has exhibited in Beirut, Dubai, London, Sao Paulo, New York, Los Angeles, Zurich, Sydney and elsewhere. Closer to home he has been head curator and director at the Palestinian Museum* and is still lead curator for the biennial Jerusalem Show. He is one of the most respected figures in contemporary art in the Arab world, and, unlike many, he has stuck tight throughout his career to Jerusalem and, specifically, to the Old City.

"Luckily," he tells me, "my father was interested in books – not only in binding them, but in learning from them. He taught himself by reading them and binding them at the same time. [He] had immense knowledge, spoke and wrote fluently in six languages. All self-taught. His first job was in Musrara at a Yiddish bookbinder. He worked there for years and learned the language. Then he grew his own business and ended up in his own shop – this place, where we are now. During its heyday there were no less than ten or eleven people working here – it was a big operation and he had huge contracts. The Einstein Institute at the Hebrew University, he was binding books for their library. I remember in the 1970s he had

---

* A national cultural institution inaugurated in 2016 in Birzeit, near Ramallah.

really good regular customers who would come from Mea Shearim [an ultra-Orthodox Jewish neighborhood outside the walls]. He took me once to the house of the head of the Neturei Karta movement there – so elegant, a fantastic house, a house where you don't see walls but only books, books, books, lining the whole place from floor to ceiling. This image never left me.

"Living here, studying here at the school next door, growing up post-1967 – I was born in '62 – there wasn't much exposure to art. At school of course nothing, and there was nothing in East Jerusalem at that time. All this neighborhood was workshops: us, the bookbinder's, a photographer, a printing shop, a wood carver, tile factory, shoe factory, all along this street and nearby. Small industrial units. Before '67 this was a dead end anyway.* Even after that, only the people who lived here would come here.

"So I remember the Israel Museum vividly. These magazines they needed binding. It was nothing anybody had ever seen, not me, not my friends at school. You never got to see magazines of photography and art. We had stacks of these magazines in the shop, and I'd go through them for the pictures. I remember when I saw Man Ray's photographs for the first time, I just…"

And even now he gasps, at the memory.

Persekian lost his father in 1988, at the time of the first intifada, the Palestinian uprising against Israeli occupation. He went to work at a photographer's studio, handling chemicals in the darkroom, and then put a couple of years into promoting and performing with the legendary Jerusalem musical group of the 1980s and 1990s, Sabreen. But then the mood shifted.

"Things were born out of need, and the possibility of making a difference. It was the middle of the intifada, and the first peace conference at Madrid was happening. Nobody was thinking of business

---

* Between 1948 and 1967 the walls of the Old City here marked the international border between Jordan and Israel. Immediately outside the walls was a strip of no-man's-land separating the two armies. New Gate was sealed shut.

– shops would open for two or three hours a day, that was it. My brother-in-law Issa Kassissieh came to me and said his family's shop on Salah ad-Din Street [the main commercial street of East Jerusalem, outside the walls] was going nowhere. 'Why don't we do something new?' he said. I said to him: 'Let's do a gallery, a commercial gallery that sells art. Now that peace is possible, all these Palestinians living abroad will want to come back and they would need art.' Of course they would!"

Persekian snorts at his own naivety, but regardless, in 1992, he and Kassissieh launched Gallery Anadiel. It was the first such enterprise in East Jerusalem and, with hindsight, turns out to have been the right people, in the right place, at the right time. Compelling images of resistance were emerging from the intifada. The international media and, broadly, the outside world were seeking to engage for the first time with the reality of Palestinian lives.

"Anadiel became a meeting place for people wanting to know and meet Palestinian artists, and for Palestinian artists to be exposed and make connections. There was no other place to do that. Issa and I had to get other jobs to keep the gallery going, but in every sense other than making money it was amazing, fulfilling to the extreme. What was super-interesting was the interest from people outside in who the Palestinians are, what they do, who the artists are. Without knowing it or planning it, I was pushed to the forefront to become the spokesperson for Palestinian art."

Persekian closely links art with the geopolitical developments of the day. The history of Palestinian art from the nineteenth century onwards is intimately tied into the region's history of imperialism, colonial conquest and occupation, particularly following the Nakba of 1948. Many artists became reliant on political patronage from the various parties and groupings that made up what could be described as the government-in-waiting, the Palestine Liberation Organization (PLO), but as a result were constrained as to styles, themes and subject matter. "Art had to work for the agenda," Persekian says.

Some managed to break the constraints, he adds, but then the Oslo peace process, launched in 1993, turned everything upside down. Suddenly, Persekian says, there was money everywhere. Vast

amounts of international funding poured into Palestine to make the
agreements happen, including cash for art and cultural projects. Yet,
under Israeli pressure, the Palestinian Authority was set up not in
Jerusalem, but in Ramallah – indeed, with a remit that explicitly
excluded a presence in Jerusalem.

"Jerusalem started being emptied out," says Persekian. "Some
international institutions decided to leave and go to Ramallah.
Others had to leave, because their staff from the West Bank were not
able to enter Jerusalem to work. Suddenly you're completely cut off.
You don't have the audience anymore, but you don't even have the

artists – the artists themselves can't reach you. From being the center of the art movement, Jerusalem became marginal."

Losing the lease on the shop in Salah ad-Din Street and splitting from his brother-in-law forced Persekian to seek a new direction. Friends urged him to follow the money and set up anew in Ramallah, but he chose to go in the other direction, back to his roots, back inside the walls. He spent the second half of 1995 clearing his father's old bookbindery at New Gate before relaunching Gallery Anadiel there – or, rather, here, since he and I are talking in the same building – and hosting a landmark show by the London-based Palestinian artist Mona Hatoum.

He sighs and puffs out his cheeks.

"That was a complete game-changer for me. Working with Mona and learning from her completely transformed my way of thinking about what running a gallery means, what it's for. Before that, what was not so encouraging was this location. Salah ad-Din Street is accessible, it's a commercial place, you can park in front of the shop, a bus will drop you right there. Here [in the Old City] you park I don't know where, and you have to walk. If it's too hot you will not come. If it's raining you will not come. If you have kids you will not come. This was in my mind at the time. But gradually I began to see this location, and the context of Jerusalem at large, as the most interesting thing about the gallery.

"The artists I've worked with are responding to the overwhelming history in the city that is experienced through being here. Artists are not your normal tourists who just come to see the city and go. Artists are people with very high sensitivity. Their capability in finding and investigating hidden issues, discovering new angles, elaborating on them, articulating them – doing that here, inside the city, was much more meaningful to them and the outcome of their work, as against being in Salah ad-Din Street or somewhere else."

Gallery Anadiel flourished – and still flourishes. That attachment to working within the walls of Jerusalem fuelled Persekian's next key innovation, moving from a privately run commercial gallery, dependent on the market and his own resources, to a sustainable public institution, a foundation for contemporary art that would be able to apply for international grants and cultural funding to spread its support more widely. Over 1996 and 1997, he and a small group of supporters developed the idea. "Everybody was saying Ramallah is the place to be, that's where you'll find meaning, audience, support, money. We said no. Not only are we going to do this in Jerusalem, but we're going to do it inside the Old City, just to make it even more difficult."

Luck granted them access to an old factory space inside New Gate, a few steps from Gallery Anadiel in Persekian's old neighborhood. Owned by the Kassissieh family, it had been operational from 1900 to 1975, producing decorative handmade floor tiles, but had fallen derelict. The structure needed work, inside and out, but it was perfect as the foundation's headquarters. They called it *Al-Mamal* (stress the first syllable) – the Factory.

It took more than fifteen years to restore the old tile factory. In the meantime Al-Mamal Foundation had to operate out of temporary premises nearby, but it finally opened in 2014. The space is cool, literally and figuratively: it's unexpectedly roomy, and contemporary art in the context of the Old City provokes thought. Al-Mamal is another beautiful, community-driven transformation of a Jerusalem building that was effectively in ruins. With its ongoing presentation of art, music, workshops and debates, this nonprofit organization single-handedly ups the ante as the only such arts space within the walls, and one of the very few in Palestinian Jerusalem.

I talked at length to Lamis Abu Aker, Al-Mamal's program coordinator, about how the foundation maintains a conversation with its Palestinian public. She acknowledged the depth of anger and frustration at the political situation, and the deprivation many experience. "A lot of Palestinians live under the poverty line," she told me. "We try as an institute to give them a platform to engage with Palestinian artists, as well as a platform to practice art and enjoy art themselves. When you're so deeply oppressed, you tend to think art is only for people who are highly privileged. I don't think so, I think art is the greatest escape we have, a way to channel energy. That's part of our role, to identify people who have potential and give them a platform, to make a connection between the artist and the audience."

I took some of those ideas back to Jack, to ask him about the value to Jerusalemites of that cultural conversation. His answers were profound, and took things much further than I was expecting. I'm going to let him speak.

"Jerusalem is becoming a mere symbol only," he said. "A religious symbol. A symbol of God and religion and nothing more. A token capital of Palestine. Holiness empties the city out, because the holiness of the symbol becomes far more important than the living [population]. There's a whole generation [of Palestinians], even two, who don't know what Jerusalem looks like. They see it in pictures, but it doesn't mean a thing. It's very disturbing. Jerusalem is becoming less and less of a place where you can see people living, enjoying their life, creating a future for the younger generation.

"Desymbolizing Jerusalem comes through education. That's what art is trying to do, to make people think outside these prescribed narratives, look at things from different ways, express ideas and thoughts and feelings. It's about liberating yourself. Once more individuals are liberated from within, you can eventually start to evolve a society that is on its way to freedom. Otherwise you can talk about freedom and liberation from here to Timbuktu, but if the people are shackled with all the baggage of religion and taboos and dominion by these bankrupt political parties, then it [won't mean anything].

"I personally believe, and the people involved with Al-Mamal believe, that we need to keep looking for ways to grow and build more of a base. It's been twenty years going strong – we have a track record now, and we have credibility. It can happen. Art can liberate.

"Yes, the people of Jerusalem are on their way to freedom and liberation, but there's a huge obstacle, and that is finding means and possibilities for those people who are gradually [realizing] their potential. They are hitting up against finding a job, affording the city, decent living conditions, being able to manage with all the complex maze of laws and regulations the Israeli [government imposes] in order to live [as a Palestinian] in Jerusalem. People see no possibility for growth here, even if you're brilliant, a creator, if you've just invented something, or you're an industralist and you want to open a factory – you can't do it in Jerusalem. You will have to go into the West Bank, or you will leave [the country].

"It's a catch-22. People who I've seen manage to liberate themselves and gain that potential opt to leave Jerusalem and make their lives abroad. Those who stay here, a good number of them are stuck, hopeless, helpless, desperate, depressed. One keeps trying and keeps working but you're pushing against a huge wall.

"We've managed to keep a voice coming out from Jerusalem in art, in all the circles that art revolves in, locally and internationally. The voice insists that Jerusalem, with all its historical, religious baggage, has a contemporary art identity, and is engaging multiple issues through the lens of art and the work of artists. It's saying that Jerusalem is worthy of attention."

EPILOGUE

A New Jerusalem

IN THE INTRODUCTION TO her study of maritime trade in the Gulf, Laleh Khalili wrote: "As sprawling as the book may be, it does not aim to be comprehensive. It does not sketch out reviews of scholarly literature, nor does it mention all possible sources about a given subject. ... [It] wanted to do something else: it wanted to tell stories." It's as if she read my mind. Stories are the point of this book, too. I wrote it to address the imbalance in stories – or narratives, or ideas – that exist about Jerusalem in my culture, English-speaking culture. Palestinian lives and voices have been too often excluded. I wanted to use my platform to try to help redress the balance.

That's a tricky word, "balance." We hear it most in relation to news media. It conjures images of a seesaw. It implies there are two sides – and in Jerusalem's case that invariably means an Israeli side, where "Israeli" is often conflated with "Jewish," and a Palestinian side. It also implies the existence of a dispassionate fulcrum in the middle, doing the balancing. Devote equal resources to both sides, this wisdom says, and the seesaw will be level. You will have achieved balance.

But as I set out to show in this book, and as I tried to suggest with its title, Jerusalem has many more sides than two, and many more quarters than the four that appear on its maps. To reduce Jerusalem to two sides, or four quarters, and then give them equal resources would be terribly misleading about the limitless complexity of this city. Those two sides – and, especially, representations of their being irreconcilable – are a convenient fiction for the disengaged or the lazy, and any balance that may result from treating them equally can never be equitable, because they do not start as equals. Israel has the overwhelmingly larger proportion of power, influence, assets, status and visibility. The seesaw is not level to begin with. To achieve an equitable balance, one must act unequally.

As for the fulcrum, that can be dealt with in one mild observation by Archbishop Desmond Tutu: "If you are neutral in situations of injustice, you have chosen the side of the oppressor."

So this book rejects equality in favor of equity. Rather than setting stories that are Jewish against an equal number of stories that are from or about everybody else, I have instead redistributed my time, energy and resources to favor those who begin less advantaged. Rather than amplifying the already-amplified, I have chosen to amplify the unlistened-to. And throughout, but for a brief excursion on the 275 bus to the Mount of Olives, I've stuck tight to my self-imposed brief to write only about people and places in or immediately beside Jerusalem's walled Old City. That was deliberate. Vendors of highest quality snake oil may laud Jerusalem's all-encompassing holiness and eternality, but take away the Old City and you're left with an overgrown provincial hill town, and not an especially pretty one at that. The meaning of Jerusalem derives from what happens within the walls, even if the business of Jerusalem is conducted mostly beyond them.

An Old City implies a New City. Is there one? Twentieth-century history was mesmerized by the idea, largely because of the last third of the Book of Ezekiel, which describes how the building of a New Jerusalem will herald the end of Jewish exile and the ingathering of all the people of Israel in harmony and blessing, keeping God's promise in Deuteronomy.

A word, if I may, about Buzi's boy Ezekiel. He was a Jerusalemite priest who was captured by Babylonian invaders as a young man in 597 BCE, torn from his home and sent into exile, along with many compatriots. He spent the rest of his life in Babylon* at Tal Abib (that

---

* Literally in his case, though the metaphor of Babylon as the iniquitous, temporal counterpoint to God's eternal, spiritual realm of Zion – meaning Jerusalem – remains familiar today, not least through Rastafari poetry and song.

is, Tel Aviv), "the hill of springtime," east of Najaf in central Iraq, communicating understandably truculent visions about calamity, retribution and divine justice. Judaism, Christianity and Islam revere him as a prophet, and his prognostications are full of creative metaphor, shaped to sustain his community in exile. Nevertheless many nineteenth-century European Zionists – and not just them – took his and others' prophetic words literally, as the blueprint for the creation of a Jewish state in Palestine.

So when the British, who invented the term "Old City" for Jerusalem's walled area, the better to objectify and preserve it, also invented "New City" for the workaday areas beyond, it had a biblical resonance. It implied progress – towards modernity but perhaps also towards the glory of the end-times, a "New Jerusalem." It felt, to many, like a fulfilment of prophecy. To others, it was a Nakba.

The Roman historian Josephus mentions Jerusalem's New City, which in his day was the hill lying to the north of what is now Al-Aqsa, encompassing the present Bab Hutta neighborhood and, perhaps also, the rising ground of downtown East Jerusalem outside the northern walls (which of course came later). He called it Bezetha, possibly deriving from a Hebrew or Aramaic term meaning "House of Olives," after the orchard slopes.

The New City for the British was centered on the commercial districts constructed along and around Jaffa Road, the main route leading northwest from Jerusalem to the coast. Ottoman legal reforms in the 1850s had granted non-Muslims and foreigners new privileges, spurring pockets of European-designed and -funded development on the hills outside walled Jerusalem – a mission school, an orphanage, a church and pilgrim hostel. In an effort to encourage Jewish communal independence British philanthropist Moses Montefiore in 1860 built the almshouses of *Mishkenot Shaananim* (Hebrew: Carefree Residences), the first Jewish neighborhood outside the walls, crowned with a working windmill. Stand outside Jaffa Gate and scan the valley opposite, and you can see it today.

By the turn of the twentieth century, as Jaffa port grew in importance and tourist/pilgrim traffic burgeoned, the area around Jerusalem's Jaffa Gate, both inside and outside the walls, had become the center of the city. This was Jerusalem's main transport hub, a whirlwind of cafés, shops, banks, tourist offices, post offices, photo studios, markets and more. A railway station – the terminus from Jaffa – was built in the valley near Montefiore's windmill. Jaffa Gate wove the city's walled and unwalled quarters together. The area's character, as historian Yair Wallach has written, "was decidedly Ottoman, cosmopolitan and nonsectarian. But British colonial rulers, who occupied the city in 1917, saw no merit [in that and] resolved to destroy much of the modern Jaffa Gate quarter in order to separate the Old City from the new. The Ottoman vision of a civic, nonsectarian and modern Jerusalem – embodied in the Jaffa Gate area – was anathema to British officials, who saw Jerusalem as an ancient city and a patchwork of ethnic and religious congregations, each in their own neighborhoods."

Scathing of modernity and fixated on the Bible, these men of empire bequeathed Jerusalem division.

I remember hearing "New City" a lot when I first visited, in the 1980s, but it seems to be used less nowadays. Even then it was only a synonym for "West Jerusalem," with the distasteful implication that "old" was Arab and "new" was Jewish. I haven't heard the term in Arabic. Anyway, there is no new/old division. There never was. The British couldn't – or chose not to – see that Jerusalem had always been one city, having conversations with itself along multiple axes of influence. Their inability to imagine its possessing an identity that superseded their own preoccupations of sect and ethnicity led directly to war and the partition that lingers today.

And let's speak plainly: partition is trauma. India and Pakistan in 1947 is one, stark example (and what a coincidence that the British had also created a "New City" for Delhi only thirty years before). Bangladesh and Pakistan again, in 1971. The Scramble for Africa, when European powers destroyed societies in partitioning a continent. Ireland 1921. Cyprus 1974. Korea after 1945. Yugoslavia after 1991. Berlin. Brexit. There are many more. Partition trauma lingers, decade after decade, rebounding onto generations and societies far removed from the rupture itself. Yet our governments of broken men continue to insist that partition, that geriatric tantrum from the 1930s rebranded as the two-state solution, is the best that Palestinians and Israelis can hope for. (Perhaps the broken men are the real problem.)

Jerusalem knows partition, and not just the clumsiness of the Old City's four quarters. For more than seventy years now, there have been two Jerusalems, neither of them old and neither new. Trumpist manipulations notwithstanding, most of the world – as well as international law – sees the division created by the armistice line following the war of 1948 as still in place. "West Jerusalem," to one side of that line, is characterized as sovereign Israeli territory; to the other, "East Jerusalem," which includes the walled Old City, is defined as occupied by Israel.*

The line between them, known as the Green Line, remains sharp, if now invisible. Israeli military checkpoints controlling the movement of Palestinians ring Jerusalem to the north, east and south, and there are even Israeli checkpoints within East Jerusalem separating one Palestinian area from another. But no physical or bureaucratic barriers hinder travel between East and West Jerusalem.

Things are subtler than that. Immediately outside Damascus Gate, a mess of multilane roads and tunnels slices through the city's undulating topography, plowing impassable furrows this way and that, alienating people from place as effectively as walls might. It is beautiful to no one. But it serves a purpose, and not merely as a car conduit. For this is Jerusalem's unacknowledged, unidentified, unmemorialized border. Walk a short way into the maelstrom and you can stand on the median dividing the main highway, Road 1. To one side, a turning leads into West Jerusalem. Opposite, another leads into East Jerusalem. Down the middle of the road run the tracks of

---

* Often, global media will burnish the division with ethno-nationalist branding, "Jewish [or Israeli] West Jerusalem" set against "Arab [or Palestinian] East Jerusalem." This is egregiously misleading. Not only does it tacitly endorse a narrative of segregation, but West Jerusalem has never been wholly Jewish, East Jerusalem has never been wholly Arab, not all Israelis are Jewish, not all Palestinians are Arab and – crucially – "Arab" and "Jew" are not mutually exclusive terms to be deployed in opposition to each other. Some Jews are Arab. Some Arabs are Jewish. Careless talk costs lives.

the Jerusalem Light Rail, a tram system opened in 2011 to link East Jerusalem's illegal Jewish settlements with downtown West Jerusalem. The ceaseless traffic and rumbling trams on both sides flow along what was the ceasefire line after the 1948 war, and the effective international border between Israel and Jordan from then until 1967.

A seam is a line of difference – gold within quartz, coal in shale, one piece of cloth set against another. Israel calls the course of the Green Line as it runs through Jerusalem "the Seam."

For nineteen years this is where the Mandelbaum Gate stood, the sole crossing-point between the two Jerusalems – not a gate as such, but fifty meters of roadway between an Israeli roadblock and a Jordanian one, flanked by barbed wire. The home of textile merchants Esther and Simcha Mandelbaum, built here in 1929 and blown up in 1948, lent its name to the crossing. In 1967, amid its euphoria at capturing East Jerusalem and "unifying" the city, Israel destroyed what remained of the Mandelbaum house. Barring an unlabelled concrete sundial, nothing now marks the crossing-point's former location. Road 1 roars with ceaseless movement. A villa nearby, still displaying war damage from its time as an Israeli military outpost, was once the home of Palestinian architect Andoni Baramki, built by him in 1932 on land he owned. It is now occupied by an Israeli art gallery – "The Museum on the Seam" – that talks about coexistence while ignoring Palestinian culture and people. (The Baramki family, forced out during the Nakba, have had their claim to the villa rebuffed by Israeli courts.)

Despite fifty years of Israeli efforts to wish the seam gone, the separation between Jerusalems remains stark – but the separation is not between a new city and an old.

Take a street in East Jerusalem, any street. Maybe it has a curb and pine trees, maybe rubble and overflowing dumpsters. For a Jewish person living there, citizenship is a right. For a non-Jewish person living there, citizenship is a privilege. They can apply for it, but Israel can refuse their application. Most non-Jewish Jerusalemites, even those born in the city and with generations of forebears also born in the city, are stateless, merely residents of Israel with no right to, for instance, vote in national elections. A Jewish citizen can leave – to study in another city or abroad, to take up a job offer or just for a change of scene – and come back whenever they like. If a non-Jewish resident does the same, the Israeli government can revoke their residency, leaving them unable to live in Jerusalem then or in the future.

Jewish and non-Jewish children in the two Jerusalems experience different education systems and curricula. The two Jerusalems have separate transport networks: Israeli buses, operating from West Jerusalem's central bus station, do not serve Palestinian neighborhoods, which have their own buses operating from East Jerusalem's central bus station. Palestinian areas lag behind in housing, roads, water, sewerage, street lighting, fire service, postal service, social welfare and other markers. They receive between 5 and 12 percent of spending from the city's budget, depending on how the analysis is done, despite being home to more than a third of the city's population. Poverty affects roughly twice the number of Palestinians in Jerusalem as Jewish Israelis.

Palestinian people who have Israeli citizenship are, in some ways, better off than Jerusalemite "residents," since their status is settled: the stress of perpetual vulnerability is somewhat eased, they pass through checkpoints and can vote for Israel's government, though they also suffer widespread discrimination in housing, education and much else. Their Israeli passport facilitates global travel, but also bars them from many Arab and Muslim countries. Israeli law downgrades their language, Arabic, to a lesser status than Hebrew, and their identity is erased in Israeli discourse – and distressingly often by foreign media – with the descriptor "Israeli Arab," a term invented by Israel's government. (Many prefer to be called "Palestinian citizens of Israel" or "1948 Palestinians," with slight variations.)

Then again, Palestinian Jerusalemites are, in many ways, better off than Palestinians in the West Bank, who cannot enter Jerusalem without Israeli permission (refused to most), cannot vote in Israeli elections, cannot use Israeli airports (to travel overseas they must apply to Israel for a permit to exit overland to Jordan, in order to fly via Amman) and whose day-to-day movement is severely restricted by Israeli checkpoints and the threat of violence from armed Israeli settlers backed by the military. In the West Bank, a Jewish Israeli and a non-Jewish

Palestinian who are arrested for the same crime in the same place at the same time face different consequences: the Israeli person is tried in an Israeli civil court, with due process, while the Palestinian person is tried in Israel's military courts, which convict more than ninety-nine times out of a hundred. A welter of political, social, judicial and economic measures hinder normal life. Different rules apply to Palestinian people depending on where in the West Bank they live.

But West Bank Palestinians are, in many ways, better off than Palestinian people living in the Gaza Strip, who suffer one of the world's highest population densities yet cannot leave: Israel seals three sides of the Strip, denying almost all applications for exit permits, and the Egyptian government keeps the fourth side closed almost permanently. Lives here are continually disrupted by an economic blockade – by land (Israel restricts goods entering or leaving Gaza), by sea (Israel permits no maritime trade and impedes fishing) and by air (Israel bombed Gaza's airport out of action in 2001 and now flies military drones daily to surveil the population). Gaza's politicians can do little to improve lives.

Yet even Palestinians in Gaza enjoy some privileges over Palestinians living in exile in the diaspora, to whom Israel denies the right to return. Many cannot even visit. Others, depending on status and country of residence, can approach but only as tourists, requesting short-stay holiday visas and facing interrogation and searches by Israeli officials.

Thus has Israel atomized the remnants of a society it destroyed. These seven distinct categories of Palestinians – citizens of Israel, Jerusalemites, West Bankers (split by the Oslo Agreement's areas A, B and C), Gazans and exiles – now all live apart, physically and bureaucratically. Each is granted fewer privileges by the Israeli state than the last. It turns out the Nakba was less an event than a process, which continues. One historian calls it "The Hundred Years' War on Palestine." And there are legitimate fears that partition, that famous solution in two states, while uniting Jewish Israel, would make Palestinian atomization permanent.

This is part of the reason why the events of May 2021 were so remarkable, catching the attention and engagement of people across the region and around the world. As families in the East Jerusalem neighborhoods of Sheikh Jarrah and Silwan – not for the first time – faced expulsion from their homes, Palestinian people across all of Israel's imposed category divisions rose together in resistance and mutual support. On 18 May there was a general strike, Palestinians nationwide stopping work for a day to protest their treatment. The unity was unprecedented.

That hints at the underlying truth: division is not the whole story. Jerusalem's lingering divide between west and east emerges from the preoccupations of diplomats and lawyers, those who have little or no skin in the game. In contrast, for many of those for whom Jerusalem really matters, there is no east or west – or, perhaps better, their internalization of the irrefutable east/west divide merely overlays a deeper, more visceral intuition of a broader and older urban identity.

To many in Israel and beyond, Jerusalem is a unified city, liberated, an "eternal and indivisible capital," as the current formulation has it.* Some even see no occupation, regarding all of Jerusalem as legitimately Israeli. They view it rather like, say, a big American city: they inhabit, focus on, value and lionize districts and suburbs they regard as theirs, or safe, while regarding all other localities with suspicion as no-go areas that should never be approached. They do not just ignore the 1948 line but erase it; younger generations may even have no knowledge of it. That's why the Light Rail was built, symbolically and literally to link the two Jerusalems in the pretense the city is one. With this mindset, divisions become defined less in political terms than sectarian ones. Or, to be blunt, racial.

Many in Palestine and beyond, too, also understand Jerusalem as a single entity, essentially whole. Some see the entire city, west and

---

* The description "eternal capital" originated in 1949, in a speech by Israel's first prime minister David Ben-Gurion. "Indivisible" was added in 1978 by then-prime minister Menachem Begin, and written into Israel's Basic Law on Jerusalem (1980) with the phrase "complete and united ... capital." Since then, variations on the wording have become ubiquitous.

east alike, as being under illegitimate Israeli occupation. Palestinian Jerusalemite psychogeography retains knowledge and memory of the prosperous residential and commercial Arab neighborhoods of what is now called West Jerusalem, whose properties – like the Baramki villa – were emptied in 1948 and then seized by the Israeli state. People sense how Palestinian identity and aspiration used to run through the undivided city before colonization and calamity struck. Current politics, local and global, that denies an Arab presence throughout Jerusalem, or that even denies the validity of a term such as "Palestine," does not diminish such feeling.

The philosopher Sari Nusseibeh wrote: "I carry a Jordanian passport, and an Israeli travel document ... When asked what my citizenship is, and what my residence is, my answers to those questions have nothing to do with who I really am. I am not a Jordanian or an Israeli. I am a Palestinian. And clearly it is hard for a person in my position to try to describe this complex situation even to myself, let alone to other people (such as to passport-controllers at airports). So that is why I often tell myself we are living a life in Jerusalem – at least in East Jerusalem – which is maybe a little bit like the one described in *The Wizard of Oz*, or, perhaps more aptly, *Alice in Wonderland* – that is, where everything is upside-down."

To return to the desiccated language of the diplomats, the status of Jerusalem has not yet been decided. The United Nations deems the expansion of the municipal boundary in 1967 by Israel, an action that created a hugely enlarged metropolis incorporating the occupied eastern part of the city (as well as suburbs and villages beyond it), and then the Israeli state's annexation of that area thirteen years later, null and void. *De jure* and *de facto* Jerusalem remains divided. There is no fait accompli. Jerusalemites do not allow it.

That's why, if you look at a global weather forecast, or a time zone app, Jerusalem doesn't (or shouldn't) fit in a "city, country" format. Until a final status is agreed, international law says Jerusalem has no country. When in 2017 the US government declared Jerusalem the capital of Israel and moved its embassy there, it was an attempt to steamroller justice and bend reality to the will of power. Every day the action remains uncorrected is another day the US tells the world "might is right." It is violence.

Then again, embassy, schmembassy. Let them salute their flags. Felipe VI of Spain calls himself King of Jerusalem.* So what?

Sovereignty over Jerusalem has long been phenomenally complicated. The changing status of the city under Ottoman rule is for another time and place, but when Mark Twain wrote a letter in 1867 he addressed it "Jerusalem, Syria." Under the British it was "Jerusalem, Palestine." After 1948 Old City addresses were tagged "Jerusalem, Jordan." Nowadays, people, companies and governments broadcast their sympathies by using "Jerusalem, Palestine" or "Jerusalem, Israel." (I remember when post to Palestinian areas would be addressed "Jerusalem, via Israel," to acknowledge the practical reality of having international mail handled by the occupying power while also affirming the city's undecided status.) Many therefore choose to remain neutral and leave Jerusalem un-countried.

You might think it obvious that Jerusalem is under Israeli sovereignty. Yet take Kufr Aqab. This Palestinian neighborhood of East Jerusalem lies within the municipal boundary but in 2003 was cut off from the rest of the city by the construction of Israel's massive Separation Barrier. The consequence is that it has become an ill-defined frontier zone, on paper part of Jerusalem, in practice part of the West Bank. Jerusalem police and municipal workers rarely venture there, but no other jurisdiction has authority. Building is unregulated. Crimes go uninvestigated and unpunished. Even

---

* Felipe's claim originated with Charles of Anjou (d. 1285), who was granted rights from Maria of Antioch, granddaughter of Queen Isabella of Jerusalem (1172–1205). Angevin titles passed to the Kingdom of Naples and, in 1441, to Aragón and thereafter the Spanish crown, hence Felipe. However, somewhat awkwardly, all the kings of Italy until the dissolution of that monarchy in 1946 were also kings of Jerusalem. At one time, so were the kings of Cyprus. In 1948 Jordan's Abdullah I had himself crowned King of Jerusalem. And until he renounced his title in 1961, "His Imperial and Royal Highness The Crown Prince of Austria, Hungary, Bohemia and Croatia" Otto von Habsburg (1912–2011) also claimed the throne of Jerusalem. Perhaps they could have had a quarter each.

though Israeli law means Palestinians with Jerusalem IDs and West Bank IDs cannot live together, Kufr Aqab is almost the only place where nobody checks, and the neighborhood has become popular with families that span the divide. Who is *de facto* sovereign there, in this liminal zone of Israel's creation?

Then there's the single most important place in Jerusalem and, perhaps, the entire Middle East. At the Haram al-Sharif (Temple Mount), the Israeli state can intervene, but with only limited effectiveness. The Status Quo is one restraint, since Jordan's monarch, as custodian of Al-Aqsa, has authority over the compound. That authority is devolved to the bureaucrats of the Islamic Waqf. They, though, do not always see eye-to-eye with the clerics of Jerusalem's religious establishment, whose opinions often hold sway. Then there's Israel's government, police, army and many politico-religious agitators. All these form a delicate balance of administrative and other interests influencing what happens at the mosque. The Israeli state may set the rules in Tel Aviv – it is sovereign there – but it cannot dictate terms at Al-Aqsa. It does not control the compound. Neither, entirely, does the Waqf. Nor Jordan. As repeated acts of popular resistance and assertions of ownership have shown – and as journalists and analysts have now started to recognize – *de facto* sovereignty over Al-Aqsa lies, extraordinarily, in the hands of the Palestinian people. They live, work, meet, study, relax and pray there. They seek refuge within the compound. They protect it. For all practical purposes, and despite the many legal instruments proving otherwise, it is theirs.

Other Jerusalems exist than those on plaques affixed to embassies.

You can, if you want to, trace an entirely other Jerusalem in the erased communities of the "New City." Ringing the hills on Jerusalem's west until 1948 were four Palestinian villages, all depopulated by threat or force during the Nakba and all now barely discernible amid the urban thicket. Where today stand a disused rail station, a giant shopping mall and the city's biggest football stadium once toiled the farmers and shepherds of Al-Maliha. Where you now find a large hospital and Israel's national memorial to the victims of the Holocaust was Ain Karim, rich with irrigated farmland. Where the villagers of Deir Yassin lived until their massacre at the hands of Zionist paramilitaries in April 1948 is now an Israeli psychiatric hospital. The hospital incorporates some of Deir Yassin's former homes, abandoned after the killing, and is famous for treating Jerusalem Syndrome, a recognized disorder in which visiting the city triggers obsessive religious delusions.

Then there's Lifta. Israel's parliament, supreme court, national museum and leading university all stand on what were once the fields of Lifta and the neighboring community of Sheikh Badr, seized by the state. Of all the Palestinian villages that were depopulated in 1948 – more than five hundred of them, thirty-eight in the Jerusalem subdistrict alone – Lifta is the only one not to have been either destroyed by Israel or reinhabited. About one-tenth of its pre-1948 stone buildings still stand, perched on a hillside beside freeways and suburbs, neglected, graffitied and overgrown. No authority protects this unique place. For now, you can walk there. In 2021 Israel's government published a new scheme to raze Lifta and redevelop it. An Israeli company has already opened a boutique hotel in one of the old buildings, in the face of long-running preservation campaigns led by architects, activists and former residents.

Those are the outskirts of the "New City." Within its core were once middle-class neighborhoods where doctors, lawyers and tycoons – Arab and not, Jewish, Muslim and Christian – built large villas for themselves and their families: Qatamon, Upper and Lower Baqa, Talbiya, and others. All, like the villages, were depopulated of their non-Jews in 1948, given new Hebrew names and built over. Once-posh Musrara, overlooking the Old City walls, was bisected by the post-1948 armistice line. Houses in its western part, crumbling from war damage and directly on the frontline, were given over to those at the bottom of Israel's social and economic heap, chiefly Jews immigrating from North Africa and the Middle East. After 1967 the pent-up tension in Musrara from years of government neglect, compounded by nineteen years of exposure to Jordanian sniper fire from the Old City ramparts nearby, coalesced in a Jewish protest movement known as the Black Panthers, which demanded justice for Israel's most marginalized. Its heyday in the 1970s, when it won headlines and voter support, is still valued on the Israeli left for laying the foundations of social movements that followed.

So Jerusalem is divided and not. One city and two. But it's never been about new or old; things are much more complicated than that. The systemic racism facing Jerusalem's bedouin and Jewish Israelis of Ethiopian or North African origin, let alone non-Jewish people seeking asylum from Sudan or Eritrea, is beyond my brief. Gender discrimination never goes away, of course, weaponized in Jerusalem's overwhelmingly patriarchal societies and turbocharged by the resentments between religious and secular. Israeli pinkwashing is another subject outside this book's focus, but I did try to talk to the Palestinian LGBTQ+ organization Al-Qaws, which builds community nationwide and advocates strongly for human rights and social change. They said – not unreasonably – their extremely limited resources were focused on working within their own constituency and they had no remit to engage with foreign media.

Meaning me.

Bashar Murad, a Jerusalemite singer-songwriter famed for "*Ana Zalameh* (I'm A Man)" and "*Ma Bitghayirni* (You Can't Change Me)," was able to be more forthcoming: "For me, as someone who's queer, there isn't a place I can go in East Jerusalem. There's Al-Qaws and honestly that's it. Growing up, there was no one who was "out," no one to look up to. I thought I was the only gay person in Palestine. You have to make your own scene, or leave for Ramallah, Haifa or unfortunately Tel Aviv. Are there queer stories in Jerusalem? No, I don't think there are."

I'm not so sure. But as Bashar was, perhaps, discreetly telling me, such stories will certainly be guarded extremely closely. Even in analyst Sa'ed Atshan's brilliant study *Queer Palestine* the city barely appears, other than in reference to events around Jerusalem Pride, a predominantly Jewish Israeli annual parade in West Jerusalem.

Among all the voices that might shed light on Jerusalem's unities and contradictions, here's just one to end with. Hiba Qawasmi is twenty-eight, born and raised in Jerusalem. She works as a translator and teacher at a language center located precisely on the invisible line between the city's east and west. In a very few years she has travelled a long way while also staying firmly rooted, as you'll see:

"Why do I identify as a Palestinian Arab? Because I was born that way. My mother tongue is Arabic and my society is Palestinian. I can never be Israeli, [even if I] speak Hebrew and join Israeli society. Yet I am constantly exposed to racism and structural oppression that tries to convince me to apply for an Israeli passport and citizenship.

"Particularly in Israeli society, where people come from so many places, it is shocking that everyone has to be the same, that Jews from, say, a Mizrahi background must forget their Arabic. As someone who lives under occupation, I am in no way willing to give up my identity. My identity is what it is. My parents are Muslim, so I'm Muslim. I'm also a vegan. A Palestinian can't be a vegan? Our society is diverse! Why not?

"I don't remember a lot from my childhood, but I do remember when Mohammed al-Durra was killed in Gaza [on 30 September 2000], hiding with his father, shot by the Israeli army. He became a symbol of the intifada. I was maybe eight … [about] the same age he was. I remember thinking he was killed because he didn't hide well. I would hide better. That's what was on my mind as a child growing up in Jerusalem. I remember understanding very clearly that I was lesser, as a Palestinian, and that I needed to be the best in order to succeed. But I never interacted with the 'enemy'. I never saw a Jewish person except for soldiers at the checkpoint. If you had asked me, 'What is a Jew?' I would have said that Jews and Israelis are the same, and that a Jewish Israeli person is someone who occupies me. I don't blame myself for thinking that way: a child expresses what they absorb in the world around them. In Israeli schools, students are prepared for the army, given intense lessons in identity. But we never learned about the Nakba.

"When I graduated school with a 97 percent average, I wanted to study in the US, like my brothers had. But my father wasn't ready to send me abroad. I was always rebellious and I insisted on university, so my father sent me to the [Israeli] Hebrew University of Jerusalem. Meeting people who were not like me did influence me a lot. I chose Middle East Studies and in my first year, I was the only Palestinian student. One of my classmates carried a gun. [Friends] would say to me, 'Oh, you are joining Israeli society, you are assimilating.' I never felt I was being corrupted, but definitions and identity categories are important in Israel and I did feel that I had to choose how to define myself. While I [studied] there, I covered my hair with a hijab.

"I am very pleased to be called an activist! You imagine activists attending protests. I did join protests when I was a student. But everyone [develops] their own form of activism. Mine, now, is teaching Israelis Arabic."

Twenty-five years ago the Haitian scholar Michel-Rolph Trouillot wrote about how history is not simply the recording of facts and events, but a process of actively enforced silences, some unconscious, others deliberate. We can be thankful that – due in part to Trouillot himself – that process and those silences are, at last, coming under new scrutiny.

It's not hard to imagine the depth of impact that work such as Hiba Qawasmi's could have on some possible future Jerusalem, freed from the nationalist fever-dream of partition, its structures of inequity dismantled. Envisioning such a place, in which Jerusalemites – and their compatriots in the wider hinterlands – live without polarization under protection of the law, their rights assured, their aspirations respected, in dignity, gives hope.

A New Jerusalem, you could call it.

Photographs

All images by the author, unless otherwise credited.
Each caption is prefixed by the relevant page number.

INTRODUCTION

x The Dome of the Rock (right) with, beside it, the smaller Dome of the Chain, thought by some scholars to predate the main building and to have served as a model for it.

7 Men playing dominoes, as seen from a walk along the Old City ramparts.

CHAPTER 1

14 The map created by English explorer Frederick Catherwood in 1835, with its key identifying sites of Christian interest (Library of Congress).

20 Visitors crowding to see the mosaic map in the Church of St. George, Madaba, Jordan. Jerusalem is visible as the oval shape at center left (Walter Bibikow/Mauritius Images/Alamy).

35 The map created in 1841 by Aldrich and Symonds, as reproduced in George Williams's book *The Holy City*, 1849 (National Library of Israel).

CHAPTER 2

42 Exterior of the Old City walls near New Gate, showing the lawns that are now protected by the Israeli government as a national park.

CHAPTER 3

52 A street sign hand-painted by Stepan Karakashian. It was originally made during the Jordanian period and showed Arabic and English only. Hebrew was added above after Israel occupied in 1967. *Frères* is the French word for brothers, referring to the Collège des Frères school on this street. The Arabic has *tariq* (road) and *al-freer*, a phonetic transliteration of *frères*, but the Hebrew translates it to read *rekhov ha-akhim*, "Street of the Brothers." It's not clear why.

59 Hagop Karakashian's photo. From left: Jamal Murad (tourist police); unknown; Anton Safieh (assistant mayor); Ghalib Barakat (tourism minister); unknown; Said al-Dajani (interior minister); Ruhi al-Khatib (mayor); unknown; Yusuf al-Budeiri (city engineer); Stepan Karakashian; unknown.

CHAPTER 4

62 Exterior of Damascus Gate. The pavilion at lower right is one of the surveillance posts installed by the Israeli authorities in 2018.

69 Mazen Izhiman in his shop in 2019, between his displays of coffee beans and grinding machines.

CHAPTER 5

72 Aqabat at-Tut, one of the stepped alleyways connecting Al-Wad Street with Khan al-Zeit Street.

82 Ayman Qaisi working hard in his hole-in-the-wall juice bar, down the street from the 2nd Station of the Cross.

94 Shadows and silhouettes outside the chapel marking the 7th Station of the Cross, on Khan al-Zeit Street.

106 The façade of the Church of the Holy Sepulchre in the 1860s, showing the "immovable" ladder at an upper window. It (or a replica) can be seen in the same position today (Frank M. Good/Jacobson Collection/The Getty).

CHAPTER 6

116 Football is one of the activities offered to the Old City's young people by the Burj al-Laqlaq community center (Rafael Ben-Ari/ZUMA Press/Alamy).

CHAPTER 7

120 Sheikh Abd al-Kareem al-Afghani (far left) listens to a lecture given by his son before leading a *dhikr* ceremony at the Zawiya al-Qadiriyya (known as the Afghaniyya) in 2019.

128–9 A panoramic image of the Haram al-Sharif, taken from a viewpoint between the Al-Aqsa mosque (at left) and the Dome of the Rock (at far right) © Børre Ludvigsen, gratefully reproduced with permission.

142 Steps leading up to the western door of the Dome of the Rock, which is framed by a free-standing arcade built around 932 CE, one of eight such arcade structures encircling the Dome.

150 Nazer Ansari, pictured in 2019 at the entrance to the room holding the cave of Baba Farid, on the grounds of the Indian Hospice.

CHAPTER 8

156 Amoun Sleem, social activist and founder of the Domari Society of Gypsies in Jerusalem, pictured in 2000 (Reuters/Alamy).

CHAPTER 9

164 Yusra Takrori, from Jerusalem's Afro-Palestinian community, greets friends before her wedding in 2007 (Eliana Aponte/Reuters/Alamy).

175 Musa Qous, who volunteers with the African Community Society, in the society offices on Aladdin Street in 2019.

CHAPTER 10

188 The exterior of the Golden Gate, showing its twin archways sealed by masonry, overlooking the Islamic cemetery of Bab ar-Rahma outside the walls.

CHAPTER 11

194 Climbing the stepped street inside Herod's Gate that leads into the residential Sa'diyya neighborhood.

198–9 Panoramic image taken inside the Byzantine-era tomb chamber of Rabia al-Adawiyya, located outside the Old City on the Mount of Olives.

CHAPTER 12

206 The plaza in front of the Western Wall, pictured at bottom center crowded with people, was created in 1967 when the Israeli government destroyed the Moroccan Quarter that filled the area (David Silverman/Getty).

215 A similar view in 1917 shows the Dome of the Rock (top left) and the Western Wall (center right), with the houses of the Moroccan Quarter, destroyed in 1967, filling the foreground (National Library of Israel).

CHAPTER 13

226 View over an excavated section of the Roman Cardo in the Jewish Quarter, showing new building above and the 19th-century Tzemach Tzedek synagogue at center right (MB_Photo/Alamy).

233 Esther Weiss in her shop on Jewish Quarter Road. Esther was one of the first Jewish Israelis to set up home in the Old City after Israel's occupation in 1967 (silverpointjudaica.com).

246 Avi Yefet, caretaker of the Old City's Karaite Synagogue and museum complex, showed me his phone as he scrolled through part of his family tree.

CHAPTER 14

 248 A sports trophy cabinet in a community center inside the Armenian convent. The poster above, whose wording is slightly adapted from a passage in the 1936 short story *The Armenian and the Armenian* by celebrated Armenian-American novelist William Saroyan, reads: "I should like to see any power of the world destroy this race, this small tribe of unimportant people, whose wars have all been fought and lost, whose structures have crumbled, literature is unread, music is unheard, and prayers are no more answered. Go ahead, destroy Armenia. See if you can do it. Send them into the desert without bread or water. Burn their homes and churches. Then see if they will not laugh, sing and pray again. For when two of them meet anywhere in the world, see if they will not create a New Armenia."

 255 Frontage of an Armenian restaurant on Armenian Orthodox Patriarchate Road, decorated with the Armenian national flag and a banner in Armenian, English, Arabic and Hebrew marking the centenary of the Armenian genocide.

CHAPTER 15

 258 An archive photograph of early tourists entering Jaffa Gate (Jeff Krotz/Alamy). As far as we know, no image of David Dorr exists.

CHAPTER 16

 266 The clocktower above Jaffa Gate looms behind Britain's victorious General Allenby as he makes his entrance into Jerusalem on foot, 11 December 1917 (Everett Collection/Alamy).

 277 At a café table inside Jaffa Gate, Judge Fawaz Altiyeh points out to me his ancestor's name, Ibrahim al-Safouti, on an archive document detailing the family's history.

CHAPTER 17

 282 Textile merchant Ibrahim Abu Khalaf, pictured in 2019 among the piles of silks and fabrics in his shop partway along Christian Quarter Road.

 292 Photographer and shop-owner Kevork Kahvedjian, pictured in 2014, holds up a print of a photograph made by his father, Elia, in 1924 (left), alongside a reproduction of the famous Visit Palestine poster created by Franz Krausz in 1936.

303 Golden-voiced nun Yostina al-Banna, pictured in 2014 while singing the Lord's Prayer inside the Syriac Orthodox Church of St. Mark.

CHAPTER 18

 310 An atmospheric alleyway leading off St. Mark's Street, in a quiet residential neighborhood located behind the Maronite church.

 315 Artist, curator and museum director Jack Persekian, pictured in 2019 in his office above Gallery Anadiel near New Gate.

EPILOGUE

 320 The view from the upper level of Damascus Gate, looking down on the heads of people entering and exiting the gate, as well as those taking the weight off for a few minutes on the low wall beside the thoroughfare.

 337 The exterior of Lions Gate showing the leopard motif of the Mamluk sultan Baybars (c.1223–1277). The motif was reimagined for this book by artist and designer Henry Iles to serve as a graphic device marking divisions between sections of text.

Notes and Sources

My intention in providing references for each chapter, beside acknowledging major sources, is to offer extra context and ideas for further reading. I cite URLs only where I think an online source might be hard to find, and favor an open link (to, for example, academia.edu, where scholars upload their own material to be read for free) over a Digital Object Identifier, or DOI (which links to a publisher, retrievable by adding doi.org/ before the number given). Everything in the journal *Jerusalem Quarterly* (abbreviated here as *JQ*) can be accessed at palestine-studies.org for free. In 2021 Dr. Roberto Mazza – *JQ*'s editor, among other things – launched *Jerusalem Unplugged*, a one-man podcast presenting interviews with scholars, activists, artists, journalists, clerics and other folk invested in the life of the city. It's often an absorbing listen.

In the notes, dates are given in the format day/month/year. "n.d." means no date. "UP" means University Press. "———" saves repeating an author's name. Where only an author's name is cited, see the bibliography (or, occasionally, a previous note). URLs were last accessed 30/11/2021. Each reference is prefixed by the relevant **page number**.

INTRODUCTION

ix Ali: al-islam.org/nahjul-balagha-part-2-letters-and-sayings/selections-sayings-and-preaching-amir-al-muminin-ali#hadith-n-10. *Coriolanus* III.1. Addonia: twitter.com/sulaimanaddonia/status/1237842328431153154 (11/3/2020).

1 My interview with Amoun Sleem 16/10/2019. ———, *A Gypsy Dreaming in Jerusalem* (Nurturing Faith, 2014).

2 John Tleel, "I am Jerusalem: Life in the Old City from the Mandate Period to the Present," JQ 4 (1999), 30-40. Short film *John Tleel/Jerusalemite* (inkcrayon pictures, 2014) vimeo.com/73337824 & longer edit (Oded Farber, 30/6/2019) youtube.com/watch?v=RZxLv6CLeUA.

2 My interview with Mustafa Abu Sway 18/10/2019.

2 Moshe Caine *et al.*, "The Riddle of the Crosses: The Crusaders in the Holy Sepulchre," Electronic Visualization and the Arts conference, Jerusalem, July 2018, 132–139, doi: 10.14236/ewic/EVA2018.28.

2 Restoring the Dome of the Rock, which included gilding the dome, began during 1959 and was completed on 6/8/1964; see Kimberly Katz, *Jordanian Jerusalem: Holy Places and National Spaces* (Gainesville: Florida UP, 2005), 107–111. Beatrice St. Laurent, "The Dome of the Rock and the Politics of Restoration," *Bridgewater Review* 17:2 (1998), 14–20, vc.bridgew .edu/br_rev/vol17/iss2/8. Robert Hillenbrand, "The Dome of the Rock: From Medieval Symbol to Modern Propaganda," in Jill A. Franklin *et al.* (eds.), *Architecture and Interpretation: Essays for Eric Fernie* (London: Boydell, 2012), 343–356. Gülru Necipoğlu, "The Dome of the Rock as palimpsest: Abd al-Malik's grand narrative and Sultan Süleyman's glosses," *Muqarnas* 25:1 (2008), 17–105, academia.edu/42016829.

4 Nan Shepherd quote from *The Living Mountain*.

5 Names are tricky things. My statement "Jerusalem is not mentioned by name in either the Quran or the five books of the Torah" is literally correct, though Jerusalem has long been understood as the meaning of the terms in the Pentateuch "Salem" (Gen. 14:18), "Moriah" (Gen. 22:2 – a problematic rendering, not agreed by all) and "the place God will choose" (Deut. 12:5), as it has of the Quranic terms "the farthest mosque" (17:1), "an honorable dwelling place" (10:93), "this town" (2:58), "the olive" (95:1) and others. Oral traditions and later texts in both religions refer to the city more explicitly under various names, e.g., "Zion," "the Sanctified House," "the Holy [Place]," "the Temple," "Jerusalem" etc.

5 Abdallah El-Khatib, "Jerusalem in the Qur'an," *British Journal of Middle Eastern Studies* 28:1 (2001), 25–53, academia.edu/38545015. F.E.

Peters, *Muslim Jerusalem... in brief* 13/4/2012: web.archive .org/web/20191023032438/fepeters .com/?p=259.

6 My Vancouver friend is Ryan Knighton, "For the Tuned-In Traveler, a Feast for the Ears Awaits in Jordan," *Afar* Nov/Dec 2019, afar .com/magazine/the-sounds-of-jordan. Also: Meera Dattani, "What does "accessible" travel really mean for blind travelers?" (7/2/2020): adventure.com/accessible-inclusive -blind-travel-jordan.

8 The 1965 photo of King Hussein is shown at: stgeorgehoteljerusalem.com/ en/hotel.

9 The 370,000 figure in: *COVID-19 and the Systematic Neglect of Palestinians in East Jerusalem*, Al-Haq *et al.* 14/7/2020: alhaq.org/ publications/17118.html. Given as "roughly 360,000" in: Nathan Thrall, "The Separate Regimes Delusion," *London Review of Books* 21/1/2021; "more than 360,000" in *Large-scale Displacement: from Sheikh Jarrah to Silwan*, Terrestrial Jerusalem 21/3/2021: t-j.org.il/2021/03/21/ insiders-jerusalem-special-edition.

9 Residency issues: "Jerusalem Palestinians Stripped of Status," Human Rights Watch 8/8/2017: hrw .org/news/2017/08/08/israel-jerusalem -palestinians-stripped-status. Manal Massalha, "Housing, rubbish, walls and failing infrastructure in East Jerusalem," *Le Monde diplomatique* 8/4/2019: mondediplo.com/ outsidein/east-jerusalem. Permits: Mya Guarnieri, "Old problems in Jerusalem's Old City," IRIN/ UNOCHA 23/11/2015: refworld.org/ docid/5656cc4c4.html.

9 Published data on hotel rooms from Israel Ministry of Tourism, Tourism Review 2019: info.goisrael .com/en/tourism-review-2019. Also: Arab Hotel Association palestinehotels.com. Unpublished data supplied to me 31/3/2020 by Jerusalem Tourism Cluster enjoyjerusalem.com.

10 My interview with Bashar Murad 26/11/2019.

10 The lawyer is Daniel Seidemann: twitter.com/danielseidemann/ status/1401296706835202050 (5/6/2021).

10 *Jerusalem Post* (18/6/2013) reported 320 CCTV cameras in Old City: jpost.com/national-news/the-eyes-of-the-old-city-mabat-2000 -captures-all-316885. Five years later Who Profits (Nov 2018) reported 400 cameras: whoprofits.org/wp-content/ uploads/2018/11/surveil-final.pdf. My calculation: approx 400 cameras for approx 35,000 population = 11.43 cameras per 1,000 people. According to research by Paul Bischoff (15/8/2019: web.archive.org/ web/20200709071027/comparitech.com/ vpn-privacy/the-worlds-most-surveilled -cities) this would place Jerusalem's Old City 19th worldwide. Alternative calculation with population of 34,140 (see note below) gives 11.72 cameras per 1,000 people, placing 18th. Compare with Dubai (17th; 12.14) and Urumqi (14th; 12.40).

10 For phone tracking and drones, see: Ben Wedeman, "Israel holds all the cards in Jerusalem," CNN 12/5/2021. For face recognition, see: Olivia Solon, "Why did Microsoft fund an Israeli firm that surveils West Bank Palestinians?" NBC News 28/10/2019. Amitai Ziv, "Israeli Face-recognition Tech Used Within Israel Against Law, NBC Investigation Finds" *Haaretz* 2/11/2019.

10 *Jerusalem Statistical Yearbook 2019*, published by Israeli thinktank Jerusalem Institute for Policy Research, gives Old City population 2017 as 34,140, of which 90 percent "Arab": jerusaleminstitute.org.il/ wp-content/uploads/2019/05/shnaton_

C0519.pdf. Breakdown of Jerusalem population by age: jerusaleminstitute .org.il/wp-content/uploads/2019/05/ shnaton_C1419.pdf.

11 Overcrowding: John Reed, "Jerusalem: city of ruins," *Financial Times* 1/10/2015.

11 Average population density (2007) in Old City: 47.12 people per dunam = 47,120 per sq km; in Muslim Quarter: 80,670. Source: *Al-Quds/ Jerusalem 2015 Program: 2008 Report* (Istanbul: Organization of the Islamic Conference, Research Center for Islamic History, Art and Culture, 2009), 19–20: academia .edu/20112181. Compare with the most crowded districts of Karachi 68,850; Hong Kong 51,104; Nairobi 63,777. Source: en.wikipedia.org/wiki/ List_of_city_districts_by_population_ density. Gilead Sher *et al.*, "The Legal Parameters of the Old City of Jerusalem Special Regime," in Tom Najem *et al.* (eds.), *Governance and Security in Jerusalem* (Abingdon: Routledge, 2017), doi: 10.4324/9781315619255-7, give much higher density of 119.5 people per dunam across Jerusalem's Old City, on a par with the densest districts of Dhaka and Mumbai, reaching as high as 182 per dunam in some Old City neighborhoods. Michael J. Molloy *et al*, "Governance Discussion Document," in Tom Najem *et al* (eds.), *Track Two Diplomacy and Jerusalem* (Abingdon: Routledge, 2017), 154, doi: 10.4324/9781315619231-9, state: "in some parts of the Muslim quarter, density is equivalent to that of the Calcutta [sic] slums [sic]." Sher *et al.* add: "In other parts of Jerusalem the range is from 5.2 to 26.3 per dunam."

11 Quote from 1876 Baedeker, 145: archive.org/details/02950227.5448.emory .edu. Lawrence quote from *Seven Pillars of Wisdom*, V:LIX.

11 Husam Jubran and Yuval Ben-Ami of Mejdi Tours originated the idea of Jerusalem's concentric walls centered on empty space. I am grateful to them for letting me join one of the tours they led for National Geographic Expeditions, where I first heard it. The core image, though, is very old. The 12th-century historian Ibn Asakir cited 8th-century scholar Thawr ibn Yazid when he wrote: "The holiest part of the earth is the Levant; the holiest part of the Levant is Palestine; the holiest part of Palestine is Jerusalem; the holiest part of Jerusalem is the mountain; the holiest part of the mountain is the mosque [that is, Al-Aqsa]; and the holiest part of the mosque is the Dome [of the Rock]." In: Jacob Lassner, *Medieval Jerusalem: Forging an Islamic City in Spaces Sacred to Christians and Jews* (Ann Arbor: University of Michigan Press, 2017), 36 [my rendering]. Similarly, *Midrash Tankhuma*, rabbinical exegesis collected in the 8th/9th century, comments on a line in Ezekiel 38:12 mentioning those who live "at the navel of the earth" thus: "The land of Israel sits at the center of the world; Jerusalem is in the center of the land of Israel; the sanctuary is in the center of Jerusalem; the Temple is in the center of the sanctuary; [and] the ark is in the center of the Temple." At: sefaria.org/Midrash_Tanchuma_Buber (Kedoshim 10).

13 Hisham Matar reference from *A Month in Siena*.

CHAPTER 1

15 Sources include: Adar Arnon, "The Quarters of Jerusalem in the Ottoman Period," *Middle Eastern Studies* 28:1 (1992), 1–65, doi: 10.1080/00263209208700889. I.W.J. Hopkins, "The Four Quarters of Jerusalem," *Palestine Exploration Quarterly* 103:2 (1971), 68–84, doi:

10.1179/peq.1971.103.2.68. Y. Ben-Arieh, "The Growth of Jerusalem in the Nineteenth Century," *Annals of the Association of American Geographers* 65:2 (1975), 252–269, doi: 10.1111/j.1467-8306.1975.tb01035.x. Vincent Lemire (tr. Catherine Tihanyi & Lys Ann Weiss), "The Underside of Maps: One City or Four Quarters?," in Lemire (2017), 15–38. Maps in this chapter can be viewed via the links at oldmapsonline.org.

16 The visitor was H.V. Morton, *Middle East* (London: Methuen, 1941), 111.

18 One person who lives with their family inside Haram al-Sharif is Moussab Abbas, interviewed in 2015 by Civic Coalition for Palestinian Rights in Jerusalem: lawcenter .birzeit.edu/lawcenter/attachments/ article/1389/CCPRJ_Special_Feature_Al_ Aqsa_Mosque_Compound.pdf. Sahar Hamouda, *Once Upon a Time in Jerusalem* (Reading: Garnet, 2010), writes of her family home Dar al-Fitiani, located inside the Haram at Bab al-Mathara: "The fortified gate ... to this day remains the only way in or out of the house ... which you enter from the courtyard of the Sacred Enclosure (not from the wall outside) ... After the evening prayer, the gate of the house was closed, along with the other gates of the Haram. We were locked in the Sacred Enclosure."

19 Soueif quote is from "Jerusalem," in: Ahdaf Soueif & Omar Robert Hamilton (eds.), *This Is Not a Border: Reportage & Reflections from the Palestine Festival of Literature* (London: Bloomsbury, 2017), 21–35: palfest.org/soueif-jerusalem.

24 Catherwood's account in: W.H. Bartlett, *Walks About the City and Environs of Jerusalem* (London: Hall, Virtue & Co., 1840), 148–151: archive .org/details/walksaboutcityen00bartiala.

Yehoshua Ben-Arieh, "The Catherwood Map of Jerusalem," *Quarterly Journal of the Library of Congress* 31:3 (1974), 150-160.

26 For Catherwood, Burford and the London exhibition, see Peter O. Koch, *John Lloyd Stephens and Frederick Catherwood: Pioneers of Mayan Archaeology* (Jefferson: McFarland, 2012), 74–77. Exhibition booklet: catalog.hathitrust.org/Record/100216128. Panorama building: british-history.ac.uk/survey-london/vols33-4/pp480-486#h3-0003.

29 For Mujir al-Din's *harat*, see Arnon (1992), 7–11. For 39 quarters, see Auld & Hillenbrand (2000), 129. For 19th-century quarters and census districts, see Arnon (1992), 13–26.

32 Many sources give Symonds's first name as John, but his 1816 christening record shows Julian, as does *Hart's Annual Army List* for 1846, 284.

32 Yolande Jones, "British Military Surveys of Palestine and Syria 1840–1841," *Cartographic Journal* 10:1 (1973), 29–41, doi: 10.1179/caj.1973.10.1.29. Haim Goren, "British surveyors in Palestine and Syria, 1840-41," International Cartographic Conference A Coruña 2005: *Mapping Approaches into a Changing World*: icaci.org/files/documents/ICC_proceedings/ICC2005/htm/pdf/oral/TEMA16/Session%205/HAIM%20GOREN.pdf.

34 Crusader quarters: Dan Bahat, *Carta's Historical Atlas of Jerusalem* (Jerusalem: Carta, 1983), 54–56.

36 Obituary of Robert Willis: gracesguide.co.uk/Robert_Willis.

36 George Williams, *The Holy City* (London: J.W. Parker, 2nd ed. 1849), 10-11: archive.org/details/holycityhistori00willgoog.

38 Ernst Gustav Schultz, *Jerusalem: eine Vorlesung* (Berlin:

S. Schropp, 1845), 4–5, 29, 31 [my renderings]: archive.org/details/jerusalemeinevo00schugoog.

38 My interview with Mustafa Abu Sway 18/10/2019.

38 Laura C. Robson, "Archeology and Mission: The British Presence in Nineteenth-Century Jerusalem," *JQ* 40 (2009), 5–17.

39 Michelle U. Campos, "Mapping Urban 'Mixing' and Intercommunal Relations in Late Ottoman Jerusalem: A Neighborhood Study," *Comparative Studies in Society and History* 63:1 (2021), 133–169.

39 Salim Tamari & Issam Nassar (eds.), Nada Elzeer (tr.), *The Story-teller of Jerusalem: The Life and Times of Wasif Jawhariyyeh, 1904–1948* (Northampton: Interlink, 2014).

CHAPTER 2

41 Sources include: Jack Persekian, "Past Tense," *JQ* 77 (2019), 7–109. Yair Wallach, "Jerusalem's lost heart: The rise and fall of the late Ottoman city center," in Hilal Alkan & Nazan Maksudyan (eds.), *Urban Neighborhood Formations: Boundaries, Narrations and Intimacies* (Abingdon: Routledge, 2020), 138–158: academia.edu/42607145. Simon Goldhill, *Jerusalem: City of Longing* (Harvard UP, 2008). Raquel Rapaport, "The City of the Great Singer: C.R. Ashbee's Jerusalem," *Architectural History* 50 (2007), 171–210. Nicholas E. Roberts, "Dividing Jerusalem: British Urban Planning in the Holy City," *Journal of Palestine Studies* 42:4 (2013), 7–26, academia.edu/27138467.

43 The silversmith is Hart: hartsilversmithstrust.org.uk & youtube.com/watch?v=BoTaeYPBwKo.

44 The Storrs reference to Ashbee's talk at Charterhouse is cited in, e.g., Goldhill (2008), 134; Felicity Ashbee,

Janet Ashbee: Love, Marriage, and the Arts and Crafts Movement (Syracuse UP, 2002), 155.

45 Evliya Çelebi and other details about the project to build the walls: Yusuf Natsheh, "The Architecture of Ottoman Jerusalem," in Auld & Hillenbrand (2000), 583–655.

47 George Hintlian, "An Attempt to Reconstruct the pre-48 Arab Commercial Center of Jerusalem," in: Ibrahim Abu-Lughod Institute of International Studies Ninth International Conference, *Between the Archival Forest and the Anecdotal Trees: A Multidisciplinary Approach to Palestinian Social History* (Birzeit University, 2004), 25–33: ialiis.birzeit.edu/?q=en/node/394.

47 Ashbee's "pagan" quote in Felicity Ashbee (2002), 158. His "picturesque" quote (from *The Times* 5/2/1919) in, e.g., Felicity Ashbee, *Child in Jerusalem* (Syracuse UP, 2008), xv.

49 For stone, see: Roberto Mazza, "'The Preservation and Safeguarding of the Amenities of the Holy City without Favor or Prejudice to Race or Creed": The Pro-Jerusalem Society and Ronald Storrs, 1917–1926," in: Angelos Dalachanis & Vincent Lemire (eds.), *Ordinary Jerusalem, 1840-1940* (Leiden: Brill, 2018), 403–422: brill.com/view/title/36309.

49 Wendy Pullan & Lefkos Kyriacou, "The Work of Charles Ashbee: Ideological Urban Visions with Everyday City Spaces," *JQ* 39 (2009), 51–61.

50 Ashbee's "industrialized" quote: Ron Fuchs & Gilbert Herbert, "A Colonial Portrait of Jerusalem: British Architecture in Mandate-Era Palestine," in Nezar Alsayyad (ed.), *Hybrid Urbanism: On the Identity Discourse and the Built Environment* (Westport: Praeger, 2001), 88.

50 Letchworth: Simon Goldhill, *The Buried Life of Things: How Objects Made History in Nineteenth-Century Britain* (Cambridge UP, 2014), 119–134.

51 Quote from: Yair Wallach, *A City in Fragments: Urban Text in Modern Jerusalem* (Stanford UP, 2020), 250; Owen Hatherley, "Demodernizing Jerusalem: An Interview with Yair Wallach," *Tribune* (UK) 7/4/2021.

51 The Israeli planner is Elisha Efrat, *Physical Planning Prospects in Israel During 50 Years of Statehood* (Berlin: Galda & Wilch, 1998), 116.

CHAPTER 3

53 After I wrote this chapter, I became aware of Yair Wallach's work on street-naming in his (then not-yet-published) *A City in Fragments: Urban Text in Modern Jerusalem* (Stanford UP, 2020). I am grateful to Dr. Wallach for sharing insights.

54 Sato Moughalian, *Feast of Ashes: The Life and Art of David Ohannessian* (Stanford UP, 2019).

56 My interviews with Hagop Karakashian, notably 21/10/2019 & 25/10/2019. See also Balian Ceramics armenianceramics.com and Jerusalem Pottery (Karakashian) jerusalempottery.biz. Tzoghig Aintablian Karakashian, "Armenian Pottery and the Karakashians," *This Week in Palestine* 127 (Nov 2008), 12–15.

57 Graves quote in: Maoz Azaryahu, "Name-Making as Place-Making," in Luisa Caiazzo *et al.* (eds.), *Naming, Identity and Tourism* (Newcastle: Cambridge Scholars, 2020), 16.

57 Natasha Roth-Rowland, "East Jerusalem streets given Hebrew names amid tensions," *+972 Magazine* 21/9/2015.

59 Hagop's photo: for identification of people, see page 339. Also see: facebook.com/hagopka/posts/10217895785238627.

CHAPTER 4

63 My interview with Mazen Izhiman 22/10/2019.

64 For "Urshalim," see: Nir Hasson, "The Jerusalem Anomaly," *Palestine-Israel Journal* 22:4 (2017): pij.org/articles/1805/the-jerusalem-anomaly. Also: ——, *Urshalim: yisraelim ve-palestinayim be-Yerushalayim, 1967–2017* (Tel Aviv: Sifrei Aliyat Hagag, 2017). Also: Umar al-Ghubari, "How Israel erases Arabic from the public landscape," *+972 Magazine* 22/11/2015. I am grateful to Dr. Sarah Irving for pointing out to me the use of "Urshalim" by Palestinian writers before 1948.

66 For the British piazza, see: Wendy Pullan *et al.*, "Jerusalem's Road 1," *City* 11:2 (2007), 176–198, fig. 15: academia.edu/20330998.

66 Al-Wad: Nir Hasson, "The Street That Encapsulates Jerusalem," *Haaretz* 11/11/2015.

67 My interview with Shahd Souri & Jantien Dajani 22/10/2019.

68 Family businesses in the Palestinian economy: Alaa Istaityeh, Aya Aburable & Balqees Falah, "Designing for a Better Family Business," presentation for An-Najah National University, Nablus (2013): repository.najah.edu/handle/20.500.11888/11935.

68 Izhiman case study in: Claudie S. Salameh, *Succession of Family Businesses in Palestine*, M.Sc. thesis, Birzeit University (2017), 111–114: fada.birzeit.edu/bitstream/20.500.11889/5533/1/claudi%twentiethesis.pdf. Izhiman family history: tiki-toki.com/timeline/entry/33646/My-Family-History.

CHAPTER 5

71 On Good Friday (29 March) 2013 Richard Coles, an Anglican vicar, musician and BBC broadcaster, tweeted a sequence of fourteen photojournalistic images, each captioned with a title from the Stations of the Cross. The juxtaposition between the captions and the imagery he chose is striking. He has done the same every Good Friday since (searchable using @RevRichardColes and #StationsoftheCross specifying dates). His approach was one of my inspirations for this chapter.

74 Development of Via Dolorosa & pilgrim pacing: Ilka Knüppel Gray, *The Search for Jesus" Final Steps: How Archaeological and Literary Evidence Reroutes the Via Dolorosa*, MA thesis, Towson University, 2017: academia.edu/33819798. Zur Shalev, "Christian Pilgrimage and Ritual Measurement in Jerusalem," *Micrologus* XIX (2011), 131–150.

75 Armstrong (1996), 202.

78 *Spilopelia senegalensis* can be heard in the opening scene of Dorit Naaman's interactive documentary *Jerusalem We Are Here*: jerusalemwearehere.com.

79 *A Journey from Rome to Jerusalem: Alphonse Ratisbonne 1814–1884* (Jerusalem: Sisters of Our Lady of Sion, 2010). *Journey by the Light of the Word of God: Theodore Ratisbonne 1802–1884* (Jerusalem: Notre Dame de Sion, 2010). *A House in Jerusalem: Ecce Homo* (Jerusalem: Carta, 2015).

87 Wittenberg: Joseph B. Glass & Rassem Khamaisi, "Socio-Economic Conditions in the Old City of Jerusalem," in Tom Najem *et al.* (eds.), *Governance and Security in Jerusalem* (Abingdon: Routledge, 2017), 7–72, doi: 10.4324/9781315619255-2. Also: jerusalem-old-city.org/164218/Beit-Wittenberg & israelrising.com/beit-wittenberg-is-the-key-to-jerusalem. Memoir of Wittenberg's nephew: Yitzhak

Shiryon, *Zichronot* (Jerusalem, 1943), at: benyehuda.org/read/7338 & jewishvirtuallibrary.org/jsource/Peace/YitzhakShirionMemoirs.pdf.

88 Alami quote in: Thomas L. Friedman, "In Jerusalem, Sharon Apartment Creates a Stir," *New York Times* 31/12/1987.

88 Shimon Gibson *et al.*, *Tourists, Travellers and Hotels in 19th-Century Jerusalem* (Abingdon: Routledge, 2013). Wittenberg: 46–47. Twain: 121. Nadav Shragai, "Mark Twain and Ariel Sharon Shared the Same Roof in Jerusalem," *Haaretz* 14/7/2008. Michael D. Press, "Mark Twain, Not-So-Innocent Abroad" 4/11/2019: textualcultures.blogspot.com/2019/11.

89 Abu Shukri: Rafique Gangat, "The best hummus in Palestine," *Gulf News* 25/1/2017. Also: facebook.com/1544990949100400/posts/2919445641654917.

97 Fatima & women street traders: Colleen A. Lowry, *Marriage and Divorce in Late 14th Century Jerusalem*, MA thesis, Portland State University (2007), 54: academia.edu/1756803.

98 Zalatimo: Ronit Vered, "The Vanishing of a Legendary Palestinian Pastry," *Haaretz* 19/7/2019. Shawn Tully, "How an Old School Jordanian Sweets Maker Made it to Walmart," *Fortune* 19/7/2019.

101 Holy Sepulchre, Status Quo, Holy Fire ceremony, etc.: Victoria Clark, *Holy Fire: The Battle for Christ's Tomb* (London: Macmillan, 2005). Alexei Lidov, "The Holy Fire and visual constructs of Jerusalem, east and west," in Bianca Kühnel *et al*, *Visual Constructs of Jerusalem* (Turnhout: Brepols, 2014), 241–249: academia.edu/11894139.

104 Ladder & testimony of "Andy": James E. Lancaster: coastdaylight.com/ladder.html. Video of man moving the ladder, presumably "Andy" in 1997, posted 10/1/2016 by Chris Moore: youtube.com/watch?v=qVckJs2pzH0 (in the comments Chris Moore says he is personal friends with the person who moved the ladder, but does not name him). Image of ladder moved to left-hand window: dannythedigger.com/who-moved-thy-ladder.

110 A.E. Harvey, "Melito and Jerusalem," *Journal of Theological Studies* 17:2 (1966), 401–404, doi: 10.1093/jts/xvii.2.401.

112 Hakim: Peters (1985), 258. *Qiyama/Qumama*: Peters (1985), 600, n9.

112 Sarah Kochav, "The Search for a Protestant Holy Sepulchre: The Garden Tomb in Nineteenth-Century Jerusalem," *Journal of Ecclesiastical History* 46:2 (1995), 278–301, doi: 10.1017/s0022046900011374. Seth J. Frantzman & Ruth Kark, "General Gordon, the Palestine Exploration Fund & the Origins of 'Gordon's Calvary' in the Holy Land," *Palestine Exploration Quarterly* 140:2 (2008), 1–18: academia.edu/2267901.

CHAPTER 6

115 My interview with Muntaser Edkaidek 27/10/2019. *Youth Challenges in Jerusalem: Bab Hutta Neighborhood Case Study* (Jerusalem: Burj al-Luqluq, 2015): in Arabic at burjalluqluq.org. Rafique Gangat, "A breathing space in Bab Hutta," *Gulf News* 2/5/2018.

118 "Israeli Occupation bans the Jerusalemite families football tournament," Palestine News Network 20/8/2019. Nir Hasson, "Israeli Police Break Up Arab Soccer Tournament in Jerusalem's Old City," *Haaretz* 20/8/2019. "Preventing the Jerusalemite Families League in Burj Al-Laqlaq": silwanic.net/index.php/article/news/77699.

CHAPTER 7

121 The core of this chapter originated in a version conceived and drafted by Daniel Adamson in 2013–14. I am grateful to Daniel for giving me access to his material. Any errors are mine only.

121 Mohammed Al-Ghazali (tr. Claud Field), *The Confessions of Al-Ghazali* (London: Murray, 1909), 43–46: archive.org/details/confessionsofalg00ghaziala.

123 Abu Yazid quote cited in, e.g.: Carl Ernst, "The Man Without Attributes: Ibn Arabi's Interpretation of Abu Yazid al-Bistami," *Journal of the Muhyiddin Ibn Arabi Society* XIII (1993): ibnarabisociety.org/the-man-without-attributes-carl-ernst.

123 Rumi quote: *Masnavi* 4:1407.

124 My interviews with Mazen Ahram 10/9/2018 & 25/2/2019.

127 Uri Rubin, "Muhammad's Night Journey (*isra'*) to al-Masjid al-Aqsa: Aspects of the Earliest Origins of the Islamic Sanctity of Jerusalem," *Al-Qantara* 29:1 (2008), 147–164: academia.edu/5617249.

127 I am grateful to Ian D. Morris for helping clarify for me scholarly debates concerning the meaning of the Quranic phrase *al-masjid al-aqsa* and the complex relationship between that phrase, the city of Jerusalem, the esplanade known as Haram al-Sharif and the building commonly termed Al-Aqsa.

127 Yasmine Seale, "Out of Their Love They Made It: A Visual History of Buraq," *Public Domain Review* 21/9/2016.

128 Mersiha Gadzo, "Israel normalization may partition Al-Aqsa: Analysts," *Al Jazeera* 14/9/2020.

130 Lawrence Nees, *Perspectives on Early Islamic Art in Jerusalem* (Leiden: Brill, 2015), doi: 10.1163/9789004302075. M. Anwarul Islam & Zaid F. al-Hamad, "The Dome of the Rock: Origin of its Octagonal Plan," *Palestine Exploration Quarterly* 139:2 (2007), 109–128, doi: 10.1179/003103207x194145.

131 Sufyan on bananas is from Mujir al-Din, quoted in e.g.: S.D. Goitein, *Studies in Islamic History and Institutions* (Leiden: Brill, 1966), 142, doi: 10.1163/ej.9789004179318.i-394. Muqaddasi on bananas, in: Guy Le Strange, *Palestine under the Moslems* (London: Watt, 1890), 18: archive.org/details/palestineundermo00lest.

132 Dhu'n-Nun quoted in: Mohammed Rustom, "The Sufi Teachings of Dhu'l-Nun," *Sacred Web* 24 (Winter 2009), 69–79: mohammedrustom.com.

132 Ruzbihan quoted in: Chittick (2000), 114.

133 Rumi "If you could get rid" quoted in: Dr. Nevit O. Ergin (tr.), *Crazy As We Are: Selected Rubais from Divan-i Kebir of Mevlana Celaleddin Rumi* (Chino Valley: Hohm, 1992), 4.

133 I wrote about the Aleppo *dhikr* in 2007 for the (now-defunct) airline BMI's magazine *Voyager*, and revised it in 2014 for the (now-defunct) journalism site *Beacon*: matthewteller.com/work/the-reluctant-mystic.

134 Camille Adams Helminski, *Women of Sufism: A Hidden Treasure* (Boston: Shambhala, 2013), 20 & 24. Moyra Dale, "Women in Sufism" (17/1/2018): whenwomenspeak.net/blog/women-in-sufism.

139 I'm grateful to Dr. Sarah Irving, who told me about the recurrence in the 1970s of pilgrimage festivals.

140 Video: *Father of the Kittens/Abu Hurairat* by Alyateema, posted 7/3/2015: youtube.com/watch?v=vAj-ynEu9Lw. AJ+ video 8/2/2018: twitter

.com/ajplus/status/961597257450582016.'
Emer McCarthy, "Meet the 'father
of the kittens' at Jerusalem's
al-Aqsa mosque," Reuters 9/11/2019.
Death: twitter.com/AJArabic/
status/1351492098021851136 (19/1/2021).
Basem Ra'ad, "Cats of Jerusalem," *JQ*
41 (2010), 73–88.

141 Story of Abu Zahir quoted in:
Al-Kilani (2001), 620-621.

143 Sabri Jarrar, "Suq al-Ma'rifa:
An Ayyubid Hanbalite Shrine in
al-Haram al-Sharif," *Muqarnas* 15
(1998), 71–100, doi: 10.2307/1523278.

144 The shocked Franciscan was
Eugène Roger, quoted in: Thierry V.
Zarcone, *Sufi Pilgrims from Central
Asia and India in Jerusalem* (Center
for Islamic Area Studies, Kyoto
University, 2009), 33: academia
.edu/35977579. My rendering.

144 Rafique Gangat, "Uzbek Zawiya,
keeping a Sufi tradition alive,"
Gulf News 8/3/2017. Jorg Luyken,
"Mystical transcendence," *Jerusalem
Post* 22/5/2008. Lauren Gelfond
Feldinger, "Sufi sheikh who preached
nonviolence laid to rest," *Jerusalem
Post* 3/6/2010.

145 Bukhari phone quote in:
Charmaine Seitz, "The Distracted
Sufi: The Naqshabandi *tariqa* in
Jerusalem," *JQ* 20 (2004), 57.

146 Baba Farid, Ibrahim bin Adham,
Moinuddin & others profiled at
sufiwiki.com.

148 The writer was Daniel Silas
Adamson, "Jerusalem's 800-year-
old Indian hospice," BBC News
23/11/2014.

149 My interview with Nazer Ansari
21/10/2019.

149 Navtej Sarna, *Indians at Herod's
Gate: A Jerusalem Tale* (New Delhi:
Rupa, 2014). Nourjahan Ansari, "The
Ansari Family of the Indian Hospice,"
This Week in Palestine 112 (Aug. 2007).

151 Indian Hospice's last Sufi head,
in: Zarcone (2009), 104–107.

CHAPTER 8

157 Amoun Sleem, *A Gypsy
Dreaming in Jerusalem* (Macon,
GA: Nurturing Faith, 2014). Also
domarisociety.com & domresearchcenter
.com. My interview with Amoun Sleem
16/10/2019. I am grateful to Muna
Haddad, who shared notes and
insights from her work for Baraka
Destinations (Amman) in 2019–20
with Amoun Sleem and the Domari
Society.

158 Rawan Asali Nuseibeh, "The
Social Exclusion of the Domari
Society of Gypsies in Jerusalem:
a story narrated by the women of
the tribe," *Identities* (15/3/2020),
doi: 10.1080/1070289X.2020.1738130.
"Domari Gypsies face daily racism
in Jerusalem and Gaza," *Travellers
Times* 17/6/2013: travellerstimes.org
.uk/news/2013/06/domari-gypsies
-face-daily-racism-jerusalem-and-gaza.
Jennifer Peterson, "The Last
Migration? Jerusalem's Gypsy
Community," *JQ* 18 (2003), 44–54.
Abigail Wood, "The Domari Gypsies
of Jerusalem," *The Middle East in
London* (Dec 2009–Jan 2010), 11–12.
Bruno Herin, "Domari: the Language
of the 'Middle-Eastern Gypsies,'" *The
Middle East in London* 11:5 (Oct-Nov
2015), 15–16. Yaron Matras, "The state
of present-day Domari in Jerusalem,"
Mediterranean Language Review
11 (1999), 1–58. ———, "Two Domari
legends about the origin of the
Doms," *Romani Studies* 10:1 (2000),
49–75, doi: 10.3828/rs.2000.3.

CHAPTER 9

165 Mujir al-Din, Safadi and Ibn
al-Jazari mention the blind governor
Ala ad-Din Aydughdi. I used sources
including: Burgoyne (1987), 117–126;
Donald P. Little, "Mujir al-Din
al-'Ulaymi's Vision of Jerusalem in

the Ninth/Fifteenth Century," *Journal of the American Oriental Society* 115:2 (1995), 244, doi: 10.2307/604667; Nasser Rabbat, *Mamluk History through Architecture: Monuments, Culture and Politics in Medieval Egypt & Syria* (London: I.B. Tauris, 2010), 40, doi: 10.5040/9780755697472 .ch-004 [earlier version at academia. edu/22544486, 35]; Dr. Ali Qleibo, *Mamluk Architectural Landmarks in Jerusalem* (Jerusalem: Taawon, 2019), 66–67. I used all of these in sketching Jerusalem's Mamluk history, and: Zayde Antrim, "Jerusalem in the Ayyubid and Mamluk periods," in Suleiman A. Mourad *et al* (eds.), *Routledge Handbook on Jerusalem* (Abingdon: Routledge, 2018), 102–109: academia.edu/37740881.

166 Arafat A. Razzaque, "Who 'wrote' Aladdin? The Forgotten Syrian Storyteller," *Ajam Media Collective* 14/9/2017: ajammc .com/2017/09. Richard Lea, "How Aladdin's story was forged in Aleppo and Versailles," *The Guardian* 2/11/2018. M. Lynx Qualey, "A whole new world: behind the new translation of Aladdin," *The National* (UAE) 20/12/2018. Hanna Diyab, Elias Muhanna (tr.), Johannes Stephan (ed.), *The Book of Travels* (New York UP, 2021). Yasmine Seale (tr.), Paulo Lemos Horta (ed.), *Aladdin: A New Translation* (New York: Liveright, 2018). For singular *nuit*, see: Sylvette Larzul, "Further Considerations on Galland's *Mille et une Nuits*: A Study of the Tales Told by Hanna," *Marvels & Tales* 18:2 (2004), 258–271, n1.

167 Lentin may not have been the first. In her foreword to Paul Lunde's translation of Diyab's memoir *The Man Who Wrote Aladdin* (Edinburgh: Hardinge Simpole, 2020) Caroline Stone – who was married to Lunde – says Lunde found Diyab's manuscript in the Vatican library in the early 1970s but chose not to publish his

discovery, or the translation he made of it, before his death in 2016. More at: Matthew Teller, "The 1001 Tales of Hanna Diyab," *AramcoWorld* 72:4 (July-Aug 2021), 28–33.

169 For context on *abd*, see: Nesrine Malik, "A paler shade of black," *The Guardian* 5/3/2008. Ahmed Twaij, "The A-Word," *Kerning Cultures* 18/2/2021. Sulaiman Addonia, "In Search of Beauty: Blackness as a Poem in Saudi Arabia," *Granta* 17/4/2019. Mohamed Hassan, "Blackface, racism and anti-blackness in the Arab world," *Middle East Eye* 22/6/2020.

169 For imported commodities, see: Donald P. Little, "Jerusalem under the Ayyubids and Mamluks 1187–1516 AD," in Asali (1989), 196.

172 Umar al-Naqar, "Takrur: The History of a Name," *Journal of African History* 10:3 (1969), 365–374, doi: 10.1017/s002185370003632x.

173 My interview with Musa Qous 21/10/2019.

174 Dzouyi Therese Konanga-Nicolas, "The African Palestinian Community in the Old City of Jerusalem," *This Week in Palestine* 112 (Aug 2007). Joharah Baker, "The African-Palestinians: Muslim pilgrims who never went home," *The New Arab/Al-Araby Al-Jadeed* 26/12/2014. Rosa Sariñena, "Los guardianes de Al-Aqsa," *El País* 12/1/2016. Isma'il Kushkush, "Afro-Palestinians forge a unique identity in Israel," *Associated Press* 12/1/2017. Charmaine Seitz, "Pilgrimage to a New Self: The African Quarter and its people," *JQ* 16 (2002), 43–51.

174 Ribat al-Mansuri 28 x 23m. Ribat al-Basiri 23 x 20m. My estimates.

176 Husni Shaheen on "French Sudan" quoted in: Yasser Qous, "Jerusalem's Africans: Alienation and counter-alienation," *Qantara.de*

(6/2/2019): en.qantara.de/node/34421. Republished at: goethe.de/prj/ruy/en/mig.html. *Soudan français* (French Sudan) originated in the 1880s as an extension of France's colony in Senegal. A map dated 1911 showing *Soudan* stretching from Mali to Darfur is at: gallica.bnf.fr/ark:/12148/btv1b530636240. By 1958 *Soudan français* was known as *République soudanaise* (unrelated to the Republic of Sudan far to the east that had newly won independence after colonization by the British). In 1960 the French-controlled *République soudanaise* became the independent *République du Mali*. British anthropologist Susan Beckerleg quotes one unnamed woman she spoke to in Jerusalem in the period 1995–97 as follows: "We just say [we came from] Sudan because we do not know and because the name means 'place of black people.' It could just as easily have been Congo." See: Susan Beckerleg, "African Bedouin in Palestine," *African & Asian Studies* 6:3 (2007), 289–303, doi: 10.1163/156920907X212240. ——, "Hidden History, Secret Present: The Origins and Status of African Palestinians," London School of Hygiene & Tropical Medicine (1998): yajaffar.tripod.com/african.html.

178 Mahmoud Jaddeh quoted in video *African-Palestinian Community in Jerusalem*, posted 2/11/2011 by Alternative Information Center: youtube.com/watch?v=yUsNFuQ-zLM. Ali Jaddeh conversations with author, also quoted in: *Jerusalem Conflict: The Ali Jiddah Story*, dir. Stephen Graham (31/8/2015, 53 min): stephengraham.net/jerusalem-conflict-the-ali-jiddah-story-uncut.

178 William F.S. Miles, "Black African Muslim in the Jewish State: Lessons of Colonial Nigeria for Contemporary Jerusalem," *Issue: A Journal of*

Opinion 25:1 (1997), 39–42, doi: 10.2307/1166246.

179 Nikesh Shukla (ed.), *The Good Immigrant* (London: Unbound, 2016). Nikesh Shukla & Chimene Suleyman (eds.), *The Good Immigrant USA* (New York: Little, Brown, 2019).

180 "Restrictions on movement in Bab al-Majles in Jerusalem's Old City place neighborhood in chokehold," *Btselem* (28/2/2016): btselem.org/jerusalem/20160228_bab_al_majles.

180 Yasser Qous, "The West African Community in Jerusalem: process of settlement and local integration," *Maghreb-Machrek* 235:1 (2018), 117–128.

183 The 1954–1984 guidebooks are: *Jordan: Facts and Information about the Holy Land* (Jordan State Tourist Department, 1954); *A Guide to Jordan, the Holy Land* (Jordan Tourism Authority, 1962); Ghattas Jahshan, *Guide to the West Bank of Jordan: Jerusalem* (3rd ed. n.d. 1963?); Eugene Hoade, *Guide to the Holy Land* (Jerusalem: Franciscan Printing Press, n.d. 1970?); Christine Osborne, *An Insight and Guide to Jordan* (Harlow: Longman, 1981); Kay Showker, *Jordan & the Holy Land* (New York: Fodor, 1984). One variant is: Isobel & John Fistere, *Jordan: The Holy Land* (Beirut: Middle East Export Press, n.d. 1964?): "Entrance [is] through two gates – the first one Bab Hutta, the second Bab al Atm." However, this passage discusses the "most convenient" approach to the Haram being from the east via St. Stephen's Gate – which is close to Bab Hutta and Bab al-Atm – so it may have been possible to enter the Haram through other gates as well.

183 The later guidebooks are: Shirley Eber & Kevin O'Sullivan, *Israel and the Occupied Territories: The Rough Guide* (London: Harrap-Columbus, 1st ed. 1989), 87; Kay Prag, *Blue*

Guide Jerusalem (London: A&C Black, 1st ed. 1989), 83: "Access for non-Muslims is from the Nazir, Chain or Moors gates'; Neil Tilbury, *Israel: A Travel Survival Kit* (Melbourne: Lonely Planet, 1st ed. 1989), 139: "non-Muslims are only allowed to enter through two: Morrolo [sic] (Moors) Gate and Chain Gate'; Diana Darke, *Discovery Guide to Jordan and the Holy Land* (London: Immel, 1993), 193: "The rules ... change frequently, but in general the three gates which are permitted [for non-Muslims] are the Bab an-Nadhir, the Bab es-Silsileh and the Bab el-Maghariba."

183 Soueif & Hamilton (2017), 21–35: palfest.org/soueif-jerusalem.

184 My interview with Al-Shaima al-Budeiri 21/10/2019.

185 For more on Mustafa al-Bakri, see: Gideon Weigert, "Shaykh Mustapha Kamal al Din al Bakri – a Sufi reformer in eighteenth-century Egypt," *Bulletin of the Israeli Academic Center in Cairo* 24 (2001).

186 Pilgrim accounts of 1229 & 1187, and speculation on Sabil Bab an-Nazir's source, from: Denys Pringle, *The Churches of the Crusader Kingdom of Jerusalem: A Corpus: Vol. 3 The City of Jerusalem* (Cambridge UP, 2007), 207–208. Also: Natsheh, in Auld & Hillenbrand (2000), 689–692.

CHAPTER 10

189 Peters (1985), 246–247, 409–411 & elsewhere. Sebag Montefiore (2011), 122n, 199, 233. Maria-Luisa Fernandez-Mansfield, *Golden Gate*, Institute for International Urban Development database: i2ud.org/jer/priv/html3/monuments/sites/t223_gold_gat_bab. Nir Hasson, "The Most Mysterious Gate in Jerusalem's Old City is Still Puzzling Researchers," *Haaretz* 24/3/2019.

191 Nazmi Jubeh, "The Bab al-Rahmeh Cemetery: Israeli Encroachment Continues Unabated," *Journal of Palestine Studies* 48:1 (2018), 88–103, doi: 10.1525/jps.2018.48.1.88. PASSIA, *Bab Ar-Rahmeh: The Story of the Structure and the February-March 2019 Crisis*: passia.org/media/filer_public/b2/76/b276b309-a199-466a-9b7c-fe6c0000494b/bab-ar-rahmeh-2019en.pdf. Zena Tahhan, "Closed Al-Aqsa gate reopens old Palestinian wounds in Jerusalem," *Middle East Eye* 21/2/2019. Mersiha Gadzo, "What's behind the unrest at Al Aqsa's Bab al-Rahma?," *Al Jazeera* 1/3/2019.

CHAPTER 11

193 Rkia Elaroui Cornell, "Rabi'ah al-"Adawiyyah," in Michael Cooperson & Shawkat M. Toorawa (eds.), *Dictionary of Literary Biography Vol. 311: Arabic Literary Culture 500-925* (Farmington Hills: Thomson Gale, 2005), 292–298. ——, *Rabi'a: From Narrative to Myth* (London: Oneworld, 2019). Laury Silvers, "Early Pious, Mystic Sufi Women," in Lloyd Ridgeon (ed.), *The Cambridge Companion to Sufism* (Cambridge UP, 2014), 24–52, doi: 10.1017/CCO9781139087599.004. Steven Aiello, "Rabi'a "l-"Adawiyya: Legend or Woman?" (15/10/2016), doi: 10.2139/ssrn.2852872. Also: sufiwiki.com/Rabia_Basri.

196 I don't know which Nai Barghouti video of Rabia's poem *Uhibbuka Hubbayn* ("I love you with two loves") Salwa [name has been changed] had seen, but maybe it was this: youtube.com/watch?v=YcQL3uPNwes.

196 My rendering of the poem is truncated & paraphrased. Proper translations include: Margaret Smith, *Rabi'a The Mystic and Her Fellow-Saints in Islam* (Cambridge UP, 1928),

102–103, quoted at rumi.org.uk/sufism/rabia. Martin Lings, *Sufi Poems: A Mediaeval Anthology* (Cambridge: Islamic Texts Society, 2004). Carl W. Ernst, "The Stages of Love in Early Persian Sufism, from Rabi'a to Ruzbihan," in Leonard Lewisohn (ed.), *The Heritage of Sufism, Vol. 1* (London: Oneworld, 1999), 438–439. Charles Upton, *Doorkeeper of the Heart: Versions of Rabi'a* (New York: Pir, 2004), 23. Also: remonaaly.com/media/my-two-loves.

197 Bucket and fire story quoted in, e.g.: Haifaa Jawad, "Islamic Spirituality and the Feminine Dimension," in: Gillian Howie & J'annine Jobling (eds.), *Women and the Divine* (New York: Palgrave Macmillan, 2009), 195.

198 In terms of wish-fulfilment, there are parallels between Rabia and the Sumerian poet Enheduanna (c.2300 BCE), who is popularly celebrated as the world's first named author but for whom all the evidence of literary composition comes from establishment myth-makers centuries after her death. Historian Eleanor Robson expanded on this in *Lines of Resistance* (2017), presented by Bridget Minamore and produced by me for BBC Radio 4: bbc.co.uk/programmes/b098h0f3 (06:56–11:23).

199 "Egypt: Rab'a Killings Likely Crimes against Humanity," Human Rights Watch 12/8/2014: hrw.org/news/2014/08/12/egypt-raba-killings-likely-crimes-against-humanity.

200 Jon Seligman & Rafa Abu Raya, "A Shrine of Three Religions on the Mount of Olives: Tomb of Hulda the Prophetess; Grotto of Saint Pelagia; Tomb of Rabi'a al-"Adawiyya," in *Atiqot* 42 (2001), 221–236.

201 Tunshuq in, e.g.: Burgoyne (1987), 485–512.

202 Yusuf Natsheh, "Muslim Women Patrons in Jerusalem," in Barbara Drake Boehm & Melanie Holcomb (eds.), *Jerusalem 1000–1400: Every People Under Heaven* (Yale UP, 2016), 242–243. ——, "Al-Imara al-Amira" in Auld & Hillenbrand (2000), 747–790. ——, "My Memories of Khassaki Sultan," *JQ* 7 (2000), 29–35. Zeynep Ahunbay *et al.*, "Public Kitchen of Haseki Sultan within the Takiyya Complex in Al-Quds/Jerusalem," in *Al-Quds/Jerusalem 2015 Program: 2008 Report* (Istanbul: Organization of the Islamic Conference, Research Center for Islamic History, Art and Culture, 2009), 175–191: academia.edu/20112181. Amy Singer, *Constructing Ottoman Beneficence: An Imperial Soup Kitchen in Jerusalem* (State University of New York Press, 2002). David Myres, "Al-Imara al-Amira: the charitable foundation of Khassaki Sultan," in Auld & Hillenbrand (2000), 539–581. Matthew Teller, "Five Centuries of Jerusalem Soup," *AramcoWorld* 72:6 (Nov-Dec 2021), 6–11.

203 Shaghab inscriptions: Christel Kessler, "Above the Ceiling of the Outer Ambulatory in the Dome of the Rock in Jerusalem," *Journal of the Royal Asiatic Society of Great Britain and Ireland* 3/4 (1964), 83–94.

204 Colleen A. Lowry, *Marriage and Divorce in Late Fourteenth Century Jerusalem*, MA thesis, Portland State University (2007): academia.edu/1756803. Aysha: 52. Shirin: 107. Amna: 182. Donald P. Little, "Haram documents related to the Jews of late fourteenth-century Jerusalem," in *Journal of Semitic Studies* 30:2 (1985), doi: 10.1093/jss/xxx.2.227. Qutlumalik: 231. Qamar: 241. Leila Ahmed, *Women and Gender in Islam: Historical Roots of a Modern Debate* (Yale UP, 1992). Bayram: 113–114.

205 Dror Ze'evi, "Women in 17th-Century Jerusalem: Western

and Indigenous Perspectives,"
International Journal of Middle East Studies 27 (1995), doi: 10.1017/s0020743800061869. Maryam: 163–164.

205 Tarafanda in: Tarif Khalidi, "A Family's History": khalidilibrary.org/en/Article/56/A-Family%E2%80%99s-History-By-Tarif-Khalidi. Hind al-Husseini: dartifl.org/en/en/12/69.

CHAPTER 12

208 Slimane Rezki, "Sidi Abu Madyan Chu'ayb al-Maghribi: Biographie": academia.edu/7086130. Claude Addas, "Abu Madyan and Ibn Arabi": ibnarabisociety.org/abu-madyan-and-ibn-arabi-claude-addas. A.L. Tibawi, *The Islamic Pious Foundations in Jerusalem* (London: Islamic Cultural Center, 1978), 10-15.

209 Maryvelma Smith O'Neil, "The Mughrabi Quarter Digital Archive and the Virtual Illés Relief Initiative," *JQ* 81 (2020), 52–76. See also: mughrabiquarter.info.

209 Noura al-Tijani, "The Moroccan Community in Palestine," *This Week in Palestine* 112 (Aug 2007).

210 Ibn Battuta's account of meeting Al-Gharnati: Burgoyne (1987), 213.

212 The Italian poet was Ahimaaz ben Paltiel, see, e.g.: jewishvirtuallibrary.org/ldquo-western-wall-rdquo-or-ldquo-wailing-wall-rdquo. Ahimaaz quoted in: Peters (1985), 224–225.

212 For early identification of Buraq Wall, see: Simone Ricca, "Heritage, Nationalism and the Shifting Symbolism of the Wailing Wall," *JQ* 24 (2005), 39–56. Amikam Elad, *Medieval Jerusalem and Islamic Worship: Holy Places, Ceremonies, Pilgrimage* (Leiden: Brill, 2012), 101. For changes in the Ottoman period, see: Peters (1985), 527–529. "The first testimony to the transformation of the Western Wall into a sacred site

for worship comes only from the sixteenth century," in: Ofer Aderet, "Prayers, notes and controversy: How a wall became the Western Wall," *Haaretz* 14/5/2013.

214 Translation of 1840 order from Muhammad Sharif, governor in Damascus, to Ahmed Agha Duzdar, governor of Jerusalem, denying the Jews the right to pave the alleyway in front of the Wall: UK Commission report on the Western Wall, 1930, Appendix VI: un.org/unispal/document/auto-insert-183716. Bonfils photograph from 1869 showing paving: rosettaapp.getty.edu/delivery/DeliveryManagerServlet?dps_pid=IE682845. Images from 1881 showing paving: lifeintheholyland.com/wailing_wall_1800s.

214 For Weizmann seeking to buy the Wall in 1918 (and others before him), see, e.g.: Menachem Klein, *Lives in Common: Arabs and Jews in Jerusalem, Jaffa and Hebron* (London: Hurst, 2014), 95–97. Roberto Mazza, "The deal of the century? The attempted sale of the Western Wall by Cemal Pasha in 1916," *Middle Eastern Studies* 16/3/2021, doi: 10.1080/00263206.2021.1895118. Also Mazza's talk (19/12/2019) at: facebook.com/watch/live/?v=549239398958471. Steven E. Zipperstein, "Revealed: An Arab prince's secret proposal to sell the Western Wall to the Jews," *Times of Israel* 9/1/2020.

214 Three examples of late 19th-/early 20th-century images showing benches & tables at the Wall: zionistarchives.org.il/en/Bonfils/PHAL1655564.jpg & jewishvirtuallibrary.org/jsource/images/jeru/wall2.jpg & flickr.com/photos/nationalarchives/3182899916.

215 For Duff, "duffing up" and torture, see e.g.: Matthew Kraig Kelly, "The Revolt of 1936," *Journal of Palestine Studies* 44:2 (2015), 32, doi:

10.1525/jps.2015.44.2.28. Richard Cahill, "'Going Berserk': 'Black and Tans' in Palestine," *JQ* 38 (2009), 59–68. Quote is from: Douglas V. Duff, *Bailing with a Teaspoon* (London: John Long, 1953), 36.

215 Mahmoud al-Mahdi quoted in: Naomi Zeveloff, "Palestinians remember Israeli destruction of Jerusalem's Moroccan Quarter," *The National* (UAE) 4/6/2017. Elmer Berger, *Who Knows Better Must Say So!* (New York: American Council for Judaism, 1955): catalog.hathitrust .org/Record/004681824. Iris Keltz, *Unexpected Bride in the Promised Land: Journeys in Palestine and Israel* (Taos: Nighthawk, 2017); excerpt at: mondoweiss.net/2015/06/ years-commemorating-the.

216 Dorit Gottesfeld & Ronen Yitzhak, "Normalization in a War Environment: The Mandelbaum Gate as an Allegory in History and in Literature," *Mediterranean Studies* 27:1 (2019), 86–110, doi: 10.5325/ mediterraneanstu.27.1.0086. Muriel Spark's 1965 novel *The Mandelbaum Gate* paints dramatic pictures.

216 Pre-1967 international flight timetables to Jerusalem: timetableimages.com/ttimages/list .htm#Asia (see Air Jordan, Alia–Royal Jordanian Airlines, Arab Airways, Middle East Airlines, Syrian Arab Airways). I wrote this in 2019, before becoming aware of new research by Eldad Brin, "Gateway to the World: the Golden Age of Jerusalem Airport, 1948–67," *JQ* 85 (2021), 61–80. Also: Nir Hasson, "Jerusalem's Posh Airport Had Direct Flights to Iran. This Is What It Looks Like Today," *Haaretz* 20/4/2021. Brin states 750,000 visitors to Jordan in 1965, split 70:30 in 1966 between visitors from Arab or Muslim countries (525,000) and elsewhere (225,000). Meron Benvenisti, *Jerusalem: The Torn City* (Minneapolis: Minnesota

UP, 1976), 59, states 600,000 visitors to Jordanian Jerusalem in 1966, split 71:29 (425,000 to 175,000). Both authors state Jerusalem Airport handled only 100,000 passengers in 1966. Therefore it's safe to say most tourists in this period approached Jordanian Jerusalem overland from Amman.

216 *A Guide to Jordan, the Holy Land* (Jordan Tourism Authority, 1962): archive.org/details/pgj_20190722. The 1960 Israeli guidebook is quoted in: Raphael Israeli, *Jerusalem Divided: The Armistice Regime 1947–67* (London: Frank Cass, 2002), 7. Visa restrictions stated in: *Jordan: Facts and Information about the Holy Land* (Jordan State Tourist Department, 1954), 30–31; Kay Showker, *Travel Jordan, the Holy Land* (Beirut: Librairie du Liban, n.d. 1965?), 18–19.

217 Tourists to Jordan were required to buy a visa. They could do so in advance from a Jordanian consulate. If they arrived in Jordan with such a visa, it seems that that was sufficient for entry. If they did not, and arrived with no visa, then (as a Jordanian government guidebook from 1954 warns) they had to show "a certificate of church membership or an official document proving that he [sic] is not a member of the Jewish faith." Another guidebook tells tourists arriving at a Jordanian frontier without a visa to "have a certificate of religious affiliation with you. Acceptable documents are: a letter of membership from your church, your baptismal certificate or a notarized statement of your religious affiliation." This requirement did not apply to tourists "arriving via an Arab country or holding an entry permit to an Arab country, [who] will be automatically granted a Jordan visa at any Jordan frontier post or airport." This suggests that the religious restriction may have been imposed only on those seeking to enter Jordan without a prearranged visa. If so, were visa applicants at Jordanian embassies in, say, London, Washington, Beirut or Tehran questioned about their religion and/or required to show a baptismal certificate as part of their application? I haven't been able to find out. And what about that odd phrase "profess[ing] the Jewish faith," which appears more than once in Jordanian government tourist publications from this period: was it bureaucratic waffle, or was the wording designed to acknowledge a gap in meaning between Jewish tourists who profess the faith and Jewish tourists who do not, thereby barring only the former? Again, I don't know.

217 Example quotes, all false: Teddy Kollek, *For Jerusalem* (London: Weidenfeld & Nicolson, 1978), 197: "[F]or nineteen years Jews had been denied access to their only Holy Place." Marshall J. Breger & Thomas Idinopulos, *Jerusalem's Holy Places and the Peace Process* (Policy Paper 46, Washington Institute for Near East Policy, 1998), 13: "Jews were denied access to worship at the Western Wall." Elie Wiesel, *New York Times* 24/1/2001: "[B]etween 1948 and 1967 ... Jews were denied access to the Western Wall."

217 Kimberly Katz, "Administering Jordanian Jerusalem: Constructing national identity," in: Tamar Mayer & Suleiman A. Mourad (eds.), *Jerusalem: Idea and Reality* (Abingdon: Routledge, 2008), 245. The deputy mayor was Meron Benvenisti, *Jerusalem: The Torn City* (Minneapolis: Minnesota UP, 1976), 68. The line "I knew I couldn't" is from: thelondonmom1.blogspot.com/2018/08/things-you-dont-tell-your-parents.html by writer Janine

Stein quoting her mother, named as Linda Zackon in Stein's email to me 14/6/2021.

218 Nazmi Jubeh, "Childhood Memories of a Jerusalemite," *JQ* 73 (2018), 90–100. ———, *Haret al-yahud wa haret al-magharba fil quds al-qadima / The Jewish Quarter and the Moroccan Quarter in the Old City of Jerusalem: History and Destiny between Destruction and Judaization* (Beirut/Washington: Institute for Palestine Studies, 2019): palestine-studies.org/en/node/1648299.

218 My interview with Maysoon al-Maslohi 22/10/2019.

219 The urinating boy story comes from Yaakov Yannai, head of the Israeli National Parks Authority, quoted in e.g.: Paula Kabalo, "City with no walls: David Ben-Gurion's Jerusalem vision post-June 1967," *Modern Judaism* 38:2 (2018), 166, doi: 10.1093/mj/kjy003.

219 The toilet story is quoted widely, e.g.: Uzi Benziman, "What Israel gained – and lost – by unifying Jerusalem," *Haaretz* 7/6/2017: "... the public toilets abutting the Wall." Kollek (1978), 230: "[We] tore down latrines and other structures actually attached to the Wall." Steven Carol, *Understanding the Volatile and Dangerous Middle East: A Comprehensive Analysis* (2015), writes falsely: "The Western Wall, desecrated by slums, became an outdoor public urinal."

220 Bialik quoted in: Philip Mattar, "The Role of the Mufti of Jerusalem in the Political Struggle over the Western Wall, 1928–29," *Middle Eastern Studies* 19:1 (1983), 106, doi: 10.1080/00263208308700536.

220 A toilet existed in the area of houses and the *zawiya* long before Jordanian rule. Source: "... a water closet close to the wall that is a direct continuation of the Wailing Wall to the south," in UK Commission report on the Western Wall, 1930, IV(c)1: un.org/unispal/document/auto -insert-183716.

220 The surprised Israeli contractor was Sasson Levy, quoted in: Nir Hasson, "How a Small Group of Israelis Made the Western Wall Jewish Again," *Haaretz*, 3/6/2017.

220 Herzog quoted in: Eyal Weizman, *Hollow Land: Israel's Architecture of Occupation* (London: Verso, 2007), 37: "When we visited the Wailing Wall we found a toilet attached to it ... we decided to remove it, and from this we came to the conclusion that we could evacuate the entire area."

220 For buildings used as latrines, see: C.R. Ashbee (ed.), *Jerusalem 1918–1920* (London: Murray, 1921): St. Stephens [Lions] Gate guard-house, 4; citadel moat, 21; Suq al-Qattanin, 30: archive.org/details/ jerusalem191819200ashbuoft. Ain Karim mosque as latrine: Evan M. Wilson, "The Internationalization of Jerusalem," *Middle East Journal* 23:1 (1969), 4. For public toilets, see: Ruth Kark, "The Jerusalem municipality at the end of Ottoman rule," *Asian & African Studies* 14 (1980), 117–141. I am grateful to Dr. Sarah Irving for many of these references.

220 Avigdor Hameiri, *Tnuva* (Tel Aviv, 1934), I:5: benyehuda.org/read/17295. Many thanks to Dr. Yair Wallach for alerting me to this.

221 The head of Israeli army central command was Major General Uzi Narkiss. The Israeli justice minister was Yaakov Shimson Shapira. Both quoted in Benziman (2017).

221 Jerusalem's Israeli mayor was Teddy Kollek. See Kollek (1978), 197. Quoted in, e.g.: Thomas Philip Abowd, *Colonial Jerusalem: The*

Spatial Construction of Identity and Difference in a City of Myth, 1948–2012 (Syracuse UP, 2014), 125.

221 The Israeli army engineer was Major Eitan Ben Moshe, interviewed in *Yerushalayim* (26/11/1999). Quoted in, e.g.: Tom Abowd, "The Moroccan Quarter: A History of the Present," *JQ* 7 (2000), 6–16. Also: Ghada Hashem Talhami, *American Presidents and Jerusalem* (Lanham: Lexington, 2017), 106. Talhami names Rasmiyyah Ali Tabaki.

221 Abdulhadi al-Tazi, *Awqaf al-maghariba fil-quds/Moroccan Islamic endowments in Jerusalem* (Jerusalem: private publication by Mahmoud Ahmed al-Maslohi, n.d.).

222 Graf Zeppelin image at, e.g.: jewishvirtuallibrary.org/jsource/images/ jeru/wallzeppelin.jpg. Benjamin Z. Kedar *et al.*, "The Madrasa Afdaliyya / Maqam al-Shaykh Id: an example of Ayyubid architecture in Jerusalem," *Revue Biblique* 119:2 (2012), 271–287: academia.edu/31273588. Nir Hasson, "Rare Photograph Reveals Ancient Jerusalem Mosque Destroyed in 1967," *Haaretz* 15/6/2012. Tom Powers, "Through the American Colony Lens: Graf Zeppelin over Jerusalem" (31/3/2016): israelpalestineguide .wordpress.com/2016/03.

225 The Zawiya al-Magharba stands on a lane that used to be called Aqabat Abu Madyan; a 1969 photo showing its Israeli street sign is at: gettyimages.co.uk/detail/152209376. On the sign the Hebrew reads *Rehov ha-Kotel* (Western Wall Street); the Arabic and English preserve the original name. Today, the same lane has trilingual street signs that reference only the Western Wall (*Rehov ha-Kotel* in Hebrew; *Tariq Ha'it al-Mabka* in Arabic) and omit Abu Madyan; see: gettyimages.co.uk/ detail/169371776.

CHAPTER 13

227 Bracha Slae & Ruth Kark, *Jerusalem's Jewish Quarter: Heritage and Postwar Restoration* (New York: Israel Academic Press, 2018). Haleem Abu Shamseyeh, "Settling the Old City: the Policies of Labor and Likud," *JQ* 6 (1999), 30–42.

228 Burqan judgment in, e.g.: Nadia Abu El-Haj, *Facts on the Ground: Archaeological Practice and Territorial Self-fashioning in Israeli Society* (University of Chicago Press, 2002), 193; Thomas Philip Abowd, *Colonial Jerusalem: The Spatial Construction of Identity and Difference in a City of Myth, 1948–2012* (Syracuse UP, 2014), 137; Yair Wallach, "Jewish nationalism: On the (im)possibility of Muslim Jews," in Josef Meri (ed.), *Routledge Handbook of Muslim-Jewish Relations* (Abingdon: Routledge, 2016), 333.

228 "Complete ruin" quote: Sam Pope Brewer, "11-Day Fight Over," *New York Times* 29/5/1948.

228 John Phillips, *A Will to Survive* (New York: Dial, 1977). "Malaga" quote: 45. "Charred" quote: 55.

229 Centenarian: Larry Collins & Dominique Lapierre, *O Jerusalem!* (London: Pan, 1973), 498.

229 Weingarten quote: Lynne Reid Banks, *Torn Country: An Oral History of the Israeli War of Independence* (New York: Franklin Watts, 1982), 187.

229 Al-Tal quote: Collins & Lapierre (1973), 562. "Cleansed": Abdullah al-Tal, *Karithat Filastin* (Cairo, 1959), 138: web.archive.org/web/20190825193703/creativity.ps/data/library/124814375719024.pdf.

229 Ofer Aderet, "The Jewish Women Who Posed an 'Existential Threat' to Israel by Marrying Arab Men," *Haaretz* 14/4/2021.

230 Displacement: Michael Dumper, *The Politics of Jerusalem Since 1967* (New York: Columbia UP, 1997), 67.

230 "No more than a handful" in Slae & Kark (2018), Kindle location 1143.

231 The Israeli architect was Ari Shem-Or, quoted in Slae & Kark (2018), Kindle location 1464.

231 "Not only about heritage" in Slae & Kark (2018), Kindle location 834.

232 My interview with Esther Weiss 12/6/2021.

233 "Crowds of people" quote and other details, in: Barak Brenner, "New Life in Jerusalem's Old City," *Segula* 13/5/2018: segulamag.com/articles/new-life-jerusalems-old-city.

236 Simone Ricca, *Reinventing Jerusalem: Israel's Reconstruction of the Jewish Quarter after 1967* (London: I.B. Tauris, 2007).

238 Michael Dumper, *The Politics of Sacred Space: The Old City of Jerusalem in the Middle East Conflict* (Boulder: Lynne Rienner, 2002), 42–43 & 80-81. Quote is from: ———, "Israeli Settlement in the Old City of Jerusalem," *Journal of Palestine Studies* 21:4 (1992), 32.

238 70:30 ratio from, e.g.: Betty Herschman, "Changing the Demographics of Jerusalem," Carnegie Endowment for International Peace, 13/12/2017: carnegieendowment.org/sada/75006. Current ratio given as 62.3:37.7 in: *PASSIA Factsheet 2019: Jerusalem* (Palestinian Academic Society for the Study of International Affairs), 14.4: passia.org/media/filer_public/3f/2c/3f2c6cd4-3555-4b7e-a57a-ebf4336d9041/factsheet_jerusalem_2019.pdf. Current ratio given as 62.1:37.9 in: David Koren, "On Demography and Economic Development in Jerusalem," Jerusalem Institute for Strategy & Security, 17/8/2019: jiss

.org.il/en/koren-on-demography-and -economic-development-in-jerusalem.

238 Udi Merioz interview in: *The Return To The Old City Through The Eyes of A 9 Years Old Boy*, posted by Israel First TV 28/11/2018: youtube .com/watch?v=3Y9Hcl-F_xU.

239 Disi: tj-jfe.mbarsinai.com/products/ sites/147. Sidna Omar: Burgoyne (1987), 513. Baruch Yedid, "Jordan Re-Opening Mosque in Heart of Jewish Quarter, Right on Top of the Hurva Synagogue," Tazpit Press Service 19/11/2019, tazpit.org.il/ jordan-re-opening-mosque-in-heart -of-jewish-quarter-right-on-top-of-the -hurva-synagogue.

240 Joel Haber, "A Jerusalem Landmark: Chabad's Tzemach Tzedek Shul" (22/5/2009): lubavitch .com/a-jerusalem-landmark-chabads -tzemach-tzedek-shul. Segal in: Greer Fay Cashman, "The man who sounded the shofar," *Jerusalem Post* 10/5/2007.

241 Weingarten: "looted" quote in "Two Lives," *Jerusalem Report* 12/5/2008. Loren Minsky, "Voices of Jerusalem: The man behind the Old City," *Jerusalem Post* 8/5/2013.

242 My interview with Avi Yefet 23/10/2019.

242 Meira Polliack, "Rethinking Karaism: Between Judaism and Islam," *AJS Review* 30:1 (2006), 67–93, doi: 10.1017/s0364009406000031. Shira Telushkin, "The Jews You've Never Heard Of," *Tablet* 29/9/2016. Isaac Kight, "Jewish Diversity: The Karaite Jews," *Times of Israel* 10/6/2014. Sina Cohen, "The Jews who take off their shoes for shul," *Jewish Chronicle* 23/6/2011. David A.M. Wilensky, "Near San Francisco, Karaite Jews keep an ancient movement alive," Jewish Telegraphic Agency 23/2/2017.

245 Moshe Cohen, "High Court 'Koshers' Karaite Ritual Slaughter,"

Arutz Sheva 19/7/2015. "Jews have superior rights" quote in: "Religious politics in Israel: Who's a Jew?," *The Economist* 18/5/2013.

246 Dates Avi Yefet showed me: Moshe al-Qudsi c.1810 to 9/1/1905; Biana al-Qudsi 1820 to 30/6/1905.

CHAPTER 14

249 Video: facebook.com/apo .sahagian/posts/10161900835510268.

250 My interview with Apo Sahagian 19/10/2019.

251 *The Itinerary of Benjamin of Tudela* (Cold Spring, NY: NightinGale, 2010), 84–86. This edition uses the Adler translation of 1907, viewable at teachittome.com/seforim2/seforim/ masaos_binyomin_mitudela_with_ english.pdf, 24–25. My rendering.

252 Doron Bar, "Jewish and Christian Sanctity under Israeli Sovereignty: Mount Zion, King David's Tomb and the Last Supper Room (1948–1967)," *Middle Eastern Studies* 55:6 (2019), 1037–1048, doi: 10.1080/00263206.2019.1600511. Also: Peters (1985), 421–424.

252 Nir Hasson, "Who Is "Judaizing" King David's Tomb?," *Haaretz* 3/8/2013. "David's Tomb on Mt. Zion" (25/4/2014): alt-arch.org/en/davids -tomb-on-mt-zion.

253 George Hintlian, "Armenians of Jerusalem," JQ 2 (1998), 40-44. Also: armenian-jerusalem.org. Susanne Falk, *"A Jerusalemite Armenian. That's a thing of its own": A Case Study about Identity, Agency and Structure among Armenian Women*, MA thesis, Uppsala University, 2019: urn.kb.se/resolve?urn=urn:nbn:se:uu:d iva-391479. Bedross Der Matossian, "The Armenians of Palestine 1918– 48," *Journal of Palestine Studies* 41:1 (2011), 24–44, doi: 10.1525/jps.2011 .xli.1.24. "Dar el-Masakin": Hintlian (1989), 24.

253 Contacts between Armenia & Palestine: Hintlian (1989), 1.

254 Roberto Mazza, "The Armenians of Jerusalem, their micro-identities and the history of the Armenian Quarter, with Bedross Der Matossian," *Jerusalem Unplugged* podcast 1/23 (30/6/2021). Tania Manougian, "The Armenian Community in the Holy Land," *This Week in Palestine* 112 (Aug 2007). Nancy Kricorian, "Stories from the Armenian Quarter," *The Armenian Weekly* 1/6/2017.

256 Benedict Anderson, *Imagined Communities: Reflections on the Origin and Spread of Nationalism* (London: Verso, rev. ed. 2016).

CHAPTER 15

259 A version of this chapter was published as "David Dorr's Window East" in *AramcoWorld* 70:1 (Jan/Feb 2019), 34–37.

259 Malini Johar Schueller (ed.), David F. Dorr, *A Colored Man Round the World* (University of Michigan Press, 1999). Lloyd S. Kramer, "David Dorr's Journey Toward Selfhood in Europe," in Lisa A. Lindsay & John Wood Sweet (eds.), *Biography and the Black Atlantic* (University of Pennsylvania Press, 2013), 149–171. Hilton Obenzinger, *American Palestine: Melville, Twain, and the Holy Land Mania* (Princeton UP, 1999), 227–229. Scott Trafton, *Egypt Land: Race and Nineteenth-Century American Egyptomania* (Duke UP, 2004), 22. Jieun Park, "The Multicolored Eye: David Dorr's Vision in *A Colored Man Round the World*," *Journal of English Language and Literature* (Seoul) 63:3 (2017), 465–483: jell.ellak.or.kr/past/view.asp?a_key=3548741. Sara Kakazu, *Incidental Americans: Encounter and Self-Construction in Nineteenth-Century Transatlantic Travel Narratives*, PhD dissertation, State University of New York Buffalo, 2012: pqdtopen.proquest.com/doc/925657388.html?FMT=ABS.

260 "The first African American Holy Land travel narrative was written by David Dorr," says Alex Lubin, *Geographies of Liberation: The Making of an Afro-Arab Political Imaginary* (University of North Carolina Press, 2014), 27. Did others travel to Jerusalem before Dorr without writing about it? I have been unable to find evidence. Frank Parrish visited Egypt in 1852 before Dorr, and was probably the first African American to visit Petra [says David Kennedy: eastofjordan.wordpress.com/2014/10/08], but there is no record of his having visited Jerusalem. Dorr describes (126) meeting Parrish in Constantinople in May 1852. Parrish returned to Nashville soon after, where he continued with his long-running barber shop business and bought his freedom the following year, aged 48. For Parrish, see: Loren Schweninger, "The Free-Slave Phenomenon: James P. Thomas and the Black Community in Ante-Bellum Nashville," *Civil War History* 22:4 (1976), 302, doi: 10.1353/cwh.1976.0040.

CHAPTER 16

267 Mehmet Bengü Uluengin, "Secularizing Anatolia tick by tick: clocktowers in the Ottoman Empire and the Turkish Republic," in *International Journal of Middle East Studies* 42:1 (2010), 17–36, doi: 10.1017/S0020743809990511. Ekrem Buğra Ekinci, "Ottoman-era clocktowers telling time from Balkans to Middle East," *Daily Sabah* 6/1/2017.

268 Public space & public time: openjerusalem.org/project.

268 Mahon Murphy, "The British in Jerusalem 1917–1920: The Imagined City," 2015: mwme.eu/essays. Also: thisweekinpalestine

.com/wp-content/uploads/2015/01/ then-and-now.pdf. There is film of the clocktower in 1917 at: iwm.org. uk/collections/item/object/1060008299 (00:59–01:58). Uzi Baram, "Out Of Time: Erasing Modernity in an Antique City," *Archaeologies* 8 (2012), 330–348, doi: 10.1007/s11759 -012-9209-9. Yair Wallach, "Jerusalem's lost heart: The rise and fall of the late Ottoman city center," in Hilal Alkan & Nazan Maksudyan (eds.), *Urban Neighborhood Formations: Boundaries, Narrations and Intimacies* (Abingdon: Routledge, 2020), 138–158: academia .edu/42607145.

269 Storrs's "sentiment" quote (Storrs to Ruhi Bey 23/2/1922) and "Ottoman Victorianism" quote in: Ron Fuchs & Gilbert Herbert, "A Colonial Portrait of Jerusalem: British Architecture in Mandate-Era Palestine," in Nezar Alsayyad (ed.), *Hybrid Urbanism: On the Identity Discourse and the Built Environment* (Westport, CT: Praeger, 2001), 91.

269 Sebag Montefiore (2011), 437.

270 The historian is Ilan Pappé, *Ten Myths About Israel* (London: Verso, 2017), 20.

270 Tleel (1999), 39.

273 Kamal J. al-Asali, Mamilla Cemetery in "The Cemeteries of Ottoman Jerusalem," in Auld & Hillenbrand (2000), 280-283.

274 In 2018 61 percent of all tourists to Israel were Christian: "Israel saw record-breaking 4 million tourists in 2018, says tourism ministry," *Times of Israel* 29/12/2018.

274 Sarah Helm, "By the Jaffa Gate, final showdown looms in battle over Jerusalem's historic hotel," *The Guardian* 21/7/2019. Nir Hasson, "'We Go Back 800 Years': Palestinian Fights Settler NGO's Takeover of Jerusalem Hotel," *Haaretz* 13/7/2019.

Hiba Aslan & Joe Dyke, "In Jerusalem hotel, eviction fears dampen Christmas cheer," AFP 3/12/2019.

275 Tarik Kafala, "Clinton's Mid-East peace plans," BBC News 22/1/2001. Martin Indyk, *Innocent Abroad: An Intimate Account of American Peace Diplomacy in the Middle East* (New York: Simon & Schuster, 2009), 322: "Barak ... said he was ready to divide the Old City in two, conceding complete sovereignty in the Muslim and Christian quarters to Arafat. Israel would retain sovereignty over the Jewish and Armenian quarters and the Temple Mount."

275 My interview with Fawaz Attiyeh 23/2/2019.

277 Yusef Said al-Natsheh, "Un-inventing the Bab al-Khalil tombs: Between the magic of legend and historical fact," *JQ* 22/23 (2005), 69–79.

278 Salim Tamari, "The Vagabond Café and Jerusalem's Prince of Idleness," *JQ* 19 (2003), 23–36. For Michel Moushabeck's reminiscences of his grandfather, see facebook .com/BMJerusalemitesPhotoLib/ posts/4997962580274413.

279 My interview with Nora Kort 25/10/2019. Nora Kort, "Palestinian Christians in Jerusalem," *Ecumenical Review* 64:1 (2012), 36–42, doi: 10.1111/j.1758-6623.2012.00143.x.

281 For more on Israel's efforts at Pool of the Patriarch's Bathhouse/ Hezekiah's Pool, see Tom Powers: israelpalestineguide.wordpress .com/2012/10/23, the last in a (linked) series of four posts in 2011–12.

CHAPTER 17

283 My Shapira sources included: *Shapira and I*, dir. Yoram Sabo, 2014 (documentary 57 min). Yoram Sabo, "Between Apostate and Forger: Moses Wilhelm Shapira and the Moabite Pottery Affair,"

English version of Hebrew original in *Zmanim* 123 (2013), 70–81: academia.edu/24911481. Shlomo Guil, "In Search of the Shop of Moses Wilhelm Shapira, the Leading Figure of the 19th Century Archaeological Enigma," English version of Hebrew original in *Etmol* 223 (2012, revised 2017?): academia.edu/2127379. Shlomo Guil, "The Shapira Scroll was an Authentic Dead Sea Scroll," *Palestine Exploration Quarterly* 149:1 (2017), 6–27, doi: 10.1080/00310328.2016.1185895. Aviva & Shmuel Bar-Am, "In The Footsteps of a Master Forger," *Times of Israel*, 2/11/2013. "William Shapira," *Joods Erfgoed Rotterdam*, last modified 12/9/2019: joodserfgoedrotterdam. nl/willem-schapiro. Beth Kissileff, "The Mysteries of Moses," *Tablet* 11/4/2016. Chanan Tigay, "Was this the first Dead Sea Scroll?," BBC Travel 30/11/2017. Jennifer Schuessler, "Is a Long-Dismissed Forgery Actually the Oldest Known Biblical Manuscript?," *New York Times* 10/3/2021. Idan Dershowitz, "The Valediction of Moses: New Evidence on the Shapira Deuteronomy Fragments," *Zeitschrift für die alttestamentliche Wissenschaft* 133:1 (2021), 1–22, doi: 10.1515/zaw-2021-0001. Christopher Rollston, "Deja Vu All Over Again: The Antiquities Market, the Shapira Strips, Menahem Mansoor, and Idan Dershowitz," 10/3/2021: rollstonepigraphy. com/?p=896. Jonathan Klawans, "The Shapira Fragments: An Artifact of 19th-Century Jewish Christianity," *Biblical Archaeology Society* 18/3/2021: biblicalarchaeology.org/ daily/the-shapira-fragments. I am grateful to Dr Michael D. Press for his insightful tweets on Shapira.

284 George Hintlian, "The Commercial Life of Ottoman Jerusalem," in Auld & Hillenbrand (2000), 230. Edited.

284 Nicola A. Ziadeh, "In Jerusalem," *Jordan Times* 2/12/1987: archive.org/ details/JordanTimes1987JordanEnglish.

287 Dr. Sarah Irving pointed out to me the alternative interpretation of the Dhibani bedouin's shattering of the Mesha Stele.

288 On Abu Khalaf (Bilal, rather than Ibrahim): Stephanie Saldaña, "The Surviving Threads of Syria's Textile Industry," 1/2/2016: mosaicstories. org/2016/02. Arieh O'Sullivan, "A Material World," *Jerusalem Post* 20/5/2010. Matti Friedman, "Losing the Thread of Palmyra: A cloth-seller in Jerusalem feels the effects of Syria's war," *Tablet* 2/6/2015. Shachar Atwan, "The Jerusalem Fabric Merchant Who Lives in a Material World," *Haaretz* 24/4/2018.

291 Kevork Kahvedjian, *Jerusalem Through My Father's Eyes* (Jerusalem: private publication, 1998). Also: armenian-jerusalem.org/ elia.htm. Rhonda Spivak, "Historic Photos of Jerusalem Discovered," *Canadian Jewish News* 24/9/2008. Interview with Kahvedjian: makehummusnotwar.com/characters_14 .html. Nir Hasson, "The finest photographs of early twentieth century Palestine, shuttered in controversy," *Haaretz* 5/2/2012. Issam Nassar, "Palestinian photographers before 1948": paljourneys.org/en/ timeline/highlight/10522/palestinian -photographers-1948.

292 Krausz's *Visit Palestine* poster: palestineposterproject.org/poster/ visit-palestine-original. Rochelle Davis & Dan Walsh, "'Visit Palestine': A Brief Study of Palestine Posters," *JQ* 61 (2015), 42–54. To my knowledge the Kahvedjian photograph has not been published; it can be seen at 01:31 in this video (posted 17/1/2011 by Danny Herman, an Israeli guide), framed & hanging on the wall to Kevork Kahvedjian's right, behind his gesturing hand: youtube.com/watch?v=gwmoisYUV1M.

293 My interview with Dawoud Manarious 10/12/2019.

293 For Deir al-Sultan, e.g.: Victoria Clark, *Holy Fire: The Battle for Christ's Tomb* (London: Macmillan, 2005), 40–43 & 61–62. Nir Hasson, "Coptic Church gears up for a new fight at Jerusalem's Holy Sepulchre," *Haaretz* 31/10/2018. Negussay Ayele, "Deir Sultan, Ethiopia and the Black World," 8/11/2002: ethiopians .com/Views/NegussayAyele_on_ Deir_Sultan.htm. "Deir Es-Sultan Monastery's mediation by Greek Church unsuccessful: Egypt Pope," *Al Masry Al Youm* 6/12/2018: egyptindependent.com/deir-es-sultan -monasterys-mediation-by-greek -church-unsuccessful-egypt-pope.

296 Who Profits, *Signal Strength: Occupied: The Telecommunications Sector and the Israeli Occupation* (July 2018), 12: whoprofits.org/flash -report/signal-strength-occupied.

297 My interview with Wassim Razzouk 21/10/2019. Mariam Gabaji, "Tracing Jerusalem's History With the Razzouk Tattoo Family," *Culture Trip* 5/7/2019. Anna Felicity Friedman, "Inside the World's Only Surviving Tattoo Shop For Medieval Pilgrims," *Atlas Obscura* 18/8/2016. Lars Krutak, "The Razzouks: tattooing for 700 years," larskrutak.com 2/6/2015. Ian Lee, "Ancient tattoo artists still making their mark in Jerusalem," CNN 6/9/2016. Alessandra Borroni, *Jerusalem Tattoos: Traditions and Designs* (Albero Niro Editore/ private publication, 2020). Adam Davis, "The Imprint of the Pilgrimage: John Carswell's Coptic Tattoo Designs," *Division Leap* 2/1/2017. Marie-Armelle Beaulieu, "Like a Seal on Your Arm: The Tradition of Tattooing Among Jerusalem Pilgrims," *JQ* 78 (2019), 86–92.

305 My interview with Karen Mann 24/10/2019; levantinegallery.com.

CHAPTER 18

309 My interview with Jack Persekian 25/10/2019.

313 Sabreen: sabreen.org & facebook .com/SabreenAssociation. Michael Rakowitz, *The Breakup: A Project for Jerusalem* (text, video, concert audio, radio series; 2010): the -breakup.net.

314 On Gallery Anadiel & Al-Mamal: almamal.blogspot.com/2010/04 & anadiel.com.

315 Basak Senova, "The Jerusalem Show: Jack Persekian In Conversation," *Ibraaz* 2/5/2012: ibraaz .org/interviews/19. James Scarborough, "A Conversation With Jack Persekian," *HuffPost* 18/10/2014. Hakim Bishara, "How To Organize a Biennial in Occupied Territory," *Hyperallergic* 29/10/2018: hyperallergic.com/468459.

EPILOGUE

321 Laleh Khalili, *Sinews of War and Trade* (London: Verso, 2020), 6.

322 The earliest source I could find for Tutu's quote is: Robert McAfee Brown, *Unexpected News: Reading the Bible with Third World Eyes* (Louisville, KY: Westminster, 1984), 19. Also: Gary Younge, "The Secrets of a Peacemaker," *The Guardian* 23/5/2009.

324 Yair Wallach, "Jerusalem's Lost Heart: the rise and fall of the late Ottoman city center," in: Hilal Alkan & Nazan Maksudyan (eds.), *Urban Neighborhood Formations: Boundaries, Narrations and Intimacies* (Abingdon: Routledge, 2020), 138–158: academia.edu/42607145.

325 Wendy Pullan *et al.*, "Jerusalem's Road 1: An inner city frontier?," *City* 11:2 (2007), 176–198: academia .edu/20330998.

326 Mandelbaum Gate in: Raphael Israeli, *Jerusalem Divided: The*

Armistice Regime 1947–1967 (London: Frank Cass, 2002), 95–97. Baramki house: Thomas Abowd, "The Politics and Poetics of Place," *JQ* 21 (2004), 49–58. Also: facebook.com/654018151335566/posts/4920603118010360.

327 Michael Dumper, *Jerusalem Unbound: Geography, History, and the Future of the Holy City* (New York: Columbia UP, 2014), 94–95. Rory McCarthy, "Israel annexing East Jerusalem, says EU," *The Guardian* 7/3/2009. Daniella Peled, "Jerusalem: planning makes idea of united city a myth," *Little Atoms* (n.d. 2015?). Tia Goldenberg, "Israeli east Jerusalem plan gets cool Palestinian reception," Associated Press 20/7/2018.

328 The historian is Rashid Khalidi, *The Hundred Years' War on Palestine* (London: Profile, 2020).

329 For Ben-Gurion declaration (5/12/1949) & Begin letter (17/9/1978) see: Ruth Lapidoth, "Jerusalem: Some Legal Issues," in: Rüdiger Wolfrum (ed.), *The Max Planck Encyclopedia of Public International Law* (Oxford UP, 2011): ssrn.com/abstract=2679232.

330 For a glimpse of Palestinian Jerusalemite psychogeography, see *Jerusalem We Are Here* by Dorit Naaman and colleagues: jerusalemwearehere.com.

330 Sari Nusseibeh, "Negotiating the city: A perspective of a Jerusalemite," in: Tamar Mayer & Suleiman A. Mourad (eds.), *Jerusalem: Idea and Reality* (Abingdon: Routledge, 2008), 198. Lightly edited.

331 Jaclynn Ashly, "Palestinians in Kufr Aqab: "'We live here just to wait',"" *Al Jazeera* 7/1/2018. Daoud Kuttab, "How one Jerusalem neighborhood has been left to fend for itself," *Al Monitor* 2/6/2016.

331 Abdullah's "coronation": Joseph Nevo, *King Abdallah and Palestine: A Territorial Ambition* (London: Macmillan, 1996), 166. Benjamin Shwadran, *Jordan A State of Tension* (New York: Council for Middle Eastern Affairs Press, 1959), 280.

332 Sovereignty at Al-Aqsa: Nir Hasson, "Temple Mount Crisis Shows Who's Really Calling the Shots at the Site," *Haaretz* 21/7/2017. Yair Wallach, "The violence that began at Jerusalem's ancient holy sites is driven by a distinctly modern zeal," *The Guardian* 13/5/2021. Also: twitter.com/YairWallach/status/1391731409543442433 (10/5/2021).

333 Lifta: 2018 World Monuments Watch, *World Monuments Fund*: wmf.org/project/lifta. Daphna Golan *et al*, "Lifta and the Regime of Forgetting: Memory Work and Conservation," *JQ* 54 (2013), 69–81. Sarah Ben-Nun, "Arab village of Lifta, abandoned in '48, to house new Israeli neighborhood," *Jerusalem Post* 10/5/2021. Aseel Jundi, "Saving Lifta: Palestinians rally against latest threat to depopulated Jerusalem village," *Middle East Eye* 13/6/2021. Hotel: liftaboutique.co.il.

334 My interview with Bashar Murad 26/11/2019. Elias Jahshan, "Queer life, occupation and expectations," *The New Arab* 5/3/2021.

335 Hiba Qawasmi in: "Between Al-Quds & Yerushalayim: voices from the east of the city," Emek Shaveh webinar 3/3/2021: facebook.com/watch/live/?v=4143059215705374 (30:48–49:49). My rendering, edited for clarity.

336 Michel-Rolph Trouillot, *Silencing the Past: Power and the Production of History* (Boston, MA: Beacon, 1995).

Select Bibliography

This is a list of noteworthy books that were of general help and relevance, in addition to titles cited above in the notes to each chapter. It is not intended to be comprehensive, and omits much.

Suad Amiry, *Golda Slept Here* (New Delhi: Women Unlimited, 2013)

Karen Armstrong, *A History of Jerusalem: One City, Three Faiths* (London: HarperCollins, 1996)

K.J. Asali (ed.), *Jerusalem in History* (Buckhurst Hill: Scorpion, 1989)

Sylvia Auld & Robert Hillenbrand (eds.) & Yusuf Natsheh, *Ottoman Jerusalem: The Living City 1517–1917* (London: Altajir World of Islam Trust, 2000)

Tamim al-Barghouti (tr. Radwa Ashour), *In Jerusalem and other poems* (Northampton: Interlink, 2017)

Ian Black, *Enemies & Neighbors: Arabs & Jews in Palestine & Israel, 1917–2017* (London: Penguin, 2017)

Michael Hamilton Burgoyne (ed.), *Mamluk Jerusalem: An Architectural Study* (London: World of Islam Festival Trust, on behalf of British School of Archaeology in Jerusalem, 1987)

Paola Caridi, *Jerusalem Without God: Portrait of a Cruel City* (Cairo: American University in Cairo Press, 2017)

Angelos Dalachanis & Vincent Lemire (eds.), *Ordinary Jerusalem 1840-1940: Opening New Archives, Revisiting a Global City* (Leiden: Brill, 2018): brill.com/view/title/36309

Marcello Di Cintio, *Pay No Heed to the Rockets: Palestine in the Present Tense* (London: Saqi, 2018)

Khaled Diab, *Intimate Enemies: Living with Israelis and Palestinians in the Holy Land* (London: Guardian, 2014)

Dick Doughty & Mohammed El Aydi, *Gaza: Legacy of Occupation – A Photographer's Journey* (West Hartford, CT: Kumarian, 1995)

Michael Dumper, *Jerusalem Unbound: Geography, History & the Future of the Holy City* (New York: Columbia UP, 2014)

Alistair Duncan, *The Noble Sanctuary: Portrait of a Holy Place in Arab Jerusalem* (London: Longman, 1972)

Marya Farah, *Occupying Jerusalem's Old City: Israeli Policies of Isolation, Intimidation and Transformation* (Ramallah: Al Haq, 2019): alhaq.org/publications/15212.html

Oleg Grabar & Benjamin Z. Kedar (eds.), *Where Heaven and Earth Meet: Jerusalem's Sacred Esplanade* (Austin: University of Texas Press, 2009)

Sahar Hamouda, *Once Upon a Time in Jerusalem* (Reading, UK: Garnet, 2010)

Dana Hercbergs, *Overlooking the Border: Narratives of Divided Jerusalem* (Detroit: Wayne State UP, 2018)

Robert Hillenbrand, *The Architecture of Ottoman Jerusalem: An Introduction* (London: Altajir World of Islam Trust, 2002)

Robert Hillenbrand & Sylvia Auld (eds.), *Ayyubid Jerusalem: The Holy City in Context 1187–1250* (London: Altajir Trust, 2009)

Kevork Hintlian, *History of the Armenians in the Holy Land* (Jerusalem: Armenian Patriarchate, 2nd ed., 1989)

Sarah Irving, *Palestine: The Bradt Travel Guide* (Chalfont St. Peter: Bradt, 2011)

Hunt Janin, *Four Paths to Jerusalem: Jewish, Christian, Muslim, and Secular Pilgrimages, 1000 bce to 2001 ce* (Jefferson, NC: McFarland, 2002)

Salma Khadra Jayyusi & Zafar Ishaq Ansari (eds.), *My Jerusalem: Essays, Reminiscences, and Poems* (Northampton, MA: Olive Branch, 2005)

Penny Johnson & Raja Shehadeh (eds.), *Seeking Palestine: New Palestinian Writing on Exile and Home* (Northampton, MA: Olive Branch, 2013)

Diala Khasawneh, *Memoirs Engraved in Stone: Palestinian Urban Mansions* (Ramallah: Riwaq, 2001)

Menachem Klein (tr. Haim Watzman), *Lives in Common: Arabs and Jews in Jerusalem, Jaffa and Hebron* (London: Hurst, 2014)

Vincent Lemire (tr. Catherine Tihanyi & Lys Ann Weiss), *Jerusalem 1900: The Holy City in the Age of Possibilities* (University of Chicago Press, 2017)

Merav Mack & Benjamin Balint, *Jerusalem: City of the Book* (Yale UP, 2019)

Nur Masalha, *The Palestine Nakba: Decolonising History, Narrating the Subaltern, Reclaiming Memory* (London: Zed, 2012)

Dina Matar, *What It Means to be Palestinian: Stories of Palestinian Peoplehood* (London: I.B. Tauris, 2011)

Roberto Mazza, *Jerusalem: From the Ottomans to the British* (London: I.B. Tauris, 2009)

Sato Moughalian, *Feast of Ashes: The Life and Art of David Ohannessian* (Stanford UP, 2019)

Suleiman A. Mourad, Naomi Koltun-Fromm & Bedross Der Matossian (eds.), *Routledge Handbook on Jerusalem* (Abingdon: Routledge, 2018)

Dr. Yusuf Said Natsheh, *Discovering Jerusalem's Secrets: Walking Trails through the Old City and Beyond* (Jerusalem: Jerusalem Tourism Cluster, 2015)

Colin Osman, *Jerusalem: Caught in Time* (Reading: Garnet, 1999)

Palestine & Palestinians (Beit Sahour: Alternative Tourism Group, 2nd ed. 2008)

F.E. Peters, *Jerusalem: The Holy City in the Eyes of Chroniclers, Visitors, Pilgrims, and Prophets from the Days of Abraham to the Beginnings of Modern Times* (Princeton UP, 1985)

Michael Prior & William Taylor (eds.), *Christians in the Holy Land* (London: World of Islam Festival Trust, 1994)

Mariam Shahin & George Azar, *Palestine: A Guide* (Northampton: Interlink, 2005)

Mahmoud Shukair (tr. Nicole Fares), *Jerusalem Stands Alone* (Syracuse UP, 2018)

Dennis Silk (ed.), *Retrievements: A Jerusalem Anthology* (Jerusalem: Keter, 2nd ed. 1977)

Rana F. Sweis, *Voices of Jordan* (London: Hurst, 2018)

Yair Wallach, *A City in Fragments: Urban Text in Modern Jerusalem* (Stanford UP, 2020)

Bernard Wasserstein, *Divided Jerusalem: The Struggle for the Holy City* (London: Profile, 2001)

Wujood: The Grassroots Guide to Jerusalem (Jerusalem: Grassroots Al-Quds, 2019): grassrootsalquds .net

Author's Note ...

Jerusalem is not my city and never will be. That said, there has hardly been a year in my life in which it has not played a part. Before I thank those who helped me write this book of stories, here is a bit of my own story.

Like so many of us, I am a child of migrants. All eight of my great-grandparents arrived in Britain between about 1887 and 1913, from Poland and the regions of Russia now called Lithuania, Belarus and Ukraine. All eight were Jewish. Their grandchildren – my parents – identified as Anglo-Jewish, and were determined to assimilate into middle-class English society. Home was a detached house in suburban Surrey, where I was born and grew up. Yet the first foreign holiday we ever took was to Israel, in 1980. That was my first visit to Jerusalem and I've still got the earnest report I typed up about it. The word I chose to describe the experience was "unforgettable." Little did I know. This book has been forty years coming.

After that, we kept on returning. There must have been five or six such holidays in my school years. At thirteen, my dad arranged for me to have my bar mitzvah twice, once at our regular synagogue at home, and again in Jerusalem, at the Western Wall. Jewishness remained an embarrassing add-on for myself, but I could see it defining a core identity in others, whether strangers on Jerusalem streets or, even more oddly, friends and family. My brother's first wife was Israeli; we visited them often at their apartment in the West Jerusalem suburbs.

But something else was starting to play below the surface. Once, in about 1985, a friend of my parents drove me into Jerusalem from his farm in the hills to the west. As we reached the city and stopped at traffic lights, he told me how everything before us had been Jordanian territory less than twenty years before, and how in 1967 Israel had liberated all of Jerusalem to be Jewish again. He sliced the edge of his hand sideways across the road junction to mark what had been the border, and talked to me about violence and enemies and hardship and divine justice. I listened, but could not relate. That friend later moved to a Jewish-only town in the West Bank – a settlement, illegal under international law – where he and his wife raised their kids. They live there still.

In my early twenties, I had the privilege to be able to go back to Jerusalem. The strangeness of the Israel I'd been brought up with was already showing through. Then I went to live in Cairo, where my horizons expanded so much so quickly that I got vertigo and had to leave after half a year before I lost my balance completely. The following spring, having saved a bit of money, I holed up in East Jerusalem, helping out at a Palestinian-run backpackers' hostel. For four or five months I barely left the Old City. All day, every day, was spent within the walls, out on the streets, walking, talking, watching, listening. Then I'd come back to the hostel and work the graveyard shift on the front desk. It was around this time, as a would-be journalist, that I got to interview a mid-level PLO official in Lebanon, and talk to people in Sabra and Shatila, areas of Beirut where Palestinian refugees have been mired in poverty for decades. I started hearing new ways of telling stories I thought I knew.

When I tried to get a job in travel writing, in 1995, the guidebook company in London asked me to tell them about a place I knew well, so I wrote a thousand words about Jerusalem. They hired me, and I lived a year or so in Amman, writing a guide to Jordan, where I finally grasped the size of the gap between what I had learned as a child and what I knew as an adult, and how the center of that, the key to the whole transition, was Jerusalem.

There were more trips, and more writing. I travelled the length and breadth of Israel and Palestine, as well as Syria and Lebanon again, and many times to Jordan, and Egypt, Morocco, Iraq, all across the Gulf from Kuwait and Saudi Arabia to Dubai and Oman, and I wrote about Jerusalem for the BBC and CNN and others, trying to work out my understanding of the place.

Because the discrimination of the Israeli border authorities works in my favor, meaning I have been able to come and go as I please – unlike so many – Jerusalem has always been a yardstick against which I've been able to measure the ebb and flow of identity. It took me twenty years to unlearn twenty, and it's taken ten more to feel like I'm able, now, to say something useful about the place. Or, rather, the people. I'm as much of an outsider in Jerusalem as I ever was, but at least I'm no longer a stranger.

... *and thanks*

This book originated in conversations with two friends, Raed Saadeh and Daniel Adamson, at the wonderful Jerusalem Hotel in 2013. Raed owns and runs the hotel, is co-founder and chair of both the Jerusalem Tourism Cluster and Birzeit's Rozana Association for Rural Tourism Development, co-founder of the Network for Experiential Palestinian Tourism Organizations and former president of the Arab Hotel Association. He has been building community structures to support Palestinian society and economy in Jerusalem and beyond for decades. This book would not have happened without his influence and his encouragement, his vision and his generosity. Dan, writer, thinker, storyteller, journalist, has been a rock in my life for years now, from Urfa to Bethlehem to W1A and beyond – an inspiration and a valued friend. For their wisdom, guidance and unwavering support, this book is as much Raed's and Dan's as it is mine. (Barring any mistakes, of course, all of which are mine.)

When Raed took me out into the hills around Birzeit in 2017, and we talked again about a book, I still wasn't sure how to make it happen. Peter Adamson encouraged me to pitch. Chris Brazier at New Internationalist Books was immediately keen. Around that time I was producing a documentary for BBC Radio 4 on the artist Peter Shenai; Peter, with his characteristic enthusiasm, urged me to investigate funding opportunities. I want to thank each of them for helping turn an idea into reality. The day, several months later, when Arts Council England approved my application for a creativity development grant was a very good day indeed.

Then the pandemic hit and everything fell apart. Late in 2020 I had to begin trying to sell what was by then a completed manuscript. When Mark Ellingham, who had published my travel writing twenty years before at Rough Guides, saw its potential and, with Profile Books' publisher Andrew Franklin, agreed to take it on, I danced. It's been a pleasure working with Mark; he is generous, insightful and supportive, and this book is substantially better for his editing. Thank you to him, to Andrew, and to their colleagues at Profile, including rights director Alex Elam, publicist Alison Alexanian, designer Henry Iles, cartographer Dominic Beddow and proofreader Susanne Hillen.

Many, many people in Jerusalem and beyond, over many, many years, showed me the exceptional friendship, hospitality, generosity and understanding that helped build the foundations, then the superstructure, of this book. I want to thank them all, but would need another book to do so properly. Thanks first to my dear friend Khalil Assali, who believed in me at my lowest ebb and whose perspective and enthusiasm kept me going when I was losing my way. Thank you to George Hintlian, who, from our very first conversation, sitting opposite each other in Jerusalem's wondrous Gulbenkian Library, immediately understood what I was trying to do and then so open-heartedly shared wisdom, good conversation, excellent contacts and his unique depth of insight into his home city to help me achieve it. I am grateful to all those who let me tell their stories – and to Nadine Liftawi, Naila Jwealis and especially Maram Summren, without whom gathering many of those stories would have been much harder. I would like to thank, in particular, Ali Qleibo, Yusuf Natsheh, Mazen Ahram, Mahmoud Muna, Yazeed Abu Khdeir, Manar Idris, Garo Sandrouni, Vatche Dakessian, Husam Jubran, Yuval Ben-Ami, Yair Wallach, Felicity Cobbing, Jane Taylor, Nadia Dajani, Carolyn Perry, Sato Moughalian, Joseph Willits, George Azar, Ramsey Tesdell, Anisa Mehdi and colleagues at API, Stefan Szepesi, George Rishmawi, Michel Awad, Mark Khano, Bob Bewley, Michael Fradley, Shehab Kawasmi and Karen Mann for the cover art, and – remembering those years in the 1990s of travel and (un)learning, with gratitude – Michelle Woodward.

I am more grateful than I can properly say to Dick Doughty, long-standing editor of *AramcoWorld* magazine, for the breaks he's given me and the support he's shown me over the years, with this project and many others. Many thanks to Richard Muir and Ursula Guy of the Al Tajir Trust in London for their generosity in presenting me with the Trust's publications on Jerusalem – invaluable for my research. Thank you to inspirational journalist Lizzie Porter, not least for facilitating access to her network of linguistic advisors, including Hsen Andil, Yazan Badran, Esmaeel Alebrahim and Raida Mukarked. Nick Breakspear of The Black Hats (buy their songs! blackhatsmusic.co.uk) worked wonders transcribing pigeon coos into musical notation. Sami McLaren of Friends, Families & Travellers advised on terminology. Sanad Abu Assaf helped with Sign Language. Barnaby Rogerson remains a fount of encouragement.

I am grateful to those who read parts or all of this book in draft manu-script: Sarah Irving, Alex Robertson Textor, George Hintlian, Roberto

Mazza, Raja Shehadeh, Penny Johnson, Salim Tamari, Ahdaf Soueif, Noga Tarnopolsky, Bernard Wasserstein, Stephen Griffith and Usama Hasan. All offered valuable criticism that significantly improved the book and allowed me to correct errors, omissions, misunderstandings, infelicities and misjudgments. Any that remain are entirely my responsibility.

Too many friends to name, before, during and after the writing of this book, continue to sustain, support and inspire me, in person and online. Profound thanks especially to Nancy Campbell, Toufoul Abou-Hodeib, Lisa Goldman, Caroline Eden, Sarah Irving, Niamh McBurney, Kedi Simpson, Moudhy al-Rashid, Muna Haddad, Noga Tarnopolsky, Zainab al-Refaie, Bettina Kircher, Peter Gibbs, David Symes, Pam Mandel, Mary Novakovich, Tharik Hussain, Pakinam Amer, Alisa Klein, Paul Clammer, Leon McCarron, Imad & Hanan al-Saied, Christian Imdorf, the Parkhouses, the Charsleys, the Laceys and my wonderful cousin Claudia Martin. I owe a special debt of gratitude to my father, Neville, and my brothers, Adam and Richard. Richard started the whole thing off by taking me into the Jerusalem souk for the first time, on 24 December 1980, when he was twenty and I was eleven. I still remember it. Seeing this book would have delighted – though also riled – my mother, Sheila.

Above all, to Hannah, without whose clarity, wisdom, love, support and encouragement I could have done none of what I have.

I did most of my research for this book and all of my writing in the last few months before COVID-19 changed everything. As I finished it, Britain, the place I call home, went into its first lockdown. Sometimes the memories in these pages have felt like a final record of what may turn out to be a lost world of human interaction unrestricted by the fear of mortal disease. Jerusalem, especially the Old City, suffered horribly through the pandemic – and, at the time of writing, continues to suffer. I don't know if all the people I spoke to, or even just those who appear in these pages, are OK. I don't know if every business I mention is still operating, or if every place I visited is still accessible. If you live there, or if you visit with this book in hand, I'd be very grateful if you could let me know.

Matthew Teller
January 2022
matthewteller.com

Index